REAPING THE WHIRLWIND

Ethnic Conflict, Ethnic Politics in Sri Lanka

K.M. de Silva

GW00671815

PENGUIN BOOKS

Penguin Books India (P) Ltd., 210 Chiranjiv Tower, 43 Nehru Place, New Delhi 110 019 India
Penguin Books Ltd., 27 Wrights Lane, London W8 5TZ, UK
Penguin Books USA Inc., 375 Hudson Street, New York, New York 10014, USA
Penguin Books Australia Ltd., Ringwood, Victoria, Australia
Penguin Books Canada Ltd., 10 Alcorn Avenue, Suite 300, Toronto, Ontario, MAV 3B2, Canada
Penguin Books (NZ) Ltd., 182-190 Wairau Road, Auckland, 10, New Zealand

First published by Penguin Books India (P) Ltd. 1998

Typeset in *Nebraska* by SÜRYA, New Delhi-110 011

Cover photographs: Bomb attack on Colombo's financial centre, 30 January 1996,
courtesy Associated Newspapers of Ceylon Ltd., Colombo.

PENGUIN BOOKS

REAPING THE WHIRLWIND

ETHNIC CONFLICT, ETHNIC POLITICS IN SRI LANKA

K.M. de Silva, held the chair of Sri Lanka History at the University of Ceylon, later the University of Peradeniya, from 1969 to 1995. He has been Executive Director of the International Centre for Ethnic Studies, Colombo/Kandy, from its establishment in 1982. Notable among his several books are *A History of Sri Lanka* (1981); *Managing Ethnic Tensions in Multi-Ethnic Societies: Sri Lanka, 1880-1985* (1986) and *Regional Powers and Small State Security: India and Sri Lanka, 1977-90* (1995). He edited *Internationalization of Ethnic Conflict* with R.J. May (co-editor), (1991), *Peace Accords and Ethnic Conflict* with S.W.R. de A. Samarasinghe (co-editor), (1993). His most recent publication is his edition of the documents in the Sri Lanka volume (2 parts) in the British Documents on the End of Empire series.

Contents

List of Maps   *vii*

Preface   *ix*

SRI LANKA: AN ANATOMY OF ETHNIC CONFLICT   3

1. An Anatomy of Ethnic Conflict   5

SOWING THE WIND: LANGUAGE, RELIGION AND ETHNICITY   43

2. Language Problems:
    The Politics of Language Policy   45

3. Religion and Politics in Modern Sri Lanka   69

4. Ethnic Politics, Political Violence
    and Tamil Separatism, 1951-1977   119

REAPING THE WHIRLWIND: THE INTERNATIONALIZATION
OF SRI LANKA'S ETHNIC CONFLICT   159

5. Policies of Reconciliation:
    Success and Failure 1977-1983   161

6. India and the Internationalization of
    Sri Lanka's Ethnic Conflict, 1983-1990   193

CAUGHT IN THE CROSSFIRE: SRI LANKA'S
SMALLER MINORITIES   249

7. The Islamic Factor   251

8. The Indian Tamil Community   272

9. Conclusion   297

    Appendices   333
    Notes   336
    Bibliography   363
    Index   380

List of Maps

Map I : Sri Lanka: Political   1

Map II : The distribution of ethnic communities
in Sri Lanka   10

Map III : Tamil population as a proportion of the
total population of the divisions   120

Map IV : Sinhalese and Muslim population as a
proportion of the total population
of the divisions   252

Preface

This book is, in every sense, a sequel to the many articles, books and monographs I have written over the last 10 years on the affairs of Sri Lanka, and on various aspects of the current ethnic conflict of which I have been a concerned witness. I have lived in Sri Lanka throughout, except for a few years spent in Britain and the US, when I was a graduate student, and on sabbatical leave from my University. I have been a participant in some of the efforts at managing the conflict in Sri Lanka, whether as a member of the Presidential Commission on Development Councils whose report of 1980 was an important stage in the establishment of a second tier of government in Sri Lanka (nearly 50 years after it was first mooted), or as a member of the University Grants Commission (1979-89), grappling with the problems of changing University admissions policy to make it more equitable than it was before 1978-79. In both these instances I have had first-hand experience in the making of public policy, and an awareness of the complexities of problems that I would certainly not have had as a mere academic commenting on issues and personalities alike. That practical experience has been, at once, sobering and educative.

My approach to the problems analysed in this book is historical. I make no apology for that. I am by training a historian specializing in the problems of modern and contemporary South Asia. Moreover, as the conflicts in the Balkans and the Caucasus regions remind us, ethnic and religious conflicts have a complex history, and one can neither understand them nor devise strategies and tactics to resolve or manage them without a grasp of the historical background. This book has been written in that spirit.

While concentrating here, of necessity, on the problems of Sri Lanka, I have endeavoured to compare them with similar issues and problems in other societies coping with ethnic conflict. My long association with the International

Centre for Ethnic Studies (ICES) has helped to give a comparative perspective to much that I have written on ethnic conflict even when I focus on South Asia or Sri Lanka for that matter.

Four books and monographs, which I published over the last two years are particularly relevant to the themes reviewed here. These are:

Sri Lanka: Problems of Governance, a volume I edited and to which I contributed a substantial portion; the second of a two-volumed biography of J.R. Jayewardene, Sri Lanka's first Executive President, co-authored with Howard Wriggins, (Quartet Books, London Vol I, 1988, and Leo Cooper, Vol II, 1994, London); a study of the Indian intervention in Sri Lanka and internationalization of the ethnic conflict entitled *Regional Powers and Small State Security, India and Sri Lanka, 1977-90*, (Woodrow Wilson Center Press, Washington D.C., 1995 and Johns Hopkins University Press Baltimore, Md, 1995). In addition to these there is a monograph, entitled, *The 'Traditional Homelands' of the Tamils, Separatist Ideology in Sri Lanka: A Historical Appraisal*. Published in Kandy, Sri Lanka, in 1994-95, it is a revised version of a monograph I published originally in 1987. Inevitably, the present work has drawn upon some of the material in these books, but there is a great deal here that has not been published before.

I am deeply grateful to my colleagues at the International Centre for Ethnic Studies, Kandy, with whom I have discussed many of these issues. Their critical comments have helped me to clarify my own thoughts and arguments. Among them are Gerald Peiris, S.W.R. de A. "Sam" Samarasinghe and Vidyamali Samarasinghe, K.N.O. Dharmadasa and Sirima Kiribamune. At Penguin Books India, my editor, Mrs Raj Kamini Mahadevan's incisive comments, and probing questions have helped me greatly in preparing the final version of the book. None of these people mentioned above are responsible for the views expressed there. Those views are mine, and I take responsibility for them.

I am greatly indebted to Gerald Peiris for the care with which he prepared the maps in this book.

As with everything I have written in recent years, I have benefitted enormously from the assistance I have had from the staff of the ICES, Kandy. Dilrukshi Herath prepared the first draft of this book. Iranga Atukorale prepared two drafts of the final version of the book. She had the assistance of Roshni Siriwardene. I am very grateful to her for the good cheer and efficiency with which she set about her task. Others on the staff of the ICES have helped in numerous ways, especially Kanthi Gamage and Yvette Ferdinands whose assistance in proof-reading has been invaluable; Vasantha Premaratne has helped with the statistical tables in the book. It is with great pleasure that I express my appreciation of their continued support.

I am indebted to the following persons and institutions for the photographs which appear in this book: Mr A. Ratnayake, Chairman, Associated Newspapers of Ceylon Ltd., Mr J. de Lanerolle, Managing Director of Upali Newspapers: the Jayewardene Centre, Colombo, and Mr M. Sameem for the pictures relating to the Muslim minority. The cartoons in the book appear with the kind permission of Mr W.R. Wijesoma.

K.M. de Silva
Kandy, Sri Lanka,
May 1997

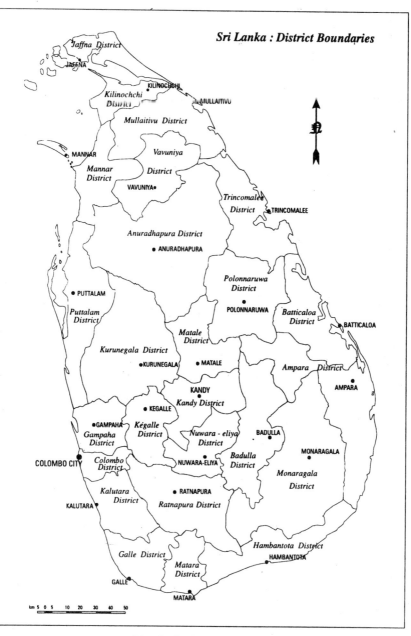

Map I: *Sri Lanka: Political*

I

Sri Lanka: An Anatomy of Ethnic Conflict

CHAPTER 1

An Anatomy of Ethnic Conflict

FROM MODEL COLONY TO EXEMPLAR OF ETHNIC STRIFE

Sri Lanka, or Ceylon, as it was called during British rule
over the island (1796-1948) and until 1972, was referred to
as the 'model' colony in the early years of independence
(1948 to the mid-1950s), where an eminently sensible
national leadership had preferred a negotiated transfer of
power, in contrast to the Indian model. Indeed, the
leadership had deliberately decided to follow the more
conventional, if unglamorous constitutional evolution of
the 'settlement' colonies of Canada, Australia and New
Zealand into independent states.

Sir Charles Jeffries, a senior member of the Colonial
Office mandarinate, was an enthusiastic advocate of Sri
Lanka's claims to the status of the 'model' colony,

> Ceylon provides the classic example of how with good
> sense and goodwill, two peoples can carry through the
> extremely difficult and delicate transition from a ruler-
> subject relationship to an equal partnership.

> Ceylon has been the prototype and model for the new
> Commonwealth of the latter part of the twentieth century.
> In Ceylon the British learnt, by trial and error, the art
> of colonial administration, but they learnt also, the
> wisdom of relinquishing control when it was no longer
> tolerable by a people willing and able to maintain itself
> as an independent state.[1]

Nicholas Mansergh, the historian of the
Commonwealth, had seen Sri Lanka's transition to
independence in much the same terms:

> Ardent nationalists from other and less peaceful lands
> might allude in tones of condescension to Ceylon's fight
> for freedom but the gentlemanly pressure for

independence exerted by its conservative nationalist leaders upon Whitehall made up in good sense what is lacked in political passion. As a result, Ceylon acquired the status of a Dominion of the British Commonwealth without bitterness, by orderly constitutional advance which made the matter of its attainment a source of unfailing satisfaction to British constitutional historians and its status in the academic world that of the model dominion.[2]

The forthright expression of approbation of Sri Lanka's path to independence by Jeffries and Mansergh are explained in part, at least, by the fact that Sri Lanka provided the *only* example, up to the mid and late 1950s at least, of peaceful and orderly transfer of power in the decolonization process of the British Empire so far as the Asian, African and Caribbean colonies were concerned. The metropolitan power had presided over long negotiations (since the 1920s) on definitions of the precise nature of the balance of power that should prevail between the Sinhalese majority and the minorities in the colony's system of government. That balance was given constitutional sanction through a succession of colonial governmental forms (1920, 1923-4, and 1928-31) culminating in the Soulbury constitution (1946-72) under which the country attained independence. However, a decade of peaceful consolidation of power by the Sri Lankan legatees of the British, the United National Party (UNP) governments of 1947 to 1956, was followed by several decades of conflict.

This book seeks to explain how the model colony of orderly, peaceful, transition to independence became an exemplar of periodic outbursts of violent ethnic conflict or, as the British political scientist, Dennis Austin has asked, how Sri Lanka's image of a 'ballot-box oriented democracy, a parliamentary democracy, a Third World democracy . . . [could] be squared with the violence between opposed communities and between terrorists and the state?'[3]

In 1931, Sri Lanka became the scene of a major

departure in British colonial administration. Sri Lanka was the first Asian colony of the British empire and, if one excluded the white settlement colonies, which later became Dominions—the peak of constitutional evolution—the first British colony to enjoy the privilege of universal suffrage. This introduction of universal suffrage just needs to be set against the British experience, where it was achieved only after several decades of agitation, to realize how revolutionary this step was. In Britain that process had stretched from 1832, the year of the great Reform Bill, to 1929 when the first general election under universal suffrage was held. Sri Lanka's first general election under universal suffrage came only two years after that, in 1931, a full 21 years before such an election was held in India. Seven times since independence governments have been changed through the ballot-box, the first such occasion being in 1956. At these Sri Lankan general elections ethnic and religious differences—and more particularly the former—have often been, focal points of political contention, a theme that is dealt with in greater detail later in this chapter, and in other chapters of this book.

Sri Lanka's descent to political instability came in three stages, beginning first of all with the period mid-1955 to 1961. Then after a period of quiescence in the mid and late 1960s, there was a second phase of confrontation, often leading to violence, in the 1970s and culminating in the riots of 1977. This time a period of relative quiescence was followed by the most violent period of ethnic conflict in Sri Lanka's recent history, beginning in 1983 and the outbreak of the anti-Tamil riots of that year, a fateful moment in Sri Lanka's political life that has had repercussions on the country that few other events of this century have had.

The island has one of the most complex plural societies in any part of the world: three important ethnic groups, and as many as four of the world's major religions (*See Tables 2, 3, 4 in appendicies*). The Sinhalese who constitute the majority of the population, have two segments, one from the south-western parts of the country—the areas subjected to colonial rule since the mid-16th century— and the Kandyans, descendants of the subjects of the Kandyan kingdom, the last of the Sinhalese kingdoms, a kingdom with a long record of successful resistance to a succession of colonial powers, the Portuguese, the Dutch and the British. Sri Lankan scholars generally believe that the Sinhalese originally came to the island, over 2,500 years ago, from northern India, Gujarat and/or Bengal, and in later times from southern India as well. The roots of Sinhala culture and civilization are thus Indian, but they have also been deeply influenced by other cultures as well, namely the Portuguese and English and to a lesser extent the Dutch, in recent times, and by the Burmese and Thai. There have always been strong cultural and religious ties between the Sinhalese and the Burmese and Thais, through their common religion: Buddhism.

The Sinhalese today constitute just short of three quarters of the island's peoples, while the Sinhalese-Buddhists are just over two-thirds of it. Yet the Sinhalese-Buddhists often tend to emphasize their minority status *vis-à-vis* the Tamils by linking the latter's ethnic affinity to the Tamils of southern India. Sri Lanka's location off the coast of South India, and specially its close proximity to Tamilnadu, separated by a shallow and narrow stretch of sea serves to accentuate this sense of a minority status among the Sinhalese. Their own sense of ethnic distinctiveness is identified through religion—Theravada Buddhism—and language—Sinhala. They take pride in the fact that Buddhism thrives in Sri Lanka while it has practically disappeared in its original home, India. Their language, Sinhala, has its roots in classical Indian languages, but it is now a distinctly Sri Lankan language, and one that is not spoken anywhere else.

Among the Tamils, there are two distinct groups, the Sri Lankan or Jaffna Tamils, whose origins go back well over 1,500 years and the Indian Tamils whose forebears were brought to the island by British planters and their agents in India in the 19th century and early 20th century. The two Tamil groups do not have much in common except their language. Both groups are mainly Hindus, but their distinctive geographical locations and the rigours of the Hindu caste system have generally kept them apart, the bulk of the plantation workers being regarded as 'low' caste by the Sri Lanka or Jaffna Tamil elite. Again, there is also the 'class' element, the Indian Tamils being, in the main, plantation workers. While there is no convergence of political attitudes and objectives between them and the Sri Lankan Tamils, especially the most activist armed groups, there is, nevertheless, considerable sympathy from the hill country or Indian Tamils for the latter in the current struggle with the Sri Lankan state. Certainly, the leadership of the Indian Tamil group has had no compunctions about openly supporting the political aspirations of the Tamil activists, including the armed separatists in the north or east of the island, a support that stops short of endorsing the demand for a separate state.

The Sri Lankan Tamil population is concentrated in the drier northern and eastern parts of the island. Two significant points in regard to its geographical distribution should be kept in mind: firstly, that over a third of them live and work in the predominantly Sinhalese parts of the island. The second point, even more significant in the context of the separatist agitation among sections of the Sri Lankan Tamils, is the close proximity of the Jaffna peninsula and the Northern Province of Sri Lanka to the state of Tamilnadu in South India. The affinity of some sections of the Tamils there for the Sri Lankan Tamils, plays a very significant and disruptive role in the affairs of Sri Lanka.

The Muslims in Sri Lanka regard themselves as, and are treated as, a distinct 'ethnic' group even though most of them are Tamil-speaking. They are closely integrated into the country's political system through the national political parties. Their rivalry with the Tamils is a long-standing one, and has frequently erupted into violence

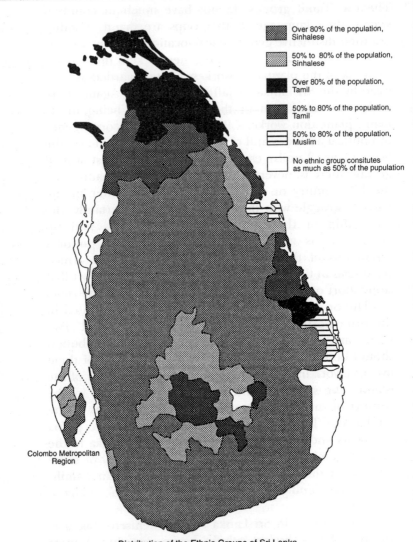

Colombo Metropolitan
Region

Over 80% of the population,
Sinhalese

50% to 80% of the population,
Sinhalese

Over 80% of the population,
Tamil

50% to 80% of the population,
Tamil

50% to 80% of the population,
Muslim

No ethnic group consitutes
as much as 50% of the pupulation

Distribution of the Ethnic Groups of Sri Lanka
Spatial Frame : Parliamentary Electorates and Polling Divisions

Map II

between the two groups in recent times. They have been strongly opposed to the establishment of a separate Tamil state, or for that matter, till recent times, even to any realistic devolution of power to district or provincial units.

The two groups, Tamils and Muslims, are split on the basis of religion; the division is seen at its sharpest in the Eastern Province where nearly a third of the island's Muslim population lives. The Muslims are as suspicious of the political aspirations of the Tamil separatists as they are of the Sinhalese majority, if not much more so. In fact, there is a striking contrast in the political behaviour of the Tamils and the Muslims. All the main Tamil political parties are ethnic or regional parties; the Muslims had no ethnic political parties till the establishment of the Sri Lanka Muslim Congress in the late 1980s. Instead they were—and are—members of national political parties and enjoy considerable influence at policy-making levels in these. Muslim candidates of the national parties are often preferred to Sinhalese opponents at the electoral level purely in terms of party alignments, a feature of Sri Lankan politics since independence.

A small country like Sri Lanka is not normally the focus of international attention. Sri Lanka has received so much attention since the mid-1950s because of several episodes of ethnic tension, erupting regularly into violent clashes between its two main ethnic groups, the Sinhalese and Tamils. The country has a long history of ethnic tensions and conflicts in pre-colonial times; indeed many scholars see these stretching back over several centuries and, as some would have it, to the very beginnings of the island's recorded history, over 2000 years ago. In addition the problem becomes more complex through the imposition of colonial rule under three western powers, in succession, from the beginning of the sixteenth century: the Portuguese, the Dutch and the British.

The current ethnic conflict in Sri Lanka is a much more complex business than a simple straightforward confrontation between a once well-entrenched minority—

the Sri Lankan Tamils—and a now powerful but still insecure majority—the Sinhalese. The Sinhalese majority and the Sri Lankan Tamil minority are not the only players in this intricate political drama even though, at present, they play the principal roles. Suffice it to say here that there are two conflicting perceptions of these conflicts. Most Sinhalese believe that the Tamil minority has enjoyed a privileged position under British rule and that the balance has of necessity to shift in favour of the Sinhalese majority. The Sri Lankan Tamil minority is an achievement-oriented, industrious group who still continue to enjoy high status in society, considerable influence in the economy, a significant if diminishing role in the bureaucracy and is well placed in all levels of the education system. The Tamils for their part would claim that they are now a harassed minority, the victims of frequent acts of communal violence and of calculated acts and policies of discrimination directed at them. Nevertheless, they could hardly be described as a beleaguered minority, the victims of regular episodes of violence—though violence admittedly has been frequent enough in recent times—given the impassioned ferocity with which sections of them have fought against the Sinhalese-dominated security forces since 1984-5, and the frequent attacks of Tamil terrorist groups, against the civilian population—Sinhalese in the main. This is quite apart from the ethnic cleansing they have indulged in at the expense mainly of the Muslim population of the Jaffna peninsula and the Mannar district (in the north-west) both in the heart of the principal Tamil settlements in the island. Most of the Tamil fears and their sense of insecurity stem from the belief that they have lost the advantageous position they enjoyed under British rule in many sectors of public life in the country; in brief, a classic case of a sense of relative deprivation.

WHAT IS ETHNICITY?

This book is about nationalism, it is about ethnicity, it is about the politicization of ethnicity. The term nationalism, is of older vintage than ethnicity, but both of them—and, in particular, ethnicity—have eluded very precise definition despite the attempts of many scholars. The present upsurge of political violence in some of the states of the former Soviet bloc, and in the successor states of the former Soviet Union, has given greater currency to the two terms, especially to ethnicity,[4] in the descriptions and analyses put forth by journalists and from politicians. The common assumption in many of these cases is that the two terms, ethnicity and nationalism, are closely intertwined, indeed that they are interchangeable.

The fact that the term nationalism has been around so much longer than ethnicity only makes the problems of definition more complex.[5] Scholars seek to distinguish nationalism from ethnocentrism; and to deny that mere evidence of the experiences of national consciousness in ancient times is proof of the existence of nationalism in the form in which western scholars understand the term. A recent scholar—and I have deliberately chosen Paul Brass, a specialist in South Asian politics—states that:

> The term 'nationalism' will be used in two senses. For the most part, it will be used to refer to the process by which ethnic groups and communities are mobilized for action to attain political ends.

He proceeds thereafter

> Another common use of the term 'nationalism' . . . the process by which loyalties are developed to the state . . . the two types of processes to which the term refers are subtypes of a more general process . . . sometimes referred to as identity formation . . .[6]

This definition is as good as any we can find in the literature today. In using it here I make no claim that it can be applied in analysis of nationalist agitations in all parts of the world. The weakness as far as I see it is that it is based on western, and especially the European experience, and it fails to consider the validity of claims being made in Asian societies for forms of nationalism before the emergence of the present European/Western model.

Over 60 years ago Pareto pointed out that the term ethnicity 'is one of the vaguest known to sociology'.[7] Despite the efforts of scholars since then, we are yet to arrive at a standard definition of ethnicity today. This is not to deny the substantial contribution of anthropologists beginning with Edmund Leach[8] in the early 1950s and Frederik Barth[9] a little over 10 years later, and of others, in clearing away some of the confusion in the use of the term. In defining ethnicity,[10] Leach and Barth adopted two distinctive approaches. Leach emphasized the structural relationships, or the relation between given institutions in a society and along with it the formation of identity, a more subjective process. Barth's important contribution lay in his emphasis on 'boundary-maintenance' as a critically important factor in ethnicity, something dependent on structural differences of groups. (In Barth's view structural relationships are more important in defining ethnicity than cultural factors. They also play an important role in the processes of state-formation and the emergence of ethnic identity.) As against this were the views associated with Edward Shils,[11] and Clifford Geertz,[12] which became especially influential in the late 1950s and early 1960s, the primordialist approach, as it was called. This emphasized the importance of culturally distinctive characteristics such as myths of origin, ritual, religion or genealogical descent in distinguishing groups and peoples from one another. The primordialists stopped short of placing these characteristics within a historical context.

These two viewpoints have been central to the debate on the term ethnicity in the 1970s, and which continues to the present day. In the early 1980s another anthropologist, Charles Keyes, in an effort at reconciling these two viewpoints began to emphasize the significance of culture as the 'primary defining characteristic' of an ethnic group, and went on to argue that 'ethnicity' is salient only to the extent that it helps peoples to determine their own distinctiveness from others who are seen to have ethnic identities of their own.[13]

The circular reasoning one sees in Keyes's efforts at straddling the contrasting views of men like Barth on the one hand and the primordialists on the other, characterizes the efforts of others as well, like the US political scientist Cynthia Enloe. Her definition of ethnicity comes close to the primordialist position in emphasizing 'an awareness of a common identity', as its principal feature. Paul Brass whom we have quoted earlier, used the term 'community' to refer

> . . . to ethnic groups whose members have developed an awareness of a common identity and have attempted to define the boundaries of the group. A community becomes a nationality or a nation when it mobilizes for political action and becomes politically significant . . . makes political demands and achieves a significant measure of success by its own efforts.[14]

An 'awareness of a common identity' brings us to three other elements essential to an understanding of ethnicity. The first of these is the vital importance of the past, an awareness of the history of a country or a people, in understanding the complexities of the present, whether in the Balkans, and Central and Eastern Europe, or the Baltic states, or in South and South-east Asia. In all of these the analyses of ethnic tensions are often framed in terms of historical legacies in which language, culture and religion are the essential points of distinctive identity. Ethnic identities often carry with them memories of deep-rooted historical enmities. Tensions and hostilities arise from attempts at a redress of historical grievances, sometimes going back several centuries into the past. Secondly, there is the 'politicization of ethnicity', a process '. . . that preserves ethnic groups by emphasizing their singularity [and yet] also [facilitates] their modernization by transforming them into political conflict groups for the modern political arena.'[15] And thirdly, there is the elasticity of the term ethnicity, and the wide variety of potential ethnic groups: F. Barth, for instance, would include 'community', 'culture', language group, corporation, association or population group,[16] while others like the historian A.J. Stockwell speaking from a scholarly interest in or experience of post-colonial South and South-east Asia—Malaysia in this instance—argue that 'ethnic identity may be perceived according to a variety of terms such as race, culture, religion, language or place or origin of the group's members.'[17]

The current reality in Sri Lanka and South-east Asia, no less than in Central and Eastern Europe, is that language, culture, religion and ethnicity stemming from pre-colonial times, and acting separately or in combination have assumed the proportions of explosive forces threatening the stability of the post-independence political settlement. The separatist threat in South and South-east Asia, dangerous though it may be in some parts of these regions, is not as ominously menacing to peace as that in the Balkans and Central and Eastern Europe. Nevertheless, four factors, either acting on their own or in combination, have stimulated forces of separatist agitation, in all these regions. These are: religion, language, the redress of historic grievances, and the question of disputed territorial boundaries, external and internal.

A key to understanding the strength of separatist forces is to identify the stages by which empires were constructed, and to examine the nature of the administrative and other mechanisms of control devised to absorb the new territories thus acquired within the wider colonial political structure. The British empire in India was unique in controlling the whole Indian subcontinent. But in welding it together, and consolidating it, the empire builders of the *raj* incorporated within it peoples and territories which Indian rulers of the past had seldom been able to control. The North-east and North West Frontier territories of the *raj*, acquired through the conquest of Burma and the subjugation of the Sikhs are examples of these. From them spring some of India's most troublesome separatist movements.

The difference in the manner of British conquest and rule in Burma and Sri Lanka underlines the importance of the colonial experience in understanding the nature of the problems confronted by these societies. Burma was absorbed in three chronologically distinct phases viz, 1826, 1852-3, and 1886 and ruled as part of the *raj* till 1937 when it was given a separate administration, the first such successful and peaceful venture in South and South-east Asian history in modern times. British colonial administration strengthened the forces of ethnic separateness within Burma, between the Burman majority (generally the more advanced people of the plains and the Irrawaddy delta) and the minority peoples, the Karens, the Shans, the Kachins and others. The Burmese kingdom of Ava had been on the crest of a wave of success in the 17th and 18th centuries as it triumphed over its Thai rivals culminating in the invasion of the principal Thai kingdom and the destruction of its capital Ayuthiya in the 1760s. But in just over 50 years of that great success, the Burmese rulers met their match: defeat by the British meant that they—the Burmese rulers—did not have time to consolidate their conquests, and to get the various minority ethnic groups living within their newly expanded territories to acknowledge their position as subjects of the Burmese kings. Thus, conquest by the British served to emphasize the differences between these peoples—the Karens in particular—and the Burman majority.

In Sri Lanka a very early attempt at rule through the Madras administration of the English East India Company led to a major rebellion in 1797-8. Thereafter, whenever British officials were tempted to treat the island as a unit of the British *raj* in India, the memory of this rebellion served as a warning against the perils involved. Thus, Sri Lanka was administered through the Colonial Office. But though the patterns of absorption in the colonial system were different in two countries, Burma and Sri Lanka, they had much the same consequences. In both a sense of separation from India was strengthened; and in both they deeply influenced the nature of post-colonial ethnic tensions and separatist agitations.

The process of colonial consolidation and integration in Sri Lanka left behind a legacy of an overcentralized state, a legacy which accounts, in part at least, for the difficulties post-independence governments have had in introducing measures for the devolution of power to regional units of administration. This pattern of colonial administration was in contrast to that adopted in Burma, and most other parts of the British *raj* in the Indian subcontinent where there was a much greater tolerance of regional and local identities.

British policy in Burma had kept peoples and territories apart, in matters of administration; in Sri Lanka on the other hand, peoples experienced greater integration, and the island's administration was made more cohesive. The second feature—and here there was greater similarity in the policies pursued in the two territories—was an increase in the elements of ethnic and religious diversity, a significant Christian minority in Burma and a dominant one in Sri Lanka, and in both the entry of a large Indian minority, more economically powerful in Burma than it became in Sri Lanka.

A tendency in Sri Lanka and Burma to cherish the pre-colonial past and to yearn for its restoration has also played a role in forging ethnic problems. Peoples of these two countries have been compelled to re-live some of the agonies of their tormented past as recent events have demonstrated so tragically. In Sri Lanka the past is a powerful presence and often carries with it painful memories of invading armies, battles lost, cities destroyed, temples and palaces pillaged and kingdoms subverted. Ethnic consciousness in combination with nationalism raises expectations of restoring some of the glories of the past, especially the ancient past, and in the process, creating a new society upon ancient foundations. Attempts to restore the past often involve an obsessive concern about securing a redress of ancient grievances; in many such instances, the past is an incubus which not only dominates the present, but carries with it the added danger of jeopardising the possibility of establishing a stable political structure for the new society of the future. The politicization of ethnicity then has an historical dimension that strengthens the hands of recalcitrant activist groups and unscrupulous politicians who seek to exploit issues linked to divisive historical events of the past for their own political ends.

This tendency to seek a restoration of an imagined past is not confined to the Burmans and Sinhalese. In Sri Lanka it has affected the Tamil minority as well, and forms the basis of their claims of a 'traditional homeland', the successor as they see it of the short-lived Jaffna kingdom of old.[18] But the historical evidence the Tamil advocates of a 'traditional homeland' provide in support of their claims is so flimsy that only 'true believers' can accept them.[19] Thus the Sinhalese and Tamils (or large and influential numbers of them) meet in the dark recesses of their respective pasts and fight once more the battles of long ago.

Indeed, the burden of historical memories is the essential starting point for an analysis of the issues that divide the people of Sri Lanka. There is, first of all, the Sinhalese sense of historical destiny, of a small and embattled people who have preserved Theravada Buddhism when it was obliterated in India under a Hindu revivalist tide, and whose language, despite its roots in classical Indian languages, is uniquely Sri Lankan. Linked to this is their perception of the Tamils as a traditional 'national' enemy against whom they have fought at various times over two thousand years of a common history. There is also the perception of southern India as the source of scores of invasions of the heartland of ancient Sri Lanka.

Equally important is the historical memory of a long,

and for many centuries, successful record of retaining national independence in the face of western invaders, of survival against very heavy odds. Factionalism within the Sinhalese kingdoms enabled the Portuguese to establish themselves in some of the coastal areas of the country, but they faced strong resistance from the Sinhalese and were eventually expelled from the island with the help of the rivals of the Portuguese, the Dutch. In doing so the Sinhalese only succeeded in changing one set of westerners for another in control of parts of the island's littoral. They fought against the Dutch and preserved their independence through the Kandyan kingdom which controlled the central hills and parts of the littoral. A British army of invasion in 1803 suffered the fate of previous Portuguese and Dutch invaders of Kandy, an early and deceptive success, and then a guerrilla campaign that destroyed the invader. Eventually, the last independent Sinhalese kingdom succumbed to the British in 1815-8, ceded by its chiefs in rebellion against an unpopular ruler.

This long and successful record of Sri Lankan resistance to Portuguese, Dutch and British invaders, was essentially confined to the Sinhalese. Meantime, the short-lived Tamil kingdom of Jaffna had been crushed by the Portuguese after some early resistance and incorporated into the *Estado* by 1619-20, never to re-establish itself again as an independent entity. Thereafter, there is no record of Tamil resistance to western rule comparable to that of the Sinhalese.

POLITICAL CULTURE AND THE POST-COLONIAL STATE

Despite the strains and stresses, the turmoil and violence, especially ethnically-driven violence, that have been such prominent features of its politics and society in recent years, Sri Lanka shares with India the distinction, among the post-colonial states of South Asia, of sustaining a democratic political system throughout the four decades and more of independence. The breakdown of democratic institutions which both countries have seen, are, on the whole, short interludes in the general pattern of democratic rule rather than distinct episodes in a history of creeping authoritarianism. In Sri Lanka, as in India, the stresses of ethnically-driven conflict need to be viewed against the background of electoral politics. These conflicts and the electoral process have had a profound influence on each other. This chapter seeks to provide an analysis of the nature and extent of that mutual influence.

The immediate post-colonial period, 1947-56, saw the seemingly successful transplanting of western style democratic institutions and organizations of civil society in Sri Lanka. Apart from a vocal Marxist minority advocating a radically different political system and social order the vast majority of the educated-elite who had grown up in a political culture suffused by the traditions and conventions of British parliamentary democracy was attracted to this as if by a process of osmosis and treated it as the only model worth adopting. It was a political order in which some of the Marxist leaders were as familiar with Erskine May's classic treatise on British parliamentary practice as they were with the works of Marx.

Within a decade of the attainment of independence the legatees of the British were under systematic attack by populist nationalists and by the Marxists. The fundamentals of the political order of the post-colonial system and especially its emphasis on pluralism, ethnic harmony, and secularism were systematically challenged by populist nationalists through their reassertion of indigenous values emphasizing an ethnic identity based on language and religion. Their campaign reached its peak in the mid-1950s and triumphed electorally in 1956. They owed some part of their success to the electoral alliance they had with the Marxist Left, but there was no doubt that the Marxists were as much the losers in this political conflict as the party that held power from 1947 to 1956.

In the period 1956-64 and again in 1970-7 the country witnessed a second phase in the transfer of power, this time from the English-educated elite to the vernacular-speaking elites. The latter placed little value on some of the principal features of the liberal tradition that had evolved under British rule in the island. This included a dominant role for the private sector in the country's economy. The local elites regarded them as either irrelevant to the needs of their political and social programmes, or as obstacles to be eliminated in the cause of cultural nationalism and the exigencies of rapid social change. In a very real sense their electoral triumphs were seen as the seizure of state power through the ballot. Once the state was in their hands it was treated as the source of redistributive justice with its own inner logic guided more by political will than concerns for economic growth. These periods of rapid political and social change placed enormous pressure on the country's institutions and its economy alike. Competing political elites used, or misused, existing institutions to impose their agendas, time-tables and priorities on them oblivious to the need to protect their independence and autonomy. In Sri Lanka, as in India, it was argued that such independence and autonomy often protected vested interests and stood in the way of delivering services to the poor. The needs of 'the people' therefore became the justification for the erosion, if not destruction, of the independence of autonomous institutions, ranging from the judiciary and the press to universities and schools.

The debate on the nature of the post-colonial state in the early years of independence was a continuation of one that was conducted in rather more strident tones in the early 1940s. Sri Lanka's first Prime Minister, D.S. Senanayake (1947-52)[20], always saw the pluralism of the Sri Lanka polity as a source of strength not weakness and identified the establishment of a sense of Sri Lankan nationalism through a resolute subordination of ethnic and religious identities as one of the principal and most urgent concerns of any transfer of power political settlement. The substance of his policies as Prime Minister was based on the recognition and nurturing of pluralism.[21]

The essence of his policies was contained in clause 8 of the Ministers' draft constitution of 1944, prepared under his leadership and drafted by his constitutional adviser, Sir Ivor Jennings, then Vice-Chancellor of the University of Ceylon,[22] and a leading authority on the British constitution and politics. Under the conditions of that clause, legislation which sought

a) to prohibit or restrict the free exercise of any religion.

b) to make persons of any community or religion liable to disabilities or restrictions to which persons of other communities or religions are not liable; or

c) to confer on persons of any community or religion any privileges or advantages which are not conferred on persons of other communities or religions; or

d) to alter the constitution of any religious body except with the approval of the governing authority of that religious body . . .

required a special two-thirds majority in the lower house of the legislature.

The debate on the nature of the post-colonial state in Senanayake's days revolved on three issues: the political form and constitutional arrangements in the transfer of power settlement, i.e., the concept of Dominion Status and membership of the Commonwealth; secondly, the security arrangements that he had devised, in the form of the defence agreements with Britain, which seemingly linked Sri Lanka to the Anglo-American bloc in those early days of the Cold War; and thirdly, the emerging conflict between supporters of the primacy of Buddhism and the Sinhalese in the Sri Lanka polity, and those who underlined the pluralism of Sri Lankan society. As regards the first two, Senanayake's critics came from the very vocal left wing of Sri Lanka's political spectrum. On the third issue the opposition was more diffused and less vocal, but it had a much wider support base although it did not seem so at that time because of Senanayake's bold and skilful handling of these criticisms.

Through his mature statecraft Senanayake thwarted these divisive forces but his immediate successors as Prime Minister, his son Dudley Senanayake (1952-5) and, especially Sir John Kotelawala (1953-6), found it more politic to come to terms with them in the hope that an accommodative policy would help the government to survive and win another term of office. By the end of 1954 and the early part of 1955, the Sinhalese-Buddhist majority, long dormant, was asserting its national dominance. It was intent on establishing the primacy of their language and religion in the Sri Lanka polity. In the process, the political validity of a Sri Lanka nationalism based on pluralism, and the essential secularity of the polity, were subjected to an emotion-laden scrutiny in which the terms of reference were drawn from the pre-colonial heritage of Sri Lankan history.

S.W.R.D. Bandaranaike (1956-9) successfully exploited this discontent in his election campaign in 1956. His decisive victory was a significant turning point in Sri Lanka's history, for it represented the rejection of the concept of a Sri Lankan nationalism based on an acceptance of pluralism as an essential feature of a democratic political system, and its substitution by a more democratic and populist nationalism which was fundamentally divisive in its impact on the country, because of its unmistakably Sinhalese and Buddhist orientation.[23] Against the background of the *Buddha Jayanthi*, the worldwide celebration in 1956 of the 2,500th anniversary of the death of the Buddha, this populist nationalism kindled visions of a revitalized society, preserving the past and transforming it into something distinctive, authentic and new. Despite the strength of a millennial form of Buddhism of this period, it was the emphasis on language that provided the sharp cutting edge of political and social change. Language became the basis of a more strident nationalism, and this metamorphosis of nationalism affected both the Sinhalese and Tamil populations.

All the major Sri Lankan political parties of Bandaranaike's day were baffled by this novel phenomenon of linguistic nationalism. Yet the imperatives of their calling compelled each in turn to define their attitude to it. Most of them eventually succumbed to the blandishments of linguistic nationalism. None understood the perils involved. They may have been less complacent if they had turned to the history of Europe where this phenomenon had appeared in the mid-19th century and had such a destructive impact on the politics of Central Europe.

A century later this same phenomenon had a powerful destabilizing effect on the successor states to the British *raj* and empire in South Asia. So strong was the pressure of linguistic nationalism in India that the internal boundaries of the provinces and 'native' states inherited at the transfer of power and the partition were drawn afresh to accommodate it. This exercise was conducted in the mid-1950s. The impact of this same force of linguistically-driven nationalism was much more destructive in Pakistan. When that geo-political oddity was dismembered and the state of Bangladesh was established in December 1971,[24] it demonstrated that language could, on occasion, be a stronger force than religion for purposeful ideological reconstruction at times of revolutionary upheaval. In Sri Lanka, as we shall see, it has contributed greatly to disturbing the civil peace since the mid-1950s.

The consequences of this transformation of nationalism for the processes of state-building in Sri Lanka may be outlined as follows. Firstly, the concept of a multi-ethnic polity ceased to be politically viable any longer. The emphasis on Sri Lanka as a Sinhalese-Buddhist polity carried an emotional popular appeal, compared with which a multi-ethnic polity was no more than a sterile abstraction. Secondly, the justification for this reversal of a central feature of the transfer of power settlement laid stress on a democratic sanction deriving its validity from the clear numerical superiority of the Sinhala-speaking group. At the same time, the focus continued to be on the island as a cohesive political entity, and Sinhalese nationalism was consciously or unconsciously equated with Sri Lankan nationalism. The minorities, and in particular the Sri Lankan Tamils, refused to endorse the assumption that Sinhalese nationalism was interchangeable with the larger Sri Lankan nationalism. As a result, 1956 saw the beginning of almost a decade of ethnic and linguistic tensions erupting occasionally into episodes of violent ethnic conflict between the Sinhalese and Tamils and religious confrontation between the Buddhist and Christians, in particular, the Roman Catholics.

Similarly, the association of Buddhism with the state, and the simultaneous reduction of Christian influence, especially after 1960, were integral features in the abandonment of the concept of a poly-ethnic polity. There was increasing but sporadic pressure for the elevation of Buddhism to the status of the state religion, but this, as we shall see in chapter three, the political leadership in both major parties, the UNP and the Sri Lanka Freedom Party (SLFP), was able to resist. Nevertheless, the secularity of the post-independence Sri Lankan polity was being undermined even if it had not become a Buddhist state, which Buddhist pressure groups wished it to be.

With Bandaranaike's victory in 1956 Sinhalese-Buddhist populism established itself as a major force in Sri Lankan politics. Its claims of supporting the interests of the ordinary people over those of the elite and the 'establishment', its emphasis on public ownership of large sectors of the economy, and its proclivity for redistributive policies, provided a politically viable substitute for Marxist ideology. Generally adumbrated in an imprecise form it drew its sustenance from its recognizably Buddhist idiom. Under his leadership the SLFP accommodated itself—as the UNP clearly had not—to an expanding 'political nation' in which Sinhalese-Buddhists sought an influence commensurate with the numbers. Ideologically hazy and politically opportunistic, Bandaranaike's 'middle way' promised people social change, social justice, economic independence from foreign powers, and the completion of political sovereignty. It gave a sense of dignity to the common people, and fortified their self-respect. But its fundamental weakness—the result of the fuzziness of its political ideology—was that its social and economic programme lacked any serious commitment to economic growth and fell back on policies of redistribution to sustain the momentum of the changes to which it was committed.

One of the notable consequences of the emergence of Sinhalese-Buddhist populism as a major political force was the setback it gave the island's dynamic Marxist movement. With independence and the first elections to the House of Representatives in 1947, the incorrigibly factious Marxist parties (divided basically between Trotskyists and Stalinists) had emerged as the most potent challenge to the UNP governments of the day, if not yet a credible alternative government. They had always aspired to this status, and in the heady aftermath of the election of 1956, they saw themselves in this role. Others also saw them in that role when Dr N.M. Perera, leader of the Lanka Sama Samaja Party (LSSP) and a master of parliamentary procedure, became Leader of the Opposition. Then came the election of March 1960 at which they made a purposeful bid for power. The electorate cut them down to size. This was unpalatable but visible evidence that the electoral gains of the past had disappeared, and the prospects for the future were much more limited. They found to their dismay and discomfiture that Sinhalese-Buddhist populism had an appeal which cut across class interests, and that it evoked as deep a response from the Sinhalese working class as it did among the peasantry and the Sinhala-educated intelligentsia. The cosmopolitan outlook of the Marxists and their enlightened advocacy of a multi-ethnic secular polity proved to be profoundly disadvantageous to them, and they were compelled to compromise on these issues without, however, any substantial political benefits.

In March 1960 a revived UNP had returned to Parliament as the numerically largest party but was well short of a majority. For three months there was even a UNP minority government. The Marxist Left helped to bring the UNP government down on that occasion by joining forces with the SLFP and the Federal Party (FP), the principal Tamil political party, to defeat it over the 'speech from the throne', the annual policy statement. The approval of this by a majority of the legislature was a *sine qua non* of Westminster style parliamentary government. Alarmed by the resilience the UNP had demonstrated and the threat this could pose to the economic if not social changes introduced under Bandaranaike, the Marxists reverted to the policy of an electoral arrangement with the SLFP, a sharing of seats and votes devised in 1955 as a prelude to the election of 1956. At the general election of July 1960 the UNP was defeated once more, but the SLFP did well enough to form a government on its own, and one which did not seem to need the support of the left to ensure its stability. It was soon evident that a revival of the SLFP's electoral fortunes did not ensure any greater degree of governmental cohesion or any substantial improvement in administrative skill than its predecessor of 1956-9 had demonstrated. Indeed things were much worse. Thus, the coalition that was established between the SLFP and sections of the Marxist Left in 1964 has a special significance. While the electoral dominance of the SLFP in national politics had resulted in a corresponding decline in the electoral fortunes of the left-wing parties, an *apertura a sinistra* was devised for two converging but different reasons. The SLFP was forced to seek the support of the Left to ensure greater governmental stability in the executive, and to harness the superior debating and tactical skills of the Left within the legislature and thereby weaken the opposition UNP, while the Marxist parties' influence on— if not control over—the public sector trade unions held out the prospect of more effective if not efficient administration. The Left saw this as an opportunity to influence governmental policies and their implementation. But more important they saw the *apertura a sinistra* as a necessity for the purpose of keeping the UNP out of power. The left-wing parties paid a heavy price for this association with the SLFP; apart from being converted, in all but name, into appendages of the centrist SLFP, they also accepted the SLFP's Sinhalese-Buddhist outlook and the policies on language associated with it, as well as a position on the minorities, which they did not jettison till the mid-1980s.

Indeed, the two Bandaranaikes between them had established a new equilibrium of political forces within the country, and their own supporters and their associates (such as the Marxist Left) as well as their opponents (such as the UNP) had to accommodate themselves to this political reality in the 1960s and 1970s at least. The primary feature of this new balance of forces had been the acceptance of the predominance of the Sinhalese and Buddhists within the Sri Lanka polity, and as a corollary of this, a sharp decline in the status of the ethnic and religious minorities. Neither the UNP nor the Marxist Left were entirely happy with the latter situation, but political prudence required them to refrain from any public repudiation of at least the first part of this arrangement. This was especially difficult for the UNP since it was the alternative government for much of the 1970s and aspiring to power. Repudiation of both these conditions came during their long term in office, from 1977 to 1994, but by this time they were confronted by a sharp radicalization of Tamil political activity in the north of the island and a burgeoning separatist movement.

Though the Buddhist movement was generally hostile to Marxist ideology, it was not strongly opposed to the adoption of a socialist programme. On the contrary, since plantation enterprise, nascent industry and the island's external trade were dominated by foreign capitalists, and the Christians (both Sinhalese and Tamils), Muslims and Tamils in general were seen to be disproportionately influential within the indigenous business class, Buddhist pressure groups viewed 'socialism' as a means of redressing the balance in favour of the Sinhalese-Buddhist majority. Every extension of state control over trade and industry—and the pace and frequency of these extensions increased markedly with Bandaranaike's victory in 1956—could be, and was, justified on the ground that it helped curtail the influence of foreigners and the minorities, quite apart, of course, from undermining the support base of the UNP. The SLFP took the initiative in much of this, but the coalition with the Marxists from 1964 onwards and the formulation of a more broad-based coalition government of 1970-5 gave an additional impetus to expanding state control over ever-increasing areas of the economy.

The Sinhalese-Buddhist section of the business class, especially those associated with the SLFP, was not averse to socialism provided, however, that its own economic interests were not seriously affected. This ambivalence to state control over the economy was reflected in the inner circles of the populist SLFP from its inception as a party, in the attempt to reconcile a commitment to an ill-defined 'socialism' with an advocacy of the interests of a section of the indigenous capitalist class—the Sinhalese-Buddhist segment of it. It weakened resistance to the imposition of state control over the dominant sectors of the economy. That resistance might have been stronger had economic interests prevailed over the divisive forces of ethnicity and religion. The result was that in Sri Lanka the economy came to be dominated and controlled by the state to a far greater extent than in other parts of South Asia. Indeed in the 1960s and 1970s, whenever the SLFP or a SLFP-led coalition was in power, state control of the economy became an end in itself and acquisition of property by the state an instrument of partisan politics. The first attempts to reverse this trend came with J.R. Jayewardene and his government of 1977, but state domination of the economy has persisted despite this, although it has considerably weakened since the liberalization of the economy was initiated with his government's budget of November 1977. The decline of state control was accelerated under R. Premadasa and appears to have survived the change of government in 1994.

Our analysis of the political effects of populist policies would be incomplete without a reference to the consequences of the overwhelming dominance of the state in social and economic life. Following the example of the SLFP and its Marxist allies and co-belligerents in the 1960s and 70s, success in electoral battle had become an obsession, a matter of near desperation, because it demonstrated that victory provided an avenue to almost unfettered power and access to the dominant source of wealth. Access to political power and powerful politicians was the principal means of acquiring wealth and controlling resources for that purpose, through the *dirigiste* economic system and its plethora of permits and licences. In addition, extension of state power and influence into areas such as the school system, nationalized in 1960-1, which had hitherto been substantially independent of the state, meant that a new set of jobs was also available and available only through the government. Thus, new avenues of patronage were being opened, and along with these, greatly enlarged opportunities for graft for politicians and middle-men.

The successive increases in polling at the general elections since 1960 is partly explained by this phenomenon of the state and politicians becoming the primary source of employment in a society which places a high premium on state and state sector employment. It is also part of the explanation for the Sri Lankans' proclivity (true of the Sinhalese more than others) to carry partisan politics to extremes, marked by occasional bursts of political violence during and after election campaigns, in short the corrosive divisiveness of Sri Lankan politics since the early 1960s.

A MULTI-PARTY SYSTEM AND COALITION GOVERNMENTS

One of the most significant features of Sri Lanka's political system is the emergence of a genuine multi-party system in which the two major parties have held power for long periods between 1947 and 1997. The UNP has been in office, on its own or in coalition, with other minor parties, for 32 years, a length of time which is exceeded only by the Congress Party in India, the Liberal Democratic Party in Japan, the constituent elements of the governing coalition in Malaysia, and of course the Peoples Action Party in Singapore. The SLFP has held office for 16 years generally in coalition with smaller parties of the Left, and for brief periods on its own. In August 1994 it began yet another period in office, as the core of yet another centre-left coalition.[25]

Another unusual, if not unique feature, is the pattern of political leadership in Sri Lanka. Over the last 45 years the UNP has had seven leaders: D.S. Senanayake from 1946 to 1952, Dudley Senanayake from 1952 to 1953, and from 1957 to 1973, Sir John Kotelawala from 1953 to 1957, J.R. Jayewardene from 1973 to 1988, and R. Premadasa from 1989 to his assassination in 1993 when the leadership went to D.B. Wijetunga (1993-4) and thereafter to R. Wickremasinghe, the present Leader of the Opposition. The SLFP, on the other hand, has had only two leaders—the Bandaranaikes, husband and wife—from the time of its establishment in 1951 to 1994 when Chandrika Kumaratunga, the younger daughter of the Bandaranaikes became Prime Minister (in August 1994) and Executive President (in November 1994). The SLFP thus remains a 'family party', one dominated by the Bandaranaike family. The record is unique in two different ways: first, it is a remarkable case of political dexterity of an 'old' family, closely associated with the British—and even earlier, with the Dutch—in short a family with a long and unbroken record of collaboration with colonialism, successfully adapting itself to a rapidly changing environment with its emphasis on nationalist and 'socialist' credentials; second, very seldom has a single family been able to retain its hold on a political party in a modern democracy as the Bandaranaikes of Sri Lanka have done through periods of government, and long periods in opposition. Under normal circumstances, the electoral defeats such as Mrs Bandaranaike suffered in 1977 and again in 1988, should have led to demands for a change of leadership. Not surprisingly the SLFP has not had even a modicum of inner-party democracy. But neither has the UNP; indeed the position of the party leader in both has seldom been challenged successfully. The leader's position in the party is taken for granted, while the party machinery is manipulated—with little or no protest—to secure the appointment or election of office bearers of the leader's choice or the adoption of policies acceptable to the leadership.

Fortunately for Sri Lankan' democracy, the electorate has proved to be much less deferential to political leaders than the party organizations to which they belong. A holder of a ministerial position was defeated for the first time in 1936. More such defeats came at the general elections of 1947 and 1952. In 1956, the governing party was routed at the polls, and most members of its Cabinet lost their seats. For the first time in a post-colonial situation in Asia/Africa power was transferred through the ballot, and peacefully, from a legatee of the colonial power to a democratic opposition party. On five consecutive occasions after 1956 the Sri Lankan electorate voted a government out of power, a record which no other post-colonial state can match. The polls at these general elections has kept increasing consistently, reaching an average of 80 per cent in the 1970s. It reached a peak of 87 per cent in 1977. There was a small decline in the poll at the presidential election of 1982 and a sharper decline at the controversial referendum of that year. It dropped to the 1947 level or lower in 1988 because of the terrifying atmosphere of violence in which the presidential and parliamentary elections of 1988 and 1989 were held. The fact that as many as 55 per cent of the electorate voted at the presidential election of December 1988, and 64 per cent at the parliamentary election in February 1989, despite the systematic campaign of violence—including the killing of candidates, supporters and voters by an ultra-left and nationalist party, the Janatha Vimukthi Peramuna (JVP)—is evidence of its deep commitment to democratic elections. At the parliamentary and presidential elections of 1994 the percentage poll reached 80 per cent (at the parliamentary election) but dropped to 70 per cent at the presidential election. As further evidence of the political maturity of the electorate one could point to the fact that except on one occasion, in March 1960, a government has been returned to power with a stable majority.

The trend in the 1970s however, was to give the winning party a lopsided parliamentary majority, far in excess of the percentage of votes it gathered at the electoral level, as was evident in the results of the parliamentary elections of 1970 and 1977. These lopsided majorities had an unexpected result in that they exacerbated ethnic rivalry; the minority Tamils could no longer serve as a swing vote as they had done in the early 1960s. Indeed elections could now be won and lost on the strength of votes polled in the Sinhalese areas alone. As a result, the alienation of the Tamils of the north was aggravated in the early and mid-1970s. The response to this was the introduction of a system of proportional representation under the Second Republican Constitution of 1978[26] which aimed to reduce if not eliminate these lopsided majorities. The first general election under proportional representation was held in February 1989. The advantages of this became immediately evident when the SLFP, with 30 per cent of the poll, secured 66 seats although it was only able to gain a majority in five polling districts, or 'constituencies'. Had the former first-past-the-post system been in operation the SLFP would have had just five or six seats at most, out of 196.

Given Sri Lanka's multi-party system, coalition governments have become the norm not the exception. It is generally forgotten that Sri Lanka's post-independence parliamentary record shows that the country has been ruled by coalitions for a longer periods of time than by dominant single party governments. The formation of coalitions has been imposed by three factors: first and most obvious of all, the requirements of a weak parliamentary or electoral base; secondly, by the search for appropriate allies on the basis of perceived national political need, the nurturing of pluralism (under D.S. Senanayake) or the exactly opposite policy of emphasizing the Sinhalese-Buddhist dominance of the polity (as in 1956); and thirdly, by concerns such as a deliberate shifting of the central focus of governmental policy in a pre-ordained ideological direction (as in 1970) with its emphasis on a radical socialist programme.

The first post-independence government which took office on 26 September 1947, was a coalition between the UNP which won only 42 seats out of 95 contested seats and independents as well as the miniscule Labour Party. This was the first example in Sri Lanka's parliamentary history of a coalition imposed by the imperatives of a weak parliamentary support base. There were two other occasions in which a party sought to establish a coalition because of its minority status within Parliament, one of which was in March 1960 when the UNP with about a third of the seats in Parliament searched in vain for allies to establish a viable coalition. The other case was in August 1994 when the People's Alliance (PA) secured a majority through the support of minor and minority parties.

The UNP-led coalition widened its support base by bringing the Tamil Congress (TC) into the coalition—and its leader into the cabinet—on 3 September 1948. Not only was the parliamentary base of the government strengthened and consolidated but Senanayake had demonstrated his, and his government's commitment, to pluralism. This ·move from opposition to government caused a split within the Tamil Congress and a minority formed a new Tamil communal party, the Federal Party (FP) in 1949. At the general election of May 1952, the

UNP campaigned in association with the Tamil Congress, the first and only occasion in Sri Lanka's recent parliamentary history when a Sri Lankan Tamil leader played a leading role in a general election campaign throughout the island as a recognized national political figure in alliance with the major party of the day. The coalition between the UNP and the Tamil Congress continued till the early part of 1956 when sharp differences on language policy brought the coalition to an end. It had survived the dropping of the Tamil Congress leader from the cabinet on 23 October 1953.

For most of the period since 1956 the country has been ruled by coalitions. Indeed every government of this period—except the short-lived UNP government of March-July 1960, and the SLFP government of July 1960 to June 1964—was a coalition government. Moreover, at every election from 1956 to 1970 with the exception of the election of March 1960, the SLFP had come to an electoral agreement with the LSSP and CP to avoid contests among themselves against the UNP. The SLFP fought the general election of 1956 as part of a coalition (the Mahajana Eksath Peramuna or the MEP) whose common interest was a fundamental change in language policy; they came together because of, and were held together by, a common commitment to Sinhalese-Buddhist populism. Once this coalition came apart in the latter half of 1959, and the SLFP recovered from the shattering effects of the assassination of its leader, its interest in electoral agreements and coalitions continued, but coalitions with left-wing parties and not with its traditional allies in the language and Buddhist movements. The latter now drifted into absorption by the SLFP and the UNP, or into the periphery of the political system in minuscule parties.

By the middle of 1964 the SLFP had reached an understanding with the Marxist parties on an agenda based on ideological interests. The LSSP entered a coalition with the SLFP in June 1964. Although this alliance was defeated in Parliament when a faction within the SLFP crossed over to the opposition and voted against the government in a crucial no-confidence motion in December 1964, this alliance continued through the general election that followed the defeat of the government, and in opposition to the seven party coalition led by the UNP which took power in March 1965. Thus a governing coalition confronted a cohesive centre-left opposition coalition. A common programme adopted by the SLFP, LSSP and CP in 1968 heralded a consolidation of the ideological coalition first constructed in June 1964. The UF government which triumphed at the election of May 1970 was intent on implementing a common programme which aimed at a radical reform of every aspect of Sri Lankan society, the economic system, and the polity. Needless to say the achievement did not match the aspirations, but the UF government did implement a series of radical measures between 1970 and 1975 by which time the coalition began to unravel. On 2 September 1975 the LSSP was expelled from the government, and its three representatives in the cabinet were removed from office. The CP remained in the government till February 1977 by which time the UF coalition had collapsed, and the SLFP faced the electorate on its own at the general election of July 1977.

For the first time since March 1960 there was no electoral agreement between the SLFP and the parties of the Left against the UNP.

The general election of July 1977 gave the UNP such a lopsided victory, 140 seats out of 168, that the need for coalition partners need not have crossed the minds of its leaders. The SLFP was in total disarray, its parliamentary representation reduced to a mere 9 seats, and the Marxist Left was in terminal decline. Yet the UNP also had its electoral alliance. The Ceylon Workers Congress (CWC), the principal political party cum trade union of the Indian plantation workers had been associated with the UNP since 1964 in one of the most long-standing, mutually beneficial, political alliances in Sri Lanka's history.[27] In recognition of this its leader, S. Thondaman[28] was brought into the cabinet in September 1978. The electoral alliance between the two parties has continued thereafter at every level, at local government elections, provincial and district council elections, parliamentary and presidential elections till the presidential election of 1994. And, more significantly, for most of this period, CWC candidates fought under the UNP label. Nevertheless, the CWC maintained its distinct identity—at the trade union level.

Electoral systems based on proportional representation generally lead to coalition governments. The first such election held in Sri Lanka, the parliamentary election of February 1989, however gave the UNP a substantial majority over its principal rival, the SLFP, and an overall majority of 20 seats in a parliament of 225 members. Thus while its coalition with the CWC continued, the UNP did not think it necessary to bring other parties into the government. The present People's Alliance (PA) is a coalition between the SLFP and the surviving elements of the traditional Left, but more significantly with a Muslim party, and with other minority representatives including the CWC.

The peculiar demographic profile of the country with a concentration of Tamils in the north and to a lesser extent in the east of the country, has given Tamil parties, beginning with the Tamil Congress of the 1940s a solid regional base which they have generally succeeded in protecting against intrusions by national parties such as the UNP, the SLFP and left-wing parties, fielding candidates of their own. As we have seen the Tamil Congress joined the UNP in a political and electoral alliance between 1948 and 1956. Only on two occasions did the UNP on its own win a seat in the Northern Province: at the general election of 1952 when a Tamil candidate of the UNP defeated the Federal Party leader, and at a by-election in February 1974 at Mannar through a Muslim candidate. Apart from this only once has a national party won a seat in the Northern Province against Tamil parties: at the general election of April 1956 when the Communist Party

(CP) candidate, also a Tamil, won the Point Pedro seat. The seats in the Northern Province and in particular the Jaffna peninsula have been shared by the Tamil Congress, the Federal Party and its successor the Tamil United Liberation Front (TULF) apart, of course, from a few independents. The Federal Party, the principal political party of the Tamils since the mid-1950s and the TULF generally sought an independent role in national politics and the national legislature, although the Federal Party formed part of Dudley Senanayake's coalition government of 1965-70, from 1965 to 1968 when it had a member in the cabinet.

The Eastern Province with its strong Muslim minority and an increasing Sinhalese population presents a different picture. Neither the Tamil Congress in its heyday nor the Federal Party and the TULF has had a dominant position there electorally; they have had to share the seats there with the national parties and independents. The UNP and SLFP have both won seats through Muslim candidates and in recent years through Sinhalese candidates. Up to the time of the parliamentary elections of 1994 the UNP's links with the Muslims there had always been stronger than that of the SLFP. Apart from that the UNP has had a strong base among the Tamils there, and some prominent Tamils have won seats as UNP candidates.

But the main interest in the Eastern Province in the 1980s lies in the emergence of a Muslim communal party, the Sri Lanka Muslim Congress (SLMC) with its base among the Eastern Province Muslims (who constitute about a third of the Muslim population of the island) and aspirations to a national status. Its expectations of achieving such a status very early were not fulfilled at the general election of 1989 and it was unable to shake the traditional pattern of Muslim membership of the UNP and SLFP which had given them cabinet representation since 1947. The situation changed in 1994 when the SLMC joined the People's Alliance coalition through its success in the Eastern Province and in the north of the island. Elsewhere the SLFP and UNP still have support among the Muslims, but no longer can the SLMC be dismissed as a mere regional party.

LANGUAGE AND RELIGION AS DIVISIVE FACTORS

The issues involved in the relationship between religion—principally Buddhism—and the State take us back to the beginnings of Sri Lanka's recorded history over 2,000 years ago. Here we are concerned with the issues in their more recent and contemporary forms.

The complexities in the relationship between religion and the State stem from the introduction of Christianity as Roman Catholicism into the island in the 16th century. Portuguese colonialism was very much the child of the Counter-Reformation and if its emphasis on the principle of *cujus regio illius religio* perpetuated a central feature of the Sri Lankan political system—the link between state and religion which had originated as long as the third century BC—the zealotry and harsh intolerance which characterized the imposition of Roman Catholicism on Sri Lanka's littoral were something new and unfamiliar. Sri Lanka's Buddhist society and civilization seldom confused the obligation to encourage adherence to the national religion with the discouragement of the public practice of other religions or suppression of other faiths.

Very few parts of Asia have a longer record of Western influence and control than Sri Lanka's coastal regions. The legacy of that colonial experience, of which the confrontation between Buddhism and the intrusive Western culture and civilization and Christianty is a central theme, has a vital current significance in Sri Lanka. The role of religion as a divisive factor in Sri Lanka's contemporary politics is inextricably linked to the history of the last few centuries. Chapter three seeks to mesh the contemporary situation with that historical background.

The current ethnic violence in Sri Lanka leads many observers—academics no less than journalists—to assume that it is all the result of a lack of recognition of multi-culturalism by the State and by a dominant majority. They take the easy way out by describing the conflict as one between Sinhalese Buddhists and Tamil Hindus. As we shall see, this is not a religious conflict. The religious conflict in Sri Lanka preceded its current ethnic conflict by several centuries. The shadows of that conflict still lie across Sri Lanka's political landscape: contemporary foreign observers mistake the shadows for the substance. A study by a reputed research institution in the US, includes Sri Lanka in one of its six case studies—along with the Ukraine and the Sudan[29]—of conflicts in which religious intolerance was a significant if not major factor. The third chapter of this book therefore delves deeper into the history of Sri Lanka and aims at the felt need to dispel these illusions.

Despite the tensions and sporadic violence in the encounter between the Sinhalese and Tamils historically, Buddhist-Hindu relations did not witness the sort of rift seen in many parts of India—or states of India—in the parallel encounter between Hinduism and Islam. On the contrary, Hinduism has had a profound influence on Sinhalese-Buddhism, the evidence of which is seen in the present day absorption of Hindu gods and goddesses, and Hindu practices in Buddhist worship. Part of the explanation for this lies in Buddhism's tolerance of other religions, the religious policies followed by the island's Buddhist rulers over the ages and in part the syncretism that has been an essential feature of Sri Lankan Buddhism. Thus, the fundamental fact of Sri Lankan history is not a perpetual conflict between Buddhism and Hinduism, Buddhist and Hindu. And the current hostilities between the Sinhalese and Tamils one needs to repeat, are not a religious conflict: it is more complex than that. Religion does not define the divisions between people in the current conflict: for example, the Christians are divided on this issue, with the Sinhalese among them identifying with their Buddhist counterparts, just as the Tamils among them identify with their Hindu counterparts even more emphatically. Language, as we shall see in chapter two, has been a sharper point of division, and is an essentially contemporary issue. Disputes on language policy triggered the first two rounds of riots between the Sinhalese and Tamils in 1956 and 1958, the first violent encounters between the two groups since independence.

What, if any is the nexus between religion and language? Part of the evidence for a close nexus lies in the events of the mid-1950s where, as we shall see in chapters two and three, the two movements converged, one seeking a position of greater salience for Buddhism in the Sri Lankan polity, and the other intent on the elevation of Sinhala to the position of the single official language of the country. Moreover, many of the prominent individuals and groups in the two campaigns treated them as facets of a single policy of societal change. Yet, the nexus was more complex and subtle than that. In the mid-1950s language policy change was given greater prominence partly at least because its objectives seemed easier to fulfil. Once the legislative changes that gave effect to the policy were in the statute book the campaign for language change lost much of its fervour. The campaign for a change in the state's religious policy, of which an important feature was a re-definition of the relations between state and religion, diverged from the campaign for language policy change in the late 1950s and thereafter became a distinct movement, or at best a parallel movement. The divergence continued in the 1960s and 1970s and, as chapter three will show, the campaign for a re-definition of the state's relations with Buddhism lost much of the momentum it had enjoyed in the mid-1950s.

II

Sowing The Wind: Language, Religion and Ethnicity

CHAPTER 2

The Language Problem: The Politics of Linguistic Nationalism

At independence the successor states of the British *raj* in South Asia confronted the crucial issue of deciding which language—or languages—should replace English as the language of administration, in education, in the law courts, in short, as the official language. The debate on this potentially and—as it eventually turned out to be— inevitably divisive issue had begun in the two decades before Sri Lanka's independence. Unlike in most parts of the British *raj*, in Sri Lanka the official decisions on changes in language and education policy had been taken in the late 1930s and early 1940s, in the last decade of British rule in the island. In May 1944 the national legislature adopted a policy resolution to the effect that Sinhala and Tamil should replace English as the official languages within a reasonable time.[1] Indeed, the two decades from 1930 onwards also marked a decisive phase in the evolution of Sri Lanka's modern education system. Language was a central issue in the controversies of educational reform. But just over 10 years later, and less than a decade after independence, the agreement reached in 1944 was unilaterally abrogated, setting in motion a train of events that marked the first phase in Sri Lanka's recent history of violent ethnic conflict.

Some of the principal political figures involved in the language controversies of the forties—J.R. Jayewardene, who was later to be the first Executive President of Sri Lanka (1978-88) and S.W.R.D. Bandaranaike, Prime Minister of Sri Lanka in the years 1956-9, to name just two of them—were to play a similarly prominent role in the controversies on language of the mid-1950s when language became the primary political issue of the day and when, indeed, language was the very core of the ethnic conflicts that erupted and nationalism itself took on a linguistic form. For them this was historically and—although they would not know it at that time—a dress rehearsal for the political dramas of the late-1950s and later in which, the roles they played were often quite different from what they did in this first phase. Jayewardene's involvement in the resolution of the language problem continued into the 1960s and during the whole period of his tenure of office as Prime Minister (1977-8) and Executive President (1978-88), in short, throughout his long political career.

Pressure for the replacement of English as the official language by Sinhalese and Tamil began in 1920s. The *swabasha* movement, as this came to be called, was, in its origins, a protest against the privileges of the English-educated—and English-speaking—elite and its monopoly of all important positions in public life and in the bureaucracy. Between the English-educated and the vernacular-educated was a formidable class barrier with its contrast in status and wealth accentuated by a growing contrariety in culture. The island's education system was notable for its bifurcation between a privileged English education sector to which access was limited, and the vernacular schools, the largest segment in the school system. From the outset, agitation for education reform—and in particular for the use of the 'mother tongue' of the students in the education process—was an integral part of the *swabasha* movement.

There was, naturally enough, greater momentum for *swabasha* with the constitutional reforms of 1931 and a greater sense of urgency for all this within the national legislature. Even so the progress made did not match the enthusiasm for the cause and the public support it was generating in the country, especially for the use of the 'mother tongue' in education.

The adherents of the latter cause were severely criticized. Their critics pointed out that while English education had become the badge of social and cultural superiority, and had elevated the English-educated to the position of a privileged minority—'the national establishment'—the English language served a politically useful role as an important unifying factor in the country. The first principal of Ceylon University College—and as usual at this time, a British expatriate—Robert Marrs, pointed to the possibility that while the triumph of *swabasha* might bring to an end the presumed divisiveness of the existing education system it could create a potentially much more dangerous division, detrimental to national cohesion, through an education system based on two languages, Sinhala and Tamil, operating on parallel lines with little effort to bring the two language streams together as part of a larger whole.

What today would be seen as an unusually prescient observation was dismissed by *swabasha* enthusiasts then as arrant nonsense or worse as coming from a prejudiced and hostile source. They believed that bi-lingualism— Sinhalese and Tamil—would be an ideal unifying force, and in the beginning there were encouraging signs of this actually happening. But the viability of Sinhalese-Tamil bi-lingualism was largely impaired by the general lack of enthusiasm for Tamil among the Sinhalese including educationists and the elite, the natural complacency of a majority community. The result, as we shall see, was that the agitation for *swabasha* continued, and succeeded—in the 1950s and 1960s—in its objective of replacing English as the medium of instruction with Sinhalese and Tamil, quite oblivious to the need to establish a unifying link in place of that language. Two 'nations' on the basis of class and language, were indeed eventually replaced by a similar division on the basis of Sinhalese and Tamil. But this, so far as the 1940s and 1950s were concerned, was yet to be.

'SINHALA ONLY'—RHETORIC AND ACTUAL POLICY, 1956-66

The pivotal role of language policy in the election campaign of 1956—although it was only one of several issues—made the governing UNP vulnerable to the groundswell of popular dissatisfaction which S.W.R.D. Bandaranaike succeeded in channeling to the electoral advantage of the Mahajana Eksath Peramuna (MEP), the party he led to victory. The mechanics of the election campaign revealed some of the contradictions that were to bedevil the formulation of language policy after the MEP's landslide victory.[2] The MEP and the Marxist Left advocated and adhered to two diametrically opposed language policies, 'Sinhala-Only' for the MEP and parity of status for Sinhala and Tamil on the part of Marxists. The UNP on the other hand was publicly pledged to a policy of 'Sinhala Only'.

But what in fact did 'Sinhala Only' and 'parity of status' really mean? One could search in vain in the speeches and statements of the MEP leadership—and Bandaranaike in particular—for any clear definition of these terms. Some of their statements ranged from the Delphic to the opaque. Since the politicians did not provide much more than rhetoric as slogans, it was left to the ideologues on both sides to define the issues, and clarify the objectives. On one point there was agreement between the 'Sinhala Only' ideologues and the political leadership of the MEP, namely that the language settlement reached in 1943-4 would be unilaterally abrogated.[3]

Nor were advocates of 'parity of status' very forthcoming by way of definition of the term either, beyond saying that it meant full equality before the law for the Tamils, equality of opportunity for the Tamils and an equality of status for the two languages throughout the land. That is how the Marxist Left saw it, and indeed how most of the Tamils in public life associated with the main Tamil political parties, the Tamil Congress and the Federal Party, saw it. A leading Tamil lawyer-politician, S. Nadesan, cogently argued a case for parity of status for Tamil with Sinhala; one of the key features in this was the linkage he made between bi-lingualism and a federal or quasi-federal political structure for the island.[4] For Nadesan, as for so many other advocates of parity of status, the models set out for emulation were the larger federal states of the world. They also turned to Switzerland and Belgium among the smaller European democracies, but to the Swiss example to a greater extent than others. Nadesan went on to explain what he meant by bi-lingualism:

> [It] implies that every single public officer in this country should have an adequate knowledge of both languages so that he may be able to take up employment in any part of the island, and that all citizens should have equal opportunities of entering the Public Service.
>
> To enable this to be done the necessary changes must be made in the education system so that those who aspire to the Public Service may acquire an adequate knowledge of both official languages. It is not necessary for those who do not desire to join the public services to learn both languages.[5]

Explanations of this sort added to the confusion, and enabled 'Sinhala Only' activists to give

> parity the misleading connotation that all Sinhalese would have to learn Tamil or that it was a device to make it necessary for the government to appoint two government servants to every post—one Sinhalese and one Tamil.[6]

Nor was the linkage between federalism and of Sinhala and Tamil parity more helpful. Indeed, ever since the Federal Party was established in 1949 as a major Tamil political party, there had been a conscious or unconscious obfuscation of the precise meaning of the federal concept in the Sri Lankan context. The Federal Party had contributed greatly to this by their own lack of precision in setting out the nature of their objectives. To many federalism was a political catchphrase which connoted separatism.[7]

While Bandaranaike had come to power in 1956 through a successful exploitation of a wave of Sinhalese-Buddhist emotion, the sobering realities of governance compelled him to impose restraints on the more enthusiastic supporters of language reform. He had promised to lead the way for a new language policy, and to do it swiftly. A draft bill for effecting this anxiously awaited change in language policy was ready before the end of April. The bill was in the nature of a balancing act and reflected his coalition's official line, incorporated in its manifesto, of combining a strong commitment to Sinhala as the sole national language with protection for the language rights for the minorities. When the government's parliamentary group met on 3 May to consider this bill, it was evident that its careful balancing of the interests of the Sinhalese and the minorities had upset the more vociferous defenders of 'Sinhala Only'. The latter set about the business of ensuring the primacy of the Sinhala language in Sri Lanka, betraying a singular lack of understanding of the nuances underlying the governing coalition's language formula put forth at the general election. Their opposition was so great that the Prime Minister was compelled to withdraw this draft bill and to appoint a sub-committee of the parliamentary group to draft a fresh one. This sub-committee's draft bill was ready by 16 May, and was presented for discussion by the government's parliamentary group on 23 May. After a discussion lasting three and half hours the group approved the bill with some slight modifications. But there were still distinct rumblings of discontent among the ideologues of 'Sinhala Only' within the government parliamentary party, who complained that the concessions made to the minorities undermined the governing coalition's own promises to the electorate on the changes to be introduced in language policy.

This second draft bill, like its predecessor, was a pragmatic concession to political realities, and adhered scrupulously to the MEP's manifesto for the 1956 election campaign. But the 'Sinhala Only' ideologues, not given to reading the small print of the election manifesto, viewed it as a great betrayal and reacted to it with a passionate hostility that eventually frightened the government and the Prime Minister to backing down. Pressure was applied on both through a formidable combination of *bhikkhu* activists and 'Sinhala Only' ideologues acting in unison. Two of the most prominent of the latter engaged in a public fast in the precincts of Parliament itself. The pressure had the desired effect. The Prime Minister and the government yielded to their demands, and the draft bill was withdrawn.[6]

A few weeks later a new bill was introduced, the Official Language Act No. 33 of 1956 (the 'Sinhala Only' act as it came to be known popularly). Its most notable feature was its stark brevity; a brevity which constituted a tactical retreat in the face of unrelenting pressure from within the government's own ranks and from forces which had worked so hard to bring the government to power. Bandaranaike had coined the popular slogan 'Sinhala Only' and in 'twenty-four' hours; and in his hour of victory he was compelled to admit that it would take considerably longer than that to implement that policy. In retrospect, it would appear that within less than two months of his massive electoral victory his main interest lay in the very limited task of securing parliamentary acceptance of the principle of one national language rather than two. That done, the process of implementation could be on a step-by-step basis. Thus an important feature of the Official Language Act, introduced and successfully piloted through the legislature in June 1956, was that its implementation would be stretched out over a period of five years, a period which Bandaranaike expected to use to devise or negotiate modifications and adjustments to make the change in language policy palatable to the Tamils. The riots that broke out in the wake of the debate on this bill in Parliament, reviewed in chapter four, underlined the combustible nature of linguistic nationalism in Sri Lanka's plural society. In the debate over the bill, the electoral alliance between the SLFP and the Marxist Left came apart. On this acrimonious occasion the UNP voted for the bill with the government while the Marxist Left joined the Tamil parties in opposition to it.

The vigour with which the Tamils fought back on the

language issue, and the zeal they demonstrated on it are often seen as a rearguard struggle of a privileged minority at bay. Their fears were for their future, not the immediate present. As with their previous campaigns on the language issue the agitation spread over two years, 1956 to 1958, demonstrated afresh that none fight more passionately than those who have a world to lose.

FROM LANGUAGE POLICY TO DEVOLUTION OF POWER

In August 1956, the Federal Party, at a convention held in Trincomalee, set out a list of demands on behalf of the Tamils, which linked language policy with other controversial issues, including the establishment of a second tier of government using the existing system of provinces for this purpose. Indeed, they placed the latter demand ahead of language policy thus giving it a prominence that it has retained ever since. The first of their demands was autonomy for the Northern and Eastern Provinces under a federal constitution; next came parity of status for Sinhala and Tamil as official languages; and a satisfactory settlement of the citizenship rights of the Indian plantation workers in the island. (This third theme is discussed in detail in chapter nine.) The threat of a *satyagraha*, or organized peaceful resistance to the government was held out, if these demands were not conceded.

While the extremists in the ranks of the coalition could think only in terms of maintaining pressure on the Tamils through a policy of confrontation, Bandaranaike began negotiations with the Federal Party for an accommodation between the two parties, as representatives of the Sinhalese and the Tamils respectively. After weeks of discussion a settlement was reached. In July 1957, the terms of the accommodation reached were published. It soon became evident that they went well beyond the language dispute *per se*; the Tamil language was to be given the status of an official language for administrative purposes in the Northern and Eastern Provinces; just as important, Bandaranaike agreed to amend a draft Regional

Councils Bill, which his government had prepared, to accommodate some of the demands of the Federal Party; and, thirdly, he agreed to place limits on the settlement of Sinhalese 'colonists' in irrigation schemes in the Northern and Eastern Provinces so that the indigenous Tamils could maintain their majority position in those areas. While our main interest in this chapter is on language policy,[9] the fact is that by agreeing to discuss the terms of a settlement more or less on the priorities set by the Federal Party, Bandaranaike had succeeded in linking one exceedingly controversial issue—language policy—with another that was equally, if not more, controversial—devolution of power.

Not surprisingly the announcement of the terms of the settlement was greeted with a storm of protests. These came principally from the die-hard language loyalists in Bandaranaike's own camp. And the UNP looking for a means of staging a comeback was provided with an ideal opportunity to embarrass the Prime Minister on a politically sensitive issue, as well as to demonstrate their commitment to a 'Sinhala Only' policy to an electorate skeptical of their motives. 'Sinhala Only' ideologues argued that the concessions to recognize Tamil as an official language vitiated the 'Sinhala Only' Act. This opinion the UNP shared. Their concern extended to other main points in the settlement, i.e., modifications of the Regional Councils Bill and the presumed threat to halt colonization in the Northern and Eastern Provinces.

In retrospect it would seem that the pact was doomed from the moment its contents were revealed. Confronted with mounting opposition to it, within the coalition he had led to victory in the electoral campaign of 1956, the Prime Minister played for time. The UNP sought to exploit the situation by staging a march to Kandy on 2 and 3 October 1957, in protest against the pact, led by J.R. Jayewardene. This march made little impression on the country and none at all on the government which succeeded in stopping it before it proceeded very far.[10]

However, having easily overcome the UNP's political initiative, the government succumbed to pressure from within its own ranks. Led by a group of *bhikkhus* who performed *satyagraha* on the lawns of the Prime Minister's private residence in Colombo on 9 April 1958, the extremists in his own party compelled him to abrogate the pact, a full eight months after the UNP's protest march had fizzled out. Once again the tension generated pressures and counter-pressures which erupted in the 'race' riots in May 1958. Later in the year—in August—Bandaranaike secured Parliamentary approval for the Tamil Language (Special Provisions) Act No. 28 of 1958. The Regional Councils Bill was abandoned, along with the pact which it came to be associated.

The Tamil Language (Special Provisions) Bill was debated in Parliament and approved by it in unusual circumstances. The Federal Party MPs, and the leadership of an extremist Sinhalese group were placed under house arrest at this time: the FP and the Sinhalese party referred to above, the Jatika Vimukti Peramuna, (not to be confused with the Janatha Vimukti Peramuna) were proscribed at this time. Incorporating most of the safeguards on the use of the Tamil that had been included in the preliminary draft legislation proposed by the MEP in 1956 which the government itself had abandoned in the face of opposition from 'Sinhala Only' activists, the new bill sought to give legal recognition to an existing situation. These included the right of Tamils to use their language in correspondence with the government, and in local government affairs, to continue educating their children in Tamil and to take the competitive examinations for entry into the government and local government service in Tamil, with the proviso that they would be required to gain proficiency in Sinhala to continue in service and to secure promotion. Despite the Official Language Act No. 33 of 1956, all of these continued as before. The regulations necessary for the effective implementation of the Tamil Language (Special Provisions) Bill were ready for debate in Parliament, but the political instability of the last phase of Bandaranaike's administration, and his assassination in September 1959, prevented their being presented for parliamentary approval. Nevertheless, the situation ante-1956 prevailed in regard to all of the matters for which regulations under the 1958 bill had been drafted.

THE DILUTION OF 'SINHALA ONLY'

Within six months of her assumption of office as Prime Minister in July 1960, Mrs Bandaranaike's government was totally alienated from the Federal Party. This was principally because of her insistence on Sinhala becoming the language of administration throughout the island from 1 January 1961 as envisaged in the 'Sinhala Only' Act of 1956, but without any substantial modifications or adjustments or concessions to the Tamils, despite the understanding reached with the Federal Party before and during the general election of July 1960 on such modifications and adjustments. No attempt was made to honour the promise to introduce the regulations required to give effect to the Tamil Language (Special Provisions) Act No. 28 of 1958. Once again there was the familiar pattern of a civil disobedience campaign in the north and east of the island in March-April 1961, with the government responding with the imposition of a state of emergency in the Northern and Eastern Provinces. Within Parliament the Federal Party moved from responsive cooperation with the government to staunch opposition. Over the next few years it became more receptive to overtures from the UNP.[11]

The regulations under the Tamil Language (Special Provisions) Act of 1958 which Bandaranaike had not lived to introduce, and his widow and successor had failed—or refused—to introduce, were eventually introduced and piloted through the national legislature successfully, in January 1966, by a UNP-led coalition. But the new government was placed on the defensive from the moment the FP opted to join it. The Tamil Language (Special

Provisions) Regulations of 1966 were drafted for, and approved by, the government by M. Tiruchelvam, a distinguished lawyer, who was the FP's nominee in the Cabinet. Parliamentary approval for them was secured against the background of massive demonstrations led by the SLFP and its left-wing allies, the LSSP and CP. The Marxist parties were recent but enthusiastic converts to 'Sinhala Only'. Together this new coalition of the centre and the left argued, despite all the evidence to the contrary, that these regulations introduced by the government violated the spirit and principles of the 'Sinhala Only' Act. Once more a state of emergency was clamped down, but any prospect of 'race' riots was nipped in the bud by decisive action taken by the government. A pledge to the FP had been honoured although at great cost in the erosion of public support for the government.

The realignment of forces on the language question was remarkable. Indeed, the wheel had come full circle. Here was the UNP adopting the language policy outlined by Bandaranaike and the MEP in the latter's controversial first draft proposal on language reform submitted just after the general election of 1956. The UNP had not shown any great enthusiasm for it on that occasion. Mrs Bandaranaike and the SLFP under her leadership were now rejecting a line of policy associated with her late husband and her party during his leadership of it. As for the left-wing in the form of the Marxists parties, by the early 1960s they had jettisoned their own language policy of parity of status for Tamil with Sinhala, as official languages. On the face of it this seemed to be the price these Marxist parties were called upon to pay for entry into a coalition with Mrs Bandaranaike's SLFP, which brought the LSSP into the Cabinet in 1964-5. The defeat of this coalition, in Parliament in December 1964 and in the general election of March 1965, did not bring the centre-left alliance to an end; it was strengthened and expanded to include the Communist Party, and as a broadened coalition they had all opposed the regulations under the Tamil Language (Special Provisions) Act introduced in 1966. In regard to the FP itself, in opting to join the UNP in a coalition—the so-called National government established in 1966—they were, in effect, acknowledging the end of parity of status as a viable policy option, if not as an objective.

Turning to the Marxist Left, this change of policy now seems in retrospect as a desperate bid to stop the erosion of public support that commitment to parity of status had entailed in the late 1950s, an erosion that was so stunningly demonstrated to them in their dismal performance at the general election of March 1960 at which the LSSP had made a bid for power on their own through the ballot. There was no public announcement about a change of policy, only a slow drifting away from what was clearly seen as a disastrously unpopular stand on national language policy. Once the FP joined a UNP-led coalition in March 1965 any lingering doubts in the minds of the political leadership of these Marxist parties about the wisdom of moving away from parity of status for Tamil with Sinhala were removed. Why adhere to a policy which the Federal Party itself was tacitly, if not openly, abandoning in the give and take of political bargaining? The FP had joined the coalition of parliamentary forces that had voted to bring down the SLFP-LSSP coalition in the last weeks of 1964, and thereafter it had thrown its support behind the UNP in the formation of a government after the general election of March 1965.

The fact is that the Marxist Left no less than the UNP and the Federal Party were responding to a changed situation in which the reality of actual policy on language rights was significantly different from the rhetoric that political parties indulged in. What indeed was this reality? Firstly, despite the lack of regulations giving legal teeth to the Tamil Language (Special Provisions) Act of 1958, the modification of the policy of 'Sinhala Only' embodied in it had been implemented in a wide area of public life. This was despite the rapid political changes of the period

1958-66: three changes of government at three general elections, the short-lived UNP minority government of 1960, the SLFP government of 1960-4, and the ill-fated SLFP-LSSP coalition of 1964-5. Secondly, despite the sanguine expectations of the 'Sinhala Only' activists of the mid-1950s, Sri Lanka remained very much a bi-lingual state (or a tri-lingual one if English is added, as it must be, to Sinhala and Tamil) and, despite the dominant Sinhalese-Buddhist cultural ethos, as much a multi-cultural society as it was before the 'Sinhala Only' agitation began. Many if not most of the advocates of 'Sinhala Only'—Professor G.P. Malalasekera for one—also argued the case for assimilation of the minorities of Sri Lanka to the dominant Sinhalese-Buddhist culture,[12] but no government sought to adopt such a policy on any systematic basis, and no major politician in power advocated it as a national objective to be imposed on the minorities. And this, at a time when assimilationist policies did not have the sinister connotations they have today. The minorities—the Tamils especially—were sensitive in regard to language and education policies and viewed these with deep suspicion on account of the potential such changes had for assimilationist ends.[13]

Bi-lingualism (or indeed tri-lingualism) was seen in the use of the Tamil language in the national insignia, coins and currency, postage stamps, in road signs and in all official and semi-official documents at every level—many if not most of these documents were in both Sinhala and Tamil, or in Sinhala, Tamil and English versions—in broadcasting over the national radio and this principle was extended to television when that medium was introduced to the island in the 1980s. The right of Tamil-speaking citizens to correspond with state officials, and with employees of state-owned corporations and public sector autonomous bodies was protected, but the snag was that quite often their right to receive a reply in Tamil was observed in the breach. Even when the government has shown the political will to implement this policy the lethargy of lower-level bureaucrats in combination with a shortage of bi-lingual officials have proved to be formidable obstacles to giving the Tamil minority satisfaction on this sensitive issue. The result is that a sense of grievance continues in regard to language policy, focussing on this gap in the system, while ignoring the reversion to a policy of parity of status for Tamil and disregarding altogether the advantages that Sri Lanka's Tamil minority have had in the field of education.

Bi-lingualism has been at its strongest in the most sensitive area of ethnic relations, education. One of the vitally important features of the education reforms of the 1930s and 1940s was the use of the students' 'mother tongue' in education. One result of this policy was the evolution of two separate language streams in the education process, beginning first of all in the primary schools, and extending through the 1940s into secondary education, and culminating in the 1960s in university education. Tamil parents were guaranteed the right to educate their children through the medium of the Tamil language, and this right was not restricted geographically to areas which were predominantly Tamil-speaking; it applied to all parts of the island. This right stemmed from the education reforms of the 1930s and 1940s, and was well-entrenched by the mid-1950s. The 'Sinhala Only' Act of 1956 did not imperil their right; indeed the education of Tamil children through the Tamil language proceeded apace over the decade 1956-66. Linked to it was the right that those educated in Tamil could take public examinations, ranging from general education certificate examinations and university entrance examinations, to examinations for entry to public sector employment, in that language.

The right to an education in Sinhala or Tamil was treated, from the very inception, as a right of an individual within a community or ethnic group rather than an individual right.[14] Both Sinhalese and Tamil politicians were agreed on this, and were insistent on it, the Sinhalese for fear that if the wishes of individual parents were conceded it would help perpetuate the primacy of English education, the Tamils for fear that some parents would opt to educate their children in Sinhala, and thus begin a process of assimilation. Children of mixed marriages were in a more advantageous position: their parents could choose the language medium in which such children were to be educated, Sinhala, Tamil or English. (The English medium continued in schools till the 1970s.) Over the years the resistance to permitting individual parents to decide the medium of instruction of their children has persisted, especially on the part of the Tamils. The Sinhalese are much less opposed to such a change of policy now, but no attempt has been made by governments in power to make such a change a matter of government policy.

Special provision was made for the Muslims. There has been a noticeable sensitivity to the special needs of the Muslims, themselves a Tamil-speaking group although quite distinct from the Tamils in ethnic identity. This sensitivity had begun in the 1940s, and was continued in the years after independence, and received a great impetus with the appointment of a Muslim, Badi-ud-din Mahmud, as Minister of Education by Mrs Bandaranaike on two occasions, 1960-3, and 1970-7.

Muslim children had the right (till 1974) to pursue their studies in any one of the three language media in the education system—Sinhala, Tamil or English—a privilege no other group in the country enjoyed. Special government Training Colleges have been set up for the Muslims. Arabic is taught in government schools as an optional language to Muslim pupils, and taught by *maulavis* appointed by the Ministry of Education and paid by the state. More important, in recognition of the cultural individuality of Muslims as distinct from the Tamils whose language is the home language of the large majority of them, a new category of government schools has been established. The usual practice had been to categorize schools on the basis of the language of instruction in them and the Muslims formed part of the Tamil-speaking school population. In the new 'Muslim' schools the sessions and vacations are determined by the special requirements of the Muslim population in particular the annual Ramadan fast. The establishment and expansion of these schools, it must be emphasized, vitiates the principle of non-sectarian state education which has been the declared policy of all governments since 1960.

Although the rhetoric of language policy did not conform to the living reality, that rhetoric had a life of its own. There was, for instance, the virulent campaign waged by a combination of the SLFP and the Marxist parties against the regulations under the Tamil Language (Special Provisions) Act of 1958, introduced in Parliament by the UNP-led coalition in January 1966. The opposition unleashed a sustained barrage of racialist propaganda in which the SLFP, the traditional advocates of the Sinhalese-Buddhist domination of the Sri Lanka polity, was joined by the Lanka Sama Samaja Party and the Communist Party, recent but enthusiastic converts to a cause they had once despised. The massive demonstrations organized by these parties on this occasion marked the triumph of the rhetoric of language policy over the hard reality of its practical application. This attitude has had lasting effects as was seen in 1972 when these parties formed the government and were in the throes of introducing a new constitution. The constitution of 1972 unequivocally consolidated the 'Sinhala Only' policy of the 1950s and emphasized the essentially subordinate role of the Tamil language: thus while the use of the Tamil language was recognized and permitted within the limits set out in the Tamil Language (Special Provisions) Act No. 28 of 1958, regulations drafted under the provisions of the act were 'deemed subordinate legislation'. The reference was quite deliberately directed at the Tamil Language (Special Provisions) Regulations adopted by Parliament in 1966. The rhetoric not the actual policy had become—to the constituent parties of the governing coalition—the political reality. This was much more so in the case of the Tamils who often, if not generally, preferred to judge the government by what it said, not by what it actually did. The irony was that this ostentatious elevation of rhetoric over political reality had little or no effect on official policy on language whether in education, administration or public life. That did not change in any significant way from what it was prior to 1972; indeed there was no change at all.

LANGUAGE RIGHTS: THE PRESENT POSITION

The framers of the constitution of 1978 deliberately sought a more conciliatory language policy and gave it very high priority. The terms of accommodation incorporated in the new constitution are, at the least, a consolidation of the *modus vivendi* on language rights that had emerged after two decades of strife. They are, in fact, much more than that, as would be clear by a comparison of the provisions of the constitution of 1978 relating to language rights with those of its immediate predecessor.

We have seen how the constitution of 1972 unequivocally consolidated the 'Sinhala Only' policy of the 1950s and emphasized the essentially subordinate role of the Tamil language. In contrast, Chapter IV of the 1978 constitution, while maintaining the status of Sinhala as *the* official language (Article 18), recognized Tamil as a national language[15] (Article 19), a significant modification of the 'Sinhala Only' policy.[16] Chapter IV of the constitution is an elaboration of Articles 14(1)(f) and 27(6), which, respectively, guarantee the freedom to use one's own language, and lays down as a principle of state policy, that 'no citizen shall suffer any disability by reason of language'. Moreover, all the rights enjoyed by the Tamil-speaking people of the island under the Tamil Language (Special Provisions) Act No. 28 of 1958 were incorporated in the constitution and cannot therefore be changed except by way of a constitutional amendment.

Most of these language rights existed in the past, derived from the language legislation of the 1950s and regulations connected with it such as those approved by Parliament in 1966, or from legislation relating to education, public administration and justice, to mention only the most important areas of public interest relevant to the use of the Tamil language. Yet in theory, if not in practice, ordinary legislation could override them, and although this had seldom happened, the more important point is that no real remedy was available against denial of these rights through regulations or even administrative decisions. The language provisions of the 1978 constitution changed all that.

Ten years later, the 13th amendment to the constitution, discussed in chapter seven, introduced, as part of Sri Lanka's obligations under the Indo-Sri Lanka Accord of July 1987, and certified on 14 November 1987, raised Tamil to the level of an official language, with English being given the position of a link language. Although there is some ambiguity about the position of English, its legal position appears to be almost equal to Sinhala and Tamil in many areas. The provisions of the 13th amendment were clarified and indeed consolidated by the 16th amendment (certified on 17 December 1988). Article 25A introduced on that occasion stated that in the event of any inconsistency between the provisions of any law and the provisions of Chapter IV of the 1978 constitution, the latter shall prevail.

There is some poignancy in the fact that the 16th amendment was more or less the last piece of legislation of J.R. Jayewardene's administration. Ironically, the first piece of legislation which he initiated a few months after he won the election to the State Council in 1943, had been the language law of 1943-4, in which lay the roots of the later language controversies.

With the introduction of a new constitution in 1978, and a new language policy, the Official Languages Department was re-established, this time to implement a policy of bi-lingualism (if not tri-lingualism) instead of 'Sinhala Only'. That department had lost much of its importance and influence in the early 1970s. Indeed, in 1973, its obligations and responsibilities had been dispersed among other ministries and departments on a directive of the Minister of Public Administration, Local Government and Home Affairs. The department itself had been reduced in status to a mere division in the Ministry of Public Administration.[17]

Its revival on 1 January 1979 marked a new phase in the implementation of the language policy in Sri Lanka. Indeed, that policy had come full circle: from English only under colonial rule, to Sinhala and Tamil from 1944 to 1956, to 'Sinhala Only' from 1956 to 1978, and on to Sinhala and Tamil with English as well from 1978 onwards. Much of the ambiguity in the language law, and hence in official language policy, had been settled with the constitution of 1978 despite the lack of precision in the terms such as 'official' and 'national language', and 'link language'.

In 1989-90, under President R. Premadasa, the UNP government took the important policy decision to establish an Official Languages Commission with wide powers to oversee the implementation of the official language policy. The proposal for the establishment of such a commission had been made in 1945-6 by the Select Committee on Official Language Policy of the State Council under the chairmanship of J.R. Jayewardene. Such a commission had been established in 1951 and its initiatives in language planning and implementation from 1951 to 1953 had marked one of the more creative phases in Sri Lanka's experience in implementing key features of the language reforms of 1943-44. The Official Language Commission appointed on 21 December 1991 with the passage of the Official Language Commission Act No. 18 of 1991 has wider powers than the Commission of 1951-3 enjoyed in regard to the implementation of language policy since the latter was the creation of the administration and not a legal entity.[18] Based on a Canadian model, the Act of 1991 provides a legal framework to monitor and supervise the implementation of the country's official language policy. It has been in existence now for just over five years and it is too early to pass judgement on its performance.

The establishment of Sri Lanka's Official Languages Commission in its present form is a manifestation of a contemporary phenomenon, the import of institutional models from a particular political culture and political environment to a totally different one in the hope that similar institutions would take root and even flourish there. The institution is new even in Canada. The chances of a successful adaptation seem difficult enough at first glance: the Canadian situation involves a conflict between two international languages which share a common script; in Sri Lanka the conflict is between a purely Sri Lankan language, and a regional one which has two centres, one in Sri Lanka and the other in Tamilnadu. To complicate matters even further there is the 'link' language, English. There are, thus, three scripts, and those who seek bilingual proficiency in Sinhala and Tamil needs to master two scripts, and a third as well if they are proficient in English. Nevertheless, the willingness to consider another institutional model is evidence of a strong political will to seek an accommodation on an issue which destroyed civil peace when it first erupted four decades ago.

Looking at the situation as it exists today, the language rights of Sri Lanka's Tamil minority are on par with those of the French in Canada, substantially better than those of the English-speaking minority in Quebec, and immeasurably superior to those of the Tamils of Malaysia who form an overwhelming majority of the Indian community in that country. A more appropriate comparison is with the language rights of the minorities in the cantons of Switzerland. The comparison is appropriate because Switzerland is often cited by Tamil critics of Sri Lanka's language policy, as the most important success story of modern pluralist democracy, and they identify Switzerland's language policy as one of the keys to this success.[19]

There are two principles in operation in Swiss language

policy: the principle of personality at the federal level, and the principle of territoriality at the cantonal level. It is at the cantonal level that the more relevant comparison with the Sri Lankan situation lies. These cantons are not only remarkably homogenous, but they are more or less unilingual, and persons 'moving to a new canton are obliged to use its local languages for the transaction of official business.'[20]

The case of Switzerland shows up the language policy of Sri Lanka in a more favourable light than argued by its critics, and the comparison would be even more favourable if one were to focus attention on education. Sri Lanka's Tamil minorities—indigenous and Indian—have always enjoyed the right to an education through the medium of the Tamil language in whatever part of the country they live.[21] This right extends to university and technical education as well. Apart from the University of Jaffna—in the Tamil-speaking Northern Province—which teaches in Tamil and English, and the Eastern University of Sri Lanka located in the largely Tamil-speaking Eastern Province (i.e. Tamil and Muslim) which also teaches in Tamil and English, the University of Peradeniya is unique in providing instruction through three languages, Sinhala, Tamil and English. Some of the departments at the University of Colombo provide instruction in Tamil besides teaching in Sinhala and English.[22] Thus, so far as education is concerned the Tamil minorities of Sri Lanka have enjoyed advantages which minorities in the Swiss cantons do not enjoy or have seldom enjoyed.

Again, because the language rights guaranteed to the Tamils are operative in all parts of the island, and not merely in the north and east, their practical value is at least on par with, if not superior to language rights available to the minority population groups in the cantons of Switzerland. The great majority of such cantons are 'officially unilingual.'[23] Indeed while

. . . Switzerland maintains more than one official language, the languages are spoken in clearly defined territorial areas.[24]

Sri Lanka, by a curious irony, is the only sovereign state in which Tamil is recognized as an official language, apart, of course, from the unusual and somewhat unreal situation in Singapore where Tamil is recognized as one of four official languages, the other three being Mandarin Chinese, English and Malay. In reality Tamil has a distinctly subordinate position there to the others, and especially to Mandarin Chinese and English. The use of Tamil in education at the primary and secondary levels is very limited, and there is no tertiary education in Tamil available in Singapore.

RETROSPECT

On the post-independence controversies over the language issue, the Tamils started with the moral advantage accruing to an aggrieved party in the unilateral abrogation of a policy outlined and accepted only three years before the grant of independence, and which could therefore, be regarded as an integral element of the transfer of power settlement. The advocates of the policy of 'Sinhala Only' were intent, implicitly if not explicitly, on abrogation of the language settlement reached in 1943-4 and used many arguments to support their case. Our concern here is with one of these, the fears expressed about Sinhala, a uniquely Sri Lankan language, being doomed to unequal competition with Tamil, a thriving Indian language, should parity of status be conceded to Tamil as an official language. That argument was not new; it had been used during the debate on language policy in 1944. While these fears were understandable, they tended to exaggerate the competitive edge that Tamil would have from association with the Indian version of that language.

Looking back on these controversies one feels that the price the country has paid in the breakdown of ethnic harmony, and in the distortion of the national priorities, outweighed the undeniable benefits the emphasis on indigenous languages brought to the people at large. After a century and half of British rule less than 10 per cent of the people were proficient in English. Had the Sinhalese political leadership that succeeded D.S. Senanayake not forced the pace of language change by seeking to give Sinhala pride of place through an abrogation of the settlement on language reached in 1943-4, had they been more patient and eschewed the path of unilateral change, they may well have ensured the primacy of their language on a much more solid basis, without the rancour and bitterness that was the price of the 'Sinhala Only' policy. Quite apart from the natural advantages accruing to Sinhala as the language of over two-thirds of the population, there was the powerful attraction of economic necessity—the Sinhalese areas offered by far the greatest opportunities of employment and trade. As it was the objective of 'Sinhala Only' has been pursued at the cost of conceding to the Tamils all the advantages of proclaiming to a sympathetic world that they, as a minority, have suffered greatly in the change in language policy imposed on them by an unsympathetic majority. More important, 'Sinhala Only' in its starkest form has proved to be an elusive object, an abstraction the pursuit of which has had the double effect of destroying the political careers of many who sought to give it life, and of provoking similar passionate commitment to the defense of their language by the Tamils. At the same time, adjustments and accommodations on language rights made to the Tamils through political necessity and a realistic adjustment to life in a plural society and democratic state from as early as 1958 had all but granted parity of status to the Tamil language by 1978. Yet the political benefits of these working arrangements proved to be just as elusive as the quest for 'Sinhala Only' because the main representatives of Tamil political opinion in the country never officially acknowledged that the reality of language policy had deviated from its rhetoric over the years.

CHAPTER 3

Religion and Politics in Modern Sri Lanka

COLONIALISM AND SRI LANKAN CHRISTIANITY

Modern Christianity came to Sri Lanka with the arrival of the Portuguese in the littoral parts of the island in the 16th century. To this day Sri Lankan Christianity bears the stamp of its colonial origins. In the 16th and 17th centuries Europe's religious conflicts—the hostilities of the Reformation and Counter-Reformation—were extended to Asian soil and Asian waters, Sri Lankan soil and Sri Lankan waters specifically. The Counter-Reformation in the form of Portuguese Roman Catholicism, in fact, came here before the Reformation in the form of the Dutch Reformed Church. With the British in the 19th century came a wider range of Protestant groups. From the mid-16th century, Roman Catholicism, Calvinism and Anglicanism have had, in succession, a special relationship with the ruling power and with this the prestige and temporal authority of the official religion of the day, whereby converts to the orthodox version of Christianity— especially under the Portuguese and the Dutch—came to be treated as a privileged group.

With the entry of the Portuguese on the Sri Lankan scene in the 16th century, bigotry and religious intolerance typical of the Counter-Reformation were introduced into an island whose Buddhist society was well-known for its religious tolerance. The earliest victims of the Portuguese in their role of Christian fanatics were the Muslims of Sri Lanka's coastal regions, once again a transfer to Asian soil and Asian waters of Mediterranean Europe's traditional hostility to the Muslims. The Muslims, fleeing the Portuguese, found refuge in the interior where the Sinhalese kings permitted them to settle, and the large

Muslim settlement on the east coast of Sri Lanka was, in part at least, the result of emigration to those parts—then under the control of the Sinhalese kingdoms. The Buddhists (and Hindus) did not fare much better under Portuguese rule, but so far as the Buddhists were concerned, they could always seek the protection of Sinhalese kings. The point, however, is that the religious intolerance that came to Sri Lanka with the Portuguese was as unusual as it was virulent, leaving behind a memory of temples destroyed, temple properties confiscated and turned over to the church, of prohibition of Buddhist and Hindu worship, and of induced if not forced conversions. As we have seen in the previous chapter, Sri Lankan society and civilization had seldom confused the obligation to encourage adherence to the national religion with the suppression of other faiths. In time, once the Dutch had established themselves on the coasts, having expelled the Portuguese, it was the turn of the Roman Catholics to feel the sting of religious intolerance—from the Dutch Protestants. Once more it was to the Sinhalese kings that the harried Portuguese clergy turned for refuge. A settlement of Roman Catholics at Wahakotte in the hills of central Sri Lanka (close to Matale) going back to the 17th century, still survives, as a monument to the traditional religious tolerance of the Buddhists.

Just as the Roman Catholics were a privileged group under the Portuguese, and severe restrictions were imposed on the practice of the indigenous religions—Buddhism and Hinduism—and Islam, so under the Dutch, it was the adherents of the Dutch Reformed Church who enjoyed a privileged existance. Both sought converts, both used a mixture of force and material benefits to attract converts, and both Portuguese and Dutch came to believe that the majority of people in the territories they controlled were Christians—Roman Catholics under the Portuguese and Protestants under the Dutch. Conversions to Protestantism under the Dutch proved to be far more ephemeral than the cognate process under the Portuguese.[1]

Through much of the 19th century and all of the 20th the Roman Catholics constituted nine-tenths of the Christian community in Sri Lanka, conversions to Roman Catholicism under the Portuguese having stood the test of persecution under the Dutch and the indifference of the British. Besides, unlike the Protestants and more especially the Anglicans who were an elite group, the Roman Catholics came from all strata of society. But put together, the Roman Catholics and the Protestants were never more than a tenth of the island's population under British rule.

This peculiar demographic configuration, about which we shall have more to say later in this chapter, has had a distorting effect on the relationship between the Christian minority and the rest of the Sri Lankan society. For much of the first half of the 19th century the Roman Catholics had little or no influence on official policies and attitudes and which in turn affected that relationship. There the pace was set by the Protestants in general and not necessarily the elite Anglican group. But with the passage of time the Roman Catholics asserted themselves and with numbers very much on their side the interaction between Christianity and indigenous society became more complex with a divided Christian community confronting a religiously segmented local population. The situation became even more complicated when the government entered the scene with interests of its own, which very often were not entirely to the satisfaction of the missionaries.

Although British rule saw the entry and establishment of a greater variety of Protestant missionary groups in the island, the British were more latitudinarian in their attitudes to religion than their predecessors, the Dutch and the Portuguese had been. While the Anglican church aspired to the role of the established church, it enjoyed few of the privileges and powers of either the Roman Catholic clergy under the Portuguese or the clergy of the Dutch Reformed Church under the Dutch. Indeed, the early years of British rule saw the recovery of the Roman Catholics from their suppression under the Dutch to their current position of being the principal Christian group in the island (90 per cent of the Christian community has been Roman Catholic from the 1840s onwards). Under the British, the state was generally neutral in religious affairs, but many of its officials were not. Thus the picture of the Christians as a privileged group, and of the Anglican church as the church of the elite persisted, even after the disestablishment of the Anglican church in 1881.[2]

During British rule, the Christian community constituted as much as 10 per cent of the population. In contrast, in British India *as a whole*, it was as little as 2 per cent. More important, the Christian minority was a powerful elite group, with a commanding position in public life. The result was that Buddhist revivalism was, from the beginning, directed against the privileged position of this Christian minority. It was also a reaction against the aggressive proselytizing activities of the Protestant missionaries.

Many of the issues that became so politically divisive in post-independence Sri Lanka had their roots in the mid and late 19th century as Buddhist activists began their agitation against British missionaries, and some of the political decisions of the British government. Of the latter, none was more important than a decision taken in the late 1840s, in response to missionary pressure in London, at the Colonial Office, through the missionary centre then known as 'Clapham House' and under missionary pressure in Sri Lanka. The formal link which the British colonial government in Sri Lanka established with the Buddhist religion in 1815 when the Kandyan kingdom, the last independent Sinhalese kingdom had been ceded to the British, was severed. The terms of the cession were set out in the Kandyan Convention of 2 March 1815; under its fifth clause the British negotiators had undertaken to protect Buddhism, its *bhikkhus*, places of worship and the properties of the temples—the *viharas* and *devales*.[3] From the moment the severance of this link was announced the

Buddhists in Sri Lanka began, what turned out to be, a decades-long agitation for a restoration of this link, if not on the terms set out in the Kandyan Convention, at least in some more tenuous form acceptable to the Buddhists and one that would enable them to secure legal protection of the rights of the *viharas* and *devales* over their properties.[4]

Most colonial administrators in Whitehall, and many in the island, did not understand that Sri Lankan Buddhism had no central organization that could either formally appoint heads of *viharas*, or give formal recognition to the validity of appointments made by others, a minimal requirement to ensure legal protection to the property rights of *viharas* and *devales*. The agitation for a restoration of the link with the state was essentially designed to persuade the British government to make some formal legal arrangements for these purposes, something that the Colonial Office had promised to do, and which Colonial Governors of the 1850s had urged it to,[5] when the severance of the link with Buddhism was forced on a reluctant colonial administration in Sri Lanka in the mid-1840s. The delay in providing the legislation required for this purpose and the inadequacies in the legislation that was eventually provided became a grievance among the Buddhists and contributed greatly to the strength of the Buddhist revival in the late 19th century.[6]

The Buddhist revival in the mid and late 19th century Sri Lanka was a reaction against the early success of the British missionaries. Indeed—by the 1850s—the British missionaries and the more prominent Sinhalese Christians all believed that Buddhism was doomed to early extinction. Their prophecies were made at precisely the moment that Buddhist revivalists launched their first campaigns against Christian influence and privilege. Some of the British governors of the late 19th century were sympathetic to the Buddhists' demands, and indeed sought to turn or manipulate the emerging Buddhist revival into a conservative force that would support the British. Two Governors, William Gregory (1872-7) a Liberal, and Arthur

Gordon (1883-90) a Conservative, between them, helped evolve a new religious policy towards Buddhism, one which emphasized the neutrality of the state, and yet conceded that the colonial state in Sri Lanka had a special obligation to the Buddhists of Sri Lanka. When this same formula was revived in the 1950s onwards by Sri Lankan politicians, they were unaware of its colonial rights.

Most of the Protestant missionaries in British Ceylon shared some of the basic assumptions of the secular advocates of Empire—faith in the permanance of British rule being one of them—and identified themselves with the processes of colonial rule to the point that the indigenous population saw them as the spiritual arm of the ruling power. To be sure there was no total identity of interests between the missionaries and the state, and the former seldom entirely ceased to be critical of the government, but their association, a blend of collaboration and critical appraisal of each other's work, was close enough for the missionary movement to suffer when colonial rule came under attack, just as much as it benefitted enormously from its association with the colonial system.

With the Buddhist revival of the last quarter of the 19th century[7] the indigenous element became more assertive if not yet the dominant one in determining the balance of forces in the complex interaction between the Christians and the rest of the Sri Lankan society. The government responded with an attempt to turn the Buddhist movement, which it viewed as an intrinsically conservative force, to its own advantage. The government's neutrality in religious affairs, asserted so often in the mid-1870s and thereafter, was demonstrated in a manner at once open and vigorous by the disestablishment of the Anglican church in 1881. More important still, it had become politic to underscore the principle of judicious patronage of Buddhism, a policy that was easily transformed into a special responsibility towards Buddhism. Buddhist opinion was not satisfied with this. They wanted the state to assume responsibility for the maintenance of Buddhist temporalities, and a more positive, in the sense of formal, link between the state and Buddhism, in brief a reversion to the position that had existed up to the 1840s when the link had been severed under missionary pressure. In time, the Buddhist revival became, the catalyst of nationalism. '[One] of the most serious aspects of the Buddhist revival' the World Missionary Congress in Edinburgh (in 1910) reported with alarm:

> is the attempt to identify Buddhism with patriotism and to urge upon people that loyalty to the country implies loyalty to the religion.[8]

> The Buddhist movement . . . is hostile to Christianity, representing it as alien, and Buddhism as national and patriotic . . .[9]

Though the diagnosis of the malady was swift and accurate it was, as usual, more difficult to prescribe a remedy. And no remedy was likely to be effective so long as the root cause of the ailment, the 'westernness' of Sri Lankan Christianity was not eliminated. The concepts used in the interpretation of Sri Lankan Christianity were essentially European and all Christian groups were generally oblivious to the value of indigenous art-forms such as music, drumming, dance and even the architecture of churches to Christian worship. They had come to Sri Lanka as the apostles of a new faith, as critics of indigenous society and in preaching the gospel—Christianity whether Roman Catholic or Protestant, had generally been an aggressively proselytizing faith—their missionaries had been fortified usually by an unquestioning faith not merely in their rightness but also in the intrinsic sinfulness or even depravity—a word they often used—of many traditional customs and beliefs. Indeed, there had been a conscious attempt to undermine traditional customs and beliefs and to impose in their place Christian values of the Victorian age. All this had given the Christian community in the island a characteristic feature of cultural intolerance. They made no attempt—at least up to the early years of the 20th century—to blend with the local culture. And, more serious still, the soul-searching about the relationship between Christianity and national identity which appeared in many parts of Asia and Africa at the end of the 19th century, either did not emerge at all, or did so a full generation later and on a more modest and diffident note.

Although the stirrings in the other indigenous religions, Hinduism and Islam, had much in common with the processes of Buddhist resurgence, certain features in them set them apart from the Buddhist experience. The principal contrast was that neither the Hindu nor the Islamic recovery developed any political overtones in the sense of a potential anti-British or anti-imperialist attitude.

THE CHRISTIAN RESPONSE TO NATIONALISM

In the early 1920s the Christian groups in the island began at last to face up to the implications of the changes brought about by the rise of nationalism. The aim now was to make the missions and churches indigenous institutions, less conspicuously under European leadership and direction, a change at variance with the whole trend of missionary thinking and practice in the 19th century.

This process of coming to terms with nationalism may be described as a 're-indigenisation' movement,[10] the revival of indigenous names, forms of dress and cultivation of the native arts and crafts among the Christians. In most Protestant churches a Sinhala or Tamil prayer book—a faithful translation from the English—had been the only concession to the native culture, and no attempt had been made to adapt the form of worship to a national, that is to say Sinhalese and Tamil, form. The Anglicans, surprisingly enough, were in the forefront of the 're-indigenisation' movement, in the use of forms of worship native to Sri Lanka, and in the adoption of the traditional architecture in church building.

A second aspect of this trend was the attempt to seek an autonomous status for the Christian missions and churches, self-supporting, self-propagating and indigenous. This was a long-drawn out process largely because of the practical and mundane problem of financial independence from the parent societies in Europe and the United States. The degree of independence achieved varied from mission to mission but it would be true to say that at the time the island achieved its independence none were substantially self-supporting. Besides the most articulate spokesmen of the 're-indigenization' movement were more often than not British missionaries rather than native Christians. And almost up to the time of independence indigenization in the top rungs of the hierarchy of the Christian churches in the island proceeded much more slowly than in the cognate process in politics and the bureaucracy.

Thirdly, the Buddhist resurgence and the growth of nationalism led to a sober realism about the limits of evangelical activity. Expansion gave way to consolidation and contraction. Besides, the missions could no longer afford to dissipate their energies in sectarian disputes. Up to the turn of the century there had been little co-operation among the Christian groups working in the island. The greatest achievement of the World Missionary Conference held in Edinburgh in 1910 was the establishment of the first permanent instrument of Christian co-operation outside the Roman Catholic Church; its impact began to be felt in Sri Lanka in the 1920s and after, and its influence fitted in neatly with the practical necessity of closing ranks in the face of a resurgent Buddhism. Nevertheless, this co-ordination of activity did not encompass the Roman Catholics who stood aloof from the other Christian groups. Indeed, the 're-indigenization' movement as a whole was essentially a Protestant one, and the Roman Catholics lagged well behind.

In retrospect it would seem that the period between the two world wars was the most decisive phase in the reconciliation of the Christian minority to a diminished role in the affairs of the country—if not yet a ready acceptance of Buddhist dominance in the Sri Lanka polity.

That is not to say there were no differences or obstacles to this policy of accommodation. Most of them had to do with education and the schools, and the conflicts over these, determined the pattern of relations between the Buddhist majority and Christian minority both in the later years of British rule and in the years after independence.

In the 1940s there were purposeful efforts to give the island's education system a new orientation, more secular and less elitist in outlook and to enlarge considerably the role of the state at the expense of the missions which up to this time dominated education. The mission schools organized on denominational lines came increasingly under attack because these schools had been seen, for long, as instruments of religious conversion and regarded, not unfairly, as needlessly wasteful of resources in an unhealthy rivalry and competition among the missions for enlarging their spheres of influence in education. This concentration of attention on education as a means of religious conversion tended to divert attention from the more constructive achievements of the missionaries in their role of educators. If the mission schools were seldom designed for purposes unrelated to evangelization, their students nevertheless did find new vistas of secular knowledge opened to them, and their intellectual horizons were widened.

The resistance organized and led by the Roman Catholics to these reforms succeded in delaying their implementation and in softening if not eliminating some of the more far-reaching aspects which were regarded as being especially inimical to denominational interests. A significant difference between the attitudes of the Roman Catholics and Protestants to education needs to be explained. The Roman Catholics brought pressure to bear on their adherents to send their children to Roman Catholic schools and the larger (and better) of such schools had a majority of Roman Catholic pupils: there were no such pressures exerted by Protestants and in few if any Protestant schools was there a majority of pupils who were Protestants (even using the term widely to cover all

Protestant denominations). Thus the Roman Catholic resistance to secularization and state control of education was much stronger and more determined than that of the Protestants. The fact that the opposition to these reforms came mainly from the Roman Catholics largely explains the irony of the situation where the bitterness of the Buddhists against the slights and neglect suffered at the hands of the Christians during the centuries of western rule should be directed at them rather than Protestants who for the last two centuries or more had enjoyed special favours if not a privileged position.

Fortunately for the Christian missions, the pressure from the Buddhist movement relaxed somewhat in the inter-war years. There was even less pressure from the Hindus and the Muslims both of whom were in the position of sharing whatever gains the Buddhists were able to extract.

In the early years of the century, the Buddhist movement in the hands of men like Anagarika Dharmapala (1864-1933) was almost the mirror image of Protestant Christianity in its techniques of propaganda. Dharmapala, the new Buddhist revivalist, was the old missionary writ large.[11] A protean, and much misunderstood figure, Dharmapala, grasped as few of his contemporaries did the political implications of the Buddhist resurgence and he never lost sight of the need to set the latter within the wider framework of the rise of nationalism in Asia. His principal role in the public life of colonial Sri Lanka was in helping to organize the Buddhist resistance to Christian influence in the island, a point which is totally ignored by many of his late 20th century critics. Moreover, his career as Buddhist activist extended beyond the island, in the long struggle he waged to secure control of the Buddhist centres of worship and the historic *bodhi tree* at Bodh Gaya in India. There he faced the full brunt of the opposition of Hindu obscurantism. A man less vigorous in his commitment to Buddhism and to a Sinhalese ethnic identity could easily have been overwhelmed by the opposition he faced in India and Sri Lanka.

After the First World War this brand of militant Buddhism receded to the background for over a generation. This was not owing to any decline of interest in Buddhism or Buddhist activity. Indeed by the 1920s, the British missionary groups in Sri Lanka, not to mention the Roman Catholics were under great pressure from Buddhist activists. Fortunately for the missionaries, there was a mood of restraint and excessive caution in Sri Lankan politics which spilled over into religious activity when the new leaders of the political reform movement, F.R. Senanayake (1884-1925) and D.B. Jayatilaka (1868-1944) took control of the Buddhist movement as well and kept a tight rein on religious enthusiasm. Their approach to the religious problems of the day was in every way a contrast to Dharmapala's—he was living in India at this time and appears to have lost much of his influence with the Buddhist movement in the island—and they set the tone in Buddhist activity right up to Jayatilaka's retirement from active politics in 1942. Jayatilaka was the most prominent Buddhist leader of the day. His dual role of elder statesman in political and religious affairs enhanced his prestige in both and this he used with considerable finesse to curb what he regarded as extremism.

With the political and constitutional changes which followed on the introduction of the Donoughmore Constitution in 1931 and universal suffrage gave the Buddhist activists greater influence; the political leadership and legislators alike were, unlike their predecessors in the old Legislative Council, subject to the pressures of a democratic electorate. They were more sensitive to the demands of Buddhist revivalists than their predecessors who had been elected by the votes of the educated elite. Significantly; the demand that Buddhist opinion had made for several decades that the administration of Buddhist temporalities be brought under state supervision was conceded in 1931.[12] The Ordinance which was passed in 1942 for the preservation of the sacred city of

Anuradhapura, in the heartland of the ancient irrigation civilizations of Sri Lanka, was based on sober necessity but lent itself to some recrudescence of Dharmapala's ideas. The duumvirate of D.B. Jayatilaka and D.S. Senanayake (1884-1952), F.R. Senanayake's younger brother and political heir, soon to be the island's first Prime Minister after independence, accepted and defended these as parts of the state's special obligation to Buddhism but they were at all times conscious of the need to reconcile this with the official policy of neutrality in religious affairs. The distinction they drew was between a government of Buddhists and a Buddhist government, in brief, a careful demarcation of the boundaries between state power and religion.

The Burmese influence on Sri Lankan Buddhism entered the country at this time in the form of *bhikkhus* educated in India (Bengal, in particular) who had become converts to Marxism and socialism. The Sri Lankan political establishment and the more orthodox *bhikkhus* reacted with considerable hostility to the new phenomenon of 'political' *bhikkhus* who were demanding a voice in political decision-making and were intent on radicalizing the country's political agenda. The role model for the 'political' *bhikkhus* was their Burmese counterparts who were in the forefront of nationalist agitation in their country. While the 'political' *bhikkhus* had less influence in Sri Lanka than they believed they had—partly because of the successful opposition of some of the principal Sri Lankan politicians of the day—they nevertheless succeeded in changing the agenda of Buddhist activism to a greater degree than their critics within the *sangha* were originally willing to concede. The classic exposition of their viewpoint, Walpola Rahula's *Heritage of the Buddha*, had considerable influence among the *sangha* in Sri Lanka. This polemical work published originally in Sinhala in 1946, translated into English in 1974 (published by Grove Press) was less intellectually rigorous than his later work, the well-known *What the Buddha Taught*, but it had served the purpose for which it was intended, of gaining greater acceptability for unorthodox ideas.

At Jayatilaka's death in 1942, the Buddhist movement passed into more militant hands, of men nursing a sense of outrage and indignation at what they regarded as the historic injustices suffered by their religion under western rule. They led the attack on the Roman Catholics on the schools issue, but found a major obstacle to the success of their enterprise in D.S. Senanayake, the most influential advocate of Sri Lankan nationalism which emphasized the common interests of the island's several ethnic and religious groups, and sought the reconciliation of the legitimate interests of the Sinhalese-Buddhist majority and those of the minority.

'SECULARISM' AND ITS CRITICS

In view of the often acrimonious controversies between Buddhist activists and the Christian minority during the 1930s and early 1940s a definition of the nexus between state and religion in the post-independence Sri Lankan polity was treated as a central feature of the transfer of negotiations which took place between 1943 and 1947.[13] The principles of a new constitution to be prepared by the Sri Lankans in the then Board of Ministers were set out by Whitehall on 26 May 1943; these were further clarified by another statement issued on 11 July 1943. The requirement that such a draft constitution should have the approval of three-quarters of all the members of the State Council ensured that it would have to be nothing less than a national consensus on constitutional reform.[14]

For D.S. Senanayake who took the lead in the transfer of power negotiations, and in the drafting of this constitution, the principal objective was to allay the fears of minorities with regard to their position in an independent Sri Lanka. This could have been done by introducing a comprehensive and justiciable Bill of Rights. Senanayake himself was not unsympathetic to the incorporation of such a bill in the constitution, but he was dissuaded from supporting it by the arguments of his principal adviser on constitutional affairs, Dr (later Sir) Ivor Jennings, for whom the applicability of the Westminister constitutional model to the Sri Lankan situation was an unalterable article of faith. Jennings would not give any serious consideration to the incorporation of a Bill of Rights in the new constitution. Instead, he recommended a provision based on section 5 of the Government of Ireland Act of 1920 prohibiting legislation infringing on religious freedom or discriminating against persons of any commodity or religion. This advice was accepted by Senanayake and the draft constitution prepared by the Board of Ministers in 1944, the Ministers' Draft Constitution as it came to be called, contained a clause (clause 8) which prohibited Parliament from enacting laws which discriminated against any ethnic or religious group, restricted or prohibited the free exercise of any religion or conferred on 'persons of any community or religion any privileges or advantages which are not conferred on persons of other communities or religions.' This was transferred, with only minor additions, as section 29(2) of the constitution on which the transfer of power was effected in 1947-8.

The constitutional settlement reached at the transfer of power negotiations incorporated, as an integral feature, an emphasis on secularism, defined in terms of the limits to the power of the state in religious affairs. This pragmatic compromise was based on two principles: the state was prohibited from discriminating between persons on the basis of religion; secondly, it was enjoined to treat all religions alike. In his commitment to these provisions in the new constitution, D.S. Senanayake successfully postponed, what now appears to have been, the inevitable confrontation between the more assertive sections of the Buddhist movement insisting in the establishment of a Buddhist government, and those who were committed, as he was, to a careful demarcation and scrupulous observance of the boundaries between state power and religion.

Senanayake and his associates faced strong opposition from a section of radicalized *bhikkhus*,[15] deeply influenced by Burmese Buddhist activism,[16] who combined a commitment to social and economic reform on Marxist principles with a demand for a closer association of the new state with the Buddhist religion and the restoration of its traditional patronage along with the precedence and prestige that would accompany such patronage.

Senanayake's great achievement was that he thwarted all efforts to abandon the concept of a 'secular' state as defined in the constitution and the state's religious neutrality. He succeeded to the extent that during his period as Prime Minister, there was little evidence of the upsurge of religious fervour and linguistic nationalism that burst to the surface in the mid-1950s.

Nevertheless, the confrontation between the advocates of a secular state and those who sought to underline the primacy of Buddhism and the Sinhalese was renewed in the 1950s. The year 1951 is crucial in this regard. It saw the establishment, by S.W.R.D. Bandaranaike, of a new political party, the SLFP which vowed to espouse the Sinhalese-Buddhist cause. In July that year Bandaranaike resigned from his Cabinet position in the first post-independence government and crossed over to the opposition. The second event is less well-known but just as significant. This was the publication in April that year of the resoluions adopted at the 32nd annual sessions of the All Ceylon Buddhist Congress. The resolutions were published, along with a memorandum, as a pamphlet entitled *Buddhism and the State* and addressed to D.S. Senanayake as Prime Minister of Sri Lanka. The memorandum stressed the

> . . . disappointment, almost resentment, growing among the Buddhists with regard to the present position of Buddhism in [Sri Lanka] . . . the present Government . . . is legally and morally bound to protect and maintain Buddhism and Buddhist institutions. The Buddhists feel, however, that our present rulers have shown a marked reluctance to acknowledge this fact . . .

It went on to argue that while politicians were not

> slow to exploit the unique position which [Sri Lanka] enjoyed among the nations of the world, by reason of her proud heritage of Buddhism and Buddhist culture . . . [they] have shown no earnest desire to rescue Buddhism from the great state of neglect to which it has been deliberately reduced by foreign rulers of this country nor to secure for the Buddhists the paramount position which should be theirs in the life of the nation.

This theme of restoring Buddhism to 'the paramount position of prestige which rightfully belongs to it' was repeatedly emphasized in this document, and along with it the demand that the Buddhists

> be given all-out (sic) assistance to rehabilitate themselves and to resuscitate their institutions . . .

The document asserted that

> It is incumbent upon the present Government of Free Lanka to protect and maintain Buddhism . . .

and added that the

> definite steps to be taken by Government to discharge this duty and obligation is (sic) a matter for decision after thorough investigation by a competent Commission.

The final paragraph of the memorandum made a specific request: that 'measures be taken at once' to provide the Buddhist religion with an 'autonomous constitution'. 'For this purpose,' the memorandum went on

> [the] Buddhists ask for the immediate enactment of an Act on lines similar to the Buddha Sasana Act 1312 B E (1950) of Burma, relevant extracts from which are given as an Appendix to this [document]. To secure the enactment and implementation of such an Act, they ask that a Buddha Sasana Department be forthwith established under a suitable Ministry by the Government of [Sri Lanka].

These demands were to be repeated with greater frequency but not with any greater clarity over the next few years. While Senanayake's UNP government in power at this time tended to ignore them, they attracted wider and stronger support from activist sections of the Buddhist public with each passing year.

D.S. Senanayake would give no satisfaction to the All Ceylon Buddhist Congress and, indeed, rejected its demands. He did not concede even the need for a Commission of Inquiry to report on the state of Buddhism. But politicized Buddhism was already a powerful force which would upset the equilibrium of forces he had endeavoured to establish. When Bandaranaike moved out of the government he was essentially seeking to exploit this new force and to provide the Sinhalese-Buddhist majority, long dormant, with a political party for the fulfilment of their aspirations. This was to be the role of the SLFP. From the outset the new party offered a home to those who rejected the concepts of a multi-ethnic polity, of a Sri Lankan nationalism, and of a secular state. It welcomed to its ranks *bhikkhu* activists, and some of them held positions of influence in its executive committee. At issue in the confrontation that emerged in the 1950s between the Buddhist activists and the Christian minority, was the privileged position the Roman Catholics continued to hold in Sri Lankan society, and the threat this was presumed to pose to Buddhist—and the national—interests.

With Senanayake's death in 1952 the commitment to the concept of a secular state on the part of his successors in the leadership of his party became less than wholehearted. The pressures they confronted from a resurgent Buddhist movement were also much greater than any he had faced. The position of Buddhism and Buddhists had improved quite substantially at independence and in the first decade after independence but these advances only served to give an exaggerated salience to the narrowing gap between aspiration and achievement. Thus, despite the education reforms introduced in the 1940s, Christian schools still retained much of the prestige and influence they had enjoyed in the days of British rule. The preponderance of Christians and other minorities in the higher bureaucracy, in the professions and in public life, in general remained intact although under increasing pressure. While the balance was shifting in favour of the Sinhalese-Buddhists, this process was inevitably slow and, in what seemed to be, measured stages. As a result, Buddhist activists were not only thoroughly dissatisfied with the pace at which the balance was shifting, but they also attributed the survival of the privileged position of the Christian and other minorities to the existing rules of the political game which were believed to bear a heavy and unfair bias against the Sinhalese-Buddhists.

In 1956 the Buddhist world was scheduled to celebrate the 2500th anniversary of the death of the Buddha—the *Buddha Jayanthi* as this was called. There was at this time 'a common belief in all Buddhist countries that this anniversary [would] initiate a great revival of Buddhism throughout the world when the Buddhist way of life and thus universal peace [would] prevail.'[17] Buddhism was being hailed as a new cross-national political force. U. Nu's Burma had taken the leadership in this, intent on establishing itself as the pre-eminent Theravada Buddhist country. The new institutions he had established in 1950, the Buddha Sasana Council and the Ministry of Religious Affairs, were being regarded by the All Ceylon Buddhist Congress as appropriate models for Sri Lanka to emulate. In 1951 U. Nu had decided on a more ambitious project emphasizing the international aspects of the Buddhist revival and linking it to the historical past of Buddhism in its ancient Indian setting: he convened the Sixth Great Buddhist Council emphasizing its role as the latest in a series, the first of which went back in time to just after the Buddha's death. Initiated eventually in 1954, it lasted for two years and inevitably established Rangoon as the main centre for Buddhists from all over the world, as well as from the five principal Theravada Buddhist nations: Burma, Cambodia, Laos, Sri Lanka and Thailand. The Council's work came to an end in May 1956, by which time Buddhism appeared to be establishing itself as the new political force in the world that U. Nu had envisaged in convening the Council.

The Hindus for their part had closed ranks with the Christians of the Tamil community and began a process of presenting a united front against a resurgent Buddhist movement. This has continued to the present day.

BUDDHIST ACTIVISM AND THE SRI LANKA POLITY, 1956-1972

The run-up to the general elections of 1956 in Sri Lanka had been characterized by a frenetic stimulation of nationalist feelings, focusing on language and religion. The purposeful intervention of the *bhikkhus*, converted a conventional election campaign into an emotional evocation of the traditional values associated with the country's Buddhist heritage. The political objectives of the campaign were clear enough: to establish, once and for all, the primacy of the Sinhalese-Buddhists in the Sri Lanka polity. The cutting edge of this resurgence of nationalism was language and the political impact of the transformation of nationalism into a linguistic form was a central theme in the evolving relationship between state and religion. While politicians, Bandaranaike included, gave pride of place to the language issue over the more complex question of the status of Buddhism in the Sri Lankan polity, *bhikkhu* activists saw them as inextricably linked together in the re-establishment of a Sinhalese-Buddhist society on traditional lines. Bandaranaike's electoral coalition of 1956, owed more to the campaign skills of the *bhikkhus* than they were willing to concede. The latter provided most of the eloquent campaign orators, and indeed very few of the leading politicians of the Mahajana Eksath Peramuna (MEP) coalition, of which the SLFP was the core, could match them in this regard. Even more important, the *bhikkhus* stepped out of their temples, literally in their hundreds if not thousands, in all parts of the Sinhalese areas of the country, to urge the masses to turn the UNP out of office, and to substitute for it a government led by Bandaranaike, a government that would reflect the views and aspirations the *bhikkhus* were articulating on public platforms.[18]

In the meantime a committee of inquiry appointed by the All Ceylon Buddhist Congress—the UNP government had refused to accede to its appeal for an official Commission of Inquiry—was preparing a major report on the state of Buddhism in the country. Issued on 4 February 1956 it contained a detailed exposition of the disadvantageous position—as they saw it—of Buddhism in the mid-20th century Sri Lanka, which they attributed to the cumulative effect of several centuries of foreign rule and, not less important, the neglect of post-independence UNP governments of Sri Lanka. The demands it made on behalf of the Buddhists were an expansion of those originally presented for the consideration of D.S. Senanayake's government in 1951. The report made it abundantly clear that the redress of Buddhist grievances was a matter of the utmost urgency and that this could only be achieved through the political process. The fact that the report was presented to the 'People of Lanka' and not to the government signified that, in the committee's view, the solutions lay with the former and not the latter. The English version of the report carried a pithy and provocative title: *The Betrayal of Buddhism.*

The MEP election manifesto issued on 7 March 1956 was clearly influenced by that document. The manifesto had pledged: to elevate Sinhala to the status of the official language of the country; to accept the recommendations of the Buddhist Committee of Inquiry; to foster *ayurveda* (traditional herbal medicine); and to reorganize the education system in accordance with national culture. Once the MEP coalition secured a decisive victory, it found the implementation of its policies a matter of the utmost difficulty. As we have seen in the previous chapter, this was especially so with regard to language, where the Bandaranaike government sought to reconcile its commitment to make Sinhala the sole national language, with the political and indeed practical necessity to make some concession to the Tamils about the use of their language. Certainly, none of the *bhikkhu* activists paid the slightest attention to that latter aspect of the MEP manifesto during their campaigns. They concentrated entirely on the elevation of Sinhala to the status of the sole national language. The *bhikkhu* activists in association with lay supporters of an extremist viewpoint on language policy drew first blood when they compelled Bandaranaike to withdraw the draft bill on language that had been prepared in April/May 1956, and to frame another more to their taste, or at least one to which they were not so opposed.[19]

Even as the new government was seeking to consolidate itself in the first two years of its existence in the wake of the violent ethnic conflicts of that time—reviewed in chapter four—it had to cope with the pressure for stronger links between Buddhism and the state, and for a corresponding reduction if not eradication of Christian influence in the Sri Lanka polity, in short the pressure for the elevation of Buddhism to the status of the state religion. In 1951 the All Ceylon Buddhist Congress had gone on record saying that:

> A great deal of deliberate confusion has been caused by the cry that the Buddhists want their religion made the State Religion in Free Lanka. The Buddhists have made no such demand. But the Buddhists do want legislative enactments enabling them to manage their own affairs efficiently, by means of an autonomous constitution . . . they recognize the undesirability of the Government, as at present constituted, controlling the internal affairs of any religion.

There were no such inhibitions in 1956-7 about the elevation of Buddhism to the status of the state religion. But the new government, entangled in the coils of the language crisis of 1956-8, preferred to delay consideration of this latter issue and resorted to the appointment of another Commission of Inquiry on this subject as a delaying tactic. The existence of the report of the Committee of Inquiry appointed by the All Ceylon Buddhist Congress in 1955-6 and which report the government had, promised, in its election manifesto, to adopt and implement, complicated the issue. Was not this new Commission superfluous? Bandaranaike did not think so.

When in February 1957, Bandaranaike proceeded to appoint the Buddha Sasana Commission, its terms of reference were seen to be much wider than that of its non-official predecessor of 1956-9.[20] The word *sasana* encompassed the institutions, property, including monastic lands and the rights, obligations, duties and privileges of the *bhikkhus*. It generally covered doctrine as well, but that seemed less relevant on this occasion. The terms of reference of the Buddha Sasana Commission included an examination of the implications of the general but vague principle of 'according Buddhism its rightful place in the country' to which the government was publicly committed. The Commission was also asked to make recommendations for a reform of the *sangha*, one of the crucially important aspects of the ruler's, and the state's, traditional responsibility in regard to the maintenance and protection of Buddhism as the national religion, and one which had been in abeyance since the fall of the Kandyan kingdom in 1815.

Viewed in historical perspective, the appointment and deliberations of this Commission were an attempt by Buddhist activists to identify the solutions they had in mind to the problems that emerged from the severance of the historical link between the state and the Buddhist religion which had occurred in 1840. British Governors of the colony and Sri Lankan politicians alike had come up against the impossibility of returning to the *status quo ante* 1840. For all of them the religious neutrality of the state was a major premise of their thinking; and for many of them—including men like Gregory and Gordon, on the

British side, D.B. Jayatilaka and D.S. Senanayake, on the Sri Lankan side—the only adjustment possible to the reality of the burdens of past history and perceptions of national destiny seen as an unfolding of Buddhism's inextricable links with the state, was a pragmatic recognition of an ill-defined special status for Buddhism. To recognize this officially was worrisome enough in the context of those times; to spell out a policy of action based on this was as problematic in the years 1957-8 as it had been under British rule.

Bandaranaike had been all too aware of the legal and constitutional difficulties to be overcome if Buddhism were to be declared the state religion. Above all there was the formidable hurdle of section 29(2)(c) of the Soulbury constitution which laid down that no law enacted by Parliament shall:

> . . . confer on persons of any community or religion any
> privilege or advantage which is not conferred on persons
> of other communities or religions.

It was not at all certain that the legislature would provide the special majority required for the purpose of overcoming this constitutional obstacle.

There was a greater chance of success with regard to the quest for increasing state control over the schools, in brief, for a completion of the work begun in the 1940s. Strong support for this reform came from Marxists and other left-wing groups. But the Minister of Education, W. Dahanayake, was adamantly opposed to a take-over of the schools run by the Christian missions and other religious organizations. And he had the support of the Prime Minister on this. It would appear that the government was not at all eager to get embroiled in another contentious issue while coping with the political fallout from the language crisis.

The report of the Buddha Sasana Commission was submitted to the Prime Minister in mid-1959, and was scheduled for publication in November 1959. There was the prospect that with its publication the government would turn, at last, to the intricacies of defining and implementing a policy on the 'rightful place' of Buddhism, and to grasp the nettles of Buddhist institutional reform.

Meanwhile, the coalition of forces that had done so much to ensure the success of Bandaranaike's own political career, was crumbling in the face of the turmoil that had characterized the last two years (1958-9) of his administration. *Bhikkhu* activists were divided on a number of issues, and some of the most prominent among them, most notably the *viharadhipathi*—the head—of the Kelaniya temple, Mapitigama Buddharakkita, had become extremely controversial because of their involvement in the ugly factionalism within the SLFP, of which they were such prominent members.

The Buddhist public was now becoming increasingly soured by the spectacle of *bhikkhus* engaging in political infighting, and using pressure for financial gain—for kinsfolk if not for themselves—through influence-peddling and the manipulation of bids for contracts. Their disillusionment turned into deep consternation when the Prime Minister was assassinated on 26 September 1959, the first political assassination in Sri Lanka's hitherto peaceful political history. The chief figure in the conspiracy to murder Bandaranaike was Mapitigama Buddharakkita, who had played a crucially important leadership role in organizing grassroots support for him at the 1956 election, and the actual shooting was done by another *bhikkhu*, a close associate of the principal conspirator.[21]

The assassination of Bandaranaike, with its powerful mix of political and sordid commercial motives, not to mention some sexual overtones, underlining as nothing else did so sharply before or after, the perils involved in *bhikkhus* engaging in partisan politics. Never again did *bhikkhus* wield the same influence in political affairs at a governmental level as they did in the years from 1943 to 1959. Reformist groups among Buddhist activists were provided with the opportunity they needed to initiate moves for far-reaching institutional reforms in the *sangha*. But the political confusion that followed on his death prevented any such initiatives. Unfortunately, there was nobody to provide the leadership in coverting the upsurge of revulsion against the excesses of the political *bhikkhus* into a constructive programme of reform of the *sangha*.

At the time of Mrs Bandaranaike's accession to power in 1960, the process of elite displacement, Christian by Buddhist, had stopped well short of the objectives set by Buddhist activists in the mid-1950s. That considerable progress had been made towards the achievement of these objectives during this period only rendered the survival of vestiges of Christian privileges of the past all the less palatable to them. The struggle for the establishment of Buddhist primacy was resumed on terms, and in areas of activity which S.W.R.D Bandaranaike had hesitated to endorse or support in his period of office: he was unwilling to enforce the demand that Buddhism be raised to the status of the state religion and he had been lukewarm in regard to the extension of state control over the school system. As the new leader of the SLFP, Sirimavo Bandaranaike pressed ahead in continuing the language policy initiated by her husband, and on doing so with as few concessions to the Tamil minority as possible; she displayed greater rigidity on principles underlying this policy than he may have shown had he been alive. Even more important, although the times seemed hardly propitious to enlarge the area of conflict from language to religion and education as well, she embarked on this two-pronged attack on behalf of Sinhalese-Buddhist interests. At the initial stages, she was not interested in the complicated question of the status of Buddhism in the Sri Lankan polity so much as in education reform and the completion of the changes initiated in the 1940s.

But, first of all, it was necessary to formulate a response to the recommendations of the Buddha Sasana Commission. Its principal recommendations included the creation of an incorporated body with wide powers over the *sangha*, empowered to regulate entry into it, and to supervise the education and residence of *bhikkhus*; it would also regulate their engagement in social and political activities, and in paid employment outside of their temples. That body could adjudicate disputes between *bhikkhus*, especially on matters relating to succession as heads of temples, issues on which *bhikkhus* generally sought legal remedies in the civil courts. Among the other areas of activity which would come under its purview were: the collection of funds for temples and Buddhist activity, the building of temples, and publications relating to Buddhism.

The two chapters of the prestigious Siyam *nikaya* (sect) of the Buddhist order raised immediate objections to the recommendations of the report. (The prominent *bhikkhu* political activists were too discredited to voice any opposition to these recommendations). There was considerable irony in this because historically the Siyam *nikaya* has had close links with secular authorities since its establishment in the 18th century. It generally had sought centralized control over the order of *bhikkhus*—which was more or less what the Buddha Sasana Commission report recommended—while the other *nikayas* had emerged into autonomous existence partly because there was no central authority to regulate the affairs of the *sangha* in colonial times.[22] Despite the opposition from the more orthodox *bhikkhus*, the new government could well have embarked on an implementation of a programme of Buddhist institutional reform but Mrs Bandaranaike's government had other priorities, and it turned to these. Thus, a historic opportunity was missed for lack of the political will to seize it and to exploit its potential for a purification of the *sangha*. To move into educational reform was certain to engender conflict with the Roman Catholics in Sri Lanka. But Mrs Bandaranaike calculated on support from the Marxists and other left-wing groups in Parliament and outside it, which may not have shown the same enthusiasm for moves to make Buddhism the state religion. For them state control over education was a desirable end in itself. The Buddhist activists, however, saw it as nothing less than the restoration of a balance that had been tilted far too much in favour of Christians. Indeed, they looked upon the existing education system as historically the principal source of Christian privilege in Sri Lanka. There were also more practical considerations. There were groups within the government and outside it who believed that once the schools came under greater state control, Buddhist influence on the education process would be greatly increased. Politicians welcomed the creation of yet another area of influence and patronage—and opportunities for graft—in appointments of teachers and support staff, and admissions of students to schools.

Once again the Roman Catholics led the resistance and bore the brunt of the attack from the government and its allies. Though all the religious groups—including the Hindus and Muslims, not to mention the Buddhists themselves—were affected by the decision to bring the state-aided secondary schools directly under state control, the Roman Catholics were the biggest losers. Most of the state-aided denominational schools accepted the painful decision to be absorbed by the state. A few big schools, mostly Roman Catholic institutions in the urban areas, decided to retain their independence by becoming private institutions without the benefit of state-aid. Deprived, by law, of the right to levy fees from their students, they maintained a precarious existence under very severe financial handicaps, unlike the elite Protestant Christian—mainly Anglican—schools which had opted to remain independent of the state from the 1940s and who were entitled to levy fees. The long drawn-out Buddhist agitation for state control over education had, at last, achieved its goal.

The fact that the vast majority of the mission schools were almost totally dependent on the government for their finances while in all but a handful of them the majority of students were Buddhists (or Hindus) made it nearly impossible to meet the arguments of the advocates of state control. There was also the zealous care with which all denominations of Christians avoided recruitment of non-Christians to the teaching staff in their schools although the salaries were provided largely, if not entirely, by the state.

The constitution afforded no protection to the minorities against these changes in language and education policy, though they were adversely affected by both. The constitutional obstacle of section 29(2)(b) would not operate as long as legislation was so framed that there might be a restriction in fact but not in legal form, and the restriction was made applicable to all sections of the community and not to a specific group. Besides, no compensation of any sort was paid to the Christian missions, and other religious organizations for the acquisition of land and buildings of the schools taken over by the state. There was no provision in the constitution for the expeditious payment of adequate compensation for property acquired by the state when ventures were nationalized whether they were business enterprises, or houses and buildings, or as on this occasion, schools with all the property attached to them. Thus, the government was under no legal compulsion to do so. Nevertheless, the proven ineffectiveness of section 29(2)(b) as a check on encroachments on the interests of the minorities did not make that clause any more palatable to Buddhist activists. They continued to view it as an ostentatious concession to minority influence, and persisted in an agitation for its elimination. Indeed, one of the reasons given, in 1972, for the adoption of an autochthonous constitution rather than a revision of the Soulbury constitution, the constitution under which Sri Lanka moved to independence, was the need to eliminate this clause.

In the course of Mrs Bandaranaike's first term of office (1960-4), the primacy of Buddhism and Buddhists in Sri Lanka's political system and public life had become a reality. Significantly, this achievement was won by the lay Buddhist leadership within the government and governing party, and outside it, and not by the *bhikkhus* whose contribution was by now very limited. This is not surprising considering that the *sangha* in general had suffered a substantial loss of prestige after the assassination of S.W.R.D. Bandaranaike and had not sufficiently recovered to return to its pre-1959 level of political activism and influence. The *bhikkhus* themselves were sharply divided, with some of the most prominent political *bhikkhus* of the mid-1950s switching their political loyalties to the UNP. Thus during the election campaign of 1965 many erstwhile supporters of the SLFP appeared on UNP platforms.

The issues in dispute in this realignment of political forces demonstrate the ambiguities inherent in the uneasy and shifting relationship between Buddhist activists and the new government. In the response to the recommendations of the Buddha Sasana Commission there were contradictory impulses between the lay and *bhikkhu* leadership of Buddhist revivalism. On the whole the lay leaders responded more positively to these proposals but, without a strong political leadership committed to their implementation, they lacked the nerve to campaign for them in the face of almost unanimous opposition from the *bhikkhus*.

As for government and political leaders within the government and the major national parties alike, the interaction with Buddhist activists, both lay and *bhikkhu*, called for great delicacy, in practice, because all parties were subject to conflicting pressures. Thus, the SLFP's coalition with the Trotskyist LSSP negotiated in 1964 provoked determined opposition from many of the 'political' *bhikkhus*. Some of the latter were quite prepared to tolerate the association as long as the gains of the immediate past were not threatened, and the new Marxist allies of the SLFP abandoned their advocacy of a secular state. However, not all their critics were won over or even mollified by these seemingly accommodative attitudes of the Marxists. The coalition government's attempts to bring the national press under state control led to renewal of fears that Marxist influence within the government was inherently erosive of Buddhist values. The SLFP sought to demolish the overwhelming dominance enjoyed by the Associated Newspapers of Ceylon—Lake House as it was called—in the island's newspaper industry. Lake House was politically associated with the UNP and was regarded as a bastion of capitalist enterprise and political conservatism. Buddhist activists including some leading figures in the orthodox establishment found common cause with the SLFP because they regarded Lake House as a stronghold of Christian influence on public life. The Marxist parties loathed the Lake House press because it symbolized political reaction as they saw it, economic privilege and the pinnacle of capitalist influence in the country, and so they enthusiastically joined forces in a bid to bring it under state control. The opposition to this assault on the freedom of the press was led, needless to say, by the UNP. Their campaign attracted wide support from Buddhist activists including a very vocal section of political *bhikkhus* increasingly disillusioned with the SLFP for its drift to the left and its association with the Marxists.

The ambiguities in the relationship between Buddhist activism and the government were revealed afresh with the return of the UNP to power in 1965 at the head of a coalition. In opposition the UNP had campaigned and voted against the educational reforms of 1960; in office there was no relaxation of the restrictive measures against which they had voted nor did they make any concessions to the Roman Catholics in regard to a right to levy fees from students in the schools that opted to remain outside the state educational system, despite a pledge given to them in 1967 to that effect. In a bid to prove its *bona fides* on Buddhism the government introduced the *poya* holiday scheme under which the weekly holiday was based on the phases of the moon while the traditional sabbath holiday was abandoned, with total disregard of the impact this variable weekend scheme would have on Sri Lanka's trade links with the rest of the world. Despite the acquiescence of the church hierarchy, the *poya* holiday also caused some discontent among the Roman Catholics—without any compensating support from the Buddhists for the UNP.

Bhikkhus in politics and political agitation was a constant factor during this period. A young *bhikkhu* was killed when the police opened fire on a mob demonstrating against the UNP-led coalition government's decision to introduce regulations, in January 1966, to give effect to the Tamil Language (Special Provisions) Act originally piloted through Parliament by Bandaranaike in 1958 and which the SLFP under his wife's leadership now opposed. *Bhikkhu* and Buddhist activists were divided politically on this. A large section of them was opposed to this piece of legislation and demonstrated against it in their customary role of articulators of Sinhalese-Buddhist political aspirations. But even if this particular form of involvement in politics received approbation from a large section of the Buddhist public, other instances of political *bhikkhus*' patent disregard of the tolerable limits of partisanship served to revive public memories of the excesses committed by the political *bhikkhus* during S.W.R.D. Bandaranaike's government. In April 1966 a leading political *bhikkhu* linked with the SLFP, *bhikkhu* Henpitagedera Gnanasiha, was arrested for complicity in an attempted *coup d'etat.* He was indeed one of the prime suspects, and was kept in remand for three years until, after a lengthy trial, he was found not guilty of the charges laid against him by the state prosecution.[23]

For our purposes here the most significant development was the government's attempt to construct a new policy for interacting with the Buddhists. Its central feature was an attempt to emphasize the role of what may be termed the 'establishment' in the *sangha* in the persons of the two *Mahanayakes* (chief *bhikkhus*) of the Malvatta and Asgiriya chapters of the prestigious Siyam *nikaya* who were generally acknowledged as the principal articulators of Buddhist opinion and as the most authentic representatives of Buddhist interests.[24] In doing so the UNP government took a calculated risk, but there was the undoubted advantage that the Buddhist public generally accepted these *bhikkhus* in this role. This acceptability rose in inverse proportion to the perceptible decline in the standing of the politically active *bhikkhus*. Their leadership also had a formal and institutional aspect to which the political *bhikkhus* could never aspire. The two *Mahanayakes* were traditionally the highest dignitaries of the *sangha*, and the government's new policy sought to buttress their status with some tangible, and some intangible, forms of official recognition. The tangible forms included two official residences for them in Colombo. The intangible but very conspicuous form included the practice for all appointees to important official positions in government and public life to make ceremonial courtesy calls on the two *Mahanayakes* in Kandy, a practice which now extends to visiting dignitaries and the diplomatic community.[25]

The official recognition and buttressing of the orthodox *bhikkhus* did not inhibit their interventions on political issues whenever an occasion demanded it. Throughout the last two decades *bhikkhus*, including the two *Mahanayakes* of Malvatta and Asgiriya, have generally taken a strong stand on issues involving relations between the Sinhalese majority and Tamil minority, a stand which reflects an instinctive ethnic nationalism. There was general opposition to the concessions on language made to the Tamils in January 1966, but on this occasion the *bhikkhus* played a subsidiary role in a campaign led by the politicians and laymen. The opposition was stronger among the political *bhikkhus* of old than among the more orthodox *bhikkhus*. The latter's opposition to the government proposals in 1967-8 for devolution of power to districts, through a system of District Councils—a theme discussed in later chapters of this book—was more vocal, because it coincided with concessions made at about the same time to the Indian residents in Sri Lanka about their citizenship rights.[26]

One of the remarkable new developments of the early 1970s was the improvement in relations between the Roman

Catholics and Mrs Bandaranaike's SLFP dominated regime. On the part of the Roman Catholics there was evidence of a greater readiness towards acceptance of religious pluralism after the Vatican Council of 1962-3. While the government made no attempt to change the education policy which had been the point of divergence between the SLFP and the Roman Catholics since the early 1960s, it nevertheless became much more conciliatory towards them. When Mrs Bandaranaike, as Prime Minister, greeted Pope Paul VI, during the latter's brief visit to Sri Lanka, in January 1970, it signified and symbolized an official recognition of the new changed relationship. The Pope's visit on that occasion was limited to the national airport, conveniently located near a concentration of Roman Catholic towns and villages. He stayed for a few hours. The ceremonial platform for the Pope was designed by a *bhikkhu*—Mapalagama Vipulasara—who was to perform the same function in 1995 for the visit of Pope John Paul II to Sri Lanka.

The Roman Catholics responded by seeking a constructive accommodation with nationalism and accepting the new balance of forces in the country, the key feature of which was the dominance of the Sinhalese-Buddhists in Sri Lanka as a political reality. This the Protestants had done a generation earlier, with some reluctance at first but with greater conviction in the years before the transfer of power and thereafter.

RELIGION AND THE STATE, 1972 TO 1997

The defeat of the UNP in 1970 and the return to power of Mrs Bandaranaike at the head of the centre-left United Front coalition saw the final phase of the process of redressing Buddhist grievances and establishing Buddhist ascendancy in the Sri Lanka polity. This phase was all the more significant because the support given by the principal Marxist parties of the country to this process in virtual repudiation of their general commitment to the concept of a secular state. Chapter II of the new Republican

Constitution of 1972 read as follows:

> The Republic of Sri Lanka shall give to Buddhism the
> foremost place and accordingly it shall be the duty of
> the state to protect and foster Buddhism while assuring
> to all religions the rights guaranteed by section 18(1)(d).

When this proposal was originally made in the
Constituent Assembly, its supporters included the UNP
whose spokesmen argued in favour of the inclusion of the
fifth clause of the Kandyan Convention of 1815, referred
to earlier in this chapter, in the new constitution. It was
rejected by the new government only because of its political
implications in regard to the protection of property rights
of the temples over the large extents of land some of them
controlled. This time there was no opposition from the
Christians in general or the Roman Catholics in particular.
The innovation introduced in 1972 came at a time when
the Roman Catholics had themselves embarked on a
reappraisal of their role in Sri Lanka and reconciled
themselves to an acquiescence in the dominant position of
Buddhism in the Sri Lanka polity. More significantly,
when the constitution of 1972 was replaced in 1978 by the
constitution of the second republic the status accorded to
Buddhism in the previous constitution—the 'foremost
place'—remained unchanged. Nor was there any recourse
to the fifth clause of the Kandyan convention as the
distilled essence of a desirable relationship between the
state and Buddhism.

In both instances the governments concerned were
operating, strangely enough, within the limits of the
'formula' adopted in the late 19th century by the British
Governors Gregory and Gordon. Indeed that 'formula'
proved to be elastic enough to cope with the pressures of
Buddhist activists for a special status for Buddhism within·
the Sri Lankan polity, without making it the state religion.
In 1978 the All Ceylon Buddhist Congress had urged that
Buddhism be declared 'the State Religion'. Other less
prestigious, if not less vocal, Buddhist organizations
proposed that the constitution should require that the

President, the Executive Head of State, be a Buddhist. Nonetheless, the UNP government remained content with sustaining the primacy of Buddhism in the Sri Lankan polity at the level established in 1972, a primacy which fell distinctly short of declaring Buddhism to be the state religion.

Even so the special status accorded to Buddhism in the new constitution attracted criticism. This no longer came from the Roman Catholics on religious grounds but from spokesmen from the Tamil minority, Hindu and Christian, on political grounds and through the principal Tamil political parties. Their complaint that the constitution 'does not prohibit the state from providing munificent financial assistance to Buddhism or from placing restrictions on the efforts of other religious organizations to propagate their faith' contained a mixture of half-truths and exaggerations.[27]

By the late 1970s Buddhist activism was but a shadow of the vibrant force it had been in the previous seventy years. Partly this was because many of the .issues which Buddhist activists had agitated about had been settled very much in their favour.

While most of the gains of the mid-1950s and early 1960s were securely established, others were lost. The most conspicuous example of the latter was the abandonment of the *poya* holiday scheme in July 1971. Almost all political parties supported this move, including the UNP itself which had originally introduced it. Significantly, the SLFP-led coalition took the initiative in a matter in which a section of the *sangha* and some lay Buddhist activists adamantly opposed the abandonment of a change for which they had long agitated.

With time, too, came wider government financial assistance to schools run by religious minorities, largely Christian, but also Hindu and Islamic, all of which lay outside the national schools structure. This bold initiative taken by the UNP government in 1979 aroused surprisingly little opposition from Buddhist activists. The apparent equanimity with which Buddhist activists accepted this decision is evidence of changed priorities in their demands and their perception of the potential harm to the interests of Buddhists and Sinhalese. The Roman Catholics, it would appear, had ceased to be regarded as a threat to Buddhist interests—perhaps because the former had accepted the political reality of Buddhist dominance in Sri Lanka.

Marxist and radical critics of Buddhist activism often question the *sangha*'s lack of interest in social issues, in particular with the condition of the urban poor. Buddhist activism is charged with the lack of a social conscience. There is some justice in this criticism, but again this lack of interest in social issues is more apparent than real. Buddhist pressure groups working through successive governments have been among the most powerful influences in the establishment and consolidation of a welfare state in Sri Lanka. A pragmatic improvization of a Buddhist state ethos preserved in the Buddhist historical tradition and in Buddhist folklore with its compassionate concern for the poor has accomplished this task even though the linkage between Buddhist activist thought and socialist doctrine in all its forms was never as strong in Sri Lanka as it was in Burma.

Radicalized 'political' *bhikkhus*, for all their occasional outbursts of militancy, are no longer the revitalizing force they were in the 1930s and 1940s. Every passing decade brought a few into prominence but they have tended to be individuals working in isolation rather than members of a cohesive group. The lay leaders of the Buddhist movement demonstrate this same loss of vitality. There were a number of overlapping reasons for this. The most significant of these is the success they, and their predecessors, achieved since the 1960s in securing the adoption by successive governments of the causes they have espoused. The institutional framework built over the last century has survived but it, too, seems bereft of much sense of purpose and idealism. The only purpose it now serves is to defend Sinhalese-Buddhist interests against the threat posed—as they see it—by Tamil forces within and outside the country.

The relationship between state and religion, surveyed in some detail in earlier sections of this chapter, becomes somewhat murky during the prolonged ethnic conflict of the mid and late 1980s and the political turmoil of the late 1980s. So much has happened and with such rapidity that it is still too early to judge whether their impact will radically transform the relationship between the state and religion that we have sketched or whether it is strong enough—or flexible enough—to withstand the pressures it has been subjected to and retain its essence without substantial change.

In the aftermath of the anti-Tamil riots of July 1983, as the processes of negotiating a settlement matured, an All Party Conference (APC) was convened in 1984 by the then President, J.R. Jayewardene. What is important for the issues being considered here is the list of invitees to the APC. It included representatives of the *bhikkhu* establishment. The invitation was extended to them, no doubt, in recognition of their general hardline views on issues vital to a possible agenda of management of the ethnic conflict, and in the hope that such views would become more moderate once they heard the wide range of opinion expressed there and once they had to set out their own views with greater precision than they were hitherto accustomed to do. Some, but not all, of these *bhikkhu* participants did become eloquent voices for moderation and pragmatism; even the more rigid upholders of Buddhist-Sinhalese primacy in the Sri Lanka polity did moderate their views.

The APC had another remarkable feature. Among the participants invited were delegates representing all the important religious minorities in the country—Hindus, Muslims and, above all, the Christians. All of them were invited to send delegates, and did so. The fact that there were no protests from Buddhist activists, lay or *bhikkhu*, was indicative of a striking change in attitudes since the religious controversies of the recent past: the Buddhists seemed secure enough in their position of primacy in the Sri Lankan polity to accept Roman Catholic and Protestant

Christian representatives engaging officially in an essentially political process of developing a national consensus on the current ethnic crisis.

This innovation of representatives of religious groups lay and 'clerical'—participating in negotiations on issues relating to the management of ethnic conflict was not pursued for very long. Representatives of religious groups were not invited to participate in the second of the major national conferences on Sri Lanka's ethnic conflicts. Held in Colombo in 1986 it was deliberately restricted to political parties and was called the Political Parties Conference (PPC). The absence of *bhikkhu* representatives at this conference, and of any vocal protests at this omission of a group who had participated in the previous conference, provided a telling demonstration of one of the vitally important strands in the state and religion relationship, namely, that the country's political leadership often disregarded the wishes and opinions of the *bhikkhus* when the national interest, as that leadership perceived it, or political expediency, demanded.

This could well have been because of evidence of a renewal of *bhikkhu* militancy and radicalism. Indeed, these emerged as a major factor in national politics a year later in the prelude to the signing of the Indo-Lanka Accord of July 1987—discussed in chapter six— and in the widespread riots that broke out in opposition to it. Radicalized younger *bhikkhus* pushed their seniors into violent opposition to the government on this. *Bhikkhu* extremism reached the cover pages of international newsmagazines in August 1987, and figured prominently in leading articles in them. One cover picture was specially significant; a Colombo lawyer, a leading figure in the articulation of Buddhist-Sinhalese views, was seen trying desperately to calm an agitated young *bhikkhu* intent on a violent expression of opposition to the Indo-Sri Lanka accord. Nevertheless, unlike in 1958 when the Prime Minister and the government capitulated in the face of a far milder demonstration of *bhikkhu* opposition, President Jayewardene proceeded with the signing of the accord. This *bhikkhu* agitation continued when the 13th amendment to the Constitution, incorporating a package of reforms involving combustible issues such as language rights and devolution of power through the establishment of provincial councils was debated in the national legislature and adopted in November 1987.[28] Once again the government stood firm, and proceeded with the implementation of a policy of reforms despite the vocal opposition of *bhikkhu* opinion, 'establishment', moderate and radical. If the last phase of President Jayewardene's government saw a continuation of these strains in the relationship between the state and large sections of the *sangha* in general, much of it could be explained by the unusually turbulent events[29] associated with the JVP insurrection of that period.

There were other factors as well, one of which was his commitment to maintaining a distance between state and religion, and to protecting what was left of the secularism which UNP leaders, and in particular, D.S. Senanayake had treated as an essential feature of public life. Ministries of Hindu and Muslim Religious Affairs had been established during his (J.R. Jayewardene's) administration. The impulse behind the decision was a desire to demonstrate a continued commitment to the principle of religious tolerance and to religious and ethnic pluralism, despite the special status accorded to Buddhism since 1972. The Jayewardene government refused to accede to the somewhat tentative requests that were made for the creation of a Ministry of Christian Affairs for that would have revived dying controversies over the issue of the privileged position of Christians in the past. More significantly, it refused to create a Ministry of Buddha Sasana which Buddhist activists urged should be done. But with his departure from office and the election of R. Premadasa as the country's second executive president the links between state and Buddhism were dramatically strengthened.

On 2 January 1989, President Premadasa took the oath of office from the Chief Justice in the octagon of the Temple of the Tooth in Kandy, in a conspicuous manifestation of a strengthening of the linkage between ruler and religion, and in a deliberate deviation from the patterns of the past when heads of government took their oaths of office in a purely secular setting. His predecessor had taken his oath of office in 1983, on his election to a second term as president, on Galle Face green, in Colombo, as open a secular setting as one could possibly get. Marking a departure from this practice, one of the first acts of President Premadasa's government in 1989 was the creation of a Ministry of Buddha Sasana, with the President himself as Minister-in-charge. Again, an advisory committee to the Ministry, bringing together representatives of the *bhikkhu* establishment and prominent Buddhist laymen was established in 1990. While Premadasa continued, and went well beyond, his predecessor's policies of giving conspicuous positions on public occasions to religious dignitaries of other religions as well, this prominent affirmation of a commitment to religious tolerance was clearly overshadowed by an unmistakable precedence and visibility given to Buddhist practices on official occasions, including affairs of state. On a more political level, some of the leading *bhikkhu* agitators against the Indo-Sri Lanka accord of 1987 became the beneficiaries of official support in their religious and secular ventures.[30]

From the beginning of 1989, an increasing amount of television time has been given to Buddhist religious events many of them with some political connotation. The most significant development was a daily television programme of 15 minutes of family worship for Buddhists. Besides, the Premadasa government deliberately distanced itself from practices deemed to be un-Buddhistic—one such example being the decision taken to discontinue state involvement and support of inland fisheries, a decision taken in response to a demand from an official Buddhist delegation led by the two *Mahanayakes*, to the President at his office.

Once the government began to extend the scope of its patronage for Buddhism and to deliberately evoke aspects of traditional practice governing the relations between the head of state and Buddhism, it was all too easy for *bhikkhus* to use pressure to have the scope of the patronage extended to more sensitive areas. In 1990, a major controversy among the Buddhists could have occurred when a prominent *bhikkhu* who had become or claimed to have become a Mahayanist *bhikkhu*, attempted to establish a Mahayanist centre in the island. Large sections of the Buddhist establishment, *bhikkhu* and lay brought such pressure against him that he gave up the venture. Of significance was the *bhikkhus'* attempts to draw the head of state and the government itself into the dispute on the grounds that it was their duty, following upon traditional lines of action, to protect the *sasana* from schism and schismatics. The head of state and the government did not have to take a stand because the controversy did not evolve into a major crisis.[31] But, while it lasted it did demonstrate the perils involved in too close an association between state and religion.

Under R. Premadasa, *bhikkhus*, both within the establishment and outside it, enjoyed greater influence with the government, in their role of articulators of Sinhalese Buddhist opinion, than at any time since mid-1950s and the days of S.W.R.D. Bandaranaike's government. The form and substance of the relationship between the state and Buddhism is not likely to change very greatly from what it was under President Premadasa partly because the institutional framework he established is still in place, especially the Ministry of Buddha Sasana. Nevertheless, his successor D.B. Wijetunga did not share his penchant for public demonstrations of religious commitment and the use of state television for this purpose. With the change of government in the latter part of 1994, the new head of government and head of state Chandrika Kumaratunga has adopted much the same line of action in regard to this sensitive issue as Wijetunga. Thus, the interplay between the individual views and inclinations of the head of state and those of the Buddhist establishment will continue to influence the relationship between state and Buddhism. In the present circumstances it would take a very courageous politician to emulate J.R. Jayewardene in his defiance of activist *bhikkhus*; it will take a very foolhardy one to make any attempt to go beyond the limits of a secular state as defined by D.S. Senanayake's advisors at the transfer of power in the mid-forties.

THE CHRISTIAN MINORITY—THE CONTEMPORARY SITUATION

In the first decade of independence there was every prospect that Sri Lanka would have and could have developed a homogenous political culture. The tensions caused by linguistic nationalism put paid to that. Nevertheless, despite the current sharp contemporary ethnic divide and the violence of ethnic conflict, the island's political culture has not been fragmented to the point of rendering her democratic structure totally unstable. Divisions in Sri Lankan society are not mutually reinforcing points of divergence: thus while language remains the essence of ethnic identity, religious contentions are featured among the Sinhalese themselves—between the Buddhist majority and the Roman Catholic minority— and not between them and the Tamils. The conflict between Sinhalese and Tamils is not a clash of religions so much as one between two versions of linguistic nationalism, even though the proportion of Christians to Hindus among the Tamils is much larger than the proportion of Christians to Buddhists among the Sinhalese. Christians have a more prominent leadership role among the Tamils than their counterparts have secured among the Sinhalese since the 1920s. S.J.V. Chelvanayakam, the leader of the Federal Party, and later of the Tamil United Liberation Front (TULF) was a Protestant Christian.

The following tables derived from the last census held in the island, the census of 1981, provide us with some striking features of the demographic composition of the Christian minority. Firstly, only 6.5 per cent of the Sinhalese are Christians, while the proportion among the Tamils is as much as 16.7 per cent for the Sri Lanka Tamils, and 7.6 per cent for the Indian Tamils. Secondly, the Sinhalese are a fraction short of two-thirds of the Roman Catholics, while the Tamils are 25.1 per cent or 29.8 per cent if one

includes the Indian Tamils. The ethnic profile of the
Protestant population is even more remarkable. The
Protestants are only 10 per cent of the Christian population
who are only 7.6 per cent of the total population. Among
the Protestants the Sinhalese are a distinct minority (43.4
per cent), while 37.1 per cent of the Sri Lankan Tamils
and 9.4 per cent of the Indian Tamils are Protestants.
Thus, Protestant Christianity is a minority religion in every
sense of the word. The Protestants are a small minority in
the country (0.76 per cent), just as they are a small
minority among the Christians, and the Tamil minority is
a, if not the, dominant influence in the Protestant churches.

Figure I

ETHNIC COMPOSITION OF RELIGIOUS GROUPS, 1981

Ethnic Group	Percentage distribution in each religious group					
	Budd-hist	Hindu	Muslim	Roman-Catholic	Other Christian	Other
Sinhalese	99.5	0.5	0.6	66.0	43.4	18.8
Sri Lanka-Tamil	0.3	64.5	1.1	25.1	37.1	23.5
Indian-Tamil	0.1	31.5	0.4	4.7	9.4	9.3
Sri Lanka-Moor	0.0	3.3	92.8	0.4	0.7	5.7
Burgher	0.0	0.0	0.1	3.3	5.7	3.3
Malay	0.0	0.0	3.6	0.1	0.6	15.9
Other	0.0	0.2	1.4	0.4	3.4	23.5
Total	100.0	100.0	100.0	100.0	100.0	100.0

(Source: *Census of Population and Housing, 1981*, General Report, Vol. III.
Department of Census and Statistics, Colombo)

Figure II

RELIGIOUS COMPOSITION OF ETHNIC GROUPS, 1981

Religion	Percentage distribution in each ethnic group						
	Sinhalese	Sri-Lanka-Tamil	Indian Tamil	Sri Lanka-Moor	Burgher	Malay	Other
Buddhist	93.3	1.8	1.8	0.2	2.9	2.1	7.5
Hindu	0.1	80.7	90.0	6.7	0.4	3.4	15.3
Muslim	0.1	0.7	0.5	92.6	1.6	89.2	48.7
Roman-Catholic	6.1	14.3	6.2	0.4	79.3	2.2	11.6
Christian	0.4	2.4	1.4	0.1	15.3	0.6	12.1
Other	0.1	0.1	0.1	0.1	0.5	2.5	4.8
Total	100.0	100.0	100.0	100.0	100.0	100.0	100.0

(Source: *Census of Population and Housing, 1981*, General Report Vol. III, Department of Census and Statistics, Colombo)

Thirdly, there has been a steady decline in the percentage of Christians in the Sri Lankan population, down from 9.1 per cent of the census of 1946 to 7.6 per cent at the last census, i.e. in 1981.

Figure III

CHRISTIAN RATIO IN THE TOTAL POPULATION

1946	9.1%	1963	8.3%
1953	9.0%	1971	7.8% (Roman Catholics 6.9%, Protestant, 0.8%)
1981	7.6% (Roman Catholics, 6.8%, Protestants, 0.76%)		

Some part of the decline may be attributed to the emigration of the Burghers who were a Christian community, but the Burghers were always a minuscule element of the population, and a drop of 1.5 percentage points needs to be explained on a more realistic basis.

Available evidence does suggest that many Christians are abandoning their religion, some of them moving to Buddhism and Hinduism. It would also appear that most of the lapsed Christians are Protestants. The Roman Catholics are not unaffected by these trends, but they are making converts among the Indian plantation workers. At the census of 1981 it was seen that 6.2 per cent of the Indian Tamils were Roman Catholics, and all the evidence seems to suggest that these numbers have gone up considerably since then.[32]

The Roman Catholic Church itself is less cohesive and monolithic than it was during much of the period of its rivalry and confrontation with the Buddhists.[33] Today ethnic identity divides the Roman Catholics into two groups, one Sinhalese and the other Tamil, each more than a little suspicious of the other. The divisions stem from divergent attitudes to the ethnic conflict, and which work themselves through the various levels of the hierarchy of a once self-confident and assertive priesthood.[34] The priesthood, in fact, displays at least some of the ideological divisions seen in other Roman Catholic societies: the popularity of liberation theology at all levels of the hierarchy is one factor in this, but there are others, including a vigorous debate on an appropriate response to the indigenous cultural environment.

The Roman Catholics and Protestants have both been trapped in an anguished conflict of interests and emotions in confronting the ethnic violence in Sri Lanka, especially after the escalation of the conflict after 1983. The Roman Catholic diocese of Jaffna, once a bastion of social and political conservatism, has been radicalized in response to the ferment in the politics of the peninsula, and as a reaction to what it regards as a repressive policy against the Tamils pursued by Sri Lankan governments. The church always had individual erudite priests with a strong commitment to Tamil studies, and indeed well-known for their celebration of Tamil culture and Dravidian civilization. But the commitment has grown stronger in recent decades and individual younger priests, in particular, have been associated with separatist agitation and support of the LTTE. The present Roman Catholic Bishop of Jaffna, the Revd Thomas Savundranayagam and the Revd S.J. Emmanuel, Vicar-General of the Diocese of Jaffna, have been eloquent spokesmen for the rights of the Tamils, and are seen among the Sinhalese, in general, as supporters of the LTTE, much to the embarrassment of the church hierarchy in Colombo. Indeed, the Vicar-General has been associated so often and so closely with propaganda activities of the LTTE, in Britain, and in Europe and in Australia that he is widely regarded as an apologist for the LTTE, if not a 'fellow traveller'.[35] The tensions caused within the church by the public pronouncements of the Bishop and Vicar-General of Jaffna have called for great tact and diplomacy on the part of the Archbishop of Colombo, to prevent open exchanges of conflicting views on Tamil separatist activism.

The hierarchy is fully aware of the potential dangers to the church of the residue of anti-Roman Catholic feeling among sections of the Buddhist population, and have endeavoured therefore to steer a careful course between expressions of concern for peace in the country, and anything that could be construed as sympathy for, much less support of, Tamil separatism and the violence associated with it.

The intricacies of the relationship between the Roman Catholics and the Buddhists were revealed when Pope John Paul II visited Sri Lanka in January 1995 as part of an Asian tour which took him also to the Philippines and Papua-New Guinea. This time it was no airport meeting, but an elaborate ceremony in Colombo which included a formal visit to the offices of the head of state, an evening mass at the principal Roman Catholic Church in Colombo, and an open-air mass on one of Colombo's most prominent sites, the Galle Face green. The expenses—and they were substantial—were borne by the state, and all the ceremonies, including the public mass, were relayed live by state television.

The visit was not without its embarrassing moments, to which we shall return later in this chapter. No papal visit could be entirely without reference to memories of the past: the Pope was participating in ceremonies that had to do with the beatification of Fr Joseph Vaz, a Konkani brahmin, who had ministered to the harried Roman Catholics of the littoral during Dutch times, making use of the hospitality shown to him by the Kandyan kings of the 18th century. Fr Vaz was a beneficiary of the traditional Buddhist tolerance. This event brought both sections of the Roman Catholic church together and, as one more demonstration of its external links, a Roman Catholic bishop from South India, the region from which Fr Vaz had hailed, joined in the celebrations.

The Pope's visit led to some strong criticisms from sections of the *sangha*, not indeed to the visit *per se*, but to some of his comments on Buddhism in a book he had recently published on the role of the church in the world. As a result of this the principal *bhikkhus* of the Buddhist sects refused to meet the pontiff. The weight of historical memories was too much to bear yet another seemingly critical comment from the principal spokesman of the Roman Catholic church, a comment which was seen to be offensive to the Buddhist religion.

The position of the Protestant churches in Sri Lanka is more invidious than that of their Roman Catholic counterparts as regards Sri Lanka's ethnic conflict because the Sinhalese are a minority in many of the Protestant churches unlike among the Roman Catholics. Two Anglican Archbishops of Colombo, the Late Revd Lakshman Wickremasinghe, and the current holder of that position, the Revd Kenneth Fernando, have sought to play a mediatory role; they have had their critics not only among the Buddhists but also within their own flock, critics who believe that the principal representative of the Anglican church should also be more critical of the violence of Tamil separatists. The comments on Sri Lankan affairs by the World Council of Churches, and of individuals like

Bishop Desmond Tutu, a prominent figure in International Alert, often seen to be one-sided if not misguided by Sinhalese and Buddhists, have also not helped the Protestant churches in their bid to steer clear of their external links and the latter's political attitudes.

The traditional Protestants face the challenge of the increasingly popular charismatic churches—the Seventh Day Adventists and others—now making heavy inroads among their adherents. It is believed that the charismatic churches are now actually numerically larger than these others. They are more dynamic and are better funded than the traditional Protestant groups because of their links with their parent churches in the Bible belt of the United States. Indeed, the charismatic churches are beginning to pose a challenge to the Roman Catholic dominance of the Christian community here in Sri Lanka as they do in parts of Latin America.

There is one significant difference between the charismatic churches and all the other Christian groups in Sri Lanka. All the others have accepted the necessity of a more limited role for the Christian community than in pre-independence times and have long since given up proselytization. The charismatic churches refuse to do this. In engaging in subtle and sometimes quite aggressive proselytization, they come up against protests of the vocal spokesmen for the Buddhists who in turn demand action from the state—in the form of legislation—against it. The Roman Catholic hierarchy, and the leadership of the Anglicans have responded to these increasingly vocal protests by asserting that they had long since given up proselytization. They lay the blame for this current revival of Buddhist fears on the charismatic churches.

At the tail-end of the fourth decade after independence the Christians in Sri Lanka have seen a reduction in status from an elite if not privileged minority to a beleaguered group struggling to keep intact its identity and to protect its flock from serious attrition. As they look to the future and reflect on the challenges that confront them, there is naught for their comfort. Given their historically proven resilience in the face of adversity, one can assume that the Roman Catholics would survive as a numerically smaller group than in the past but it is likely that the ethnic divide among them will harden and the Roman Catholic church in Sri Lanka will have to reconcile itself to its being virtually two independent units.

The Protestant groups face a harsher future. The Anglican church is likely to go the way of the Dutch Reformed Church, after the expulsion of the Dutch in the early years of the 18th century and, generally become a forgotten irrelevance in Sri Lanka's religious history. The other traditional Protestant churches face the challenge of the charismatic churches who are more self-confident, wealthier, and less conscious of the self-restraint as regards proselytization that the former observed since the 1930s. For the charismatic churches the path ahead is a stormy one if they ignore that policy of self-restraint, since it will bring them into confrontation with Buddhist activists.[36] But they will, in all probability, absorb the traditional Protestant groups, and also win 'converts' from among the Roman Catholics. Even so, it is unlikely that one could envisage any substantial increase in the number of Christians in Sri Lanka, Protestant or Roman Catholic.

CHAPTER 4

Ethnic Politics, Political Violence and Tamil Separatism, 1951-1977

The two previous chapters have shown how the mid-1950s are a watershed in Sri Lanka's post-independence political evolution, marking as they did the first phase in the eruption of ethnic conflicts that have been such a prominent feature in the island's recent history. When the language legislation of 1956 was introduced in the House of Representatives, the debate on it took place against the background of the first post-independence outburst of ethnic strife. Sinhalese-Buddhist activists who had campaigned so enthusiastically on behalf of the new governing party in 1956, were now intent on getting the government to honour its pledges on language policy change which it had made to the electorate. Tamil politicians led by the Federal Party directed an equally fervent agitation against the new legislation. Thus the riots of June 1956 provide a classic example of the disturbing effects of conflicting linguistic nationalisms on a multi-ethnic society.

In South Asia the earliest signs of political tensions inherent in introducing language change had come in the 1930s and 1940s, in the then Madras Presidency where there was an anti-Hindi movement.[1] Then the earliest phase of Pakistan's post-colonial history was marked by opposition to the imposition of Urdu as the national language in East Pakistan. This emerged as early as 1948 and continued through the early 1950s. Eventually, the opposition to Urdu was one of the principal factors in the rout of the Muslim League government of East Pakistan at the general election held in 1955. The Chief Minister and his Cabinet colleagues were overwhelmed by a wave of popular opposition directed against the official language policy adumbrated by the West Pakistan leadership.[2]

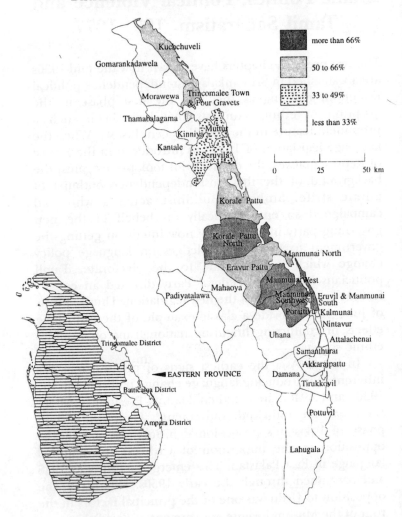

Distribution of Tamils in the Eastern Province

- more than 66%
- 50 to 66%
- 33 to 49%
- less than 33%

Kuchchuveli
Gomarankadawela
Morawewa
Trincomalee Town & Four Gravets
Thamahalagama
Kinniya
Muttur
Kantale
Seruvila
Korale Pattu
Korale Pattu North
Manmunai North
Eravur Pattu
Mahaoya
Manmunai West
Padiyatalawa
Manmunai Southwest
Manmunai South
Eruvil & Manmunai
Poraitivu
Kalmunai
Nintavur
Uhana
Attalachenai
Samanthurai
Akkaraipattu
Damana
Tirukkovil
Pottuvil
Lahugala

0   25   50 km

Trincomalee District
Batticaloa District
Ampara District
EASTERN PROVINCE

Tamil population as a proportion of the total population of the administrative divisions

Map III

There is no evidence to suggest that the East Pakistan general election, its issues and results, had any part to play in the thinking of the Sri Lankan politicians as they prepared for the election campaign of 1956. Even if this had been considered, many of the Sinhalese politicians who campaigned for the elevation of Sinhala to the status of the national language would have argued that there was a world of difference between the position of Urdu in Pakistan and Sinhala in Sri Lanka. The former was a minority language spoken by around 7 per cent of the population, while the Sinhala-speaking majority of Sri Lanka numbered nearly 70 per cent of the population. Nevertheless, just as the Bengali-speaking population of East Pakistan—an overwhelming majority of the population—resisted the imposition of Urdu on them, so the Tamil minority of Sri Lanka opposed the unilateral abrogation of the language policy agreed upon in 1943-4, and the imposition of Sinhala on them as the sole official language. Thus, while the losers in Sri Lanka's general election of 1956—the UNP—were disoriented by the electorate's rejection of their credentials as authentic adherents of 'Sinhala Only', the winners were taken aback by the tensions provoked by their efforts to implement the language legislation of 1956. While the debate on that legislation commenced against the background of protests by Tamil groups led by the Federal and the Tamil Congress acting as co-belligerents rather than as allies, the government, was being held to ransom by language loyalists within its own ranks, working in association with *bhikkhus* and prominent public figures insisting on a purist version of a language bill that would make no concession to the use of the Tamil language in the administration of the country.[3]

By comparison with the riots that broke out in Sri Lanka in the late 1970s and 1980s, those of June 1956 were a minor affair. The death toll on this occasion was around 150,[4] small by South Asian standards in the number of casualties in the course of violent ethnic and religious conflict but the shock felt by the Sri Lankan polity was very great. Over four decades of orderly, if unexciting, political evolution after the Sinhalese-Muslim riots of 1915 came to an end.[5] There was also a recognition that this violent encounter between the Sinhalese and Tamils, the first in Sri Lanka's modern history, was an avoidable, self-inflicted wound.

A group of around 200 Tamils led by Tamil parliamentarians gathered at the Galle Face green just opposite Parliament for a silent, symbolic protest against the legislation on language policy introduced for debate in Parliament by the government. Surprisingly, the police had been instructed not to provide any security to those engaged in this protest. A mob which had gathered at Galle Face attracted by this protest, was naturally encouraged to resort to physical violence to break up the gathering since the police were not around to check them. This deliberate and successful attempt at disturbing the peace emboldened mobs in and around Colombo to engage in violence against Tamils. Violence soon spread to other parts of the country. With the prospect of the violence getting out of control, the police were at last called in and their intervention, supported by the armed services, brought the situation under control within a few days. The riots of 1956 damaged the reputation Sri Lanka had earned for its success in handling a double transfer of power so peacefully, the first from British to Sri Lankan rule in 1947-8, and the second in 1956, the transfer of power from one political party to another, in short the fall from grace of the 'model colony'.

It did not take long for the second episode of violent ethnic conflict to erupt. This was in April 1958, less than two years after the first.[6] These riots were associated with attempts to modify the language policy adopted in 1956. This time there was a substantially higher death toll— between 500 and 600. The violence followed yet another intervention in national politics at the highest level by a small group of *bhikkhus* associated with the government.

The campaign was led by *bhikkhu* Baddegama Wimalawamsa. They organized a sit-in on the lawn of the Prime Minister's private residence in Colombo on 9 April 1958 and compelled Bandaranaike to tear up the agreement he had reached with S.J.V. Chelvanayakam, the Federal Party leader, on language policy, devolution of power to regional bodies, and settlement of Sinhalese peasants in parts of the Northern and Eastern Provinces. In doing so they demonstrated the weakness of the Prime Minister and his government and underlined their own position of a rigid adherence to the policies on which they had campaigned for him in 1956. Once more it required a combination of the police and the armed services to bring the situation under control.

Unfortunately, neither of these riots, those of 1956 nor those of 1958, became the subject of an official inquiry as they should have been. An official inquiry was planned in 1956 but was quickly abandoned on the grounds that it would only exacerbate an already tense situation. This gap in our knowledge of these events has been filled to some extent by two contemporary works: Howard Wriggins's pathbreaking study, *Ceylon: The Dilemmas of a New Nation* (1960) and Tarzie Vittachy's *Emergency '58: The Story of the Ceylon Race Riots* (1958). Wriggins, an American political scientist, spent three years researching the background to these events in Sri Lanka while Vittachy was a distinguished Sri Lankan journalist. His account gives much more detail on the actual riots themselves—the riots of 1958—than does Wriggins who concentrates instead on the complex issues that gave rise to these outbreaks of violence.[7]

After the riots of 1958, there was a decade or more of relative peace in so far as ethnic politics—Sinhalese versus Tamils—is concerned. This is not so say that there was no trouble at all. Trouble came in the form of two failed *coups d'état* which we shall review later in this chapter.[8] What is important is Wriggins's observation—in 1960—of the possibility of interventions in politics by leaders of the security forces:

The army has remained aloof from politics and has loyally served whatever governments the electorates have chosen. The army itself is small . . . [and] has no great tradition of combat . . . . This is not to say it is ineffective. When it was called out in the 1958 communal riots, it promptly mastered the disorders and re-established public peace. But no recollections of past grand missions tempt its leadership to dominate affairs. Moreover, while its officer corps no doubt has that firm disdain for the men of politics that is common to many professionals, they themselves have been men deeply imbued with British ideas of the limited place of the military man in public life . . .[9]

Wriggins warned presciently that:

. . . If public disorders became frequent and if the men of politics appear chronically incapable of effective government, some leaders in the army might become persuaded that they were indispensable in the domestic area. But matters would have to be dire indeed before this lurking temptation would become a political reality.[10]

As we shall see later in this chapter, 'this lurking temptation [had] become a political reality' by 1962.

Despite these botched attempts at military-police *coups*, the country enjoyed a decade or more of freedom from ethnic conflict or political violence. The situation changed in the early 1970s after Mrs Bandaranaike returned to power in May 1970 at the head of the United Front (UF) coalition between the SLFP, LSSP and the Communist Party (Moscow wing). Together they won 120 seats (out of 168) in Parliament, the first Sri Lankan government since independence to command a two-thirds majority in the national legislature without the need for support of the Tamil political parties. The election of 1970 was a setback for the FP, its worst performance since the debacle of 1952; its leader came through on a mere plurality of votes, and two of its leading members including A. Amirthalingam, who later became the leader of the Tamil United Liberation Front, lost their seats. But as in the mid-1950s the lost ground was recovered, on this occasion much earlier than on the previous one; in both cases the recovery came from leading the opposition to governmental policies perceived as being discriminatory to the Tamils.

Despite the enthusiasm with which the Marxist parties, the LSSP and CP, had succumbed to the attractions of ethnic or communal politics in opposition to the UNP-led coalition government in the period 1965-70, the sharp reversal of electoral fortunes which saw them now in an influential position within the new government, raised the hope that their presence would mark the beginning of a more constructive phase in devising policies and mechanisms for dealing with the problems of the minorities. This did not happen, and more to the point, there was very little evidence that the Marxist Left made a determined bid to guide the new government to take a less hostile attitude to the main Tamil parties than may have been expected from a SLFP government without Marxist coalition partners. Instead, the SLFP-dominated coalition applied old policies of the period 1956-64 with regard to the Tamil minority, both indigenous and immigrant Indian, and applied them with renewed fervor. If this was only an accurate reflection of the great strength of the SLFP in the government as the principal political force in the UF coalition of the years 1970-5, it also demonstrated the ineffectiveness of the Marxist cabinet ministers—there were four in all, 3 LSSP and 1 CP—as a brake on the communalism that was rampant within the SLFP and through it within the UF government.

Of the acts of commission of the new government two in particular, discussed below, were decisive in widening the breach between itself and the Sri Lanka Tamils: the new Republican constitution of 1972, of which Dr Colvin R. de Silva, a LSSP stalwart and Minister of Constitutional Affairs was the mastermind; and a change in the system of admission of students to the island's universities. Relations between the government and the leadership of the Ceylon

Workers' Congress (CWC), the principal trade union cum political organization of the immigrant Indians were as hostile as the government's attitude to the Federal Party. Indeed, the period of office of the UF government was singularly barren of any political initiatives directed at defusing the ethnic tensions of the 1970s. Decentralization of administration through District Councils which had figured so prominently in the post-1956 period in discussions on structural changes to reduce ethnic tensions and manage conflicts driven by ethnic politics lay forgotten throughout these years. It was revived only after the electoral rout suffered by the remnants of this once powerful coalition at the general election of 1977.

The new constitution was in many ways the consolidation of the linguistic nationalism that had dominated Sri Lankan politics since 1956.[11] This was how many of its advocates preferred to see it, and the form in which its strongest opponents—the Tamil political leadership—preferred to see it too. The latter argued that the new constitution gave validity and confirmation to the second-class status of their citizenship by consolidating the position of Sinhala as the official language while Tamil was granted a distinctly inferior and hazy position, as well as by elevating Buddhism to 'the foremost place' among religions.

In retrospect, the adoption of the first Republican constitution on 22 May 1972 was clearly the critical starting point of a new phase in ethnic conflict in Sri Lanka, in which the triumph of the linguistic nationalism of the Sinhalese, consolidated through a new political and constitutional framework, soon confronted a Tamil version of it which was taken to its logical conclusion in the form of a separatist movement. Between May 1972 and end of 1976 we see a momentous shift in the political aspirations of the Sri Lanka Tamils, from demands for structural changes and constitutional reform, to an assertion of the right to self-determination on the basis of a Tamil state in Sri Lanka. As we shall see this latter change marked the culmination of a process of political thinking which began with the foundation of the Federal Party in 1949. The FP's political campaign attracted a wider range of political support than usual, extending to groups not identified with, or hostile, to it—the Tamil Congress, the FP's traditional rival, mainly, but also for a brief period the Ceylon Workers' Congress.[12]

Opposition to the new constitution brought the two main Tamil political parties—the Federal Party and the Tamil Congress—together for the first time since 1948. Along with the leadership of the Ceylon Workers' Congress (CWC) and other Tamil politicians they established the Tamil United Front (TUF). The CWC was the weakest link in this chain; its ties to the TUF were intrinsically fragile and the association between it and the two other parties was seldom as cordial as the founders of the TUF claimed it was. Nevertheless, all previous attempts to bring the leadership of the Indian plantation workers to the point of coordinating their political activities with those of the indigenous Tamils had failed, and so even a brief and fitful association, as this proved to be, was a considerable political achievement.

By the early 1960s some of the framers of the constitution of 1946-7 were expressing concern about its ineffectiveness in protecting the rights of minorities and they were now arguing that only a bill of rights could guarantee the minorities a measure of protection against the pervasive pressures of Sinhalese-Buddhist extremism. In a notable reversal of attitude Sir Ivor Jennings, 'candidly admitted that a comprehensive chapter of fundamental rights was very desirable in Ceylon's constitution particularly in the conditions [then] prevailing in Ceylon.' In 1963, Lord Soulbury himself expressed similar views in response to the comments of Sir Charles Jeffries, a senior official at Colonial Office, who in his book *Ceylon—The Path to Independence* had claimed that: 'the Soulbury Constitution . . . had entrenched in it all the protective provisions for minorities that the wit of man could devise.'[13] Soulbury

would not endorse this view; he argued, on the contrary
that

> . . . in the light of later happenings—I think it is a pity
> that the [Soulbury] Commission did not also recommend
> the entrenchment in the constitution of guarantees of
> fundamental rights, on the lines enacted in the
> constitutions of India, Pakistan, Malaya, Nigeria and
> elsewhere.[14]

In the early 1960s the SLFP was committed to the
amendment of the Soulbury constitution, not its
replacement by another, and its election manifesto of
1960 spelled out the desired changes: '. . . a reconsideration
of the position of the Senate, the definition of democratic
and economic rights, and the establishment of a democratic
republic . . .' Its manifesto of 1965—which had the
endorsement of the LSSP and CP (Moscow wing)—
reiterated the theme of republican status and the need to
revise the constitution 'to suit the needs of the country'.
There was, in fact, a substantial similarity in attitude on
this between itself and its principal rival, the UNP. That
party also advocated the revision of the Soulbury
constitution; in particular, that Sri Lanka should become
a republic within the Commonwealth. But when in power
(1965-70) it lacked the parliamentary majority (two-thirds
of all members of the Lower House) necessary to amend
the constitution.

During their years in opposition between 1965 and
1970 the constituent parties of the United Front coalition
government had made a far-reaching re-appraisal of their
stand on the question of constitutional reform: from a
mere revision of the existing constitution to a new policy
of establishing a Constituent Assembly deriving:

> authority from the people of Sri Lanka and not from the
> power and authority assumed and exercised by the
> British Crown and Parliament in establishing the present
> [Soulbury] constitution . . . nor from the constitution
> they gave us.'

This was no more—and no less—than the adoption by the then coalition government of the orthodox and doctrinaire LSSP and CP attitude on an autochthonous constitution for the island. From the mid-1940s these parties, and especially the LSSP of that time, had argued that the transfer of power should be preceded by or should be followed by the convening of a Constituent Assembly which would draft a constitution for the country. They had watched this happen in India. Now, over two decades later they were instrumental in getting a similar process initiated here.

How did the SLFP come to acquiesce in, and indeed enthusiastically endorse, this line of action? The answer one suspects lies in a notable *obiter dictum* of Lord Pearce in a case—the Bribery Commissioner versus Ranasinghe[15]—which came up in 1964 before the Judicial Committee of the Privy Council in London. This *obiter dictum* related to section 29(2)(b) of the Soulbury constitution and it made the point that it [i.e., section 29(2)(b)]:

> entrenched religious and racial matters which 'shall not be the subject of legislation [and] represent[ed] the solemn balance of rights between the citizens of Ceylon, the fundamental conditions on which *inter se* they accepted the constitution; and these are therefore unalterable under the constitution.

He added that

> the Court has a duty to see that the constitution is not infringed and to preserve it inviolate.

To the SLFP—the party most committed to the Sinhalese-Buddhist domination of the Sri Lanka polity—this would have been ample justification for the replacement and not merely a revision of the Soulbury constitution, and replacement by an autochthonous constitution drafted by a Constituent Assembly. The overwhelming electoral victory of May 1970 gave the coalition the opportunity it sought to put this new policy into effect.

The process of constitution-making proved to be controversial and not merely among the Tamils. The Federal Party moved out of the Constituent Assembly in June 1971 and did not participate in its proceedings thereafter. The UNP participated in the proceedings but eventually voted against the constitution because of the extension of the life of the Parliament elected in May 1970 by two years through this device of a Constituent Assembly.

If the UF government made no positive contribution to easing emerging ethnic tensions, it aggravated them through its policy changes in the matter of university admissions. While other issues—such as the new constitution—have contributed more substantially and dramatically to the sharp deterioration of ethnic relations in Sri Lanka in the last decade, none did more in radicalizing the politics of the Tamil areas in the north, and in particular the Jaffna peninsula, than this.

One aspect of this university admissions policy needs to be mentioned here. It was piloted through to implementation in the face of Tamil opposition by Badi-ud-din Mahmud during his second term of office as Minister of Education (1970-7). As a Muslim, he was always conscious of the special needs and interests of the Muslims in the vitally important area of education, and many policy decisions in his tenure of office as Minister of Education reflected his concern for these special needs and interests. In so doing he sharpened the competitive instincts of the Muslims in their traditional rivalry with the Tamils in education, and just as important contributed greatly to generating tensions between the Muslims and Sinhalese.

Significantly enough, the years 1970-6 were notable for sporadic clashes between Sinhalese groups and Muslims in several parts of the island. In fact, these clashes constitute the worst phase in Muslim-Sinhalese rivalries, tensions and resort to violence, since the 1915 riots. Fortunately, these clashes were not only sporadic, but also limited to a few localities. Causes of these clashes varied from locality to locality but the single common factor was the perception that too much concern was shown for Muslim interests in educational opportunities and employment as teachers in the government service.

The Tamils managed, up to 1970, to hold their own in some of the more prestigious professions, the medical, scientific, technical and engineering fields. This is largely a reflection of the superior facilities for science education in the Jaffna peninsula which enabled the Tamils to enter the medical, science and engineering faculties of universities in much larger numbers than their population ratio *vis-à-vis* the other ethnic groups in the island. In 1969-70 the Tamils, mainly from Jaffna and Colombo, constituted 35 per cent of the admissions to the science-oriented courses, and in the engineering and medical faculties the figure was as high as 45 per cent.

Entrance to the universities had been on the basis of academic achievement tested through rigorous competitive examinations. In the early 1970s B. Mahmud, as Minister of Education, succeeded in committing the UF government to a fundamental change in policy, to a system of standardization by language media at the University Entrance Examination.[16] The effect of this was to place the Tamil students at a great disadvantage in that they needed to obtain a higher aggregate of marks to enter the universities—in the medical, science and engineering sections—than the Sinhalese. Not only was the system maintained since 1970, but other schemes were introduced, all of them representing a departure from the practice of selecting students on the basis of actual marks obtained at an open competitive examination. Among these was the district quota system which seemingly involved a balance in favour of rural areas and backward communities. But there is no mistaking the fact that it gave a decided advantage of weightage to the Kandyan segment of the Sinhalese and the Muslims.[17]

No longer did academic ability *per se* suffice to ensure entry to the university, and those who suffered most from the change were undoubtedly the Tamils of the north (although the Sinhalese in the city of Colombo and the crowded Colombo district fared badly too). They regarded this change in university entrance policy as patently and deliberately discriminatory. The Tamils have been so dependent on state employment that even a quota system which gives them a slightly higher proportion of places than their numbers in relation to the ratio of Sri Lankan Tamils to the total population of the country, would in practice, be a hardship. The new university entrance policy of the 1970s made entry to the professions and to scientific and technical education much more difficult for the Tamils. Nothing has caused more frustration and bitterness among Tamil youth than this, for they regarded it as an iniquitous system deliberately devised to place obstacles before them.

This unilateral change in the policy on university admissions is thus a fundamentally important factor in the seventies' breakdown of ethnic relations in the island, and in radicalizing the politics of the Tamil areas of the north and east. Professor C.R. de Silva's outstanding scholarly work, sheds light on the complexities of the politics of university admissions of the 1970s. He delineated the nature of the issues at stake:

> Education, especially university education, is a key channel of social mobility in most developing countries and hence the distribution of opportunities for higher education is often regarded as the distribution of future wealth, status and power. In countries where university education is available only to a small minority, the competition therefore becomes very intense. Further problems arise, when in the context of a plural society each ethnic and religious group tends to evaluate the ratio of university admissions obtained by its members as an index of equality of opportunity or of discrimination. University admissions thus cease to be the exclusive preserve of academics and become the concern of politicians and leaders of various groups and interests.[18]

It was really in the 1960s, once Sinhala and Tamil replaced English as the medium of instruction in the higher classes of the secondary schools, that political and sectional pressures on university education began to build up.[19] The rapid growth of secondary education resulted in intensified competition for entry to the universities, especially to the prestigious University of Ceylon at Peradeniya. Such political pressure as there was in the 1960s had been for the expansion of the universities to accommodate ever-increasing numbers of students; the procedure for admission to the universities was not yet a matter of dispute or even discussion. That happened after 1970 with the victory of the UF coalition. Its occurrence was soon seen as part of the wider problem of Sinhalese-Tamil rivalry in the areas of language, employment and education.

The crux of the problem was that the indigenous Tamils who constituted just over 11 per cent of the population had for years enjoyed a position of predominance in the science-based faculties. This was facilitated by their higher rate of literacy in English and the excellent facilities for science education in the schools of the Jaffna district from which many of them entered the universities. With the changeover to *swabasha* there were, in effect, two distinct streams of students seeking admission to the university, one educated in Sinhala and the other in Tamil. There was also a much smaller English stream consisting of students of almost all ethnic groups. Since examiners did marking in one or other of those streams and not in both, it was only a matter of time before the superior performance record of the Tamils would be attributed to deliberate over-marking or grade inflation on the part of Tamil examiners. Late in 1970, there was a rumour that the Tamils had obtained almost 60 per cent of the admissions to the engineering faculty (or school as it would be called in US universities) of the University of Ceylon at Peradeniya, the only such faculty in the country at that time. The source of the rumour, which had appeared before the admissions list was officially announced, was never satisfactorily established but it was widely suspected that these inaccurate figures had been leaked to the student leadership at Peradeniya by some officials in the lower rungs of the administration at that university.

The consequences were truly momentous. The allegation of favouritism among Tamil examiners was investigated but there was no evidence to substantiate such a charge. Nevertheless, the government decided on changing the hitherto accepted basis of admission and to introduce a lower qualifying mark for Sinhala medium students, so that a politically acceptable proportion of Tamil-to-Sinhalese students could be admitted to the university. The significance of this step was that

> at long last the principle of choice of candidates for university education on the basis of their academic performance as reflected in the raw marks had been successfully challenged.[20]

Although the Tamil political leadership protested strongly against the

> iniquitous nature of differential 'qualifying marks' for Sinhalese and Tamil candidates the immediate effect of the change in terms of the number of Tamil students admitted to the science-based faculties was merely marginal, a drop from 35.3 per cent to 33.6 per cent, an actual increase in the aggregate from 337 to 359.

But as Professor C.R. de Silva points out

> the real significance of the change in 1971 does not lie in these figures. It marked the ascendancy of a group of Sinhalese [officials, and advisors] in the Ministry of Education, a group which firmly believed that some adjusting mechanism was necessary to give Sinhalese students a chance in competing for the coveted places in science-based courses at the University. It was this group which came up with the suggestion for media-wise standardization for [the 1973 admissions].

In 'media-wise' standardization all marks were reduced to a common scale in order to ensure that the number qualifying from each language medium would be more or less proportionate to the number sitting the examination in that medium. The result was to neutralize the superior performance of the Tamil medium students in science subjects, as depicted by 'raw marks'. Those who proposed the measure argued that the difference in performance between Sinhalese and Tamil students must necessarily be attributed to differences in facilities, better teachers and equipment and that standardization was merely a devise to compensate for such imbalances. The fact that differences in facilities and teaching available to students within any one medium were often as great, if not greater, than any overall difference between the two media was glossed over.

Once again however the immediate effect on numbers of Tamils entering the university was marginal, and far less damaging to Tamil interests than the acrimony which the change caused would appear to support. As Professor de Silva explains:

> The Sri Lankan Tamils, though they constituted just 11.1 per cent of the population provided about 30 per cent of the science students in the secondary schools and the scheme of [media-wise] standardization ensured that this proportion of places in the university accrued to them.

In the next year came 'the district quota' system, introduced, it would seem, to satisfy two interest groups, the Kandyans, and the Moor/Malay group. Both groups regarded themselves as educationally backward, and both were not content with the changes in admissions policy effected since 1970. Since the Moor/Malay group were educated mainly in the Tamil medium, standardization pitted them against the Tamils in the competition for places in that medium of instruction, and they saw the contest as an unequal one. Mahmud, leader of the Islamic Socialist Front, was not unmindful of their interests.

Sri Lanka soon earned the doubtful distinction of becoming a frequently quoted example of the perils of affirmative action in multi-ethnic societies, especially where the affirmative action was designed to benefit the majority group as against the minorities. Well-known US political scientists such as Donald Horowitz, Myron Weiner and Thomas Sowell would cite the Sri Lanka example prominently in their studies on ethnic conflict and especially the destructive impact of affirmative action policies in situations of energetic competition for desirable posts in state and professional employment.[21]

More ominous for the long-term future of the Marxist parties, and the concept of a political alliance between the centrist SLFP and the former, was the challenge it faced from another quarter. The pace of change and reform in the first 10 months of the UF government's tenure of office was inadequate to satisfy the aspirations of the more articulate and militant young people whose political appetite had been whetted by their zeal in working to bring the government to power. By the middle of March 1971 it was evident that the government faced a deadly threat from the Janatha Vimukthi Peramuna (JVP), an ultra-Left organization dominated by educated youths, unemployed or disadvantageously employed. The insurrection that broke out in April 1971 was, from beginning to end, a revolt of youth, an unusual, if not the first, instance of tension between generations breaking out into military conflict on a national scale.[22] The creed of generational war was linked to eradicating a colonial status which had ended two decades previously but was presumed to be still in existence. It was a movement of the new Left and the ultra-Left against the established Marxist parties, the LSSP and CP, and the populist SLFP. The insurgents were, in general, the children of the rural poor, Sinhalese and Buddhist. The ethnic and religious minorities of Sri Lanka played no significant part in the insurrection. The traditional Marxist parties of Sri Lanka had preached class warfare but had never resorted to political violence to overthrow the elected governments of the day. The JVP's contribution to Sri Lankan politics was to engage in revolutionary violence as an essential feature of their political activity.

In the immediate sense the 1971 insurgency failed. Once the momentum of their original thrust had been absorbed and repelled the insurgents were unable to sustain their attacks although they had the numbers to do so. The insurrection was crushed but the defeated rebels played a part, indirectly if not directly, in shaping the future. They did this through the marked influence they had on policies adopted by the UF government: in hastening proceedings begun in 1970 for an autochthonous constitution for Sri Lanka to replace the Soulbury constitution and in the impetus the insurrection gave to radical social and economic reform in the years 1972-5. As a result of these reforms state control was extended to every sector of the economy, from trade to industry, and to the island's efficiently-run plantations, foreign-owned and locally owned (which provided over two-thirds of the island's foreign currency earnings annually). Meanwhile, restrictions were placed on size of land-holdings and the ownership of houses; land in excess of the ceiling imposed was taken over by the state with the promise of compensation, and in the case of houses and apartments, those in excess of the limit of one house or apartment per family and one per child were re-distributed, in the first instance, among tenants in occupation of them. In brief, the rebels strove towards pushing Sri Lanka more rapidly towards becoming a socialist society.

However, these purportedly socialist measures did very little to improve the position of the poor, and the restructuring of the economy which the government attempted did nothing to stimulate economic growth and little to check inflation. The economy remained stagnant, while inflation reached levels never experienced before in Sri Lanka, and unemployment rose to unprecedented levels. In a tight employment market and a state-dominated economy the struggle for jobs became fiercer than ever, and contributed greatly to the aggravation of ethnic tensions between the Sinhalese and the Tamils, not to mention the Muslims.

We need to turn, at this stage, to the politics of the Jaffna peninsula. In retrospect it does seem that the militancy among Tamil youth there, a striking feature of this period, stemmed from similar, if not the same causes that led to the JVP insurrection and that the shock waves set off by the JVP were by no means limited to the Sinhalese areas of the country. These included the bleak employment prospects that faced Tamil youth. The frustration and anger this gave rise to turned to a profound alienation because of their perception of themselves as victims of deliberately devised policies of discrimination, and above all alienation from a political system which appeared to symbolize not merely class privileges but— and here lay the divergence from the JVP—also the dominance of an unsympathetic majority community. Thus, while the Sinhalese youth in the JVP insurrection rose against a system which appeared to them as the embodiment of class privileges, and social and economic stagnation, the Tamil youths' perception accommodated all these but went beyond them in their sense of an ethnic alienation. It was this alienation that made them so responsive to separatist sentiment. This new generation of young and impatient Tamils were soon the most militant supporters of the separatist cause, and the most volatile element in Tamil society. Beginning as foot soldiers of the separatist campaign, and the vital link between the established politicians of the TULF and the Tamil people in the north and east of the country, they were soon—by the late 1970s—much more than that: they helped fashion the ideology of separatism while emphasising radicalism and various forms of Marxism, and which served to influence the strategy and tactics of the campaign for separatism. By the early 1980s, the parliamentarians of the TULF seem to have ceded to them, or were compelled to cede to them, the principal leadership role in the separatist movement. They were also—and here again there was a remarkable similarity with the JVP—the catalysts of revolutionary violence. In resorting to violence they were following the example of the JVP. At the core of the Tamil separatist movement, and from the very outset, were terrorist groups.

The five years from 1972 to 1977 were a sterile phase, unproductive in initiatives and policy options on improving relations between the island's main ethnic groups. It was as though the UF government exhausted its political resources in confronting the JVP and the insurgency of 1971 and in devising a response to these. Despite the speed with which that insurrection was crushed, the government's morale never recovered from having to deal with so formidable a threat from left-wing groups. A right-wing *putsch* could have been handled just as easily but with much less damage to the government's morale, and without any erosion of its credibility as a socialist regime.

A by-product of the increasing alienation of the Tamils from the Sinhalese since the adoption of the new constitution was the conversion of a large section of the Tamils of the north to the idea of a separate Tamil state in Sri Lanka, an indication of the intensity of feeling in the Tamil areas of the country at what they regarded as a deliberate attempt to reduce them to subordinate status. The Federal Party itself was a recent, but not entirely reluctant, convert to this policy, and its—and subsequently the TUF's—enthusiastic advocacy of a separate state for the Tamil-speaking areas of the Northern and Eastern Provinces introduced a new dimension of hostility into relations between themselves and the UF government.

At the heart of the separatist agitation was the Tamil youths' desperation at the prospects of long periods of unemployment or under-employment. Increasing competition from the Sinhalese with the expansion of education facilities in the Sinhalese areas of the country would in any case have reduced the prospects of the

Tamils in their traditional search for positions in the bureaucracy and the state's technical and educational services. With the change of government in 1956 and the new language policy adopted shortly thereafter, the number of Tamils entering the public sector began dropping and this reduction has not been reversed.[23] The teaching profession in the Jaffna peninsula was overcrowded and afforded few opportunities for young graduates, especially after the take-over of the schools by the state.

Similarly, one of the detrimental if unintended effects of the expansion of the public sector and the pre-eminence it achieved in all areas of economic activity was a contraction in employment prospects for the Tamils because entry to most sections of it lay through political patronage. Since the vast majority of Tamil parliamentarians were in the opposition, they were effectively excluded from access to these sources of political patronage.

SEPARATISM, VIOLENCE AND THE SECURITY FORCES

From the early days after independence a combined service force had been located in the Jaffna peninsula with the twin objectives of checking illicit immigration into the island from Tamilnadu and Andhra Pradesh, and curbing the very profitable and highly organized—indeed, centuries old—smuggling trade through the northern ports, in particular Velvettithurai. The smuggling trade will be discussed later, but suffice it to say here that it linked the economy of the Jaffna peninsula with that of the southernmost parts of Tamilnadu.

There had always been Sinhalese officers of all ranks in the police force in the Jaffna peninsula. For most Sinhalese police officers, service in the Jaffna peninsula was a punishment posting; not infrequently officers with a record of transgression of the disciplinary code of the police force were sent there. But Sinhalese policemen were not unwelcome in Jaffna; on the contrary in the caste-ridden society of Jaffna they were, as outsiders, impartial arbiters in conflicts which had a caste connotation.

The Sri Lankan police and the armed services had earned a reputation in the country, not least among the Tamil minority, for impartiality during the riots of 1956 and 1958. The attitude of the Tamils to the security forces however changed in the mid and late 1960s and with it their view of the role these forces played. They began to be seen as part of the state's security network devised to keep the Tamils down; and these forces themselves were often compelled to take hard decisions for perceptibly political reasons. Once the phenomenon of youth unrest and violence came to dominate the political scene in the north, the police force found that the boundary between the routine business of maintaining law and order on the one hand and political activity on the other became increasingly blurred. Tamil officers in the police force faced an impossibly difficult conflict of loyalties, between their commitment to their duties, and their own ethnic identity. The result was that by the early 1970s more Sinhalese officers were sent to the north, for the government regarded Tamil officers as either ineffective or unreliable. Thus, the police force in the north and the security forces in general became overwhelmingly Sinhalese in ethnic composition. Few were proficient in Tamil and this widened the gulf between them and the people among whom they served. But more important, once political violence, politically motivated armed robberies and open intimidation of potential or actual witnesses of these crimes became a feature of life in the Jaffna peninsula, the security forces confronted a wall of silence among the people, a wall which they found impossible to penetrate. Gang robbers in Jaffna arrogantly demonstrated their immunity from arrest—because no one would dare to stand witness against them—and their nonchalance, in brash daylight incursions in which a common push bicycle was their mode of conveyance to and from the scene of their depredations.

The security forces were perceived now as a Sinhalese army of occupation, and in their frustration at their inability to bear down effectively on the perpetrators of these robberies and acts of violence they often turned violent themselves. A force perceived as an army of occupation was driven by the inexorable logic of their ambiguous position in Jaffna to behaving like one. And that in turn was a factor of great importance in the late 1970s and 1980s in the breakdown in communications and understanding between the Sinhalese and the Tamils not merely in Jaffna but in all parts of the island.

The crux of the problem was that there had been, by the beginning of the UF's tenure of power, a remarkable change in the ethnic composition of the security forces in the island. In the officer corps of the security forces and the police, as in the higher bureaucracy of the early post-independence years, there had been an under-representation of Sinhalese-Buddhists. This was less so in the rank and file. War service had contributed greatly to the *esprit de corps* and *elan* of this small security force and it had proved its worth as an impartial peace-keeping force during the ethnic disturbances of the mid and late 1950s, both on its own as well as in support of a hard-pressed and thinly spread police force. The frequency of their use as a peace-keeping force had contributed to a growing contempt for the incompetence and cynicism of politicians, culminating in the abortive coup of 1962.[24] Not surprisingly one consequence of the abortive coup had been a purge of the officer corps. The guiding spirit in this was religion not ethnic identity. The decades long conflict between Buddhists and Christians in Sri Lankan society had reached its denouement. The police force had seen this same crisis of identity a few years earlier—in 1958—when Bandaranaike had quite deliberately chosen a civil servant as Inspector General of Police—because that individual was a Buddhist— overlooking the claims of all the Deputy Inspectors General, once again on grounds of religion, all of whom were Christians. He had less reason for thus disturbing the normal patterns of promotion and preferment than his widow had in confronting an abortive coup. Thus by the mid-1960s the security forces and the police reflected more accurately than in the past, the ethnic profile of Sri Lankan society. When the UNP-led coalition was in power, there was yet another abortive coup—in 1966.[25] Significantly, it was not the senior officers who were prosecuted as the conspirators but—with one exception—junior officers, and non-commissioned officers, Buddhists to a man, and intent on protecting the Sinhalese-Buddhist identity of the armed services from any possible dilution by the new government. They were by now ethnic soldiers.

The third phase in the changing composition of the armed services came in 1970 when the UF was returned to power. The commissions of a number of officers were withdrawn. This time the guiding principle was political conviction not religious affiliation. Anyone suspected of not toeing the new political line was removed and for the first time influential political appointees were introduced into the army, at least one of whom was an active politician. The rank and file both in the police and the armed services were by now largely Sinhalese and Buddhist.

THE TAMILNADU CONNECTION

Within the Indian Union, Madras, or Tamilnadu as it became later, had been witness to a separatist movement. The rise of the Dravida Kazhagam (DK) and later the Dravida Munnetra Kazhagam (DMK) in the early 1950s reflected the same powerful force of linguistic nationalism that was to transform the politics of Sri Lanka in the same period. By the early 1950s the Congress Party in Madras had become more Tamil than it had been ever before, but this transformation did not prevent its being supplanted by a more authentic instrument of Tamil regional sub-nationalism, the DK and later DMK. Between 1952 and 1967 the DMK had risen from challenger to the Congress to the ruling party there.[26]

Confronted by this force of linguistic nationalism in many parts of India Jawaharlal Nehru responded by appointing the States Re-organization Commission. He had done so with considerable reluctance for he was appalled by the parochialism and worse still the communalism of this potentially state-destroying force. The creation of Tamilnadu was an outcome of the Commission's efforts. This concession to linguistic nationalism did not help the Congress save its position as a regional force in the new state. On the contrary, it strengthened the DK and DMK and seemed, at first, to do little to dampen the forces of separatism which had been encouraged in the struggle for the creation of a linguistic state. In 1957, provocative political gestures encouraged by the DK and DMK led to the passage of the *Prevention of Insults to the National Honour Act* aimed at stopping the practice of burning the national flag or the constitution. Then in March 1963 came the 16th Amendment to the Indian constitution which placed a legal ban on secessionist parties and the advocacy of secession. By now the DK had abandoned its official goal of Dravidistan and its separatist agitation. Its official policy now was one of greater autonomy for Tamilnadu. The central government itself made a major concession in the form of a three-language formula by which Tamil was guaranteed the status of an official regional language for Tamilnadu. By 1969, the DK had changed its name to the DMK, and the Tamilnadu unit of the Congress itself had come to terms with this regional party after it had conformed to the requirements of the 16th Amendment and changed its political goal to one of advocating a greater measure of autonomy.

For present purposes the important point is that the DK and the DMK were even more conscious of the rights of Tamils in South Asia than the Congress-dominated state governments of Madras had been. But both DK and DMK can be accused of having acted with much less restraint than the Congress in demonstrating their concern about the Tamils. So much so that by the early 1960's the increasingly turbulent politics of the Jaffna peninsula began to be treated as an integral part of the internal politics of Tamilnadu. The DMK, effectively checked from pursuing its separatist goals in India, took vicarious pleasure in giving encouragement and support to separatist tendencies among the Tamils of Sri Lanka. To the latter, worsening relations with the SLFP dominated governments of the 1950s and 1960s, and more so the UF government tended to make ties with Tamilnadu more attractive than they had once been. The links, however, were still fitful and tentative.[27]

Tamil politics in South Asia thus had a regional rather than a purely local impact. One important instrument of this regionalization, if not, internationalization, was the convening in 1966 of a Conference of the International Association for Tamil Research. One of the leading figures in its establishment was a Sri Lankan Tamil, Fr Xavier Thaninayagam, a Roman Catholic priest who had been a lecturer at the University of Ceylon, Peradeniya, and had moved to Kuala Lumpur as the Foundation Professor of Indian Studies of the University of Malaysia. Since 1966 these conferences have become a regular feature, held either in Europe, or in South and South-east Asia. Whenever they were held in South Asia they took on a political dimension and were 'by no means limited to the congregation of scholars'. An American scholar described the Fifth International Tamil Conference held at Madurai in 1981 as a three-pronged affair, with the 'research' and 'public' conferences accounting for two parts, and the third 'being devoted to the domain of public spectacle'.[28] Seven years earlier—January 1974[29]—when this conference was held in Jaffna the three-pronged nature of the event was seen for the first time.[30] The organizers had hoped that the government of Sri Lanka would either sponsor or give its official support to the conference, but neither sponsorship nor support was forthcoming and they had to rely entirely on local resources and support from the Tamil communities overseas.

From the outset organizers of the conference were under pressure to convert it into a great public event with a heavy political content. In the end that was precisely what happened. The grand finale of the conference was scheduled for 19 January 1974 and the conference was shifted from the original venue to a more capacious one to accommodate the large crowd expected. Eventually, the size of the crowd—about 50,000 by some estimates—far exceeded the most sanguine expectations of the organizers. They packed the hall in which the conference was due to take place, and crowded into the vicinity of the hall and on to the roads that led to and from it. An academic conference had become a public spectacle with obvious potential for conversion into a massive political meeting.

The conference took place at a time when the state of emergency declared over the whole island in the aftermath of the JVP insurrection was still in force. Stringent restrictions were in force in regard to the holding of public meetings. The shift of venue had been approved by the police under the emergency regulations, and on the understanding that the meeting would be held inside the hall, using only the public address system therein, and also that only those in the list of speakers submitted by the organizers would be entitled to speak, and that 'no political or controversial' speech would be made. The organizers agreed to comply with those requirements.

But what actually happened at this meeting? The meeting was an orderly one, but there was always the danger that someone would use the occasion for a provocative political speech. There was just such a person waiting in the wings, a youth leader from Tamilnadu, Janatharan by name, who was neither a delegate to the conference nor an invitee. The police regarded him as a 'security risk', and as a foreigner, he was not permitted to address public meetings. He had addressed meetings in Jaffna and in nearby towns in breach of the law, and had been warned by the police about persisting with this. It was known that some youth groups in Jaffna had planned to get him to address the crowd on this present occasion. The organizers of the meeting were intent on honouring their agreement with the police, but they failed in their efforts to prevent him from appearing at this meeting. Some senior TUF politicians played a more ambiguous role: instead of supporting the organizers on this issue, at least one of them—A. Amirthalingam—in a gesture that was regarded by the police as a signal for a breach of the law, garlanded Janadharan. The police were intent on seeing that the latter did not address the meeting. When he seemed likely to do so, they moved in to prevent that from happening. A stampede ensued, and in the resulting mêlée seven persons were killed. The police party was a small one, and although they carried arms no shots were fired. But the use of teargas caused panic. People fleeing from the meeting in myriad directions, dislodged an electric wire. This live wire either fell on the crowd, or persons in the crowd trampled on it, resulting in seven deaths.[31]

The whole incident was in the nature of a tragedy waiting to happen. All the elements that possibly could ignite Jaffna's volatile politics were there: a celebration of Tamil language and culture, an assertive youth element setting the pace in politicizing the event, Tamil politicians exploiting the situation for political advantage, the Tamilnadu presence in a very provocative form, and a handful of police seeking to maintain law and order and in the process triggering a totally unintended result that provided the separatist cause with its martyrs. The event itself, in a distorted form, is now part of the political mythology of Tamil separatism: police brutality, a Sinhalese-dominated government which acted in total disregard of a conference that had come to mean so much to Tamils in Sri Lanka, and the shadow of Tamilnadu in Sri Lankan Tamil politics.

To return to Jaffna and the incidents of January 1974. An unmistakable intensification of separatist agitation, as well as an increase in terrorist activity was observed in their wake. The security forces found the search for actual and potential troublemakers a frustrating experience as the local population would not voluntarily help in apprehending these young men; besides when there was the slightest chance of capture, they moved across the Palk Straits to Tamilnadu which served them as a refuge, and as a bridge-head for raids into the Jaffna peninsula. It was at this point—the passage to and from Jaffna to the Tamilnadu coast—that the smugglers entered the picture both as transport agents for fugitives and as sources of ready money. Also the safe houses established on both sides of the Palk Straits for the traditional smuggling trade were now put to other uses—as havens for men on the run, and for storing arms—in support of the separatist cause. Very soon the more politically conscious smugglers and the terrorist groups had joined forces. Each needed and used the other. There was the inevitable metamorphosis of the smuggler into 'guerrilla' and 'freedom fighter' and indeed two of the most dynamic and powerful leaders in recent times thrown up by this blending of clandestine trading activity and militant and violent political agitation were prominent smugglers.

By the mid-1970s radicalization of politics in Jaffna was an established fact, and with radicalization came violence, including the beginnings of a terrorist campaign that was to pervade the next two decades. In the beginning, the targets in these carefully chosen acts of political violence were Tamils associated with the government, culminating in the attempted murder of a pro-government Tamil MP, and the murder of the SLFP Mayor of Jaffna, Alfred Durayappah, the most prominent of the Tamil supporters of the UF government in the north. This was the first political assassination conducted by the leader of the Liberation Tigers of Tamil Eelam (LTTE), V. Prabhakaran, then a youth of 21. He later claimed that it was his 'first military encounter'.[32] Soon there was what came to be a familiar cycle of escalation ranging from: political rhetoric, symbolic acts of violence, the killing of carefully chosen supporters of the government in the Jaffna peninsula, all aimed at conveying the chilling political message that opposition to and indeed deviation from the TUF's programme carried fearful risks, and culminating in systematic acts of violence directed at the police and security services.

THE RISE OF TAMIL SEPARATISM: 1948-55

Separatism,[33] defined as a concerted attempt at the creation of a new sovereign political entity out of a larger one, is alive and well in South Asia. South-east Asia may boast of separatist movements with a longer history such as the agitation of the Malay/Muslims of southern Thailand, or the Moro campaigns[34] in the Philippines (which have roots in the anti-colonial resistance against the Spaniards and the Americans[35]), but it cannot match the success achieved by separatism in South Asia. The process began in the last decade of British rule. The separation of the province of Burma from the *raj* in 1937 (ending a connection that went back to the 1820s) was a deft piece of damage control by the British, a concession to separatist sentiment—i.e. separation from the *raj*—before the latter could be converted into a political movement that threatened the British connection and not merely the incorporation into a British-Indian political entity of a former Burmese kingdom. The nearest we have to such a peaceful post-colonial parallel is the separation of Singapore from Malaysia, an exercise in the management of a potentially dangerous political manoeuvre. By and large, however, separatism has been successfully thwarted by the post-colonial state system of South-east Asia whether it be Myanmar (Burma), Thailand or the Philippines.

No doubt South Asia has its own examples of thwarted separatist movements, but it has at least two successful—and bloody—exercises in the creation of new states out of an existing one. The first, of course, was the creation of Pakistan in 1947-8 from the former British *raj*, a tumultuous event that took place simultaneously with the transfer of power from the British to the political leadership of their legatees in India and Pakistan. The second successful exercise in separatist agitation was the partition of Pakistan in 1971 into two states, Pakistan and Bangladesh. The creation of Bangladesh in 1971 was, up to very recently, the only successful separatist movement in the post-colonial world, indeed almost anywhere in the world, for that matter, since the end of the Second World War. The world community had been inclined to treat state boundaries as sacrosanct. The partition of Pakistan was a rare example of a successful intervention by a regional power on behalf of separatists in a neighbouring state. But as chapter six will show, Indian intervention in 1987-90 in Sri Lanka failed in most if not all of its objectives, and the Sri Lankan separatist movement, or rather Tamil separatism in Sri Lanka, ranks as one of the thwarted separatisms of South Asia.

Where an ethnic (or religious) minority is concentrated in a region or regions of a country, and where in addition it constitutes the overwhelming majority of the population there, as is the case with the Tamils of the Jaffna peninsula and Jaffna district in Sri Lanka (and to a lesser extent in the other component districts of the Northern Province), geography and demography combine to provide an ideal breeding ground for a separatist movement. Ethnic cohesion and a heightened sense of ethnic identity, important ingredients for the emergence of separatist sentiment, had existed in Jaffna and the Jaffna district since the mid-1950s; indeed some would argue that these had been in existence since the 1940s in the last decade of British rule. However, the striking feature of the emergence of Tamil separatism in Sri Lanka, in contrast to contemporary separatist movements in Burma, Thailand, and the Philippines, is its late development. Early expressions of separatist sentiments (in the late 1940s and early 1950s) developed into a full-fledged separatist movement over a period of twenty-five years or more, and that transformation was the result of the operation of a number of factors. These included a perceived threat to the ethnic identity of the Tamils from political, economic and cultural policies; perceived grievances of a political or economic nature or both; and a sense of relative deprivation at the loss of, or the imminent loss of, an advantageous or privileged position the Tamil minority enjoyed under colonial rule under the British.

Separatist agitation went through several stages and phases, beginning with peaceful political pressure, moving on to civil disobedience, and then to violence, and that violence itself graduated from sporadic acts to more systematic attacks directed against state property and police and security forces until, in the early 1980s, it assumed the form of a dangerous threat to the integrity of the post-colonial Sri Lankan state. The avowed objectives of the agitation began with demands for securing greater autonomy for a region or a people within the Sri Lankan polity, to pressure for conversion of its unitary structure to a federal or quasifederal one, and on to its current phase of an agitation for a separate state encompassing most or parts of the northern and eastern littoral regions, and their hinterlands.

The case for Tamil separatism in Sri Lanka was built upon the modern doctrine of self-determination of people, and linked with it came, in time, the concept of the 'traditional homelands' of the Tamils, 'homelands' that needed to be protected from 'outsiders', themselves citizens of the same country. It is important to remember that the concept of the 'traditional homelands' of the Tamils of Sri Lanka emerged in the late 1940s and early 1950s at a time when the first post-colonial government in Sri Lanka under D.S. Senanayake was taking great pains to foster a pluralist, secular democracy.

The concept of the Tamil 'traditional homelands' was itself based on a fragile foundation of pseudo-historical data and a cavalier disregard of the composition of the demography of the 'homelands', past and present. Every version of the concept of the 'traditional homelands' of the Tamils of Sri Lanka since that time has been built on a foundation of 'historical' data and has a superstructure of 'historical' data as well. In the late 1940s and early

1950s, it was inextricably linked with the political ideology of the Federal Party, the progenitor of the Tamil United Front (TUF) and the Tamil United Liberation Front (TULF), and was immanent in the principal political resolution adopted when the Federal Party was established in 1949. At the first national convention of the Federal Party in 1951 a claim was made that

> the Tamil-speaking people in Sri Lanka constituted a nation distinct from that of the Sinhalese in every fundamental test of nationhood . . .

and the 'separate historical past' of the Tamils was emphasized as an essential part of this.

It was a claim based on a hazy 'historical' memory of statehood in centuries past, remembered and newly interpreted (and generally misinterpreted) as a continuous and continuing tradition of independent statehood and an unbroken national consciousness. In less than a decade of its first enunciation this theory, refined as 'the traditional homelands' of the Tamils, became an indispensable and integral part of the political ideology of the Tamil advocates of regional autonomy and separatism. At this point, there was very little by way of definition of the boundaries of these 'national areas' of the Tamils except for occasional references to the Northern and Eastern Provinces. The definition of the boundaries came in the mid-1950s and it was based on a single piece of 'historical' evidence, contained in a document prepared by Hugh Cleghorn, a British academic, who had been in the island in the very early years of British rule in the last years of the 18th century as political troubleshooter, and later on as the island's first colonial secretary.[36]

Tamil politicians and ideologues looking for historical data and evidence in support of their case for the 'traditional homelands' of the Tamils seized upon one short extract from a minute prepared by Hugh Cleghorn— the Cleghorn Minute as it has come to be called. It read as follows:

Two different nations, from a very ancient period, have divided between them the possession of the island. First the Cingalese[sic] inhabiting the interior of the country, in its southern and western parts, from the river Wallouve [Walawe] to that of Chilow [sic], and secondly the Malabars [Tamils], who possess the northern and eastern districts. These two nations differ entirely in their religion, language and manners. The former, who are allowed to be the earlier settlers, derive their origin from Siam, professing the ancient religion of that country.'[37]

The last sentence, an egregious solecism, would have alerted readers to the limitations of this extract as historical source material, but ideologues of Tamil separatism generally carefully omitted it in their resolutions and documents on the theme of 'traditional homelands'. They used the rest of this extract. One sees this in claims advanced by the Federal Party, its successor the TULF and by other Tamil separatist activists, in defining the territorial limits of the 'traditional homelands' of the Tamils. This single extract from Cleghorn's Minute in support of their territorial claims has gained the status of scriptural sanctity among the advocates of a separate state for the Tamils of Sri Lanka, accepted almost as an act of faith, in the face of scholarly criticism of its reliability as a historical source.

From the outset the concept of the Tamil-speaking peoples of Sri Lanka sought to bring the Muslims, who were Tamil speakers generally, under the umbrella of Tamil politics, on the assumption that a common language linked them, despite a fundamental difference in religion. It was a linkage which the Muslims have persistently rejected because of its assumption of a Tamil tutelage over them, but one which constantly reappears in Tamil agitational activity. Secondly, the Tamil agitation was linked to the purposeful opposition of the Federal Party and its successors in the leadership of Tamil politics, to the entry of Sinhalese into those parts of the country regarded as 'traditional' Tamil areas. Thus, at the inaugural convention of the Federal Party (or *Ilankai Thamil Arasi Kachchi* in

Tamil-ITAK) in April 1951, a resolution urged that

> Inasmuch as the Tamil-speaking people have an
> inalienable right to the territories which they have been
> traditionally occupying, the first national convention of
> the ITAK condemns the deliberately planned policy of
> action of the Government in colonizing the land under
> the Gal Oya reservoir and other such areas with purely
> Sinhalese people as an infringement of their fundamental
> rights and as a calculated blow aimed at the very existence
> of the Tamil-speaking nation in Ceylon.

The change of political mood in the country in the mid-1950s and early 1960s, especially among the Sinhalese majority should have given greater salience to separatist sentiment among the Tamils. Surprisingly, the advocacy of separatism did not lead to a shift from peaceful agitation to mass protest or sporadic violence among the Tamils. Nevertheless, separatism was part of the political agenda, not so much as an agitation for the creation of a separate political entity but as an emphasis on regional autonomy, the creation of a Tamil, or Tamil dominated, ethno-region in the north and east of the island; if not in the whole of the Northern and Eastern Provinces. There was, however, a new leadership among the Tamils. The Tamil Congress which had been the principal political group among the Tamils since the 1940s was overtaken by the Federal Party. The objectives and title of the Federal Party were ambiguous at best. In Tamil, the title of the party meant the Tamil Kingdom Party, or Tamil State Party. The Federal Party was deliberately vague about its objectives: it would stress the case for a federal constitution in place of Sri Lanka's unitary structure, in all their negotiations and pronouncements in the Sinhalese areas of the island; for the Tamil dominated Jaffna peninsula, the emphasis was less on regional autonomy than on the creation of a separate state.[38]

Despite the tensions of the mid-1950s and early 1960s, there was no full-blooded separatist movement among the

Sri Lankan Tamils in the mid and late 1960s. Even the rise of Tamil separatism in southern India did not have as much of an impression and influence on the thinking of the Tamil intelligentsia in Sri Lanka as one may have anticipated in a period of ethnic strife, and the clash of linguistic nationalisms, Sinhala and Tamil. The situation changed in the 1970s, and changed decisively in the course of the years 1970 to 1976 when a centre-left coalition of the SLFP and the Marxist Left ruled the country.

THE MATURATION OF TAMIL SEPARATISM—THE 1970s

The adoption of the first republican constitution on 22 May 1972 was clearly the critical starting point in the growth of Tamil separatism. Between May 1972 and end of 1976 we see a momentous shift in the political aspirations of the Sri Lanka Tamils, from demands for structural changes and constitutional reform, to an assertion of the right to self-determination on the basis of a Tamil state in Sri Lanka. As with the Federal Party in the 1950s, now in the 1970s too, the claim for a separate state looked back to the distant past, and endeavoured to link the present with that past through a misinterpretation of historical events and data. Once more the emphasis was on a continuing tradition of independent statehood and unbroken national consciousness. Above all the territorial dimensions of 'Eelam' were defined in the Vaddukodai resolution of 1976 in terms which clearly showed an unacknowledged dependence on Cleghorn:

> Whereas throughout the centuries from the dawn of history, the Sinhalese and Tamil nations have divided between them the possession of Ceylon, the Sinhalese inhabiting the interior parts of the country in its southern and western parts from the river Walawe to that of Chilaw and the Tamils possessing the northern and eastern districts . . . [the TULF resolves that] Tamil Eelam shall consist of the Northern and Eastern Provinces (of Sri Lanka).

In its manifesto for the general election of July 1977, the TULF elaborated further the concept of the 'traditional homelands' of the Tamils. The claim now was that:

Even before the Christian era, the entire island [of Sri Lanka] was ruled by Tamil kings . . .

From this claim which was, in fact, a falsification of history,[39] the manifesto proceeded thus:

From this background of alternating fortunes [of the Sinhalese and Tamil rulers of ancient Sri Lanka] emerged, at the beginning of the 13th century, a clear and stable political fact. At this time, the territory stretching in the western seaboard from Chilaw through Puttalam to Mannar and thence to the Northern Region, and in the east, Trincomalee and also the Batticaloa Regions that extend southwards up to Kumana or the northern banks of the river Kumbukkan Oya were firmly established as the exclusive homeland of the Tamils. This is the territory of Tamil Eelam.

Tamil Eelam, the manifesto asserted, is the successor to the Jaffna kingdom. At this stage and till 1980 or so the TULF was still a dominant force in Tamil politics in Sri Lanka.

A Tamil kingdom was in fact a historical reality, but its lifespan had been short—from the 13th century to the early part of the 17th—and except during the brief heyday of its power in the 14th and early 15th centuries it seldom controlled anything more than the Jaffna peninsula, and some adjacent regions on the coast and some parts of the interior. Set against Sri Lanka's recorded history of over 2,000 years the independent existence of this kingdom was a brief episode during a period of political decline of the Sinhalese kingdoms of that time. At times the kingdom of Jaffna had been very powerful; at others it had been reduced to the status of a satellite of expanding Dravidian states across the Palk Straits, and at times it had been subjugated by the Kotte kingdom the principal political entity in the island in the 15th and early 16th centuries, and generally it acknowledged the suzerainty of the principal Sinhalese kingdom. It disappeared from the historical scene in the early 17th century[40] and while its memory was kept alive in the 20th century there was neither an unbroken 'national' consciousness nor a continuing tradition of independent statehood among the Tamils of Jaffna in particular or of Sri Lanka in general.

There were, besides, contradictions and ambiguities in the claims made in the 1970s and 1980s. The Vaddukodai resolution of 1976 defined the boundaries of Tamil Eelam in terms of people: 'Tamil Eelam shall consist of the people of the Northern and Eastern Provinces'; while the TULF manifesto of 1977 adopted a spatial definition in which the territorial limits were extended to cover part of the North Western Province in addition of course to the Northern and Eastern Provinces. The lack of consistency in these claims was demonstrated afresh in the amendment to the Statement of Government Policy in the national legislature moved on 18 August 1977 by A. Amirthalingam as the Leader of the TULF and Leader of the Opposition in which he referred to the 'mandate given by the people of Tamil Eelam to the Tamil United Liberation Front for the restoration and reconstitution of a free sovereign socialist state of Tamil Eelam.'

On that occasion there was no reference to the boundaries of the state, no reference to provinces, or to peoples, no reference to the exclusive rights of the Tamils to such territory, and no reference implicit or explicit to that extract from the Cleghorn Minute which plays such a vital role in the claims of Tamil politicians. There was merely a reference to the '[Tamils'] traditional occupation of a separate and well-defined territory in the Northern and Eastern parts of Ceylon.'

Within 25 years of the adumbration of Tamil separatism by the Federal Party, its lineal descendant, the TULF, hitherto the principal exponents of the ideology of the separatism, were being overtaken by a variety of younger political groups who were more radical politically and more violent in their methods. As chapters five and six will show the LTTE stormed its way to pre-eminence in the early and mid-1980s, in a series of bloody encounters with their rivals, and have retained that position since then, virtually unchallenged by the latter. They became the principal exponents of Tamil separatism in Sri Lanka.

III

Reaping The Whirlwind: The Internationalization of Sri Lanka's Ethnic Conflict

Policies of Reconciliation: Success and Failure 1977-1983

TO REAP THE WHIRLWIND

All freshly elected governments, especially those which secure a landslide victory, assume that they can set the agenda for their term of office. They learn soon enough that the agenda is likely to be set for them by the actions of their predecessors in office. And so it was with the UNP government which came to power in July 1977, acutely conscious of the tensions and occasional eruptions of violence between the country's several ethnic and religious groups in the 1970s and the damage inherent in this to the stability of the polity.

There was some consternation in the ranks of the new government when riots broke out in August 1977,[1] especially at the speed with which they spread to parts of the country which had not been affected by the riots of the mid-1950s. How was it that the Tamil minority had come under attack in so many parts of the island? The new government could console itself with the thought that, they could not be blamed for what had happened, that they were reaping a whirlwind, which was itself the direct consequence of the wind that their predecessor had sown. Even so it was difficult to deny the validity of the argument that the violence of the Sinhalese reaction was largely a visceral opposition, if not the inevitable reaction of large numbers of Sinhalese, to the separatist agitation in the Tamil areas of the north and east of the island, and the threat it appeared to pose to the country's territorial integrity.

Soon after its election victory the new government had given positive evidence of a more accommodating policy in regard to the grievances of the Tamil minority than had its predecessor. Thus, in the first formal statement of policy in the National State Assembly on 4 August 1977 the government made a pledge to introduce far-reaching changes beginning with a fresh look at the status accorded to the Tamil language. Again, and once more before the riots of mid-August broke out, a major change of policy was announced in regard to a grievance of more recent vintage—a declaration that the controversial system of standardization of marks for admission to universities would be abandoned with immediate effect. This announcement was made almost as soon as the new government took office.

The TULF's response to these gestures of reconciliation was rigidly doctrinaire. An amendment to the government's statement of policy of 4 August 1977, moved by the TULF on 18 August, after the outbreak of communal rioting, was both tendentious and provocative—an insistence on proclaiming the TULF's commitments to the establishment of a separate Tamil state in Sri Lanka. The amendment itself could hardly have been more ill-timed for this reiteration by the TULF literally fanned the flames of Sinhalese communal feeling. An extravagant exercise in rhetoric, part of the ritual of parliamentary politics, was seen by the Sinhalese as the launching of a major political campaign directed from the office of the Leader of the Opposition and all the more dangerous and sinister for that. The Sinhalese had hardly had time to get accustomed to the idea of a Tamil in the role of Leader of the Opposition—the SLFP had only 9 seats in Parliament and thus its leader did not have the numbers to claim the post—when this ill-advised amendment to the government's policy statement appeared to suggest that conciliatory moves were so many sops to a particularly intransigent Cerberus. But the TULF's reaction is explained, in part at least, by a change of leadership that occurred in the course of 1976 and 1977.

In the course of those two years the Sri Lanka Tamils had lost not one but three outstanding leaders: S.J.V. Chelvanayakam, leader of the Federal Party since

1948 and of the TUF (later, TULF) from its inception, very much the father figure of Tamil politics; the silver-tongued G.G. Ponnambalam who had led the Tamil political campaigns up to 1956, when Chelvanayakam established his supremacy, and was the latter's main rival; and M. Tiruchelvam, the only TULF politician with any recent experience of Cabinet Office. All of them were distinguished senior lawyers, capable of negotiating on equal terms with the Prime Minister of the day and—this was particularly true of Chelvanayakam and Ponnambalam—of securing acceptance of an agreement by the Tamil electorate.

The new and untried TULF leadership thus faced an enormous challenge in taking over from these senior politicians. Their task was rendered all the more formidable by the volatility of Jaffna's politics since the early 1970s. The transition from the second rung to the top of the leadership may have been easier in less troubled times. The change in political style, from a charismatic leadership, to a more low-key one was a realistic adjustment to a new situation: the Tamil masses in Jaffna held Chelvanayakam in great respect as a principled, incorruptible politician and indeed they referred to him as *Perayar* or the great leader; his successor, A. Amirthalingam, was referred to as an elder brother, suggesting thereby the head in a collective leadership, a chairman of a board rather than an unchallenged single leader. Besides, there were the TULF's links with Tamil youth groups who were intent on radicalizing the new politics of the north and east of the island, and intent also on holding the new leadership to the objective of a separate Tamil state in Sri Lanka, Eelam, on which it had secured so resounding a mandate in the Jaffna peninsula and the Northern Province if not in the Eastern Province. Thus, there was an amazing parallel between the early 1930s and the late 1970s in the politics of Jaffna, and the Northern Province—the pace-setters were youth groups. In 1931, a group of youthful enthusiasts succeeded in cajoling the Tamil politicians of the day into a boycott of elections to the national legislature, the State Council. Within a few months of this, it was evident that they had driven their seniors, reluctantly or not, into a *cul de sac* and it was to take two years or more before the politicians re-established their hold on the electorate in the Jaffna peninsula. The latter's counterparts of the present day never succeeded in establishing anything approaching a similar independence of action.

In the circumstances the TULF leadership's failure to reciprocate the conciliatory gestures on the part of the new government, by holding back its separatist demands for a few months, at least, till the new regime had time to convert its proposals for a settlement of the problems of the indigenous Tamils, was understandable as a tactical move designed to retain the confidence of its youthful and radicalized supporters. But it contributed not a little to the spread of communal disturbances in 1977 to parts of the island that had been spared the worst of the ethnic violence of the mid-1950s.

POLICIES OF RECONCILIATION

The riots of August 1977 could not deflect the government's attention from other pressing issues for very long. High on its priorities was a fresh and searching look at Sri Lanka's constitutional framework. We focus attention here on some of the principal features of the new constitution, beginning with the issue of fundamental rights.[2]

These were more strongly and genuinely entrenched and afforded greater protection than the equivalent clauses of the constitution of 1972. They were more detailed and more precisely formulated, apart from being more numerous. Moreover, provision was made for their protection through and by the Supreme Court against the infringement or even imminent infringement of such rights by either executive or administrative action. Again, the constitution provided for the creation of a post of Parliamentary Commissioner for Administration (Ombudsman) with powers to investigate and report on allegations of infringement of fundamental rights, but in practice this, unlike the protection afforded by the Supreme Court, proved to be much less effective than its advocates claimed it would be.

All fundamental rights enumerated in Article 14(1) of the 1978 constitution were extended by Article 14(2) to a large category of non-citizens resident in the country—the stateless Indian Tamil minority. The scope of fundamental rights was now expanded to incorporate all the permanent and legitimate residents of Sri Lanka within their purview, for a period of ten years from 1978 long enough, it was hoped, to resolve the vexed question of the citizenship rights of the stateless persons of recent Indian origin. In contrast, under the constitution of 1972, only citizens had been entitled to the rights enumerated in section 18(1) (c), (d), (e), (f), (g) and (i).

In addition, most of the fundamental rights in the new constitution were free of any restriction, and even those that are not, were far less circumscribed than those of the previous constitution were by provisions such as section 18(2) of that constitution. There are some however, Article 12(1) of the 1978 constitution, for instance, which are not so well protected. The provisions of this article which states that

> no citizen shall be discriminated against on the grounds only of race, religion, caste, sex, political opinion or place of birth

were qualified by those of 15(7) which spells out the nature and extent of the limits imposed:

> in the interests of national security, public order, and the protection of public health and morality or for the purpose of securing due recognition and respect for the rights and freedom of others or of meeting the just requirements of the general welfare of a democratic society.

Article 15(7) similarly restricts freedom from arbitrary arrest, and detention incorporated in Article 13(1) and

(2) as well as freedom of speech, of assembly, of association, of public worship and of movement.

Language, the 'pedigree of nations', in Dr Johnson's felicitous words, had been the rallying point of Sinhalese and Tamil ethnic identity and assertiveness since the mid-1950s. Although language had lost some of its virulence as a factor in Sri Lanka's ethnic tensions and rivalries by the 1970s, the framers of the constitution of 1978 sought an accommodation on language and gave it very high priority. The essential features of this accommodation have been reviewed in chapter two. As we have seen there, the constitution of 1972 had unequivocally consolidated the 'Sinhala Only' policy of the 1950s and emphasized the subordinate role of the Tamil language. The new constitution incorporated the *modus vivendi* on language rights that had emerged after two decades of strife. Chapter IV of the 1978 constitution, while maintaining the status of Sinhala as *the* official language (Article 18), recognized Tamil as a national language (Article 19) a significant modification of the 'Sinhala Only' policy.

The first of the policies of conciliation announced was a reversal of the UF government's university admissions policy. This was announced on 4 August 1977 just after the new government took office. Given all that had happened on this issue between 1970-7, it was a bold political decision even for a government that had inflicted a stunning defeat on its opponents and now commanded an overwhelming majority in parliament. To announce the abolition of standardization was one thing: to evolve a new university admissions policy[3] viable both politically and academically was another. Before it could set about this complicated business, a time-consuming one at the best of times, the government had to cope with the communal riots that erupted unexpectedly in August 1977. There was considerable opposition to the new policy. Its salient features are reviewed below. In those details lie some of the nuances in the making of policy on this complex issue.

While the government stood firm on its decision to

abandon standardization some significant concessions to its critics among the Sinhalese were made in other areas: in a move that could be described only as one of those rare, successful attempts to pursue two diametrically opposed policies at the same time without damaging its own interests, the government decided that while standardization was abandoned, all students who would have gained admission to the universities had there been standardization, should be admitted. The 3,700 students originally admitted on the basis of 'raw' marks (the technical term for aggregate of marks) were now joined by nearly 900 others, a good many of them Sinhalese. Subsequently, more than 250 more students were admitted on a 'district' basis, with special consideration being given to students from districts regarded as under-privileged in terms of educational facilities. There were almost as many districts in which the Tamils were a majority and the Muslims a significant minority included in this list as there were those in which the Sinhalese were a majority.

This remarkable exercise in pragmatism brought advantages to everyone. As we have seen the government refused to give way to its critics on the abolition of standardization, and so the Tamil political leadership tacitly accepted the compromise that had emerged. They had good reason for satisfaction, because the number of Tamil entrants to the medical and engineering faculties rose by 250 per cent or more over the figures for the previous year, and equalled or exceeded the 35-40 per cent of the total student population in the science-based courses they had obtained under the system of open competition in 1969-70 and 1970-1.[4] Moreover, those who had been agitating for an increase in the total intake of students to the universities had reason to be satisfied: admissions were up by 25 per cent. Then, there was also an increase in the number of Sinhalese entering the universities, especially from the politically dominant rural areas.

The changes, however, were not regarded as permanent

or even long term: by mid-1978 the whole question of university admissions became once more a matter of acute political controversy because many Sinhalese supporters of standardization, distinctly unhappy with the 1978 compromise scheme, were intent on upsetting it. Their contention was that the Sri Lankan Tamil minority of 11 per cent could consistently obtain such good results—35-40 per cent of medical and engineering entrants to universities—only by unfair means. They proceeded to back up their charges with allegations that examiners in the Tamil medium had been partial in their grading of examination scripts at the national examination through which entrance to the universities was determined; in particular, the examination held at the end of 1977.

A new institutional framework for higher education adopted in 1979-80 helped to stabilize the formula adopted in 1978, that combination of a new national merit quota, regional merit quotas, and 'raw marks'. The establishment of a University Grants Commission (UGC) and Ministry of Higher Education, and above all the placing of these directly under the President of the Republic, helped guarantee this stability, and protected university admissions policy from a repetition of the series of *ad hoc* changes that had been among its principal—and most pernicious—features under the UF government.

The Commission had a membership of five till 1985, when it was increased to seven. It consisted in its first phase of three Sinhalese, one Tamil and one Muslim. The establishment of this Commission did lead to relative stability in the system of admissions; changes were much less frequent than they had been in the early seventies. More important, there was relative stability also in the ethnic proportions in university admissions; the Tamil share was consistently higher than the proportion of Sri Lanka Tamils in the population and much higher in regard to the science-based disciplines, especially medicine and engineering. They have never been lower than 35 per cent in these disciplines in the period reviewed in this chapter. The smaller minorities had yet to gain their 'ethnic quotas' in university admissions, but there was a distinct improvement in the position of the Moor/Malay group.

It was evident that the formula adopted in 1978 needed to be kept in constant review. Once more a committee was appointed for that purpose. Among the problems that attracted attention was the special allocation of 15 per cent of places to the so-called educationally disadvantaged districts. These constituted half of the island's 24 administrative districts.[5] The number was subsequently raised to 13 during 1980. The minimum mark for admission in some of these districts was lower than that for Colombo and Jaffna where the competition was keenest, by as much as 100 out of a total 400. In a situation where a single mark could make the crucial difference between admission to medicine and engineering rather than to the less desirable courses in agriculture or the pure sciences, this differential was seen to be grossly unfair. There were other disadvantages as well, especially the growing clamour from politicians in other rural districts to partake of the largesse distributed to the fortunate 13 districts, an agitation based on the argument that by any standard of assessment their districts were only marginally better off in terms of schools, equipment and teachers, than the 13 that benefited from the existing quota system for disadvantaged areas.

In late 1981 a new formula was announced for 1982-3. The merit quota was to be increased to 40 per cent; the district merit quota to 60 per cent and the 15 per cent special allocation eliminated. The abolition of the 15 per cent allocation was received with a sigh of relief by those convinced that the pendulum had swung too far toward the so-called under-privileged districts. Representatives from the latter group put up a spirited defense of their special vested interests and succeeded in preventing implementation of the new scheme. 1982-3 were election years, and the government preferred to let the existing system continue rather than persist with a change which had brought together an amazing coalition of forces—Sinhalese from rural areas, Tamils from the districts of Mannar, Mullaitivu, Vavuniya, Batticaloa, Trincomalee and Ampara; and Muslims as a whole—together in defense of the 15 per cent allocation. In 1984, another official committee was appointed to review the whole question, and one outcome of its deliberations was a recommendation for a reduction in the number of under-privileged districts to five; and a reduction in the percentage of places available to them from 15 to five. No change was made in the merit quota of 30 per cent, but the district quota went up to 65 per cent. This time the resistance to change was not as effective in yielding results as it was in 1982. The new formula was operative from 1985-6.[6]

Despite the gains that accrued to the Sri Lankan Tamils by way of a higher percentage of places in the science-based faculties after 1977 there was naught for their comfort. They could not have hoped, by the very nature of things in such a sensitive area of ethnic competition, to retain their advantageous position for long. The percentage of places they held could only go down and not up, and this had nothing or little to do with any policy of discrimination: as education facilities improved in the Sinhalese areas of the country—and this process is an inevitable one even if somewhat slow and uneven—the advantages the Tamils had did diminish rapidly in the face of the fierce competition they continued to face. Nor were the Sinhalese the only rivals of the indigenous Tamils. Within the Tamil-medium itself they faced increasing pressure from the Moor/Malay group, who generally had less than 5 per cent of the places in the universities although they form 7 per cent of the population. Besides, over the next decade or so they were also beginning to face a challenge for places by the Indian Tamils whose leaders began a steady pressure for a Sri Lankan version of affirmative action, and a system of ethnic quotas based on population, to pick members of their ethnic group even if it meant scraping the bottom of the barrel. Besides, among the indigenous Tamils themselves, those in the Jaffna peninsula and Colombo faced the competitive zeal of their fellow Tamils in the educationally backward areas such as Mannar, Mullaitivu and Vavuniya in the Northern Province, and Batticaloa and Trincomalee in the Eastern Province, a point we have referred to in the previous paragraph.

Admission on a district basis, introduced originally as an avowedly temporary device, survived into the 1990s. Indeed, in Sri Lanka seemingly temporary devices often enjoy a longevity denied to measures and institutions designed to last long. The anguish the Tamils felt and continue to feel on this issue stems mainly from a sense of relative deprivation, the feeling—indeed, the knowledge— that the halcyon days of the late 1960s when Tamils dominated the science-based faculties of the universities are not likely to return and that the gains made after 1977- 78 were temporary ones. Even if standardization and the district quota system had not been adopted from the early 1970s a reduction in the percentage of places gained by the Tamils in the science-based faculties would have come, gradually at first, but with much greater speed by the end of the decade and in the 1980s, as the Sinhalese areas caught up with the Jaffna peninsula in terms of well- equipped schools and eventually overtook it. By stepping in to force the pace of this inevitable development and doing so in an obviously discriminatory manner, the UF government of the 1970s caused enormous harm to ethnic relations and converted the university admissions issue from a controversial educational problem to a complex and emotion-charged political issue, the consequences of which confront the country even today.

The changes in university admissions policy made between 1977 and 1983, revealed the vulnerability of the government despite its intent on a principled reversal of controversial discriminatory policies given the special circumstances. In this instance, even when the changes effected were clearly beneficial to the minority principally aggrieved, the latter's mainstream political leadership did not feel it necessary, or were too insecure politically, to make any public acknowledgement of the advantages of the changes introduced. The sense of grievance, which for the most part stemmed from the implementation of a misguided and hard policy, remained long after that policy was abandoned. Vested interests intent on maintaining the fiction of disadvantages if not discrimination, had developed. Advocacy groups were often receptive to such claims based on residual grievances. Through their writings they helped spread the notion of the maintenance of the original policy long after that had been modified if not abandoned. Advocacy groups were not the only ones guilty of this. There were distinguished scholars based in the West who also helped perpetuate these misleading claims through their own writings, as is seen below.

In 1981, in her report on *Ethnic Conflict and Violence in Sri Lanka*, Professor Virginia Leary, on behalf of the International Commission of Jurists, argued that:

> Analysts of the ethnic conflict in Sri Lanka would appear to be convinced that one of the principal causes of the rise in militancy among the educated Tamil youth has been the subject of admission to higher education. The government should re-examine its policies on university admissions with a view to basing it on merit rather than on racial grounds. Tamil and Sinhalese youth alike will then have equal rights to university education on the basis of capacity rather than on racial grounds. One of the major points of tension among many Tamil youths has been the implicit racial quota under present university admission policies which has barred many competent youths from pursuing education.[7]

This extract from Leary's report was written *long after* the government had re-examined the policy that had caused so much harm and had actually jettisoned it. Clearly, her understanding of the problem was flawed as it was based on faulty data, hastily gathered from obviously prejudiced sources. Five years later, by which time so many changes had been made, another activist group, International Alert, quoted this same extract, from Leary, with approbation, in its pamphlet *Emergency Sri Lanka* as though it reflected the current reality.[8]

Then again Stanley Tambiah, the distinguished Sri Lanka-born American anthropologist, claimed in his book *Sri Lanka, Ethnic Fratricide and the Dismantling of Democracy* (1986) that,

> The SLFP and subsequently, Jayewardene, had helped in the formulation of what was called 'Standardisation Policy' that claimed a rise in the number of Tamils admitted. But since university admissions are calculated largely on the basis of district population and since the Tamils form a majority in only six of the total of twenty-four districts, the Sinhalese students enjoy a conspicuous advantage over their Tamil counterparts on the basis of demographic rather than meritocratic criteria.[9]

The first sentence here is clearly inaccurate: far from helping in what was called 'Standardisation Policy' Jayewardene's government repudiated it at the first available opportunity. The second sentence is clearly misleading because it ignores the fact that the immediate effect of the change of admission policy in 1977-78 was a steep increase in the number of Tamil students in the universities. The precise figures have been provided earlier in this chapter.

In the field of general education, the UNP government initiated a move in mid-1979, to redress a grievance of the Christians, especially Roman Catholics, which went back to the days of the nationalization of schools in 1960-1 and the administrative mechanisms devised for this. Some schools—largely Roman Catholic—remained outside the system but were not permitted to levy fees. It was now decided to grant financial assistance to all non-fee levying private schools, and to a lesser extent to fee-levying private schools as well. The major beneficiaries of this move were the Roman Catholics, but Protestant groups, and the Muslims and Hindus benefitted as well. Such assistance— though on a somewhat more modest scale—had been promised to the Roman Catholics in 1966-7 but after some hesitation and much vacillation, the then government had not honoured the pledge for fear of political consequences in the shape of opposition from Buddhist activists. The Roman Catholic Archbishop of Colombo, the Most Revd Nicholas Marcus Fernando, described the new policy introduced in 1979 as 'a long-awaited relief from a heavy and unjust burden [the Roman Catholics] had to shoulder for the past eighteen years'.[10]

This bold initiative aroused surprisingly little opposition. The apparent equanimity with which Buddhist activists accepted this decision is as remarkable as their continued opposition to modifications introduced in university admissions policy in 1977-8. It is evidence of changed priorities in their demands and their perception of potential harm to the interests of Buddhists and Sinhalese. The Roman Catholics, it would appear, had ceased to be regarded as a threat to Buddhist interests; this was rendered all the easier by the Roman Catholics' acceptance of the political reality of a Buddhist dominance in Sri Lanka. As for the Tamils, on the other hand, the separatist policies advocated by the TULF, and the expatriate Tamil pressure groups in western countries, in combination with the activities of terrorist groups in Jaffna seemed to underline a persistent threat to the territorial integrity of the Sri Lanka polity, and to the interests of the Sinhalese as an ethnic group.

The centrepiece of the government's policy of reconciliation were the District Development Councils to which it had committed itself in its manifesto for the elections of July 1977. That document made reference to the need to decentralize administration down to the village level, to 'make the people partners in planning, organisation and implementation of policy.' There was reference also to the administrative machinery to be established for that purpose. At the apex were to be District Development Councils headed by a District Minister, and consisting of MPs of the district, elected heads of local bodies, and government officials. In its statement of policy in the National State Assembly on 4 August 1977 the pledge was renewed. But the outbreak of communal violence in August 1977 proved to be a setback to the implementation of this programme. While the riots focussed the attention of the island's politicians on the urgency of devising measures to resolve the festering conflict between the two main ethnic groups in the island, they also had the effect of delaying the initiatives planned by the government on the basis of its election manifestos, and its statement of policy of 4 August 1977, on devolution of power.

It was only in the middle of 1979 and against the background of an imminent eruption of ethnic hostilities once again that the government turned its attention to the problem of decentralization of administration which the Tamil leadership had for long regarded as an essential feature in any political settlement. On 10 August 1979, a 10-member Presidential Commission was appointed to report on the decentralization of administration through the device of District Development Councils. Two TULF representatives were appointed to serve on the Commission.[11]

The appointment of this Commission was a reaffirmation of the government's commitment to a policy of decentralization of administration or, more accurately, to depart from the policy of concentrating administrative and political authorities in Colombo which had been sustained since independence, in a continuation of a trend which had begun in the early phases of British rule. With the appointment of this Commission the TULF's separatist agitation was, if not called off, at least put into cold storage.

In 1928, the Donoughmore Commission had recommended the creation of a second tier of government between the central authority and the local government bodies. That it took 52 years before such a system could be introduced—in the form of the District Development Councils of 1980-1—is explained in part by inertia. This was especially true in the 1940s, but later on the caution was induced by a suspicion that any relaxation of centralization could culminate in the dismemberment of the Sri Lankan polity. The devolution of power to regional units had been accepted in principle by the State Council, the national legislature, in 1940, without dissent if not unanimously. But legislation required for the purpose was not introduced in the 1940s. By the mid-1950s the consensus that existed in regard to this had evaporated, and instead the creation of regional bodies had become one of the most controversial issues in Sri Lankan politics because of its association with the demands of the Federal Party, the predecessor of the TULF.[12] Two previous attempts to introduce such councils, the first time in 1957-8 under Bandaranaike's government, and the second occasion in 1968, under the UNP-led coalition of the day had failed hopelessly. Neither government had been able to summon the political will to overcome the opposition to such councils within Parliament and in the country at large. The creation of a second tier of government in 1980-1 was thus a major achievement of the UNP government.

A new institutional structure generally takes a decade or more to be firmly established, and before it is possible to pass judgement on its utility. Here in Sri Lanka, the District Council system introduced in 1981 was abandoned in 1983 in less than two years after its establishment. The events that led to its abandonment are analysed in a later chapter.

Solutions to the minority problems of Sri Lanka have often been caught up in the minorities' jockeying for positions of advantage in the race for political and economic gains. There were some misgivings among the

Muslims about the creation of these District Development Councils.[13] For their part the Muslims had no special demands to make except in the field of education but their primary concern was they should not be left too far behind by the Tamils. Since the District Development Councils bill was seen as primarily a response to Tamil pressures, the balance was adjusted to the advantage of the Muslims, in the first week of December 1980, by the creation of a Department of Muslim Religious and Cultural Affairs placed under the senior Muslim member of the Cabinet. This was as good an example of a political establishment engaged in calibrating the machinery of democracy to secure a tolerable balance of interests, as we are ever likely to find in any plural society.

The political pragmatism of the Muslims was matched by that of the Indian Tamils of Sri Lanka. About the latter there had been no direct mention in the UNP manifesto of 1977. The ties between the UNP and the Ceylon Workers' Congress (CWC) had been strengthened ever since J.R. Jayewardene took over the leadership of the party in 1974, and these had been reinforced by participation in a common struggle against the UF and the SLFP core of that coalition in the years 1975-7. The links were augmented by the electoral support given by the Indian Tamils to the UNP at the general election of 1977. They survived the attacks on the Indian Tamils by Sinhalese mobs during the ethnic disturbances of 1977.

The Ceylon Workers' Congress leader joined the Parliamentary Select Committee on the constitution, and used his influence there to extract two major concessions. One of these, the extension of all eight fundamental rights enumerated in Article 14(1) to the stateless Indian Tamils resident in the island, has been mentioned earlier in this chapter. The second was the elimination of one of the long-standing grievances of the Indians in the island, the distinction between citizens by descent, and citizens by registration. Article 26 of the constitution abolished this and removed thereby the presumed stigma of second-class citizenship attached to the Indians who had obtained it through registration under the terms of the Indo-Sri Lanka agreements of 1964 and 1974. These agreements are discussed in some detail in chapter eight. The third concession had come in December 1977 through an administrative decision rather than legislative amendment or constitutional provision. This was the removal of the bar placed 40 years earlier on plantation workers resident on estates from voting in local government elections. Together, these changes in policy initiated in the wake of the victory of the UNP in 1977, conferred on Indian Tamils in Sri Lanka, in the main plantation workers, a distinct improvement in legal status, and underlined their equality with Sri Lankan citizens by descent. When the Ceylon Workers' Congress leader S. Thondaman joined the Cabinet in September 1978 it completed the process of bringing the Indian Tamils within Sri Lanka's 'political nation' for the first time since the 1930s. It consolidated the improved status of the Indian community within the Sri Lankan polity since July 1977.

For the Indian Tamils, political life and life on the plantations are inextricably linked. In recognition of this, the new government made a deeply significant gesture of reconciliation in August 1977 when a representative of the Ceylon Workers' Congress was appointed to the directorate of each of the two giant state corporations controlling the management of the nationalized plantations. These appointments had more than symbolic significance for the workers' representatives who now had a direct and influential voice in policy-making for the plantations. Their initiatives have contributed greatly to improving living conditions—especially housing—and welfare facilities on the plantations, while wages on plantations have improved substantially above what they were prior to mid-1977. A long-standing demand for equalization of wages for women, engaged in the same work as men on the plantations, was conceded by the government in 1984. Above all the woefully inadequate 'schools' in the plantations have been taken over and integrated into the national education system far more systematically than in the past, and much more is spent now by the state on education of children of the plantation workers through the Ministry of Education and through the two State Plantation Corporations, (Indeed, it is estimated that over a tenth of the gross earnings of the plantations is now diverted to welfare facilities including education.) By the mid-1980s the last of the 'registered' plantation schools were absorbed into the national educational network. These relics of the past, symbolic of the peripheral nature of 'education' and schools as a welfare measure in the plantations, have been swept away; with their disappearance there is now greater hope for the future, in the sense that education will have the same liberating effects as it has had on the poorer segments of other ethnic groups in the island. The Ceylon Workers' Congress has often raised the question of affirmative action for this educationally deprived ethnic group and, like the Muslims, have become advocates of ethnic quotas in higher education.

CONFRONTING SEPARATIST VIOLENCE

With the outbreak of communal violence in mid-August 1977 the new government confronted, very early in its tenure of office, the political fallout of policies pursued by its predecessor. The communal riots of August 1977, the first of three major outbreaks of ethnic violence during the period reviewed in this chapter, bears comparison with the last major ethnic disturbance in Sri Lanka, the riots of 1958.[14] The government brought the situation under control very quickly. An important point in this respect needs specific mention; the outbreak was handled without resorting to the proclamation of a state of emergency. In August 1977 this policy reflected the new government's doubts about the willingness of the police and the armed services—and specially the rank and file in those services— to serve as impartial enforcers of the law, given the fact that in the previous seven years (1970-7) recruitment had been on a political basis. The rank and file of the police force and the armed services, and to a lesser extent, the officer corps, had become overwhelmingly Sinhalese and Buddhist. To impose a state of emergency and to unfold the full range of emergency regulations available for use in such situations was to confer almost unlimited power on the police and armed services. This, the government was unwilling to do at this stage in its tenure of office. Over the next five years—till the first quarter of 1983—the UNP government persisted with this policy of dealing with sporadic eruptions of ethnic violence under the normal laws of the country. Curfews would be imposed in trouble spots, but there would be no declaration of a state of emergency. This policy was seen to be very effective in keeping the peace, but it had its critics, especially in the ranks of the Tamils.

Unlike the JVP insurrection of 1971, political violence in Jaffna at this stage, and till 1983 at least, was not an open confrontation with the state. Instead, there were sporadic, and more often than not carefully orchestrated symbolic acts of violence against persons and state property. Like the JVP of this period the various activist youth groups and factions, and their terrorist units among the Tamils proclaimed themselves Marxists in the style of the contemporary European and Cuban left-wing radicals, but unlike the JVP there was a wider range of non-Marxist elements represented at the leadership level, and much more so in the rank and file.

One—almost natural and predictable—effect of the ethnic disturbances of 1977 was to strengthen the extremist youth groups in the Jaffna peninsula—in particular the Liberation Tigers of Tamil Eelam (LTTE) as they came to be called—by gaining wider support for them among the Tamil people, if indeed these events did not confer a greater degree of respectability on their separatist aspirations than in the past. They were thus able to indulge in a career of violence, murder and robbery with little risk of identification by witnesses; the violence and killings were directed quite calculatedly at Tamil police officers and actual or potential defectors from the ranks of the TULF parliamentary group, and also against suspected informants. From one spectacular incident to another they moved with conspicuous impunity demonstrating that they had public support (or at least were able to extract it by threats of reprisals) and, more to the point, that the police were quite unable to cope with this threat to law and order, and the potential risk to the peace of the island. Moreover, if there was the slightest prospect of falling into the hands of the security forces they moved across the Palk Straits to Tamilnadu where they had sympathizers and supporters.

The TULF had campaigned vigorously on a separatist programme in July 1977, and had won convincing if not overwhelming victories in the constituencies of the Jaffna peninsula. In general the TULF's performance in other parts of the Northern Province fell well below that of its record in the Jaffna peninsula, and in the Eastern Province it was overtaken by the UNP. Even so it could claim, with justice, that the Tamils of the north had endorsed their programme. Having won on this separatist platform the TULF was now the main opposition party in the national legislature, and its leader was elevated to the position of the Leader of the Opposition. There was no precedent in the history of the parliamentary democracies of the Commonwealth[15] for the post of Leader of the Opposition being held by the head of a party committed to a separatist programme, and thus to the dismemberment of the polity. Naturally, questions were raised about the TULF's links, both at the leadership and the constituency levels, with activist youth groups, especially the LTTE, who had spearheaded the campaign for separatism and were now intent on holding the TULF to that programme.[16] When these activist groups persisted with their political programme in the north of the island, in the course of which they indulged in acts of terrorism, the ambiguity of the TULF's position within the country's political system was emphasized with every violent incident.

The government, for its part, faced an extraordinarily difficult situation. The normal legal machinery and police procedure were generally ineffective in meeting the challenge to the state posed by the LTTE and their activities. The ease with which these extremist groups got away unscathed with daring daylight robberies and physical violence, extending with increasing frequency to killings of carefully chosen victims including, on occasion, Sinhalese police officers stationed in the north of the island, was doubly provocative. There was, first of all, an inevitable undermining of the morale of the police who were already chafing under the restraints imposed by established legal procedures in coping with these politically-motivated acts of violence and defiance of authority. Secondly, there was the indignation felt in the Sinhalese areas that the government seemed powerless to act in the face of a deadly threat to its authority. Both could provoke a backlash, the police by retaliating with greater force than was prudent—their patience worn thin by the constant challenges to their authority—and the Sinhalese, in general, through a recrudescence of ethnic violence directed against Tamils living in their midst. Thus, whenever Sinhalese policemen were killed by terrorists in the north of the island and their bodies were brought to their homes in the Sinhalese areas, the government was compelled to take extraordinary precautions to prevent communal outbreaks in those localities.

On 22 May 1978 Parliament therefore approved 'a bill to proscribe the Liberation Tigers of Tamil Eelam and other similar organizations'. It was introduced because of the spate of incidents of politically-motivated violence in the Northern Province and the breakdown of law and order there. The new law was intended to last for one year after which the situation was to be reviewed. Not surprisingly it did not yield the results anticipated by the government. Instead, to its embarrassment, the politically-motivated violence and robberies persisted. The TULF for its part also confronted great difficulties in evolving a coherent and credible response to the problems created by the LTTE. They denied that there were any political links with this group, and also often issued statements repudiating the violence associated with them. Yet, so far as their Sinhalese critics were concerned, this denial did not carry conviction; the TULF leadership's association with these groups in the early and mid-1970s was well known, and became even better known with the publication of the report of the Sansoni Commission appointed to investigate the background and events of the riots of 1977. Perceptive observers of the politics of Jaffna realized that the TULF was in no position to place too great a distance between itself and the separatist activists operating in Jaffna, because the links between them, forged in the heat of the political struggles against the UF government, could not be easily severed. And, in fact, they made no attempt to sever such links. As a result relations between the TULF and the UNP government became noticeably strained by the end of 1978.

In the early part of 1979 this estrangement was exacerbated by the activities of groups of Tamil expatriates in a number of western countries intent on internationalizing Sri Lanka's ethnic conflict. A dimension of internationalization had begun with the Tamilnadu link, and through it, with a wider Indian one, as will be discussed further on. Internationalization of the conflict proper began in the early and mid-1970s in Britain, and later spread to the Continent and Scandinavia through the well orchestrated, and very effective, efforts of groups of Tamil expatriates protesting against the policies of the UF government. They indulged in a propaganda campaign intended to demonstrate that the Tamils were victims of a deliberately planned policy of discrimination. Quite often their aims were clearly self-serving; in many instances the objective was to obtain the right to convert their status as temporary residents in a European country to permanent resident status, or indeed to obtain full citizenship rights on the basis of their being 'refugees' from a harsh regime. But there were more immediate and less personal objectives as well; to get the media to focus attention on the problems of Sri Lanka's Tamil minority, and to use the unfavourable publicity this generated against the Sri Lankan government. An important objective was to put pressure on the Sri Lankan government through political action in the form of sustained agitation in the countries to which Sri Lanka Tamils had moved. They hoped that official pressure through diplomatic channels, by the governments of these countries would help their cause.[17]

If the UF government's policies provided the Tamil expatriates with the data for their propaganda campaigns, and gave their propaganda the element of authenticity it needed to win support from sympathetic sections of the western media, the riots of August/September 1977 gave the campaign even greater credibility. The campaign spread across Europe, but Britain continued to be the main centre. The change of government in 1977, and the reversal of the UF's policies—which had earlier been the focal point of the expatriate Tamils' campaign—the changes introduced through the new constitution of 1978, made not the slightest difference to the campaign. By now the expatriate Tamil groups were the most vocal advocates of a separatist state for the Tamils of Sri Lanka—the state of Eelam.

The activities of the advocates of separatism thus brought the country, by mid-1979, to the brink of another round of communal violence. As in August 1977, the government now adopted a blend of firmness and conciliation in dealing with a potentially dangerous situation. First of all, the legal apparatus of the state was revamped and strengthened. This happened in two steps. One, the law proscribing the Liberation Tigers and similar organizations, originally intended to last just one year, was extended in May 1979 for another year. The second step was the more significant one, and more controversial too: on 19 July parliament approved the second reading of the

Prevention of Terrorism (Temporary Provisions) Bill avowedly modelled on the British Prevention of Terrorism Act, devised as a response to the situation in Northern Ireland and terrorism unleashed by the Irish Republican Army both in Northern Ireland and England itself. Critics of the Prevention of Terrorism (Temporary Provisions) bill argued that many of the rigorous regulations generally imposed through the declaration of a state of emergency were now being incorporated as part of the legal framework of the country. Civil libertarians expressed concern about the potential dangers in this new legislation to the fundamental rights incorporated in the new constitution.[18] Government spokesmen responded to this latter criticism by arguing that Sri Lanka had to follow the example of other liberal democracies where separatism challenged the integrity of the state and where terrorism, resorted to by the more extremist groups advocating separatism, posed dangers to public security. Special legislation of this sort was a regrettable but inevitable part of the price the country was called upon to pay in resisting these threats and repelling them.

Simultaneously, a state of emergency was declared in the north of the island, and a military commander was appointed to co-ordinate security arrangements in Jaffna, and with instructions to stamp out terrorism there. Once more a state of emergency had become part of the armoury of the state in dealing with politically inspired violence. But on this occasion its operation was restricted to one part of the island, and for a limited period of time. The state of emergency was to lapse on 31 December 1979, and it was not extended beyond that date. By this time the army had become an integral part of the peace-keeping force in the restive Jaffna peninsula and other parts of the Northern Province. The pressures mounted by terrorist groups were much too great for the small and scattered police force, the normal instruments for the maintenance of law and order, to deal with. These vigorous measures served at least some of the purposes they were intended for—an impending crisis was averted in 1979. The measures of conciliation pursued simultaneously with them have been reviewed earlier in this chapter.

Elections were held throughout the island for seats in District Development Councils on 4 June 1981. The election campaign was peaceful and orderly except in Jaffna,[19] where terrorist groups directing their attack on political parties desirous of constructive change, first assassinated the leader of the UNP campaign in Jaffna, and killed others of the party prominently associated in that campaign. Extremist groups were demonstrating their opposition to the concept of District Development Councils as part of the process of decentralizing administration; more important they were expressing their determination to prevent the UNP from establishing an electoral foothold in the Jaffna peninsula. To meet this mounting violence the police force was strengthened by a large contingent of policemen and police reservists. The stage was set for a tragic sequence of events. These reinforcements checked the violence temporarily, but became themselves the target of violence. On the eve of the elections, a terrorist group shot dead four policemen who were on election duty. This incident provoked just the response the terrorists had anticipated and desired: the unfocused anger of the police in one of the worst incidents of police reprisals against the young militants and terrorists in Jaffna. The violence was inflicted on property not persons, culminating in a mindless act of barbarism, the burning of the Jaffna Municipal Library. For the government the most galling consequence of this one incident was that the psychological and political battles had been lost, at least for the moment. The immediate consequence of this confused denouement was that the hard-line opponents of reconciliation were able to set the agenda and the priorities in political activity in the Jaffna peninsula.

The violence and police reprisals compelled the postponement of the election in the Jaffna district. Fortunately, the violence was contained within the Jaffna district, and did not spread, on this occasion to other parts of the country. 1981 had seen other sporadic but localized outbursts of ethnic violence, and in one of the most serious of them, victims of mob violence included the Indian Tamils who had nothing at all to do with separatist agitation and violence. It was evidence of the brittleness of the calm that seemed to settle on the country in the wake of the emerging détente between the government and the TULF.

The elections to the District Development Council in Jaffna, postponed because of the violence, were held shortly afterwards, and the result was an overwhelming victory for the TULF who won every seat on that Council, a difficult enough achievement under a system of single member constituencies, but remarkable for an election held under proportional representation. If that victory helped consolidate the improvement in relations between TULF and the government which had begun somewhat tentatively in the last quarter of 1979, there was the nagging fear—in the government at least—that the TULF's solid position in the north was now more apparent than real.

An important feature of this period was the regular meetings held between the government—cabinet ministers and officials—and the TULF MPs and their advisers, with President Jayewardene in the chair. At these informal meetings issues relating to the management of ethnic tensions were discussed, solutions suggested and proposals that emerged from the discussions were often implemented and, if not implemented on any regular basis at least tested for their impact. Certainly, by the middle of 1982 it seemed as though the establishment of the District Development Councils had yielded the political results expected from them, namely to give the Jaffna peninsula a respite from turbulent political agitation. But it was not a durable peace, for violence continued to take its toll either in clashes between separatist groups and the police and security forces, or in the fratricidal conflicts among the fragmented separatist groups themselves, described in greater detail on chapter six. And there were also those other victims of violence in Jaffna and the north of the country—men and women suspected of being police 'informers', as well as the so-called 'social parasites'—small-time thieves and hoodlums who had been of use to the separatist activists and terrorists, but were now an embarrassment and were dispatched as ruthlessly as the informers. For them, as for the informers, the usual punishment was a shot through the head, the body left near a lamp post, or hanging from one, with a placard attached announcing to the world why this summary punishment had been meted out.

There was little the police and the security forces could do to check these killings, and the robberies associated with the militants and terrorists. All they could see was that the newly established cordiality between the government and the TULF had done little to check these either. On the contrary, it seemed to them that these cordial relations between the government and the TULF were a positive hindrance in the struggle against the more extremist Tamil groups and their terrorist associates. Worse still, in the Sinhalese areas, the failure to stem the tide of terrorism was being attributed to a political factor, the influence of the TULF with the highest levels of government, rather than to the inadequacies in the police and security forces' intelligence gathering exercises.

THE RIOTS OF JULY 1983[20]

The period from around August 1982 to the end of May 1983 was one of intense political activity: first, the presidential election was held in October 1982, to be followed by the referendum of December 1982. Secondly, this in turn was followed by 18 by-elections in the Sinhalese areas of the country and local government elections in municipalities and urban councils all over the island. This prolonged period of political campaigning, and the unusual frequency of electoral contests kept political passions and rivalries inflamed and overheated throughout these months. Inevitably too, communal tensions were aggravated by all this, especially because in the early months of 1983 terrorist violence erupted with greater frequency.

Yet, there were signs of conciliatory moves afoot in other circles. A committee of high-ranking officials had been appointed to make recommendations on strengthening and indeed revitalizing the District Development Councils. Above all, moves were afoot to summon an All Party Conference for the resolution of outstanding ethnic issues. This was explicitly intended to move beyond the stage of bilateral talks, between the government and the TULF, which had been a feature of the years 1981 and 1982 but which had ended in an impasse, to a wider national forum. A round table conference for this purpose was announced for the end of July 1983. One of the principal groups invited, the TULF, was in one of their frequent moods of introspection, unable to decide whether to participate or not (or least put up a show of doubt to satisfy their own electorate), aggrieved at the lack of an opportunity to test their electoral popularity through parliamentary elections. They were scheduled to meet at their annual conference in the third week of July where policies for the immediate future were to be determined.

While the TULF's convention was in progress in Mannar, a terrorist ambush which killed 13 soldiers in Jaffna on 23 July, led, first to army reprisals there and subsequently to the worst outbreak of ethnic violence since 1958. Unlike in the riots of 1958, the worst affected area was the city of Colombo and its suburbs. The riots were an urban rather than a rural phenomenon.

The symbolism of the terrorist attack was not missed. It was timed to coincide with the TULF convention, to upstage the latter, and to serve as a warning that a conciliatory response to the government's proposals would be quite misplaced in the current mood of youth opinion in the north; 23 July was also the sixth anniversary of the

UNP's return to power in 1977. Thus, in one decisive move, the terrorists had once again attacked the principal advocates of constructive change in the troubled ethnic scene of Sri Lanka.

Sinhalese mobs did not distinguish between Sri Lankan Tamils and Indian Tamils in their ferocious, vengeful and diffused outburst of indignation against terrorism in the north. In fact, the victims of these assaults had shown no outward sympathy for the terrorists or indeed for the TULF. Tamils living in the Sinhalese areas had voted in large numbers for the government. Yet they faced the rage of the mobs. Colombo city was the scene of a wave of arson and destruction with the Tamil enclaves in middle-class residential areas, and Tamil houses elsewhere in the city facing the brunt of the mob's fury. Much of the violence reflected a ferocious mood of disapproval of the government's handling of the terrorist threat. There was a self-destructive aspect too, most evident in the senseless burning of factories and shops owned by Tamils but providing employment for large numbers of Sinhalese.[21]

The Roman Catholic areas in the north and north-west of the city, and the Roman Catholic suburbs and towns situated between Colombo and Negombo, on the route to the national airport were among those most seriously affected. This was also one of the principal differences between the riots of 1983 and those of 1958. The violence in the Roman Catholic suburbs and towns reflected the deep chasm that had emerged over the years among the Roman Catholics themselves, between Sinhalese and the Tamil Roman Catholics, and the anger was directed against the Roman Catholic church in the north of the island where some of the younger and more activist Tamil clergy were well known for their avowed sympathy for the separatist cause.

Given the extent of the physical destruction of property—houses, shops and factories—that occurred in Colombo and its suburbs and elsewhere in the country, the death total estimated at between 500 and 600 was much smaller than was feared at first.

What marked off the riots of July 1983 from those of 1958 was the role of the security forces. The breakdown in law enforcement in the early days of the riots had no precedent in the past; it took the government nearly a week to re-establish its authority and quell the violence. The security forces were either generally indifferent to or they ignored their peace-keeping role, repeatedly refusing to intervene when their intervention could have saved lives and property. The machinery of law and order had almost totally collapsed. There are two parallels for this in recent items, the Malaysian riots of May 1969,[22] and the Delhi riots of 1984 in the aftermath of the assassination of Prime Minister Indira Gandhi. A *New York Times* report on the attacks on the Sikhs in November 1984 would serve as an amazingly accurate account of what happened in Colombo and its suburbs in that dreadful week of July 1983.

> The first is the repeated failure of the police to intervene against acts of terror and killing. The second, based on mounting evidence from witnesses, is the apparent organization behind the attacking gangs, strangers who arrive in trucks and disappear when the deed is done.[23]

The 'apparent organization' referred to in this extract were code words for the local units of the Indira Congress in Delhi and some important political figures in it. The situation in the Sri Lankan riots was much more complex. Despite the comments of some contemporary observers of these incidents suggesting a link between the mobs and influential government politicians no firm evidence has yet emerged to support that contention.[24] The fact is that the mobs that roamed the streets of Colombo and the other towns of Sri Lanka on that fateful week were composed of people professing a wide range of political views and they included supporters of the UNP. Anyone who saw them at work would have sensed the operation of something like a mass of visceral antagonisms, a frightening force fed on a diet of rumours, tensions, fears and paranoia, and a fearsome rage directed against the Tamils—any Tamil for that matter—on the assumption that they were all communally responsible for the terrorist outbreaks in the north, and in fact for the incident that sparked off this vengeful fury. The country's political structure was shaken to its foundation.

A state of emergency had been in force since the middle of May 1983. Now in the aftermath of the riots, curfews were imposed under the emergency regulations. At the outset the curfews were ignored both by the mobs and the security forces. It took a few days before the security forces began the business of restoring order, tardily and hesitantly at first, but within a week with professional competence; soon curfews and emergency regulations became vigorous instruments of peacekeeping. But not before the government had made an important concession to Sinhalese opinion, an admission on state television by the President of the republic, that the policy of conciliating the TULF and separatist forces was a mistaken one, and a promise was made of firm and effective steps to curb separatism.

Thus, one important change of policy flowed from the riots of July 1983. In August 1983, Parliament approved the sixth amendment to the constitution, imposing a ban on political parties that advocated separatist policies and penalties too on individuals that advocated separatism. An important and inevitable consequence of this was that all TULF MPs forfeited their right to sit in the national legislature unless they took an oath abjuring the advocacy of separatism. None of them chose to take such an oath.

CHAPTER 6

India and The Internationalization of Sri Lanka's Ethnic Conflict, 1983-1990

INDIA AS PRINCIPAL MEDIATOR

Sri Lanka's ethnic conflict of the mid and late 1970s and early 1980s and especially the anti-Tamil riots of 1983 created conditions for India to play a major role in the island's affairs. This was threefold. The first, which began with Mrs Gandhi's return to power in 1980, was her covert support to Sri Lankan Tamil political activists who were operating from India. This covert support continued until 1987. The second, hinged on the Tamilnadu factor which has traditionally formed an important facet of India's relations with Sri Lankan affairs. Seldom has a constituent unit (a province or a state) of one country influenced the relationship between it and a neighbouring country with the same intensity and to the same extent that Tamilnadu did and continues to do. Admittedly, India's own role is more complex than merely reacting to the pressures of domestic politics in Tamilnadu. Nevertheless, concerns about the latter have been an important consideration. Tamilnadu governments have provided Sri Lankan Tamil separatist activists with sanctuaries, training and bases. Not only did the central government under Indira Gandhi connive in this, but it also tolerated the provision of training facilities and the existence of camps and bases in other parts of the country. The origins of these camps and bases go back to the early 1980s, that is to say, well before the riots of July 1983 in Sri Lanka.

India's role of mediator—the third of India's roles—began under Mrs Gandhi as a calculated political response to the anti-Tamil riots of July 1983 in Sri Lanka and continued under Rajiv Gandhi himself. An integral aspect of this third role, that of active participant which began in late 1987 and continued to the middle of 1990, is reviewed below. Never before, or very rarely indeed, has a mediator taken on the role of combatant, and the presumed guardian of an ethnic minority's interests waged a bitter war against sections of that minority, and in a neighbouring state at that.

From the outset Mrs Gandhi's statements and actions made it clear that she regarded India as a principal mediator rather than a neutral one. Here James Laue's definition of the distinction between the two roles fits the Indian situation with an unusual degree of accuracy:

> The principal mediator is a mediator with muscle, one who is a principal in the dispute; the neutral mediator in an international conflict would be a truly uninvolved third party, with little or no actual or implied power over the disputants . . .[1]

Throughout the period 1983-90 India never abandoned her role of being a principal in the dispute, and the presumed protector of the interests of the Tamil minorities in the island.

The result was that India was at once a negotiator and an advocate. The distinction between these two roles was blurred to the point where it often disappeared altogether. There was one other consequence, and it is best stated through another extract from James Laue, this time a concise statement on the essence of conflict resolution:

> True resolution of conflict satisfies the underlying needs and interests of the parties by joint agreement. Real conflict resolution does not sacrifice any of the parties' important values. If a conflict is resolved, none of the parties will later wish to repudiate the agreement, even if power conditions change so they might be able to do so. Voluntary compliance is another major criterion. It is really not a resolution unless the agreement is self-implementing. If agreements have to be enforced, they may be managed, settled, planned or controlled, but

these differ from full resolution. A final criterion for determining whether a conflict is resolved is whether the outcome meets some mutually agreed-upon standards of fairness and justice.[2]

The eventual failure of the Indian mediation effort was because it fell far short of the exacting requirements of successful conflict resolution as outlined above.

CONFLICTING PERCEPTIONS OF SECURITY

Sri Lanka is by any definition a small state, 'a local power whose demands are restricted to its own and adjacent areas'.[3] The island is at once strategically situated and yet deeply isolated in relation to its location with South-east Asia, China, Africa and West Asia and Antarctica. Sri Lanka's geographical location also emphasizes its proximity today as in centuries past to a large regional power or powers in the Indian sub-continent.

The fact that Sri Lanka, or Ceylon as it was called then, was never part of the *raj* has had a profound impact on the thinking of several generations of Sri Lankans, and its influential politicians especially on matters of security. Thus, Sri Lanka's first Prime Minister, D.S. Senanayake, based the strategy for his country's security in the post-independence situation on the assumption that the most likely threat to her independence would come from a newly-independent India. For Senanayake no less than for Whitehall the defence agreements signed at the transfer of power in late 1947—and which he had first suggested to the Colonial Office as early as August 1945[4]—were part of the process of adjusting to the uncertainties of a new pattern of international politics in South Asia with India as an independent state. Senanayake believed that the agreements offered his country security against any possible threat to her independence from India. For Whitehall the defence agreements with Sri Lanka were important because of British strategic interests in the Indian Ocean, especially for securing her links with Australia and New Zealand.

This arrangement gave Sri Lanka a free ride in defence and external security in the crucially important early years of independence, when she had no credible defence capacity. The army, navy and air force were all built from scratch and under British supervision over the next decade.

Senanayake's policies survived his death (in 1952) but not the defeat of his party, the UNP, in 1956. The time had come to think of a national defence policy, in the new strategic situation of the late 1950s and early 1960s, the central issue being the power vacuum created by Britain's abandonment of her traditional role in the Indian Ocean region. The Sri Lankan governments of this period did little to develop even a modest defensive capacity against any external threat, or for that matter even against internal turmoil. More significantly, without ever considering the long-term implications of its actions or inaction, Sri Lanka took shelter under the security system that Nehru's India was in the process of constructing.

But even if a small power like Sri Lanka could afford to ignore the external environment, India could not. She had inherited much the larger portion of the *raj*, after the partition, and was in the process of consolidating it into a cohesive state. Nehru's India and Nehru himself had inherited from the *raj* a belief in India's 'natural boundaries'.[5] In its commitment to the defence of this inheritance, Nehru's India was assuming, tentatively at first, but with greater conviction with the passage of time, the strategic vision of the *raj*. This conviction grew stronger, especially under Indira Gandhi.

In the 60s, Sri Lanka's acceptance of India's defence umbrella was voluntary. This underwent a change in the next decades. With Indira Gandhi reflecting the views of the exponents of India's assumption of the mantle of the *raj*, India decided that small South Asian neighbours like Sri Lanka *must* take shelter under that umbrella, and that a search for an alternative would be regarded as an unacceptable, if not intolerable, challenge to the dominant regional power. This policy was made explicit with regard to Sri Lanka, for the first time, in 1983.

From the mid-1970s Indo-Sri Lankan relations were to be dominated by Indian responses to Sri Lanka's ethnic conflicts, Sinhalese versus Tamils. The mid and late 1970s mark the beginning of the second phase in the post independence violence in the island. During the first phase in Sri Lanka's ethnic conflict, in the mid and late-1950s, India had treated it as a matter of Sri Lanka's domestic politics and therefore not for diplomatic or political intervention. It was the heyday of India's perception of itself as the conscience of the Third World, and Nehru acted with a restraint in regard to domestic turmoil among India's smaller neighbours (with the possible exception of Nepal) which his daughter and successor did not show. In the 1970s the situation had changed. After the intervention in East Pakistan and the creation of Bangladesh, India was in a more self-confident mood. The debacle of 1962, when China had inflicted a humiliating defeat on India, had long been forgotten. The other factor which influenced the relationship between the two countries was the Tamilnadu connection and its impact on the Sri Lankan situation.

INDIA AS MEDIATOR: MRS GANDHI AND SRI LANKA, 1983-84

The victory of the Janata government at the elections of 1977 marked a brief period of two years when India's relations with her neighbours improved remarkably. With the landslide victory of the UNP at the Sri Lankan general election of July 1977, the two elderly leaders of India and Sri Lanka, Morarji Desai and J.R. Jayewardene, one an octogenarian and the other a septuagenarian respectively, established a very close understanding, and the two countries, a very cordial neighbourly relationship. The situation changed dramatically once the Janata coalition crumbled and Indira Gandhi returned to power in 1980.

Once she returned to power, she found herself at odds with President J.R. Jayewardene and his government on their outlook, attitudes and policies on regional and world affairs. There was, first of all, the Afghanistan issue on which the two governments adopted diametrically opposed policies: Sri Lanka, like most other South Asian states strongly condemned the Soviet invasion. India was out of step with the rest of South Asia on this issue. There was also Sri Lanka's futile attempt to secure membership of the Association of South East Asian Nations (ASEAN). This was regarded as proof of the Sri Lanka government's general pro-Western attitudes, of which, further evidence was presumably provided in the expanded facilities granted to the United States for its Voice of America (VOA) relaying station in the island, and also in the choice of a consortium consisting of Oroleum (Pvt.) Ltd., Singapore, Oil Tanking, West Germany, and Tradinaft, Switzerland, to restore to commercial use a complex of oil-tank farms in the vicinity of the strategically important port of Trincomalee. India's concern with regard to this consortium lay in the supposedly covert links between its constituent units and US interests and the suspicion that these commercial links concealed political and strategic dimensions. Then came the Falklands war where Sri Lanka alone of Third World countries backed Britain rather than Argentina.[6]

Sri Lanka, for its part, found the new Indian government less than helpful with regard to Tamil separatist groups operating from Tamilnadu. After the riots of 1977 a period of quiet and slow improvement in relations between the government and the principal Tamil party, the TULF, had seen the passage of the District Development Councils bill in August 1980 and the establishment of a second tier of government in the island. This was a major political achievement, considering that two previous attempts (in 1958 and 1968) had failed in the face of extra-parliamentary agitation and internal bickering within the then ruling party or coalition.[7] There were, nevertheless, occasional outbursts of ethnic violence (in 1981 for instance) and an ongoing conflict between security forces located in Jaffna and Tamil separatist activists and terrorists.

As in the past the latter were using safe houses, if not 'bases,' in Tamilnadu.

Given this background, the anti-Tamil riots of July 1983 gave Mrs Gandhi a totally unexpected opportunity for intervention in the affairs of the island. She moved very swiftly in launching diplomatic initiatives which saw India assuming the role of an intermediary in Sri Lanka's ethnic conflict almost as soon as the riots erupted. It began with strongly worded expressions of concern about the situation in the island, in an avowed effort to put pressure on the Sri Lankan government on behalf of the island's Tamil minority. The Sri Lankan government was invited to accept Indian mediation—the sort of offer best described as one which could not be refused—at a time when it was greatly, if temporarily, weakened politically, at home, and more so internationally, and was thus in no position to resist the pressure.

In Tamilnadu, M.G. Ramachandran, the Chief Minister, and his principal rival in the state's politics M. Karunanidhi, made demands to Delhi for intervention in Sri Lanka. During the debates in the Lok Sabha and Rajya Sabha on 16 and 18 August 1983 there were calls for action over the Sri Lanka situation especially by Tamilnadu politicians.[8] Most of them used the analogy of India's swift intervention in East Pakistan in 1971 and the creation of Bangladesh. Others referred to the Turkish intervention in Cyprus as an appropriate example for India to emulate.[9] Murasoli Maran (presently a Union Minister in the Gujral Cabinet), a DMK legislator from Tamilnadu and a nephew of M. Karunanidhi, advocated the Cyprus model for Indian intervention: 'To get a permanent solution we should send our forces there and carve out a homeland for the Tamils there. We should recognize the Tamil Eelam movement there. Otherwise, if we keep quiet history will not pardon us.'[10]

While there was no support for this from the Indian government, Mrs Gandhi made no public commitment to refrain from military intervention. The Sri Lankan government was operating on the assumption that such an invasion could not be ruled out altogether. For their part, Sri Lanka's mainstream political party the TULF, most of whose leadership moved to Madras, supported Tamilnadu politicians in the latter's calls for Indian intervention.

There were three reasons for this decision on the part of the TULF leadership; the first was a search for security from an increasingly hostile and violent LTTE intent on a ruthless elimination of their rivals in Tamil politics in Sri Lanka; and second, a calculated attempt to use this Madras base to influence Indian policy in Sri Lanka. Soon a third factor entered their calculations when over 35,000 Tamil refugees crossed the seas to Tamilnadu in the aftermath of the riots. Their numbers increased, in time, to about 1,25,000. For the advocates of Indian military intervention in Sri Lanka, such as the TULF, the refugee problem was yet another parallel to the situation in East Pakistan which had paved the way for the Indian surgical strike in Pakistan in 1970-1 and in the creation of Bangladesh.[11] As for the Sri Lankan Tamil refugees in Tamilnadu, some fled in a search for security in the aftermath of the riots of 1983. Some—a small minority—followed the example set by the TULF leadership, who went into self-imposed exile there, but many more were coaxed to move out by Tamil separatist groups in the expectation that large numbers of refugees would help to consolidate Indian support for the Tamil cause in Sri Lanka.

In intervening in Sri Lankan affairs as a self-appointed mediator in a major ethnic conflict, Mrs Gandhi was underlining India's right, as a regional power, to a say in the settlement of a potentially (and actually) destabilizing domestic conflict in a neighbouring state. Because one of the parties to the conflict—the Tamil minority—had linguistic, cultural and religious ties with a neighbouring state of the Indian union, the conflict itself was seen in India as a regional rather than a purely local one. Tamilnadu opinion was inflamed by the anti-Tamil riots in Sri Lanka and Indira Gandhi could hardly ignore this in devising her policies on the Sri Lankan situation.[12] But there was a personal factor as well. With general elections due in late 1984 and her electoral base eroding in many parts of India, including some of her strongholds in southern India, Indira Gandhi was very anxious to mollify Tamilnadu opinion in order to retain if not consolidate her, and the Congress party's, electoral base there. This explains to a large extent the speed with which she intervened when the riots of July 1983 broke out, the choice of G. Parathasarathy as a mediator, and the very significant change in the basis of India's declared interest in the affairs of Sri Lanka.

G. Parathasarathy was an experienced diplomat and administrator as well as being a trusted confidant of Mrs Gandhi with easy access to her. He had, in addition, the advantage of being a South Indian Tamil which meant that Tamilnadu opinion as well as the TULF were happy with him. To them it was a reassuring choice.

On previous occasions of ethnic conflict in Sri Lanka, India's main concern had been about the safety of the 'stateless' Indians resident in the island, and with Indian citizens generally, both categories being largely plantation workers. With Mrs Gandhi in power, in the 1980s, Indian interest in the affairs of Sri Lanka was extended to cover the Tamils, in general, and not merely Indian citizens or 'stateless' persons of Indian extraction most, if not all, of whom were also Tamils.

In the last five months of 1983, Parathasarathy travelled frequently between Delhi and Colombo seeking to devise a set of proposals that would be acceptable to the three parties involved—the Tamils of Sri Lanka primarily, the Sri Lanka government, and to the Indian government. As Mrs Gandhi's special representative he negotiated directly with the Sri Lankan President. In addition, he established close links with the TULF, with the objective of winning their support for a scheme of devolution of power, and other safeguards, that would be an acceptable alternative to a separate state in the north and east of the island for the Tamils of Sri Lanka which many of the Tamil groups, including the TULF, were now advocating. In time, Parathasarathy's closeness to the TULF eroded the confidence that President Jayewardene and the Sri Lankan government had in him originally, and he came to be regarded as an advocate of TULF policies.

Apart from the close links they had established with G. Parathasarathy, the TULF leadership was in constant touch with senior Indian officials in Delhi dealing with Sri Lankan affairs, and on occasion they met Mrs Gandhi herself. Thus, the TULF was able to re-open the debate on the devolution of power in Sri Lanka with the assurance of a sympathetic understanding and support of their views at the highest levels of the Indian government. With Parathasarathy's approval they formally withdrew their support for the District Development Councils established in 1981, claiming that these were inadequate in meeting the needs of the Tamil minority in Sri Lanka as they perceived it in the context of the changed situation. They staked a claim for a system of provincial councils, as the second tier of the governmental structure in Sri Lanka. Their main aim was to secure the establishment of a large regional council, encompassing the Northern and Eastern Provinces where the Tamils would be a dominant if not overwhelming majority, which they had advocated since the 1950s (through the Federal Party, the core of the TULF established in the late 1970s).

When President Jayewardene visited Delhi in November 1983, on a fence-mending trip for which the opportunity was provided by the Commonwealth Heads of Government meeting, he met Mrs Gandhi for the first time after the riots of 1983. He found that she had absorbed Parathasarathy's views on Sri Lankan affairs, especially the proposition that the unit of devolution should be a province rather than a district, and that the powers assigned to such units should be much wider than under the District Development Councils. The meeting with Mrs Gandhi served to underline the weakness of his position in negotiating with the Indian government on the resolution of the political crisis in Sri Lanka stemming from its ethnic conflict. He tentatively accepted a set of proposals embodied in a document which came to be known as 'Annexure C' where the framework of a settlement with the TULF and other Tamil groups was outlined. The merger of the Northern and Eastern Provinces into a single Tamil ethno-region[11], implicit in this document, was one of its controversial features. As a result, something which Sinhalese opinion had steadfastly refused to accept as a politically viable proposition was elevated to the position of a cardinal principle of a political settlement with the Tamils.

When President Jayewardene returned home it soon became evident to him that there was little support in the Cabinet for the terms of the settlement incorporated in 'Annexure C'. He called a conference—the All Party Conference (APC)—to discuss this, among other proposals. The discussions began in January 1984. The UNP's election manifesto for the general election of 1977 had made reference to such a conference to seek a resolution of the island's ethnic conflicts, but once in office there was marked preference for bilateral negotiations with the TULF. Now the scope of participation was widened to include not merely political parties but also representatives of religious groups, including representatives of the *sangha* (the Buddhist order). The *sangha* were generally hardline opponents of all schemes of devolution. The SLFP, the principal opposition party, could not be persuaded to participate in the discussions of the conference.

While the absence of the SLFP deprived the APC of some of its political credibility, the fact that all other parties—including the TULF and the Marxist parties, were participants—encouraged hopes of a compromise settlement being reached. Parathasarathy was in the island during some of these discussions and was able to meet some of the delegates informally. He was encouraged to talk to the *sangha* representatives and did so but was unable to dispel the suspicions they had of him and the proposals with which he was associated. The discussions at the APC continued over most of 1984. It became clear that 'Annexure C' would have to be jettisoned. Instead, a consensus was reached on the crucially important issue of the range of powers to be devolved to regional bodies— the District Development Councils. The *sangha* representatives accepted the need for a second tier of government something they had been unwilling to do up to that time. Nevertheless, they were still reluctant to commit themselves to. a system of provincial councils. Much progress was achieved in regard to other controversial issues such as language policy. The government published an elaborate legislative framework based on the consensus reached at the APC—this included a scheme for a second chamber—as the basis of a settlement.

In the meantime that hardy perennial in Indo-Sri Lankan discord over the last five decades—the political status of Indians resident and working in Sri Lanka—was well on the way to amicable settlement in .the post-1977 period through the operation of the democratic political process in Sri Lanka.[14] One of the more fruitful results of the APC of 1984 was the decision that 94,000 stateless persons—Indian plantation workers—be granted Sri Lankan citizenship. This recommendation was accepted in principle by the government. Legislation for this purpose was ready in 1986-7 and approved by Parliament (through the Grant of Citizenship to Stateless Persons Act of No. 39 of 1988). With its adoption, plantation workers of Indian extraction fell into two clear categories: Sri Lankan citizens, and those with Indian citizenship but resident in the island for the duration of their working lives.

Quite clearly, from August 1983, the debate on devolution in Sri Lanka had an Indian dimension. Partly this sprang from initiatives taken from India; partly it stemmed from the TULF's near-total reliance on Delhi for extracting the best deal possible from the Sri Lankan government. The TULF's reliance on the extract from Cleghorn's Minute—referred to in chapter four—in support of its claims was at last made explicit, in their letter dated 1 December 1985 to Prime Minister Rajiv Gandhi of India. That document contained a section with the subtitle 'the Integrity of the Tamil Homeland'. An extract from it is quoted below.

> The Northern and Eastern Provinces have been traditionally recognized as Tamil-speaking areas from the days of British rule. This was the position at the time of the British conquest of the Maritime Provinces of Ceylon. Sir [sic] Hugh Cleghorn in a report to the Colonial Office in 1799 stated as follows:
>
> Two different nations, from a very ancient period, have divided the Island. First, the Sinhalese in its southern and western parts, from the river Walawe to that of Chilaw; and secondly, the Malabars in the Northern and Eastern Districts (Malabars is used to refer to the Tamils).

This letter was written, as we shall later see in this present chapter, during negotiations for a political settlement of Sri Lanka's ethnic conflict then being conducted, in the wake of the disturbances of 1983, through the mediation of the Indian government and was clearly aimed at influencing the Indian government's policies. At that time the Indian government was engaged in the application of diplomatic and political pressure on behalf of the Tamils of Sri Lanka for a more thoroughgoing scheme of decentralization and devolution of power than that introduced in the island in 1980.

The problem at this stage was the unit of devolution, which had been the district since the decentralization exercise of 1980 and indeed in all political negotiations on devolution of power since the early 1960s. The upshot of India's mediatory effort was the presentation of a set of proposals by the Sri Lankan government for a radical restructuring of Sri Lanka's administrative system, in which the key feature was a system of provincial councils, nine in all, based on the provinces of British times but modelled as regards their legislative powers and administrative authority on the states of the Indian union, with the significant difference that the Sri Lankan provincial councils would operate within the framework of the country's constitutionally-entrenched unitary system.

One of the most controversial features of this endeavour to reshape the structure of the Sri Lankan polity in the 1980s was the attempt to create a supra-provincial regional unit by the fusion of, or a linkage between, the Northern and Eastern Provinces. The pressure for this came from the TULF and various other Tamil separatist groups, in the aftermath of the riots of 1983, and was a revival of a concept of regionalism introduced into the national political debate by the Federal Party in 1956-7. The Bandaranaike government of that latter period had agreed to this but the storm of opposition that erupted from within and outside the government compelled a hasty— and indeed ignominious—withdrawal of the offer. When a proposal to create a regional unit encompassing the Northern and Eastern Provinces was introduced by the TULF in late 1983 it immediately won the backing of the Indian government. As in 1956-7 so in 1983-4, the Sri Lankan government found itself hastily abandoning plans it may have had to consider this demand, once it became evident that there were divisions within the Cabinet on it, and almost unanimous—and vehement—opposition to it from the principal opposition party and other Sinhalese groups, not to mention powerful sections of the government.

The TULF's letter to Rajiv Gandhi of 1 December 1985 brought up once again the equivocal concept of the 'Tamil-speaking peoples' in which the Muslims, as a Tamil-speaking group, were involuntarily yoked to the Tamils. The TULF argued that in the Eastern Province

> 75 per cent of the population have Tamil as their mother tongue [and in] the combined Northern and

Eastern Provinces the Tamil-speaking people form over 86 per cent of the population.

From that specious piece of statistical information they proceeded to invoke the Indian experience in support of the claim for a Tamil homeland encompassing the Northern and Eastern Provinces:

> In the same way that India has solved its multilingual problem by creating linguistic states the Tamil linguistic area, i.e., the Northern and Eastern Provinces should be made into one unit.

THE EASTERN PROVINCE: 'THE TRADITIONAL HOMELANDS'

From the early 1980s to the present day, the fate of the multi-ethnic Eastern Province has been at the core of the separatist agitation of the Tamils. The Eastern Province, whether in the form it was in the period 1832 to 1873, or in its present form, consists of territories which were integral parts of the Kandyan kingdom at the time it was ceded to the British in 1815. Most of the eastern seaboard had never been a part of the shortlived Jaffna kingdom. At the height of the latter's power part of its southern boundary had extended close to Trincomalee, but this had been only for a very brief period. Nor was the Batticaloa area part of the Jaffna kingdom.[14] Indeed, not only was the eastern seaboard part of the Kandyan kingdom, but also for much of the 19th and the early 20th century, the Tamil population there was concentrated in and around Trincomalee and the Batticaloa lagoon. These littoral settlements were, as in the 18th century, in the nature of a thin strip of habitation confronting two powerful forces of nature, the sea on the one side, and the forbidding wilderness of the almost impenetrable forests of the hinterland. The overwhelming difficulties of access by land intensified the isolation of this region; land communications improved only in the late 19th century, and the early 20th century.

More important, these settlements had a large Muslim population. The littoral regions of the present Eastern Province are the home of about a third of Sri Lanka's Muslims. Some of them are descended from immigrants from the coasts of South India, but a substantial number, perhaps the large majority, are descended from Muslim refugees from Sri Lanka's own west coast fleeing the persecution of the Portuguese and afforded a safe haven on the east coast and elsewhere by Sinhalese kings of the period. While they were, and still are largely, a Tamil-speaking group, they maintain an identity distinct from the Tamils, through their religion.

In the 1880s, Sir Ponnambalam Ramanathan, a distinguished Tamil lawyer-politician caused a stir by arguing that the Muslims were, in the main, Tamils who had converted to Islam. Spokesmen for the Muslims passionately rejected this and responded by reasserting their Arab or Indo-Arab origins, and by insisting that their Islamic faith separated them from the Tamils with whom they shared only a common language. Echoes of this controversy reverberated in the aftermath of the language controversies of the 1950s when the concept of the 'Tamil-speaking peoples' of Sri Lanka became part of the political jargon of those tumultuous times. The Muslims rejected this concept then as they do now—as they did at the tail-end of the 19th century—because of its implications of a subordinate role for them *vis-à-vis* the Tamils, and the assumption of a Tamil wardship over them.

Nevertheless, we have seen TULF politicians—and radical groups to the left of them—persist in treating the Muslims as part of the Tamil-speaking population, especially in claims for the 'traditional homelands' of the Tamils encompassing the Northern and Eastern Provinces. And this despite the frequency of violent clashes in recent years between the Tamils and Muslims in the Eastern Province (and in Mannar in the Northern Province where there was till 1990 a large Muslim presence). Islamic fundamentalism which emerged as a potent force in the politics of the

Muslims in the Eastern Province in the late 1980s has sprung up largely as a reaction against the political pressure on the Muslims from Tamil separatist groups operating there.

The interior of the Eastern Province was sparsely populated and contained Sinhalese settlements in *purana* (i.e. traditional) villages with its people eking out a hard existence in this forested region. These Sinhalese settlements, although smaller in population than either the Tamil or Muslim ones, and few and far between, were scattered throughout the Trincomalee and Batticaloa districts. (The present Ampara district of the Eastern Province was created only in 1960). Writing in 1921, S.C. Canagaratnam, a Tamil official of the *Kachcheri* (secretariat) at Batticaloa, observed that:

> One of the saddest features in the history of the [Batticaloa] district is the decay of the Sinhalese population in the West and South. At one time there were flourishing and populous Sinhalese villages here, as is evidenced by the ruins and remains dotted about this part of the country.'[15]

Canagaratnam also made the point that

> The whole district formed part of the Kandyan Provinces when the Sinhalese Kings held sway and Batticaloa was then known as Puliyanduwa.[16]

It is precisely in this part of the present Eastern Province that the massive multipurpose Gal-Oya project, which the Federal Party pointedly refers to in its political resolutions of the 1950s as a prime example of state sponsored settlement of Tamil homelands, was established. This was the first new major irrigation project and settlement scheme after independence, and the first new major scheme since the 11th century, the last great age of Sinhalese irrigation engineering. C.W. Nicholas's pathbreaking monograph on the *Historical Topography of Ancient and Medieval Ceylon*[17] makes specific reference to the Gal-Oya scheme, and shows it as occupying for the greater part the ancient and important territorial division called *Dighavapi-Mandala* or *Dighavapi-Rata*. Gal-Oya and most of the other major colonization schemes of the Eastern Province are located in areas which in 1921—and at the time of the census of that year—were either the sites of remnant Sinhalese villages or were covered by forests. These settlements had survived several centuries of war and invasion, of pestilence and privation, and the ravages of nature in the form of droughts, floods and cyclones, till they were revitalized in the years after independence as peasant 'colonies,' that is to say village settlements of the Gal-Oya scheme. Nor are the Sinhalese the sole beneficiaries of this scheme. Despite the large number of Sinhalese peasants who were settled in the 'colonies' established under the Gal-Oya project, the then existing Muslim and Tamil village settlements of the Eastern Provinces more than held their own in regard to population growth and agricultural productivity. Indeed, 30 years after the Gal-Oya project was initiated, the Sinhalese are very much a minority of the population there, as shown below by the official census of 1981.

Figure IV

	Sinhalese	Tamils	Muslims
Left Bank System	61,451	42,114	18,200
Right Bank System	12,084	5,975	19,436
River Division	3,228	41,085	110,119

Furthermore, and here we quote the geographer Professor G.H. Peiris,

The sparsely settled interior of the Eastern Province of Sri Lanka was not a hinterland of the settlement cluster of the littoral and . . . there is no empirical basis for a theoretical assertion that because there was a numerical preponderance of the Tamils in the coastal areas, the inland areas, regardless of the traditional rights of other ethnic groups, should.form a 'traditional hinterland' of the Tamil areas.[18]

The 'traditional homelands' of the Tamils theory has, as we have seen, several versions. One of these as propounded in the TULF's election manifesto of July 1977 speaks of these regions as 'exclusively the homeland of the Tamils'. This claim to exclusivity has caused profound concern among other ethnic groups in the country, indeed more concern than other variants of this theory because of its implications: nearly 30 per cent of the land area of the country, and over half of its coastline with its marine resources to be reserved for a minority who constitute only 12.6 per cent of the island's population in their entirety. The share of the national resources thus claimed is grossly disproportionate to their numbers *vis-à-vis* the rest of the population, and even more so when two other factors are considered.

Tamil politicians and publicists who protest against alleged Sinhalese encroachments into the 'traditional homelands' of the Tamils have seldom shown any sensitivity to the grievances of the Kandyan Sinhalese over the massive presence of Indian—almost entirely Tamil—plantation workers, a process of demographic transformation which is historically of very recent origin, and one which converted parts of the core area of the old Kandyan kingdom into a polyethnic community; in some areas, for example in the Nuwara Eliya district, the Indian Tamils now very nearly outnumber the local Sinhalese population. Tamil politicians of the Federal Party and the present TULF see no contradiction in advocating the preservation of the 'traditional homelands' of the Tamils from Sinhalese encroachment while at the same time championing the cause of Indian Tamils settled in Sinhalese areas by British planters, meeting a demand for cheap, regimented labour on the plantations which the local population was unwilling or reluctant to meet. Population increase through immigration of Indian labour was actually greater than natural increase of population during some decades of the late 19th and early 20th century. Most, if not all, of these immigrants moved into the Kandyan areas to the tea and rubber plantations there.

Figure V

NATURAL AND MIGRATION INCREASES, 1871-1946

Period	Inter-censal increase	Births	Deaths	Natural increase	Migration increase
1871-81	359,358	708,150	588,358	119,792	239,566
1881-91	248,051	836,636	692,376	144,260	103,791
1891-1901	588,165	1,22041	896,635	225,406	332,759
1901-11	540,396	1,459,618	1,103,471	356,147	184,249
1911-21	392,256	1,648,066	1,328,656	319,410	72,846
1921-31	808,266	1,946,115	1,289,165	656,990	151,276
1931-46	1,350,468	3,209,520	1,928,604	1,280,916	69,552

(Source: *Census Reports*, 1871, 1881, 1891, 1901, 1911, 1921, 1931 and 1946)

It is clear from Figure V that with the exception of periods 1871-81 and 1891-1901, natural increase was the more significant factor in population growth. During 1871-1881 and 1891-1901, increase due to migration exceeded natural increase quite substantially. Since 1911, natural increase accounted for more than 80 per cent of the entire inter-censal increase, and after 1931 for more than 90 per cent. Immigration of unskilled labour from India came to an end by 1939-40.

Next, there is the demographic reality of a vital Tamil presence in other parts of the island. 29.2 per cent of the Sri Lanka Tamils lived outside the Northern and Eastern Provinces in 1971; this figure had increased to 32.0 per cent at the 1981 census. The Tamil areas of the north are poor in economic resources, and since the late 19th century have exported labour, generally skilled labour and professionals to the Sinhalese areas and especially to Colombo city and its suburbs. There are, in fact, more

D. S. Senanayake, Sri Lanka's first
post-independence Prime Minister.

S. W. R. D. Bandaranaike, Sri Lanka's
fourth Prime Minister. His period of
office (1956-1959) saw the beginnings
of Sri Lanka's ethnic conflict.

G. G. Ponnambalam, Tamil Congress leader, and Cabinet Minister (1948-1953).

S. J. V. Chelvanayakam, founder of the Federal Party and founder President of the Tamil United Liberation Front.

Mrs. Sirimavo Bandaranaike, Prime Minister, 1960-65 and 1970-77. Her two periods in office saw an aggravation of the island's ethnic conflict.

Tamil politicians perform satyagraha on Galle Face green, June 1956, against changes in language policy. S.J.V. Chelvanayakam is seen (second from left, front row), as also C. Suntheralingam, on early idealogue of separatism (fourth from left, front row).

S. J. V. Chelvanayakam and his political associates in discussions with Bandaranaike, 1957. These discussions culminated in the abortive Bandaranaike-Chelvanayakam pact.

Sinhalese tearing Tamil lettering in government-owned motor bus, Colombo 1958.

Tamil protesters obstruct police jeep during satyagraha in Jaffna, 1961.

Navy check point in Jaffna, during satyagraha, 1961.

S. J. V. Chelvanayakam and others in protest march, Trincomalee, 1961.

The Roman Catholic church in Jaffna was seen to be sympathetic to extremist and violent separatist groups, especially the LTTE or Tamil Tigers . From *The Island,* 6 December 1982.

A popular perception in Sri Lanka of the links between the TULF, the Tamil Tigers and Tamil Nadu. From *The Island,* 1 July 1983.

J.R. Jayewardene, Prime Minister, 1977-78, Executive President, 1978-88.

V. Prabhakaran, LTTE leader, who first rose to prominence in the period after 1982.

R. Premadasa, Prime Minister, 1978-88, Executive President, 1988-93.

S. Thondaman, leader of the Indian Tamils in Sri Lanka; Cabinet Minister, from 1978 to the present day.

Riots of 1983. Flash point—the Borella cemetery, Colombo, where the riots of July 1983 began and from where they spread. Police seek in vain to control the crowd.

Arsonists at work, attacking Tamil shops, near Borella, 23 July 1987.

A ravaged building (the former Bristol Hotel) in Fort.

J.R. Jayewardene in offical negotiations with Indian delegation in Colombo, 1985. The Indian delegation was led by R. Bhandari, then Foreign Secretary. Also in the picture are J.N. Dixit, Indian High Commissioner and P. Chidambaram.

Critical of the TULF demand that groups such as the LTTE be included in the proposed Round Table talks. From *The Island,* 11 December 1983.

Undergraduates and others protest Indian air drop of food over Jaffna, May 1987. The protesters had gathered opposite the residence of the Indian High Commissioner in Colombo.

Rajiv Gandhi clarifies India's position on separatism in Sri Lanka to the Tamil Tigers and to the TULF represented by A Amirthalingam. From *The Island,* 28 July 1985.

The signing of the Indo-Sri Lanka Accord, July 1987. Indian politicians standing in first row include, P. Chidambaram, K. Natwar Singh and P. V. Narasimha Rao.

Naval rating attacks Rajiv Gandhi at Guard of Honour prior to his departure after signing of Indo-Sri Lanka Accord.

Officers of Indian Peace-Keeping Force (IPKF) at formal token surrender of arms by Tamil separatist groups, Jaffna, 5 August 1987.

IPKF troops in Jaffna, searching a house.

President Premadasa in discussions with LTTE, 1989. The LTTE delegation includes S. Balasingham, the LTTE idealogue and his Australian wife.

President Premadasa with LTTE delegation.

Signing of formal agreement between Sri Lanka and India, on departure of the IPKF, 19 September 1989, by L.L. Mehrohtra, Indian High Commissioner, and Bernard Tillekeratne, Sri Lanka's Foreign Secretary.

Formal departure of IPKF from Sri Lanka through Trincomalee. Ranjan Wijeratne, Sri Lanka's Foreign Minister and Indian High Commissioner, L.L. Mehrotra are in the front row.

M.H.M. Ashroff, leader of the Sri Lanka Muslim Congress.

Mosque at Kattankudy, Batticaloa. Scenes of massacre of Muslims by LTTE, June 1990.

Ethnic cleansing: Muslim refugees from Mannar leave by boat, October 1990.

Muslim refugees from Mannar.

Four member government delegation of officials at talks with the LTTE in Jaffna, early 1995.

Anuruddha Ratwatte, in military uniform, with Sri Lanka troops in Jaffna.

Mrs Chandrika Kumaratunga, Executive President.

Bomb attack on Colombo's financial centre, 30 January 1996.

Tamils in Colombo and its suburbs than in the town of Jaffna.

From the 1930s, when the regeneration of the dry zone of the ancient Sinhalese kingdoms, the core of which lies in the present North Central Province, and its peripheral regions, began on a systematic basis, the Tamils who lived to the north and north-east looked upon this process of economic development with a mixture of fear and anxiety. The ebbing of the jungle tide that had submerged this region for centuries, and the moving frontier of Sinhalese settlement represented, or were seen to represent, a potent threat to the majority status the Tamils enjoyed in the north and some parts of the north-east of the island.

These fears and anxieties became more pronounced after independence and lie at the heart of the mythmaking connected with the political pressure for a demarcation of a region or regions as the 'traditional homelands' of the Tamils. That pressure ignores the facts of history as well as the hard economic reality that the forests of these regions could not serve forever as a buffer between the two ethnic groups, the one—the Tamils—anxious to preserve their ethnic dominance in the periphery of these regions, and the other moving in to do battle with the forests and the anopheles mosquito in a historic return to the heartland of the hydraulic civilizations of old. Resources of land and water are scarce in all the dry zone regions and the preservation of an uninhabited no man's land in the face of unprecedented population pressure is as unreasonable as it is inequitable. Moreover, as Professor G.H. Peiris points out, while 'state sponsorship' has 'admittedly been a vital element in land settlement schemes', this was necessarily so because such schemes

> . . . were meant for the poorest segment of the population—the landless peasantry. But neither in this nor in state responses to . . . encroachment [on state lands] do we find any evidence of discrimination against the Sri Lanka Tamils.[19]

INDIAN MEDIATION IN SRI LANKA, 1984-7

The discussions on the mechanics of devolution and the future, if not fate, of the Eastern Province took place against the backdrop of an increasing frequency of guerrilla attacks and terrorist incidents in the north of the island, and the extension of these into the eastern seaboard. The guerrilla forces were now much larger, much better trained (the training was largely in India), and much better equipped than they were before. The training and equipping of guerrilla forces in India had begun in the early 1980s, well before the riots of July 1983, but there is no mistaking that this process was intensified as a result of the violence inflicted on the Tamils in July 1983. Tamilnadu had always been a ready haven for these guerrilla forces, but now the support they received was strengthened immeasurably, as was the extent of the protection they enjoyed. Their morale was stronger, and their motivation keener after these riots than before, and by the end of 1983 they demonstrated a greater willingness to take risks, and greater resourcefulness and daring in their attacks on the security forces and on carefully chosen targets. Until about the end of 1985 they were in many ways better equipped than the small security services stationed in the north of the island.

The first reports on these training camps and 'bases' located in India appeared in western newspapers in April 1984, at much the same time that comprehensive coverage of them appeared in *India Today*.[20] More solid evidence of the use of Indian soil by Sri Lankan guerrillas and terrorists was forthcoming when a section of the Madras International Airport was accidentally blown up on 2 August 1984 by bombs due for transfer to Sri Lanka for the destruction of aircraft of the Sri Lankan national airline at Colombo International Airport: the explosion killed over two dozen Sri Lankan passengers in the transit lounge of the Madras airport on this occasion. The bombs were planted by Sri Lankan Tamils. Some of the perpetrators of this outrage were arrested but a few of them escaped from India—with the connivance of Indian officials—and at least one of them secured refugee status in London! A few years later—in 1992—K. Mohandas, the Deputy Inspector General of Police (Intelligence) of the Tamilnadu police, revealed that a 'senior policy maker' in Delhi had indicated to him,

> that we have a duty to protect the Sri Lankan militants and that, if we continue along the known lines of investigation in the airport blast case, the Sri Lanka government would take advantage of it and proclaim to the world the existence of militant training camps in India which had officially been denied by New Delhi.[21]

The Indian government generally refused to acknowledge the existence of training camps and facilities for Sri Lankan Tamil guerrillas and terrorist groups on Indian soil.[22] Instead, it sought to divert attention from Sri Lankan charges and protests about these with counter-charges of human rights violations in Sri Lanka, attributing these quite explicitly to the lack of discipline among the Sri Lankan security forces. In so doing they met an embarrassing fact with a half-truth.

The fact is that at this time Sri Lankan Tamil guerrillas and terrorists operated in Tamilnadu with a freedom and publicity for which the only parallel is the PLO and its various factions in the Arab world. Quite apart from the public support they enjoyed in such large measure in Tamilnadu, they engaged in fund-raising drives at public meetings in other parts of India as well, in particular Bombay.[23] This double standard on separatism and terrorism—to crush separatism ruthlessly when it is seen to pose a palpable threat to the Indian polity as was done in 1984 in the Punjab through Operation Blue Star, to protest vigorously at the tolerance accorded to Indian extremists and terrorist groups operating in the western world (the Sikhs in Britain, Canada and the United States for instance), and yet to feign ignorance of the existence of training camps and 'bases' for Tamil guerrillas and terrorist groups on Indian soil—was one of the great stumbling blocks to cordial relations between India and Sri Lanka during this period and on to 1987 or later.

India's policy in regard to the internationalization of Sri Lanka's ethnic conflict was a two-pronged affair. While discussions and negotiations with the Sri Lankan government on a settlement of differences between the government and the Tamil minority were proceeding, with India in her role of mediator, India was using its formidable diplomatic resources through its High Commissions and Embassies in the West—in Ottawa, London, and Washington, in particular—to accuse the Sri Lankan government and its armed forces of violations of human rights in attacks on Tamil civilians, in the course of, or in the wake of, security operations in the north and east of the island. At the United Nations Organization, Indian delegates—generally a Tamilnadu politician (a Tamilnadu minister in 1983)—would raise the Sri Lankan issue in the course of debates there.[24] The situation was even more favorable to this diplomatic offensive at the United Nations Office in Geneva, and the sessions of the Human Rights Commission where the Indian representative would either raise the Sri Lankan issue on his own, or more often back countries such as Argentina (smarting under Sri Lanka's support of Britain in the Falklands war) and Norway in raising the issue officially. Since some of the western nations—the United States and Great Britain—were represented on the Commission by non-governmental organizations, and there was in addition the conspicuous presence of Human Rights groups, Sri Lanka was under much greater pressure in Geneva than in New York.[25]

In the meantime the TULF leadership was living in self-imposed exile in Madras as guests of the Tamilnadu government. This was quite apart from more radical Tamil activists who also lived in Madras and conducted their clandestine operations and political campaigns through Madras and India, linking up with well-funded diaspora groups living in the west. These latter groups sought and received political support from Indian Embassies and High Commissions, in Washington for instance, and Ottawa, not to mention London.[26]

Then again, while persistently ignoring the provision of training facilities to Tamil activists in Tamilnadu (and elsewhere in India) and the transfer of weapons from India to Jaffna, the Indian government under Indira Gandhi used pressure on western powers to prevent the sale of sophisticated weaponry to the Sri Lankan forces. Sri Lanka purchased weapons from Pakistan and the People's Republic of China; Pakistan also provided much of the training, and in addition Sri Lanka turned to Israel for assistance in training its forces.

The TULF's sudden decision in late December 1984 to announce a rejection of the proposals placed before the APC has been the subject of much speculation. And so for that matter was the government's decision to react so quickly to this decision and to withdraw its support for a set of proposals that had been so carefully developed over two months of hard bargaining. The explanations suggested for this latter decision have focussed on the exigencies of local politics. But one explanation, and a more plausible one, is that it was a response to Mrs Gandhi's assassination, and a calculated move based on the assumption that a fresh start was possible under a new Indian Prime Minister who would be less committed to supporting the TULF.

Rajiv Gandhi made a positively encouraging impression on the Sri Lankan politicians and diplomats who met him in the early months of his prime-ministership. Among his first decisions on Sri Lankan affairs was the appointment of Romesh Bhandari, India's Foreign Secretary, as principal mediator in place of G. Parathasarathy, a move that was clearly intended to signal a search for new policies in a more cordial atmosphere.

At the time Romesh Bhandari took over as India's principal negotiator on Sri Lankan affairs, relations between the two countries had been soured by misunderstandings and misapprehensions on both sides. On the Indian side there was the feeling that President Jayewardene had not tried hard enough to win support in Sri Lanka for the agreements between him and the Indian government negotiated through G. Parathasarathy, over the last months of 1983. As for Sri Lanka, Mrs Gandhi was seen—and known—to be encouraging and manipulating Tamil separatist activists living in India to further India's strategic advantage in its quest for regional dominance. In particular, her (and the Indian government's) failure to acknowledge the existence of 'bases' and training facilities for Sri Lankan Tamil separatists in Tamilnadu and elsewhere was viewed as a cynical exploitation of separatist agitation in a neighbouring country. Suspicion of her objectives in her mediation in the Sri Lankan conflict was compounded by Parathasarathy's patent failure to distance himself significantly from the importunate TULF to give greater credibility to his role as mediator.

When President Jayewardene met Prime Minister Rajiv Gandhi in New Delhi in June 1985, for the first time, their discussions took place in a greatly improved atmosphere. This was followed by the despatch of Bhandari to Colombo for talks with the Sri Lankan President. The talks resulted in a major breakthrough with the latter being persuaded to let his government begin talks with the several Tamil separatist groups, who were engaged in violent confrontation with Sri Lankan security forces, in addition to the TULF, the mainstream Tamil party, with whom the government had negotiated hitherto. Up to this time the government had refused to talk to the other separatist activists on the grounds that doing so would give them an unwarranted legitimacy. The fact is however, that the TULF was rapidly losing ground to their younger rivals, and the President's agreement to engage in discussions with the latter was a belated recognition of political realities.[27]

The increase in the number of spokesmen for the Tamil minority had some predictable consequences, beginning naturally enough with a struggle among them for dominance, and a quest for the position of sole spokesman. The TULF, the most moderate of the Tamil groups, found itself edged out of any position of influence. Instead, the lead went at various stages to other groups, with a bewildering range of acronyms, People's Liberation Organization of Tamil Eelam (PLOTE), the Tamil Eelam Liberation Organization (TELO), the Liberation Tigers of Tamil Eelam (LTTE), and Eelam People's Revolutionary Liberation Front (EPRLF) all of whom were assiduously cultivated by the Research and Analysis Wing of the Indian Prime Minister's office. This Indian equivalent of the CIA, better known by its acronym, RAW, provided Tamil groups located in India with arms and arms training with the knowledge, if not under the aegis, of the Indian government. The TELO group was its favourite. The LTTE eventually pushed ahead to a position of dominance largely because of its strong and expanding base in Jaffna. The three leaders of the strongest of these groups, Prabhakaran of the LTTE, Uma Maheswaran of the TELO, and Sri Sabaratnam of the EPRLF, were soon engaged in a bitter and increasingly violent rivalry for the position of principal spokesman of the Tamil cause. Prabhakaran, the most astute of them all, and the most violent, eventually won the day.

Two sets of talks between representatives of the Sri Lanka government and the various Tamil groups claiming to speak on behalf of their ethnic group, took place in July and August 1985 at Thimpu, the capital of Bhutan. These talks did not yield any positive results, but Bhandari used the opportunity they provided to continue negotiations with the Sri Lankan delegation in New Delhi. These talks were more fruitful. The new agenda for ethnic reconciliation which emerged from them yielded a framework for a realistic devolution of power in Sri Lanka intended to meet some of the principal Tamil demands.

The draft accord, which came to be known in official circles as the Delhi Accord of August 1985, was based on the consensus reached on that occasion and the TULF's views were part of that consensus. One of the most significant features of this meticulously crafted agreement was that the unit of devolution was to be a province, no longer a district. Secondly, the powers to be devolved on these provincial units were much wider than those offered earlier by the Sri Lanka government in discussions with Indian mediators and Tamil representatives. The complex new structures agreed upon constituted a major concession on the part of the Sri Lankan government to the demands of the Tamils of the north and east of the island. Initialled on 30 August this draft accord became the basis of all future negotiations between the two governments on Sri Lanka's ethnic problems concerning the Tamil minority.

At the time the Delhi Accord was initialled Rajiv Gandhi was riding on the crest of a wave of popularity in India. The political settlement Bhandari had begun negotiating in Sri Lanka on behalf of the Indian government was actually the third in a series initiated in the early months of Rajiv Gandhi's prime-ministership. The first and second had been on the Punjab and Assam respectively in which the young Indian Prime Minister had been the principal negotiator. The Punjab Accord had been signed on 25 July 1985; in less than three weeks thereafter the Accord on Assam had been signed; in less than six weeks after the signing of the Punjab Accord, the Delhi Accord with the Sri Lanka government had been initialled.

The actual signing of the Accord which Bhandari hoped would crown his mediatory efforts confronted a major obstacle in the reluctance, if not refusal, of the other Tamil groups who were represented at Thimpu to give their consent to it. The longer they held out the more difficult it became for the TULF to publicly commit itself to an agreement in the formulation of which they had been consulted and to which they had given their concurrence in Delhi.

In December 1985, the TULF withdrew its support for

the Delhi Accord under pressure from their more aggressive rivals, in particular, the LTTE. By the time Bhandari left office in early 1986 only the two governments remained committed to the agreement reached and initialled in Delhi.

Meanwhile, sporadic outbursts of ethnic violence, especially in the north and east of the island, and clashes between the security forces and Tamil guerrillas and terrorist groups disturbed the peace of the island. Greatly improved relations between the two countries did not extend to any serious efforts on the part of the Indian government to prevent Indian territory being used by Tamil guerrillas and terrorists for attacks on a friendly neighbour, much less to close down the training facilities and camps. Rajiv Gandhi, so much less dependent on the southern Indian political base than his mother, and intent on taking a more evenhanded approach than she did to the problems posed by Sri Lanka's ethnic conflicts, found his options more limited than he would have liked them to be. The constraint lay in the ethnic politics of Tamilnadu. The Tamil guerrillas and terrorist groups continued to have training facilities and bases there.

The Tamil separatist groups in Sri Lanka all had their supporters among the political parties of Tamilnadu, the government and opposition parties alike, each of whom was determined to demonstrate that its commitment to the Sri Lankan Tamil cause was stronger than the other's. In locking themselves into the politics of Sri Lankan Tamil separatist agitation, they were also drawn into the fierce factionalism that was part of the Sri Lankan Tamil political scene. None of the Tamilnadu political parties was able to keep the peace among the rival Sri Lankan Tamil groups whose internecine warfare often took more Tamil lives than their frequent clashes with the Sri Lankan forces. Tamilnadu continued to serve three purposes: as a sanctuary; as a base for training and supply of arms; and as a source of funds. Thanks to the support they had in and from Tamilnadu, the Tamil separatist groups, and especially the LTTE and its ally the EROS group, had become a formidable guerrilla force, much stronger than their Indian mentors thought they would ever be.

The LTTE was also helped by a decision taken by the Sri Lanka government in July, 1985, as part of an understanding reached with India, that its forces in the Jaffna peninsula would be kept within their barracks or camps. Originally, this arrangement was to last for two months, but it was later extended, in response to Indian pressure, for three months. The LTTE took advantage of this to mine all the roads leading out of the camps and proceeded thereafter to barricade them. These makeshift barricades were converted into concrete bunkers. The result was that the LTTE established effective control over the town of Jaffna if not the Jaffna peninsula itself, since the Sri Lanka army's movements were seriously hampered thereafter by these barricades. As a result, the units of Sri Lanka army stationed in the fort of Jaffna could only be supplied by air.

Emboldened by this shift in the military balance, the LTTE embarked on a vigorous campaign against the Sri Lankan forces, and also increased its attacks on softer targets; and also engaged in a ruthless programme of eliminating its Tamil rivals. They seldom directed their attacks against the security forces in open confrontations. When they did so their attacks were generally easily repulsed. But one of the consequences of such confrontations was that quite often civilians were killed, either caught in the crossfire or—on occasion—by soldiers on the rampage seeking to avenge the loss of their comrades in landmine blasts. The LTTE, for its part, began to choose easier and softer targets such as an attack on the city of Anuradhapura in May 1985 in which 150 civilians were killed, or more frequently thereafter on Sinhalese peasants in the remoter areas of the north-central and eastern regions. These attacks became a major political embarrassment to the government.

The internecine warfare between the separatist groups

reached its peak between September 1985 and April 1986. On 1 September 1985 the LTTE assassinated two TULF stalwarts—two former MPs—who, unlike the bulk of their colleagues, had continued to live in Jaffna. It was a move designed to compel the TULF in Madras and elsewhere to toe the line, that is to say, to refrain from signing the Delhi Accord.

The opposition to the signing or initialling of the accords Rajiv Gandhi had negotiated had come very quickly; indeed, in less than a month after he had signed the accord with Rajiv Gandhi, Sant Harchand Singh Longowal the Akali Sikh leader, had been assassinated. The killing of the two TULF MPs in Jaffna on 1 September had followed shortly thereafter, effectively putting an end to Rajiv Gandhi's hopes that the signing of the Delhi Accord could be achieved in a few weeks, a month or two at most.[28] In the event it was to take a full two years before an Accord on Sri Lanka was signed.

The delay is explained by the deteriorating situation in Jaffna which compelled the Sri Lanka government to divert an increasing proportion of its annual budget to the expansion and equipping of its armed forces. Along with it there was an escalation of military action against the Tamil separatist groups in the north and east of the island.[29] The Sri Lankan armed forces were now better equipped and better trained than before. As we have seen, much of the training was done in Pakistan, while small groups of Israelis and British mercenaries honed the skills of special counter-terrorist units in the army and police.

As clashes between the security forces and the Tamil separatist activists became more frequent and casualties increased in number, India's mediatory role gave way to a return to the Indira Gandhi policy of a diplomatic offensive against Sri Lanka. Thus, a propaganda campaign was launched through its Embassies and High Commissions abroad, accusing the government of human rights violations, while Sri Lankan and Indian diplomats clashed at the UN in New York and Geneva, all part of a policy of 'moral' sanctions aimed at persuading Sri Lanka to return to the bargaining table.[30] The Indian Embassy in Washington and the High Commissions in Ottawa and London, in the meantime, continued to be centres of support for Tamil separatist groups operating in those countries.

Had the Indian government been more sensitive to its Sri Lankan counterpart's difficulties, and made some unambiguous and noticeable effort to stop the use of Indian territory by the LTTE and others for their military activities, there may have been greater political support within Sri Lanka for a resumption of negotiations with the Tamil groups, or greater readiness to stop military action against the LTTE. The Sri Lankan government had treated the Delhi Accord initialled on 30 April 1985 as an important step forward in reaching a settlement with the Tamil minority, and described it as 'a reasonable basis for negotiation and settlement'. Neither the TULF nor the other Tamil groups had responded positively to the proposals in the Delhi Accord.

It took several months of negotiations with them by Indian officials before the Indian government could send an official delegation to Sri Lanka for further discussions on possible adjustments and modifications of the Delhi Accord. By the time the delegation arrived in Sri Lanka Bhandari had retired. The delegation was led by P. Chidambaram (currently India's Finance Minister), then a young (40 years at the time) Tamil who aspired to a Congress-based leadership of Tamilnadu, and Natwar Singh, Rajiv Gandhi's Minister of State for External Affairs. The delegation arrived in Colombo on 30 April 1986 and held very intensive talks over the next five days. For the first time since Indian mediation began in late 1983 the principal negotiators for the Indian government were politicians and not bureaucrats or diplomats. On the departure of the Chidambaram delegation on 4 May it was announced that 'the Sri Lanka government had agreed to make further concessions beyond the terms of the Delhi Accord'. The decisions reached on this occasion were published on 4 May 1986.

Their arrival coincided with the LTTE's massacre of the TELO leaders and the killing of Sri Sabaratnam in the course of this clash.[31] One of the triumvirate of separatist activist leaders had been killed. The LTTE was moving ahead to complete supremacy, in bloody encounters with their rivals which, it is believed, caused as many, if not more, Tamil casualties than clashes with the Sri Lankan security forces.

Bhandari's successor as Foreign Secretary, A.P. Venkateswaran, had much less rapport with Rajiv Gandhi than had Bhandari, and far greater sympathy for the Sri Lankan Tamil cause. He placed his trust in the TULF and virtually pushed them into taking the lead in negotiations with the Sri Lankan government. The TULF leaders living in exile in Madras, were not unwilling to play the role that Venkateswaran had devised for them but they were terrified at the prospect of antagonizing the more aggressive Tamil groups. Venkateswaran called representatives of these latter groups to Delhi and persuaded them to let the TULF take the lead in the discussions with the Sri Lankan government scheduled to be held in Colombo later in the year.[32]

More important, he hit upon the idea of giving the Delhi Accord greater acceptability to the Tamils by using the Indian state system as a model for Sri Lanka's devolutionary schemes. He believed that this subtle, but nonetheless significant, transformation of the devolution package negotiated by Bhandari would appeal to the TULF because it had some features of the Indian federal system. It would also be acceptable to President Jayewardene and his advisers because the central government in India was much more powerful than in most federations. Besides, there was sufficient ambiguity in the refinement of the Delhi Accord to permit bargaining and give and take, in short, to leave room for other adjustments in the course of negotiations.

By the time the TULF arrived in Colombo for negotiations with the Sri Lanka government in June 1986, President Jayewardene had embarked on a new initiative, the Political Parties Conference (PPC), at which the Delhi Accord and the changes in it agreed to by the two governments in April 1986, were to be discussed. Once again the principal opposition party, the SLFP, refused to join the conference, but seven other parties, including the vocal but uninfluential parties of the Marxist Left participated. The TULF joined in the discussions at the Political Parties Conference, but even more important they had no fewer than 37 formal meetings with President Jayewardene and his senior Cabinet Ministers between 13 July and 26 August 1986.

The negotiations between the government of Sri Lanka and the TULF, and the discussions and debates within the conference continued over three months. In general the conference endorsed the proposals submitted for discussion by and through its committees, clarified some complex issues, and identified potential points of difficulty and ambiguities, all of which made it possible to widen the scope of the powers conferred on the provinces in the schemes of devolution submitted for discussion. These modifications and extensions were incorporated in the proposals sent to India in September 1986. They included draft constitutional amendments, a draft Provincial Councils bill, schedules setting out the 'Reserved, Concurrent and Provincial' lists on the sharing of power between the centre and the provinces, as well as detailed memoranda dealing with law and order, land and land settlement and education. Problems relating to land and land settlement, crucially important issues in Sri Lanka's ethnic conflict, had been resolved in 1984. The essence of that agreement was endorsed in the discussions in Colombo in September 1986. The subjects of finance and administration had been discussed in detail but no final agreement was reached. An official statement to this effect was issued by the Sri Lanka government on 26 November 1986. There were no insuperable difficulties in the way of reaching agreement on the financial and administrative aspects of the scheme of devolution that had emerged from the discussions of the PPC.

The real difficulty was that the TULF and the Tamil separatist groups in general continued to press for the creation of a single regional unit encompassing the Northern and Eastern Provinces as a Tamil ethno-region. The Sri Lankan government was unwilling to consider this, much less to concede it, because of its political implications. The opposition to this from large and vocal sections of the Sinhalese would have resulted in an extensive erosion of the government's electoral base, leading in turn to a rapid undermining of its stability.

There was also another problem. Although both governments were anxious to treat the TULF as the main representative of Tamil opinion in Sri Lanka, it was evident that there was more than a touch of unreality in giving them this status. By living in self-imposed exile they had cut themselves off from the Tamil people. The more activist separatist groups and those less hesitant in resorting to violence and terror, in particular the LTTE, had filled the vacuum caused by the TULF's absence. The longer the TULF leadership stayed away from Sri Lanka, the more their chances of a political rehabilitation were reduced to a chimera; indeed they already were something close to that. Thus, the negotiations with them were exercises in futility. The crux of the problem that confronted the two governments was that the LTTE was in no mood to accept anything short of a separate state. Nor were they inclined to respect the new status conferred by the two governments on the TULF.

Throughout the second half of 1986, Indian mediators were engaged in a sustained effort to break the deadlock caused by the TULF's insistence on the creation of a Tamil ethno-region linking the Northern and Eastern Provinces. Venkateswaran came up with a proposal to divide the Eastern Province into three units, one Muslim, one Tamil and one Sinhalese, with the Tamil unit being linked to the Northern Province by a narrow land corridor. When this proposal won no support, least of all from the Tamils, the Indian negotiators prevailed upon the Sri Lankan government to consider the excision of the Sinhalese parliamentary electorate of Ampara from the Batticaloa district of the Eastern Province so that the Tamil ethnic component in that province would reach a level of parity with the other ethnic groups. The LTTE, however, rejected the formula as wholly unacceptable. Nor was the Muslim minority who formed over 40 per cent of the population willing to accept it.[33]

The proposals agreed to in September 1986 formed the basis of negotiations between President Jayewardene and Prime Minister Rajiv Gandhi when they met in Bangalore at the summit of the South Asian Association for Regional Co-operation (SAARC) on 17 and 18 November. Indian officials were generally unhappy at letting Rajiv Gandhi get involved in the minutae of the negotiation process with the much more experienced Sri Lankan President whose grasp of the principles and details were so much greater than his. They had succeeded up to this point in keeping the negotiations under their control, but now they could only watch, apprehensively, as the two heads of government began and continued the discussions on their own. These heads of government negotiations were accompanied and followed by discussions at a ministerial level.

Rajiv Gandhi and his advisors were also engaged in frenetic negotiations to persuade the rival Tamil separatist groups, and in particular the LTTE, to accept the proposals that had emerged from several years of quiet diplomacy as the basis of a workable framework of an honourable peace in Sri Lanka. Most of these groups were willing to accept these proposals or at least to give them a try. The LTTE alone refused to do so.

The Indian government showed its displeasure with the LTTE by imposing restrictions on Sri Lankan Tamil activists operating from Indian territory. This was the first time that such restrictions had been imposed despite Prime Minister Rajiv Gandhi's assurances to President Jayewardene in New Delhi in 1985 in that regard.[34]

The progress made in the Bangalore discussions owed a great deal to the personal intervention of the two heads of government. They agreed on a tentative time-table for the signing of an accord by the two countries in January 1987. When Chidambaram and Natwar Singh visited Colombo—their second visit—on 24 November for further discussions with President Jayewardene, it was an admission that the time-table for the signing of an accord had to be readjusted. The political future of the Eastern Province remained the most intractable problem. No headway was made, in regard to this, on this occasion as well. When President Jayewardene called a meeting of Muslim organizations on 11 December to discuss the future of the Eastern Province, their opposition to any merger of the two provinces, or an excision of the Ampara electorate, much less the Ampara district, was made abundantly clear. Chidambaram and Natwar Singh visited Colombo for the third time on 17 December for discussions with the Sri Lankan government. While agreement was possible on all other issues, this contentious problem defied settlement. Not a single group saw any positive advantage in it. Muslim MPs who met the leaders of the Indian delegation expressed their firm opposition to any changes in the boundaries of the Eastern Province or to linking it with the Northern Province.

There was no way out of this impasse. The Indian government sought to prevent Prabhakaran, then operating from Tamilnadu, from leaving India for Jaffna. They succeeded in this until the beginning of 1987 when Prabhakaran and the LTTE ideologue Anton Balasingham slipped across the Palk Straits to the Jaffna peninsula to continue their fight from there. As expected their return to the island marked the beginning of a more activist and violent phase in the ongoing conflict between the Tamil separatist groups and the Sri Lankan forces.

In early 1987, the LTTE was believed to be on the verge of making a unilateral declaration of independence in the north of the island. Treating this as a gravely provocative move, the government sent troop reinforcements into the Eastern and Northern Provinces with instructions to clear these areas of the LTTE and other separatist groups. Contrary to expectations, the LTTE did not put up much of a fight. The LTTE's retreat was anything but orderly. They fled to the Jaffna peninsula.

The Indian government, apparently much perturbed by this turn of events, urged Sri Lanka to abandon these military moves and to continue with a search for a political solution. In response to this, the Sri Lankan government offered a ceasefire for the duration of the national holidays in April. The LTTE spurned this offer and responded with the Good Friday bus massacre where 130 people were killed by shooting with assault rifles on the road from Trincomalee to Colombo, and they followed it up with a bomb explosion in Colombo's main bus station in which over a hundred people were killed.

Faced with the prospect of a serious erosion of political support as a result of these outrages, the government decided to make an attempt to regain control of the Jaffna peninsula. 'Operation Liberation', which began on 26 May 1987 in the Vadamarachchi division on the north-eastern part of the peninsula, was directed at preventing the hitherto easy movement of men and materiel from Tamilnadu. By the end of May, Sri Lankan forces had gained control of this area. The LTTE, the most formidable Tamil separatist group, had suffered a major setback and in a region they had dominated for a long time. It was this demonstration of the LTTE's failure as a fighting force that triggered the chain of events that resulted eventually in Indian military intervention in Sri Lanka's ethnic conflict.[35]

At this point India moved swiftly to prevent the capture of Jaffna by the Sri Lankan forces. The first move came from M.G. Ramachandran in Tamilnadu with a donation of US$ 3.3 million, to the LTTE and its allies, made with great fanfare.[36] The Indian government, for its part, announced that it was sending shipments of food and petroleum products to Jaffna, which, it claimed, was facing a severe shortage of these items through a blockade imposed by the Sri Lankan forces. Despite the refusal of the Sri Lankan government to accept this offer, or concede the need for it, a first shipment in a flotilla of about 20 Indian fishing-vessels was dispatched on 3 June 1987 but was turned back by the Sri Lankan navy. When this happened, the Indian air force in a blatant violation of international law and of the Sri Lankan airspace dropped food and medical supplies in Jaffna on the following day. All these actions constituted an unmistakable demonstration of Indian support for the Tamil separatist movement in Sri Lanka. The Indian supply of food to Jaffna continued over the next few weeks by sea with the formal but clearly reluctant agreement of the Sri Lankan government. The result was that by the end of June, Indo-Sri Lankan relations were mired in mutual recrimination and deep suspicion. And the island's ethnic conflict seemed headed for prolonged and debilitating deadlock. However, the principal objective of the Indian and Tamilnadu governments had been served—the LTTE had been saved from humiliation by their intervention.[37]

THE INTERMEDIARY AS DIRECT PARTICIPANT

The tensions and dramas of the early days of June were followed by exchanges of mutual accusations between the two countries. On the diplomatic scene stalemate and immobility replaced the frenetic activity of May and early June. Yet, in the first two weeks of July an exchange of political signals set the two governments on the road to serious negotiations to break the deadlock. The initiative came from India with the offer to underwrite the implementation of a political programme that would ensure the end of the current ethnic conflict in the island. Both governments had a clear understanding of what this meant: the LTTE would have to accept the settlement negotiated by the two governments, and the Indian government would use all the resources at its command to compel them to do so. In return, the Sri Lankan government was urged to consent formally to implement the substance of the agreements reached on devolution and related subjects in the negotiations which had taken place between 1985 and 1987. There was a second proviso: the Sri Lankan authorities were asked to agree to a link between the Northern and Eastern Provinces, the large Tamil ethno-region on which the Tamil political activists had set their hearts. This was the final step in the adoption of the devolution package which the TULF as well as the armed separatist groups had demanded since 1983, and which the Sri Lankan government had refused to consider, much less to accept. A loophole was left to make the offer more palatable to the government: the link would be a temporary one, and its fate would eventually be decided by a referendum to be held in the Eastern Province. Even so, there was no mistaking the enormity of the political risks inherent in its acceptance by President Jayewardene. Once this was agreed upon, the negotiations proceeded beyond the devolution issue to foreign policy matters relating to India's security concerns and interests.

Reports that an accord was about to be signed appeared in the Sri Lankan newspapers, especially those critical of the government, and some of its contents leaked out despite all the efforts of the negotiating teams to keep the discussions as confidential as possible. The opposition parties and the Marxist—and ultra-nationalist—JVP sensed much more accurately than the government the public mood of hostility to an agreement with India so soon after the humiliation inflicted on Sri Lanka in early June. The news that an accord was to be signed ignited massive protests in the country in the last week of July. The opposition to the accord was partly a reflection of an innate hostility to Indian pressure, partly a rejection of the more controversial features of the accord such as the link between the Northern and Eastern Provinces, but much more because of the antipathy if not antagonism to Rajiv Gandhi for India's violation of Sri Lankan air space, which had occurred just six weeks earlier, President Jayewardene decided to brave the hostility of the opposition forces, and went ahead with preparations for the signing of this controversial and fateful accord. On 29 July Rajiv Gandhi arrived in Colombo to sign it on behalf of India.

On a first reading of the clauses of the accord it would appear that its main concern was with the peace-keeping aspects. The accord sought to arrange a complete cessation of hostilities, within 72 hours of its implementation; and the provision of Indian military assistance to help with peace-keeping (more than 7,000 Indian troops were drafted into the Indian Peace-Keeping Force—the IPKF—in August). There was also agreement on a general amnesty, after the surrender of arms, for all Tamil separatist activists, including those in custody, imprisoned or facing charges.

The fact, however, was that the substance of the accord lay in the clauses which dealt with the joining together of the Northern and Eastern Provinces into one administrative unit with an elected provincial council there (to be elected within three months); and the holding of a referendum in the Eastern Province to determine whether its mixed population of Tamils, Sinhalese and Muslims would support its merger with the Northern Province into a single Tamil-dominated province. There was another clause in the accord which referred to the establishment of provincial councils in the island based on its nine provincial units.

India's foreign policy objectives were secured through a clause which ought to prevent the use of Sri Lankan ports, Trincomalee in particular, by any country, in a manner prejudicial to Indian interests. Reciprocity was seemingly ensured by another clause which sought to ensure that Sri Lankan Tamil political activists would not be permitted to use Indian territory for military or propaganda purposes. India also sought assurances from Sri Lanka about employment of foreign military and intelligence personnel in the island, and there was a call for a review of Sri Lanka's agreements with foreign broadcasting organizations.

Other clauses referred to the repatriation of about 100,000 Tamil refugees then in India to their homes in Sri Lanka; and promised a resumption of the repatriation of Indian citizens from Sri Lanka under the terms of agreements reached between the governments of Sri Lanka and India in 1964 and 1974. This latter process had been stalled since the early 1980s.

The preamble of the accord which referred to the nature of the Sri Lankan polity and its 'multi-ethnic, multi-lingual, and multi-religious plural society' was more cosmetic than substantial. So was the provision that Tamil and English have equal status with Sinhala as official languages was another: it was merely an extension of the provisions on language in the Sri Lankan constitution of 1978.

Although the Sri Lanka Cabinet eventually approved the signing of the accord, the divisions among its members on this issue could not be concealed. Lalith Athulathmudali, as Minister of National Security and Jayewardene's Deputy Minister of Defence, was the most consistent critic. Prime Minister R. Premadasa was scarcely less hostile. Much of the opposition was based on personal antagonism to Rajiv Gandhi; some of it reflected a sense of despair at the political risks incurred by the government; the higher priority given to India's over Sri Lanka's security interests; as well as the use of Indian troops to supervise and enforce the ceasefire. The Sri Lankan negotiators had opted for an Indian army presence for this latter purpose for two reasons: the need for speedy implementation of the accord, two weeks to a month being the optimistic time-table spoken of at this stage by their Indian counterparts; and because such an Indian contingent would be more acceptable to the Tamils, who would more readily surrender their arms to them rather than to the Sri Lankan security forces, with whom they had been in conflict for so long, or to a Commonwealth/UN peace-keeping force.

The attempt to restrict if not ban the employment by Sri Lanka of foreign military and intelligence personnel directly impinged on Sri Lanka's own security interests and was seen as a constraint on its choices in security. The references to such personnel related to an Israeli presence in Sri Lanka, and to British mercenary groups engaged in training Sri Lankan forces. India had put pressure on Great Britain and other countries, likely to be of assistance to Sri Lanka, to desist from establishing training facilities for Sri Lankan forces in the island. The Indian offer to provide training facilities and military supplies for Sri Lankan security forces was regarded as one-sided when the threat to Sri Lankan security was seen to come from India alone.

The signing of the accord led to violent protests and widespread civil unrest among the Sinhalese majority in and around Colombo and in the south-west of the country. These demonstrations had the support of the SLFP, of sections of the *sangha*, the Buddhist order, and of a revived JVP. Rajiv Gandhi himself narrowly escaped serious injury, if not death itself, when an enraged sailor swung his rifle at him at the guard of honour ceremony prior to the Indian Prime Minister's departure from Colombo.

Although many risks were expected in any progress towards the stabilization of the accord (given the opposition of the SLFP, the Prime Minister and several other members of the Cabinet), the early indications seemed encouraging. Sri Lankan security forces in the Northern and Eastern Provinces returned to their barracks and the paramilitary forces there were disarmed as part of the Sri Lankan government's obligations under the accord. The LTTE began a symbolic handing-over of arms. However, it is in the nature of things that peace accords seldom work according to the wishes of those who negotiate them. The early signs of progress proved to be deceptive.

If a swift pacification of the north and east was envisaged by the Indian and the Sri Lankan governments, they were quickly disillusioned. The Indian Peace-Keeping Force (IPKF) entered Sri Lanka under the assumption that they would be welcomed in the Tamil areas of the north and the east as liberators and that the separatist forces would quickly and willingly surrender their arms to them. In reality, its presence was very soon resented by the LTTE, who decided to defy them. They began with attacks on their Tamil rivals, of whom nearly 150 were killed. The massacre of about 200 Sinhalese in the Eastern Province shortly thereafter (in September) led to a toughening of the Indian attitude.

Urgent discussions between President Jayewardene and Prime Minister Gandhi brought into force part of the hidden agenda of the peace accord that Indian troops would eventually be used against the LTTE. As early as 2 August 1987 Prime Minister Rajiv Gandhi had given an assurance to President Jayewardene that '. . . if Prabhakaran goes back on his word in any manner or fails to organize surrender of arms, the Indian army will move to disarm the LTTE by force.'[38] With practically world-wide condemnation of the LTTE, and severe criticism of India for its failure to maintain the peace, the Indians at last decided to disarm the LTTE, and to make an effort to destroy it as a military if not political force.

Accordingly, the IPKF now moved in to disarm the LTTE and, when faced with resistance from the latter, launched a major attack on the LTTE strongholds in Jaffna town and the peninsula in the second week of October. Despite stiff resistance from the LTTE which necessitated the deployment of thousands of reinforcements, the LTTE's hold on Jaffna and the peninsula was eventually broken. Both parties, the Indian army and the LTTE suffered heavy casualties, but those who suffered most were the Tamil people.

The Indian government which had intervened earlier in the year to prevent the destruction of the LTTE by the

Sri Lankan army were doing it themselves; the Indian government which objected to the Sri Lankan army taking Jaffna city was doing it themselves, and in that process inflicting much heavier casualties and far greater hardship than anything done up to that time by the Sri Lankan security forces. In addition, the Indian government which had accused the Sri Lankan forces of violation of human rights in their confrontation with the Tamil separatist groups, now found itself defending its own forces from similar charges and with even greater frequency.

The Indian army made a number of tactical mistakes which helped the battered LTTE forces to regroup. The latter was allowed—or able—to escape from the Jaffna peninsula to precisely those areas of the Northern Province from which the small Sri Lankan army had driven them out earlier in the year. They were also permitted to establish themselves in the Trincomalee district of the Eastern Province in which—up to that time—they had not much more than a foothold. Above all, if the LTTE had been able to survive in the jungles of the Northern Province against the massive presence of the Indian army, that had as much to do with the reluctance if not failure of the Indians to deliver a *coup de grace* to the LTTE—for political purposes linked to the byzantine politics of Tamilnadu—as with the LTTE's far superior knowledge of the terrain they were operating in relative to that of the Indians. The LTTE was permitted to maintain a small but conspicuous presence in Madras through which it channelled its official 'messages' to various parts of India, and from there to the rest of the world. This contradiction in Indian policy, was regarded in Sri Lanka as a concession to Tamilnadu sentiment.

Although the IPKF was never seen outside the north and east of the country (except in the North Central Province on their way to the east coast) its shadow lay across the country's political landscape. Its presence was exploited politically against the government, by the SLFP and the JVP acting together or separately.

The opprobrium attached to the Indo-Sri Lanka Accord was focussed on its architects within the government and especially the President himself. The JVP, the most vocal, violent and consistent critics of the accord, called for his assassination through posters and inflammatory pamphlets and speeches (transmitted through tapes). On 18 August 1987, the JVP very nearly succeeded in assassinating him within the parliamentary complex when the whole parliamentary group were gathered to discuss the Indo-Sri Lanka Accord. He had a miraculous escape. One District Minister was killed on that occasion and several cabinet Ministers (including Lalith Athulathmudali, Minister for National Security) seriously injured. Earlier one MP had been killed on 31 July by the JVP in the violence that broke out in the wake of the signing of the accord.

Over the next 15 months, the JVP assassinated one Cabinet Minister and one District Minister, as well as the Chairman and Secretary of the UNP. Several MPs narrowly escaped death at the hands of the JVP. It is estimated that over a 1,000 UNP cadres were killed during this period alone. The objective of this violence in the early stages was to prevent the implementation of the legislative programme envisaged in the Indo-Sri Lanka Accord. That this programme was implemented at all was due in the main to the political skills and personal courage of President Jayewardene. When Parliament debated the 13th amendment to the constitution (in November 1987) making provision for the establishment of a system of Provincial Councils, by far the most controversial part of this programme, the security precautions taken within and outside Parliament were unparalleled in the history of the national legislature.

Once the government announced its decisions to hold elections to the newly established Provincial Councils, the SLFP joined the JVP in organizing a boycott of these. The JVP's hitherto sporadic violence against persons and property increased in a concerted bid at intimidating all parties supporting the accord and candidates of all parties seeking election to the Provincial Councils. In February 1988, a new opposition force had emerged, an alliance, named the United Socialist Alliance (USA), consisting of the Sri Lanka Mahajana Pakshaya (SLMP) an off-shoot of the SLFP, the Lanka Sama Samaja Party (LSSP), the Communist Party of Sri Lanka, the Nava Sama Samaja Party, and (most notably) the Eelam People's Revolutionary Liberation Front (EPRLF) from the north and east of the island. The USA group expressed full support for the peace accord, and participated in elections to the Provincial Councils. At the elections to seven of the Provincial Councils (elections in the north eastern Province were postponed) held in April and June 1988, in defiance of the JVP's sustained campaign of threats and violence, the UNP won a majority and effective control in all of them, while the USA emerged as the main opposition group. A surprise 'peace agreement' in May 1988, between the government and alleged representatives of the JVP turned out to be a hoax. The government, however, decided to proceed with its decision to lift the proscription on the JVP imposed in 1983.

Apart from incorporating the new system of Provincial Councils, the 13th amendment to the constitution raised Tamil to the level of an official language (along with Sinhala), with English given the position of a link language. Although there is some ambiguity about the position of English, its legal status appears to be on par with Sinhala and Tamil. The provisions of the 13th amendment dealing with language, were clarified and consolidated by the 16th amendment to the constitution which was certified on 17 December 1988—it was more or less the last piece of legislation of President Jayewardene's administration.

In September 1988, President Jayewardene officially authorized the merger of the Northern and Eastern Provinces within a single North Eastern Province. In mid-November 1988 elections were held for seats in this Provincial Council. The politics of Tamilnadu had a great deal to do with the timing of these provincial elections.

The Indian government, through its High Commissioner in Colombo, J.N. Dixit, pressed very hard to get them held and succeeded in this pressure, in the face of opposition of the Sri Lankan defence forces who argued against it on the grounds that such an election could not be free and fair so long as the IPKF was present in those regions. The Indian government was anxious that this election be held before the elections to the Tamilnadu state legislature. They had their way, but the Congress and its allies lost the Tamilnadu election anyway.

The pro-accord, and pro-Indian, Tamil groups, the EPRLF and the Eelam National Democratic Liberation Front (ENDLF) together with the Sri Lanka Muslim Congress (SLMC), emerged strongly from these elections in the holding of which the IPKF played a prominent and controversial role.[39] The poll was boycotted by the LTTE and the TULF, the latter involuntarily.[40]

The EPRLF won the elections—given the extent of support they received from the IPKF they were bound to win[41]—and nominated a regional ministry, in November 1988, to administer the new province. As a result the IPKF had been drawn into the vortex of Tamil politics in the north and east of the island. From the outset the EPRLF was seen as creatures of the IPKF and India, and never succeeded in establishing themselves as an independent political entity. The Indian government and the IPKF now found themselves saddled with a puppet regional government which they had to sustain and protect against the LTTE. These problems became even more difficult when President Jayewardene decided that he would not contest the Presidential elections scheduled for late 1988.

THE IPKF IN SRI LANKA—THE LAST PHASE

The last few months of President Jayewardene's term of office saw almost as much violence and turmoil as July 1983. The source of the trouble was the same, Sinhalese intransigents, this time led and manipulated by the JVP. In the first two weeks of November a series of politically inspired strikes and disturbances sought to bring the government down. The JVP had made another of its changes of policy: after agitating for over a year for presidential and parliamentary elections, it now demanded that the elections be postponed till the IPKF left the island.[42] Their violence was directed at all political parties (including its erstwhile ally, the SLFP) contesting the elections. It required President Jayewardene's enormous reserves of political skill and shrewdness to hold the government and administration together in the face of this turmoil and violence, and to see that the elections were held. The presidential election of December 1988 was among the most violent ever held in a democracy. Indeed the levels of violence evoked comparison with general elections in Jamaica in the 1980s with the difference that in Sri Lanka it was not the participant parties but an entirely different group that indulged in the violence.

President Premadasa's narrow victory over Mrs Bandaranaike did not lead to anything more than a temporary relaxation of the JVP's violence; it was resumed before the end of January 1989, and continued beyond the parliamentary elections of February 1989. Moreover, the renewal of the UNP's mandate did not guarantee a return to political stability. The new UNP president faced two formidable challenges. The first of these was from the JVP which continued its career of violence, ruthlessly and relentlessly, and showed no signs of a change of attitude to the government, despite the fact that he adopted a policy of conciliation to the JVP in the face of this violence which had left over 2,000 of his supporters dead. The JVP spurned his conciliatory moves.[43]

The second of these related to the Indian presence in the island, and the Tamil problem. As Prime Minister, the new President had never been enthusiastic about the Indo-Sri Lanka Accord. As the UNP's presidential candidate he had pledged to have it replaced by a friendship treaty more acceptable to Sri Lanka. He was also committed to ensuring a speedy departure of the IPKF. President

Premadasa saw the early departure of the IPKF as essential to the restoration of political stability in the country. He scored an early but ambiguous success when the LTTE in a surprising *volte face* accepted his invitation to talks. These began in April 1989. Opposition to the IPKF's presence in the island had brought two old adversaries—the UNP government and the LTTE—to the bargaining table. The ambiguity lies in the fact that the LTTE was driven to the bargaining table because of a perceived weakening of its military strength, sapped in the course of a long and debilitating struggle against the IPKF.

This sudden change in the political situation was bound to have its impact on the affairs of the IPKF. With the departure of President Jayewardene from office, the commitment to the Indo-Sri Lanka Accord at the highest levels of the Sri Lanka government was bound to ebb, especially because his successor had never shown much enthusiasm for it. The Indian High Commissioner J.N. Dixit himself left for his next assignment, to Islamabad, in April 1989 and with his departure the Indians themselves appeared to lose interest in their struggle against the LTTE; certainly the pace with which the IPKF pursued the LTTE began to slacken.[44] Moreover with President Premadasa's election to office in December 1988, the IPKF's continued presence in the island had become a point of contention between the Sri Lankan and Indian governments. The ensuing negotiations on the removal of the IPKF from the island were both long drawn-out and acrimonious. Eventually, the vicissitudes of electoral politics in India, the defeat of Rajiv Gandhi's government and the formation of a new coalition under V.P. Singh, helped ease the situation. The IPKF was withdrawn on a time-table determined by V.P. Singh's government. The key negotiator for India was Inder Kumar Gujral, then Minister of External Affairs. The process of withdrawal was completed in March 1990.

Earlier, under Rajiv Gandhi, the political changes in Sri Lanka had created anxieties in India and in the IPKF about the fate of the EPRLF government and EPRLF cadres once the IPKF left. These anxieties had driven the Indian government, and the IPKF on to a most short-sighted decision, to create an IPKF-sponsored Tamil National Army (TNA) linked to the EPRLF, and to supply it with sophisticated weapons, all in the hope that the TNA could stand up against the LTTE in the inevitable conflict between them. Mistake followed mistake in the pursuit of this disastrous policy. The TNA succumbed to the LTTE literally without firing a shot, leaving their arms to the LTTE. The Sri Lankan authorities, civil and military, were aghast at this new development, but their protests against establishing the TNA and arming it were not heeded. The irony of it appeared lost on the Indian government. A peace-keeping force brought in to disarm Tamil separatist groups, not only failed to do so but, worse still, actually ended its stay in the island by arming a rag-tag force linked to its puppet regime. The principal beneficiary was the LTTE.

As we have seen, there was by this time a surprising *rapprochement* between the government of Sri Lanka and the LTTE, drawn together by a common opposition to the IPKF, and in the hope that the animosities and hostilities of a decade could be overcome through negotiations.[45] These were cordial enough at the beginning and this brief period of peace (after May 1990) enabled the army to devote its attention to meeting the challenge posed by the JVP. It is grimly ironic, but nevertheless true, that the continued presence of the IPKF in the island, and the peace talks between the government and the LTTE, helped the Sri Lankan security forces, and in particular the army, to meet and overcome the threat posed by the JVP.

The IPKF's presence in the north and east of the island was therefore not without its advantages to the Sri Lanka government. Sri Lanka's defence expenditure dropped noticeably after mid-1987. The Indian government bore the heavy expenditure involved in the pacification—such as it was—of the north and east. This decline in defence spending on the part of Sri Lanka might have been more substantial had the threat posed by the JVP not proved to be so serious.

In retrospect, the IPKF's presence in the island and in such large numbers, proved to be a self-defeating exercise.[46] Its size was variously estimated at between 75,000 and 100,000 at its peak, larger than the *whole* British element in the Indian army in the days of the *raj*,[47] more than half the size of the Soviet army in Afghanistan. Indeed, the well-known Indian defence expert, Ravi Rikhye, estimated the IPKF, at its peak, to have been as large as 150,000 if para-military forces were included.[48] And besides, it was all located within an area of about 10,000 sq. kilometres. The Indian policy seemed to be one of saturating an area by throwing in enormous numbers of troops into action, and seeking to submerge the LTTE that way. But this action was only partially successful. The IPKF was unable to disarm the Tamil separatist groups, and especially the LTTE, one of the principal objectives of the Indo-Sri Lanka Accord, even if one disregards the time-frame set out in it as hopelessly optimistic and therefore unrealistic. Nor did the IPKF succeed in eliminating the LTTE as a fighting force once it was decided to turn its guns on them, thus opening itself to the charge that it was incapable of doing that or that it was never intended to do so. The LTTE survived in the jungles of the north and east of the island, and even in Jaffna the peninsula—areas 'pacified' by the IPKF and were under its control—it maintained a shadowy existence and compelled an adherence to its dictates through its cadres. Above all, the LTTE maintained a presence in Tamilnadu throughout the whole period of the IPKF's stay in the island and continued to use its safe houses there.

The IPKF exercise cost India something like Rs 50 billion (in Sri Lanka rupees) or US$ 1.25 billion. While it may be argued that a great deal of this money would have been spent on this force even if it had remained in India, the additional costs involved in moving troops to and from

Sri Lanka and in maintaining them there would have been very considerable. Besides, over 1,000 Indian soldiers were killed, and over double that number were injured, many of them crippled by landmines and other improvized explosive devices in the laying and making of which the LTTE were experts. That expertise had been gained in India.[49]

There is also that great intangible—the loss of prestige, and the sense of failure, in short a propaganda disaster. At the time the IPKF arrived in the island, only the Sinhalese were hostile and opposed to its presence. Within a short time of the IPKF's presence in the north and east, even the Tamils who originally welcomed them as liberators were alienated from it, all save the political groups associated with the marginalized EPRLF. The gains were few, if any.

In June 1990, a LTTE execution squad operating in Tamilnadu had raided a block of apartments in Madras, housing the leadership of the EPRLF who lived there as refugees, killing 13 of them including the Secretary-General of the party and one of its MPs in the Sri Lanka parliament. The LTTE raiders had carried AK-47 assault rifles. While the immediate reaction in Tamilnadu was one of shocked dismay, little was done to curb the LTTE's activities, until the assassination of Rajiv Gandhi, a year later, compelled a re-appraisal of attitudes and policies.

When Rajiv Gandhi was assassinated by the LTTE in May 1991 in Tamilnadu the tragic failure of the Indian intervention in Sri Lanka which his mother had initiated and which he himself had raised several notches higher was underlined for all the world to see. At last India itself woke up to a realization of the full extent of the price she had been called upon to pay for the support extended to Tamil separatism in Sri Lanka. The LTTE had established a government within a government in parts of the Tamilnadu coast; its smuggling enterprises included narcotics; it had infiltrated the Tamilnadu administration; and it had introduced the culture of violence into parts of India which had not known it before.

MEDIATION WITH MUSCLE

Through all these experiences one bitter lesson emerges: it is often easier to end an international conflict than a civil conflict especially when the latter is essentially an ethnic one. In situations of prolonged ethnic conflict fashioning an outcome that is intermediate between victory or defeat for one of the combatants becomes extraordinarily difficult. Because civil violence is often less well-organized than in international war, conflict resolution requires an outcome that has something for everyone. Parties to the conflict cannot be expected to give up their claims without receiving some compensation, and this implies a willingness to compromise on some at least of the underlying issues. The LTTE, like the JVP, has never shown any readiness to compromise. Conflict resolution is much more difficult in such situations, because even a small number of unsatisfied participants can make it impossible to end the quarrelling. All these are lessons that emerged from the Sri Lankan conflict, and the Indian involvement.

In Sri Lanka one saw an extreme form of the mediation-with-muscle version of conflict resolution—the use of the Indian army in a calculated demonstration of military power to impose the will of the Indian government in support of what were seen to be India's national and strategic interests in Sri Lanka. We have seen similar exercises in Punjab and Kashmir. The difference was that in Sri Lanka the use of the Indian army followed the signing of an accord and flowed from its clauses, while in Punjab the accord itself had to deal with the consequences that flowed from the army's intervention. In both instances the use of the army did little to resolve the conflict; on the contrary, the consequences were well-nigh disastrous for India's own national interests, and not least for the two leaders who ordered the resort to force. Mrs Gandhi was assassinated by her Sikh bodyguards within a few months of 'Operation Blue Star' as the army assault on Amristar's Golden Temple was called; Rajiv Gandhi was assassinated nearly four years after he sent the Indian army to the north and east of the island, an assassination which was carried out by the LTTE presumably to avenge the deaths caused by the Indian army in Jaffna and elsewhere in the north and east of the island.

The use of the Indian army in Punjab on that fateful occasion was a purely internal matter for the Indian state; and for which there were some precedents in India's recent history. There were very few precedents in international politics for the decision to use an army in an attempt to resolve an ethnic conflict in a neighbouring state. One such precedent was the Indian intervention in East Pakistan which led to the creation of Bangladesh, and the other was the Turkish intervention in Cyprus. These were unilateral decisions of the two governments, India and Turkey. In contrast, the use of the Indian army, in the north and east of Sri Lanka had the support of the Sri Lankan government and of its President at that time, J.R. Jayewardene.

It has been seen how Indian intervention began as a comparatively low-key business, giving aid to some of the participants in Sri Lanka's conflict—the Tamil separatist groups. Assistance was given in order to encourage the continuation of the struggle, in order to compel or persuade the Sri Lanka government to change some features of its foreign policy. The next stage in the escalation of Indian involvement came in India's decision to help resolve the conflict itself by acting as a mediator, in the course of which it sought to apply sanctions to some or all parties, and eventually ended by underwriting a settlement negotiated with the Sri Lanka government. The Indian intervention reached its denouement in 1987 with the mediator transformed into a combatant; by 1989-90 a startling change saw the Sri Lanka government, under its new leadership, and the LTTE drawn together against India. The mediator had become the common enemy.

IV

Caught in The Crossfire: Sri Lanka's Smaller Minorities

CHAPTER 7

The Islamic Factor

Among the most poignant features of Sri Lanka's current
ethnic conflict are the episodes of violence directed by
Tamil activist groups, principally the LTTE, against the
Muslim minority in the north and east of the island. The
violence which began in the years 1984-7 drew national
and international attention to the complexities of Sri
Lanka's ethnic conflict. But those events paled into
insignificance in comparison with the scale of violence
against the Muslims in 1990. In August 1990 nearly 300
unarmed Muslims were slaughtered by the LTTE in several
incidents in Batticaloa; the most notorious of these was
the cold-blooded shooting of 120 or more Muslims at
prayer time in a mosque at Kattankudy, a Muslim suburb
of Batticaloa. Then in October 1990 came a concerted,
and successful, attempt to expel the Muslim minority as an
entity from the Jaffna peninsula, and from their traditional
villages in the strategic district of Mannar which has had,
for centuries, a large Muslim settlement.

Two conflicting views of the Muslims' role in the Sri
Lanka's polity lay at the heart of the problem. For decades,
Tamil leaders or politicians spoke of the Tamils and
Muslims as one people united by language but divided by
religion. That is at best a half-truth, and in any event it is
passionately rejected by the Muslims for whom the language
they speak is much less important than the religion and
culture that divides them from the Tamils. The Muslims
and Tamils pursue different goals and have adopted
different strategies in the Sri Lankan political process. The
Tamil-Muslim conflicts of the 1980s and 1990s reflected
these differences.

To a certain extent the roots of these differences lie in
the demography, the numbers and the distribution of Sri
Lanka's Muslim minority. Never more than six to seven
per cent of the island's population, they are geographically

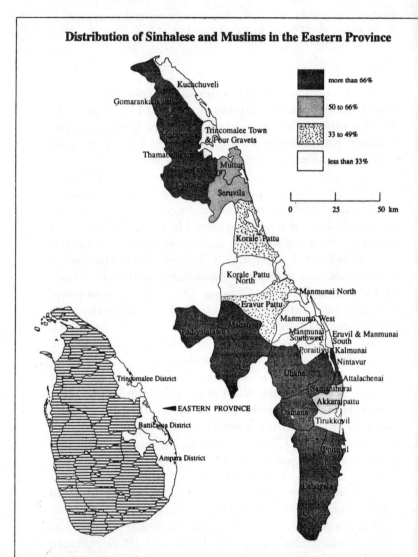

Distribution of Sinhalese and Muslims in the Eastern Province

more than 66%

50 to 66%

33 to 49%

less than 33%

0   25   50 km

Kuchchuveli

Gomarankadawala

Morawewa

Trincomalee Town & Four Gravets

Thamabalagamam

Kantalai

Kinniya

Muttur

Seruvila

Korale Pattu

Korale Pattu North

Manmunai North

Eravur Pattu

Manmunai West

Paddiyatalawa

Mahaoya

Manmunai Southwest

Eruvil & Manmunai South

Poraitivu

Kalmunai

Nintavur

Uhana

Attalachenai

Samanthurai

Akkaraipattu

Damana

Tirukkovil

Pottuvil

Labugala

Trincomalee District

◄ EASTERN PROVINCE

Batticaloa District

Ampara District

Sinhalese and Muslim population as a proportion of the total population of the administrative divisions

Map IV: *Sinhalese and Muslim population as a proportion of the total population of the divisions*

dispersed, unlike Sri Lanka's Tamils who form a clear majority in the Jaffna peninsula and most other parts of the Northern Province as well as in the Batticaloa district of the Eastern Province. In no district do the Muslims constitute a majority; in all except the present Ampara district of the Eastern Province (until 1960, Ampara was part of the Batticaloa district), they are a small minority. There is a concentration of Muslims in the capital city, Colombo. Generally, they define their ethnicity in terms of religion and culture, not language. Today, most Muslims speak the language of the district in which they live, while a great many are bi-lingual, speaking both Sinhala and Tamil while a few speak English as well. Before Sri Lanka regained her independence almost all Muslims spoke Tamil and very few were proficient in Sinhala. Indeed, Tamil had long been the *lingua franca* of maritime trade in the Indian Ocean region; as a trading and seafaring community, Muslims had been exposed for centuries to the influence of that language. More importantly, the Koran had been translated into Tamil; thus even Sinhala-speaking Muslims had perforce to be proficient in Tamil up to now. (It is only recently that the Koran was translated into Sinhala). However, unlike Tamils—and the Muslims of Tamilnadu—Muslims in Sri Lanka have no great emotional commitment to the Tamil language. They have demonstrated little reluctance to adopt Sinhala as a medium of instruction in schools and as the principal, if not sole, national language. But they have also found it exceedingly difficult to abandon Tamil altogether.

In the 1930s, a controversy broke out among the various Islamic groups in the island over the use of the terms 'Moor' and 'Muslim'.[1] Which of the two was more appropriate for the community? Those who preferred and indeed took pride in calling themselves 'Moors' emphasized the historical origins of their community, stretching back to the 9th century AD, and its strong indigenous roots in Sri Lanka. They were clearly the majority group. Others felt this term was too exclusive, and more elitist than the term 'Muslim' which would help bring in a number of other Islamic groups who had come to the island in Dutch and British times. Most of these groups were small in number, but many of them—like the Borahs, Memons, Sindhis and others—were very powerful economically through their control of a great deal of the island's import and export trade. Also included were the Muslims of Indian origin, generally traders, who lived in the island; as well as, of course, the small Malay community whose origins go back to Dutch times. The distinction between Moor and Muslim led to the formation in the 1930s of two separate political groups, the All Ceylon Muslim League and the All Ceylon Moors Association.

Ethnic stereotypes popular in the island portray the Muslims as largely a trading and business community. While this depiction tends to ignore the fact that most Muslims are cultivators (as in the Eastern Province) or part of the urban poor (as in Colombo), it would be true nevertheless to say that, to a larger extent than all the other ethnic groups of the island, the Muslims had—and continue to have—a penchant for trade at all levels. This explains why they played no part at all in the rivalry for places in the bureaucracy in the pre-independence period, and why Muslim representation in the professions was minuscule at that time and has not expanded substantially since.

Through most of the 19th century Sri Lanka's Muslims were an apolitical group. Even the process of religious revival among the island's Muslims, initiated during the last quarter of the 19th century and continued during the first quarter of the 20th century, made no difference in this; there was little or no political content in it in the sense of an opposition to British rule,[2] much less any anxiety to see it replaced by a national regime. The Muslims were generally well behind the Tamils and Sinhalese in the formulation of political demands and pressure for constitutional reforms. The situation did not change much even after the Sinhalese-Muslim riots of

1915, by far the most serious outbreak of communal violence on the island since the establishment of British rule.

For a decade or more after the 1915 riots, the mood of the Muslim community was determined by a mixture of fear and suspicion of Sinhalese nationalism. Thus, there was very little support from the Muslims for the Sinhalese and Tamil leadership's major constructive political initiative in 1917-9, the establishment of the Ceylon National Congress. The Muslims stood aloof, more than a little apprehensive of this new political organization.

PRE-INDEPENDENCE POLITICAL ATTITUDES

A prominent feature of Muslim political attitudes in the early 1920s was an alliance of convenience between the Muslims and Tamils. While Muslims' acceptance of Tamil leadership at this stage was a natural result of the 1915 riots, their acquiescence in the leadership of Ramanathan (who had turned against his erstwhile Sinhalese allies and supporters in the early 1920s) is more surprising. It is evidence of the depth of their disillusionment with the Sinhalese. Ramanathan had been at the centre of a controversy in the mid and late 1880s over his publicly expressed views on the ethnic identity of Sri Lankan Muslims, or Moors as he preferred to call them. Ramanathan argued in 1885 that the Moors of Sri Lanka were Tamils in 'nationality' and 'Mohammedans' in religion, a contention which greatly offended the Muslims, and which was vigorously refuted by M.C. Siddi Lebbe, the main spokesman for Muslims at that time. Ramanathan made a more comprehensive restatement of these views in 1888 in a public lecture on 'The Ethnology of the "Moors" of Sri Lanka', delivered in Colombo.[3] As the representative of the Tamil community in the Legislative Council (1879-91), Ramanathan was often inclined to talk expansively on behalf of the 'Tamil-speaking peoples' of Sri Lanka, a categorization which enabled him to place Muslims within the scope of his tutelage as a legislator. In this claim, as in so many other ways, Ramanathan was the precursor of views and attitudes of mainstream Tamil politics of the future, of the Federal Party and the TULF. Then, as now, however, the Muslims rejected this claim and refused this tutelage.[4]

But in the 1920s the Muslims' acceptance of Ramanathan's leadership—just a few years after his spirited defence of the Sinhalese leadership in the aftermath of the 1915 riots—was a triumph of hope over experience. On this occasion the hope was fulfilled in ample measure. The Muslims remained Ramanathan's allies until his death in 1930. Indeed, their acceptance of Tamil leadership on political issues lasted for some time after Ramanathan's death.

None of the Muslim representatives in the Legislative Council were major political figures. All were conservatives in political attitude; they were either somewhat diffident when they expressed their views or gave silent but unswerving support to the British administration and, later, Ramanathan. The impression one has of them is of men who were distinctly uncomfortable in the parry and thrust of debate in the national legislature.

The keynote of Muslim politics of the inter-war period was one of self-preservation; to safeguard, sustain and advance their distinctive cultural identity. They sought and obtained state support for this in two distinct fields, the first of which was the consolidation and recognition of the personal laws of Muslims. The Muslim Marriage and Divorce Registration Ordinance 27 of 1929, which became operative from 1937, set up a system of domestic relations courts presided over by Muslim judges (*quazis*). These courts explicitly recognized orthodox Muslim law pertaining to marriage and divorce; the same process was instituted for inheritance in the Muslim Intestate Succession and Wakfs Ordinances of 1931. Second, there was the field of education. The divisiveness of education—dividing Muslims from Tamils—began in the 1940s, and has continued to the present day.

The early 1940s marked the beginnings of a significant change in the Muslims' attitude to the nationalist movement as well as a reappraisal of their position on the impending transfer of power. The key figure in this change of attitude was a newcomer to the national legislature, A. R. A. Razik, whose father W.M.A. Rahiman had served in the Legislative Council during the years 1900-17 i.e. during the period of the riots as well. From the early 1940s onwards, the Muslims' response to political and constitutional changes can be viewed in terms of the attitudinal differences between T.B. Jayah, a Malay and senior Muslim member of the national legislature, on the one side, and Razik, on the other. Subtle and muted at first, these differences, became more pronounced in time as Razik gained more confidence as a political leader and greater influence within the national legislature. Some of these differences were inherent in the controversy that broke out over the terms 'Moor' and 'Muslim', with Razik emerging as the advocate of the first and Jayah of the second. In 1942, a third Muslim, Dr M.C.M. Kaleel, entered the legislature; in time he became one of the most respected Muslim politicians, who retained a prominent position in national politics till the time of his death in 1994.[5] Equally important, Razik, who had been a member of the Executive Committee of Local Administration[6] under the Donoughmore system of government, switched over to the Education Committee on 10 March 1942, and that Committee thus had two Muslim members (the other being Jayah).

This concentration of attention on education, in a bid to give a boost to Muslim education, brought Razik into conflict with the Tamils. This was especially so with regard to the Eastern Province where Muslim schools had mostly Tamil schoolteachers or where Muslims attended Tamil schools. Razik deplored this state of affairs. He used his influence, through the Education Committee, to build the resources of Muslim schools and secure the appointment of more Muslim teachers. The insensitivity of Tamils to these Muslim concerns brought home to men like Razik the need to emphasize a Muslim identity in the national education system.

The change of mood was illustrated by the voting patterns in the State Council on J.R. Jayewardene's motion, debated in May 1944, to make Sinhala the national language of Sri Lanka, and especially in the contrasting stands taken by Razik and Jayah in the debate and in the voting on the motion. When Jayewardene first introduced his motion in 1943, there was much opposition to it on the grounds that it made no provision for Tamil. By the time the motion came up for debate in 1944, Jayewardene had agreed to amend it to include Tamil along with Sinhala as the national languages. With the mover's consent a Tamil member, V. Nalliah, moved an amendment 'that the words "and Tamil" be added after the word "Sinhalese" wherever the latter occurs.' The amendment was debated and put to a vote on 25 May 1944. It was carried by 29 votes to 8. Jayah voted for the amendment; Razik joined four Sinhalese in voting against it—they wanted Sinhala as the sole national language.

Razik's speech on this occasion[7]—a brief one—is worth quoting:

> I feel that in the best interest of Lanka, my mother country, I must stand up for the motion of the honourable member for Kelaniya [J.R. Jayewardene]; that is that Sinhalese should be the official language of the country. However, there is not the slightest doubt that this cannot be done in a hurry, in a year or two, or even in 10 years. I certainly feel that in the best interests of Lanka and her people one language will bring unity among our people. We are really divided at the present moment. Each community has its own language. But if we all take to one language, then we will not think in terms of Tamils, Moors, Sinhalese, Burghers, Malays, and so on.

The Tamils could no longer take Muslim support for granted in their political campaigns. By the early 1940s the political alliance between Tamils and Muslims came apart over conflicting attitudes to the transfer of power, with the Muslims supporting the Sinhalese leadership on this and the Tamils acquiescing in it with unconcealed reluctance. This contrast in political attitudes has persisted in the post-independence period.

POST-INDEPENDENCE PERSPECTIVES

In post-independence Sri Lanka, the political attitudes and behaviour of the Muslim community provided a strong contrast to those of the Tamils. First, since 1956 mainstream Tamil leaders have emphasized the distinct and separate identity of their community. With a solid territorial and demographic base in the north and some parts of the east, their politics generally emphasized regional autonomy based on ethnic identity; later on this took a separatist or secessionist form. Their separatist claims were perceived as a threat both to the legitimacy of majority rule and the integrity of the polity. In contrast, the Muslims generally chose to support the Sinhalese majority on some critical issues and were supported in turn by the Sinhalese on issues regarded by the Muslims as necessary for maintaining their culture and identity (on education, for instance). They were helped in this quite substantially by the volatility of the island's political system in which, from 1956 onwards, the ruling party was defeated on six consecutive occasions (including 1956). The result was that Muslims were offered opportunities for political bargaining which they used to the great advantage of their community.

There is also the crucially important fact that the island's Muslims never faced the prospect, much less threat, of assimilationist policies. All governments respected the ethnic identity of the Muslims and have, in fact, helped to protect and foster this.

Until the late 1980s, the Muslims had no 'ethnic' political parties of their own. Neither the All Sri Lanka Muslim League nor All Ceylon Moors Association became Muslim political parties in the years after independence;

by contrast their contemporary, the Tamil Congress, continued as a Tamil political party and was indeed the principal Tamil political organization on the island until the mid-1950s. Muslims sought and obtained membership and achieved positions of influence in all major national political parties, the UNP and SLFP in particular. They were not well represented in the governing bodies of Tamil political parties. The link with the UNP had given that party a majority of the Muslim vote at every election since 1947 till the presidential election of 1994. The UNP has always had more Muslim Members of Parliament than the SLFP till the parliamentary elections of that year. Within the party, Colombo-based Muslims have been, until very recently, the dominant element.

The UNP's defeat in 1956 presented some difficulties for Muslims because of their strong commitment to the party. But soon the SLFP, as the party in power, began to attract substantial Muslim support, especially under the leadership of Badi-ud-din Mahmud. A man of considerable influence within the party he demonstrated the value of a place in the Cabinet as a political base for a national leadership role in the affairs of the Muslim community. Mahmud had two periods of Cabinet office, from 1960 to 1965 and from 1970 to 1977; on both occasions he was an appointed Member of Parliament, not an elected one. On both occasions he was a key figure in the SLFP, but during his second period of office he sought to expand the political organization, the Islamic Socialist Front, which linked the SLFP with an articulate but numerically small group of Muslims to the left of the traditional SLFP supporters in that community. Mahmud has earned a measure of notoriety in the annals of Sri Lanka's ethnic conflict as the man who introduced the change in university admissions policy in the early 1970s, from open competition to a form of affirmative action of which his own community and the rural Sinhalese were the principal beneficiaries.

Since 1947, every Cabinet has had a Muslim in it; the UNP government of 1977-94 generally had three. The first

Cabinet after independence had two Tamils; there was one between 1952 and 1956, but none at all from then until 1965. Thereafter every Cabinet has had a Tamil representative, generally a Sri Lankan Tamil; since 1977 there have been two or three (1978-89) one of whom has been the leader of the Indian Tamils. Even more remarkable is the ready acceptance of Muslims by Sinhalese voters in electorates where Muslims comprise less than a fifth and quite often less than a tenth or a twentieth of the total voting strength. Muslims are regarded as being so clearly integrated into the Sri Lankan political community that the Sinhalese will vote for them on party grounds against Sinhalese opponents.[8] In contrast, not a single Tamil candidate has won a seat in a predominantly Sinhalese area since independence, except for Indian Tamils who have won seats in the plantation districts or in the periphery of such districts.

As in the inter-war period, so now in the post-independence era Muslims have striven to sustain and advance their distinctive cultural identity. They have sought and obtained state support for this in two distinct fields: the consolidation and recognition of the personal laws of Muslims, and in education. In the first area, this trend has continued after independence. The provisions of the Muslim Intestate Succession and Wakfs Ordinance of 1931, which relates to Muslim charitable trusts (Wakfs), was superseded by the Muslim Mosques and Charitable Trusts or Wakfs Act of 1956; meanwhile the Muslim Marriage and Divorce Registration Ordinance 27 of 1929 was replaced by the Muslim Marriage and Divorce Act 13 of 1951 (operative from 1954), which enhanced the powers of the *quazis* who were given exclusive jurisdiction over marriages and divorces as well as the status and mutual rights and obligations of the parties concerned. The Wakfs Act of 1956 established a separate government department with an executive board all of whom were Muslims. During the period of the first and second republics (i.e. from 1972 onwards) the personal laws of Muslims were maintained and, more to the point, unlike in India remain unchallenged.

The most important gains have been made in education, especially since 1956. The list of advantages secured by the Muslims is quite substantial. Special government training colleges have been set up for them. In government schools Arabic is offered as an optional language to Muslim pupils, taught by *maulavis* appointed by the Ministry of Education and paid by the state. In fact, the sensitivity to the special concerns of Muslims in education had begun with C.W.W. Kannangara as Minister of Education from 1931 to 1947, and was continued by W. Dahanayake in the same role from 1956 to 1959 in S.W.R.D. Bandaranaike's Cabinet. It received greater emphasis with Badi-ud-din Mahmud, who served as Minister of Education from 1960 to 1963 and again from 1970 to 1977.

In the first period Mahmud piloted the landmark education legislation of Mrs Bandaranaike's first government; in the second his role was more controversial, especially with regard to a crucial change in university admissions policy, which adversely affected Tamils and, to a slightly lesser extent, Sinhalese in urban areas, especially Colombo. Muslims and Tamils have pursued diametrically opposed objectives on university admissions, with Muslims among the most persistent advocates of ethnic quotas and Tamils advocating open competition and academic merit as the main criteria for admission to universities. As in the 1940s, rivalry between Tamils and Muslims in education has been an important feature of the island's ethnic disharmony: apart from the Muslims' anxiety to break away from Tamil tutelage in schools of the Tamil medium, they have successfully lobbied for more Muslim schools and more Muslim schoolteachers. Mahmud's tenure of office as Minister of Education was an important landmark in the gains Muslims achieved both in literacy and a notable improvement in educational standards at the secondary level.

Equally significant has been the divergence of views on devolution of power. Till the appearance of the Sri Lanka Muslim Congress in the late 1980s Muslims have been inveterate opponents of any attempt to tamper with Sri Lanka's existing unitary political structure. Two examples of this are: the opposition mounted by A.R.A. Razik, later Sir Razik Fareed, within the government parliamentary group to the District Councils scheme which Prime Minister Dudley Senanayake sought to introduce between 1966 and 1968. Similarly, two Muslim members of the Presidential Commission on District Development Councils wrote a lengthy note of dissent against the main recommendations of that commission in its report published in 1980.[9]

Neither the UNP nor the SLFP could take Muslim support for granted. While each has large reserves of Muslim support—the UNP's has traditionally been larger than the SLFP's—they were aware that Muslim voters could tilt the balance, in not less than 15 electorates in all parts of the country, in the days before the proportional representation system was introduced. Often they did precisely that. Muslims have seldom hesitated to vote against a governing party if it appeared to them to be inconsiderate to or negligent of their interests. Thus in 1964-5, the then SLFP-dominated government's failure to remedy the legal deficiencies which the Supreme Court pointed out concerning *quazis* courts was a significant enough factor in turning large numbers of Muslims against them in the general election that year. Then again, some of that support returned to the SLFP and its allies in 1970 as part of a national trend against the UNP, which was seen to have done more for Tamils than Muslims.[10] They turned against the UNP once more in 1994 much more emphatically than in the past because of the perception that the party's leadership at that time was not as sensitive to the interests of the minorities as their predecessors had been.

Briefly, then, while Muslims have not been reluctant to consider themselves as a counterweight to Tamils in communal rivalries that have been so prominent in political developments in post-independence Sri Lanka, they have seldom hesitated to express their displeasure at signs of neglect of their interests, or hostility to them, by a government. And Sri Lanka's electoral system has provided them with all the opportunities they need to make this displeasure felt. Governments have changed with remarkable frequency in Sri Lanka, and the Muslim community, small though it is, has contributed mightily to these swings of the electoral pendulum.

It would be too naive to assume that these advantages were secured as a result of Sinhalese altruism. On the contrary, one has the feeling that quite often Sinhalese politicians have used state resources to build the Muslim community or sections of it as a counterweight to the Tamil community in a game of checks and balances, an intrinsic element in the process of government in any plural society. As we have seen, Muslims—in striking contrast to Tamils—have had no distinct ethnic or religious political parties of their own till the appearance of the Sri Lanka Muslim Congress to contest seats to Parliament in competition with, if not in opposition to, the main national political parties. Instead, their political organizations preferred to work in association with and as adjuncts of the latter. The result is that the Muslim community, although numerically much smaller than the Tamils, had far greater bargaining powers electorally than their number seemed to warrant.

THE POLITICS OF THE EASTERN PROVINCE

In resisting the temptation to form an ethnic or religious political party, a theme that has been commented upon by a number of political analysts, the Muslim community has demonstrated an astute understanding of the mechanics of politics in Sri Lanka.[11] Not all Muslims were happy with this state of affairs. Indeed, in the early 1970s some—especially those from the Eastern Province—began to argue the case for a Muslim political party, independent of existing national parties and pursuing the sectional interests of Muslims with single-minded commitment to Islamic principles.[12] With the creation of the Sri Lanka Muslim Congress (SLMC) in the late 1980s that wish was fulfilled. The new political party's base was the Eastern Province.

About 30 per cent of Sri Lanka's Muslims live in the three districts of the Eastern Province; of these the largest concentration (nearly 15 per cent of Sri Lanka's Muslims) live in the Ampara district. This naturally encouraged the hope that an ethnic political party would be a viable entity in the Eastern Province—at least as effective at protecting Muslim interests, if not potentially more so, than the prevailing system of Muslim representation through and within the main national political parties.

The Eastern Province Muslims have always had their own style of politics: a mixture of regional loyalties, disregard for party ties and a continuing loyalty to a powerful family group overriding party ties—the Kariapper family. Thus, Muslim political figures of national importance have frequently been rejected by Eastern Province constituencies in favour of local Muslims. A.R.A. Razik was defeated in Pottuvil in 1947, and B. Mahmud was much more comprehensively rejected in 1977 in Batticaloa. Then again, Eastern Province Members of Parliament have shown a cavalier disregard for political consistency, measured in terms of party loyalty, that the celebrated Vicar of Bray of 18th century England would have appreciated. The interested reader has only to turn to the political careers of M.E.H. Mohamed Ali and M.M. Mustapha for striking evidence of this. Moreover, over the last 40 years the Kariapper family has enjoyed a remarkable, if somewhat unobtrusive, dominance in Eastern Province politics. Many, if not most, Eastern Province Members of Parliament of all political parties including M.H.M. Ashroff, the leader of the Sri Lanka Muslim Congress have kinship ties with this family. It goes to show that Eastern Province Muslims have their own peculiar priorities.

In the mid-1950s, some Muslims in the Eastern Province actually joined Tamils in the latter's attempt to build an organization of Sri Lanka's 'Tamil-speaking peoples', on whose behalf the Tamil political leadership campaigned, to preserve their language rights. Some Muslims contested on the Federal Party ticket in 1956 and won election to Parliament.[13] But their loyalty to the Federal Party did not survive the bitter conflicts over language that broke out from the very first months of the third Parliament. Soon the Muslims reconciled themselves to the new language policy introduced by the Bandaranaike government; the fragile alliance of Tamils and some Eastern Province Muslims as the 'Tamil-speaking peoples of the island' was shattered, never to be put together again.

M.H.M. Ashroff and the SLMC took the established Muslim political leadership associated with the UNP and the SLFP by surprise by a very successful entry into national politics at the provincial council elections of 1987 and 1988. The new organization had outmanoeuvred and out-polled the Muslim organizations associated with the UNP on this occasion. Ashroff claimed that over 75 per cent of the Muslims had voted for his party. While this was clearly an exaggeration, it was nevertheless true that even if only 35 per cent to 40 per cent of the Muslims had voted for his party, it was still a remarkable political achievement. Ashroff had emerged as a politician to be reckoned with.

Much of the success Ashroff achieved at this time could be attributed to a clever exploitation of a feeling of disenchantment among the Muslims with President Jayewardene and the UNP. The signing of the Indo-Sri Lanka Accord and its most conspicuous result, the entry of the Indian Peace-Keeping Force (IPKF) to the north and east of the island, had brought the Muslims in the Eastern Province and the Mannar district of the Northern Province into conflict with the LTTE and its allies.[14] Attacks on them by Tamil separatist groups increased in frequency and intensity and the IPKF had proved to be totally ineffective in protecting them. Ashroff's argument that if the Muslims, like the Tamils, had a political party of their own, instead of being linked to the country's main political parties, their voices would be heard more readily and their wishes less likely to be ignored had a ready reception especially in the Eastern Province. The SLMC was first and foremost an Eastern Province organization. Its most substantial achievement lay in making the politics of the Eastern Province, and the fate of the Muslims there a live issue among Muslims in other parts of the country. Thus, early in 1987, Muslim traders in parts of Colombo had, for the first time, closed their shops in response to a call from the SLMC to protest the killings of Muslims in the Eastern Province by the LTTE. Also a large section of the Muslims, the more articulate younger people, were upset at President Jayewardene's Israeli initiative, that is to say the approval given to the establishment of an Israeli interest section of the US Embassy in Colombo and the use of a small group of Israelis in the training of the Sri Lanka army.[15] The SLMC exploited this sense of discontent with the UNP in gathering protest votes from the Muslim community.

The SLMC's electoral success appeared to give added significance to other developments within the Muslim community, especially in the spread of a militant, some tended to call it fundamentalist, form of Islam. The appeal of the new Islamic message was somewhat blunted by the range of conflicting political interests, from Saudi Arabian to Libyan and Iranian, at work, within the Muslim communities, with money available for political and religious activities from all these competing sources. Sri Lankan political analysts began to take notice of the spread of a new 'Islamic' garb adopted by female Muslim students—school children—an ensemble of cotton trousers, blouses and headgear, generally all white. Up to very recently, the 1980s in fact, all female school children in the island, Sinhalese, Tamils and Muslims usually wore the same white cotton garb, a frock. The more conservative Muslim males have now begun to insist on a form of the *chador* for their wives.

At the time of the elections to the North Eastern Provincial Council, which as we have seen in an earlier chapter was boycotted by the LTTE, Ashroff and the SLMC were active participants. They won all but one of the Muslim seats in the Eastern Province in the council. When the presidential election of 1988 came around, Ashroff and the SLMC were courted by the two main contenders, the SLFP and its allies, and the UNP. After associating with the former for a while, the SLMC swung to a more neutral posture, which was interpreted as a pro-UNP stance. Once President Premadasa secured victory, Ashroff and the SLMC contested the parliamentary elections and secured election for himself and a small group of supporters. While the UNP had enough of a majority to do without their support within the legislature, Ashroff and the SLMC were not without influence there. When President Premadasa abruptly terminated the link with the Israelis in March 1990, it was widely attributed to the lobbying skills of the SLMC. The Muslims had established a lock on one aspect of Sri Lanka's foreign policy, a virtual veto on diplomatic links with Israel.

The SLMC, as we have seen, was associated with the North Eastern Provincial Council dominated by the Eelam People's Revolutionary Liberation Front (EPRLF). As a result it earned the hostility of the LTTE. The hostility was aggravated by the cordial relations maintained by the SLMC with the IPKF. This was one of the reasons why the Muslims of the Eastern Province came under attack from the LTTE the moment it became clear the IPKF was scheduled for an early departure.

The attack came in August 1990 in a most horrifying form, the butchery of nearly 300 Muslims by the LTTE, over 120 of them in one ghastly incident inside a mosque at prayer time. The idea at this stage was to force the Muslims out of some of the strategic villages which separate Tamil settlements in the east coast. The LTTE failed in this but succeeded in the north and north-west of the island, the Jaffna peninsula and the Mannar district.

Political analysts attributed the hostility of the LTTE to the Muslims of the Eastern Province in part at least to Ashroff's own views on the future of the Muslims in the region covered by the North Eastern Province. He was staking a claim for a Muslim Provincial Council, with the Ampara district of the Eastern Province as its core, and with 'cantons' covering the principal Muslim settlements in the Batticaloa and Trincomalee districts of the Eastern Province and, more ominously for the LTTE, in the Jaffna peninsula and the Mannar district of the Northern Province as well. To the LTTE, as the exponents of the Tamil dominance of the north and east, and as advocates of the case for the 'traditional homelands' of the Tamils, this was an intolerable challenge.

Having failed in their attempt to expel Muslims from strategic villages in the Eastern Province, the LTTE turned to the more vulnerable and less numerous Muslims of the Jaffna peninsula and the Mannar district. In the latter part of October 1990 the entire Muslim population of the Northern Province (around 75,000 people at that time) were driven from their homes at gun-point.

A flavour of this exercise in ethnic cleansing by the LTTE comes through in this extract taken from a contemporary account:

> The mass expulsion of the Muslims from the north was carried out in the following manner. On 22nd October 1990, quite unexpectedly, the LTTE announced over loudspeakers in the streets of the Muslim settlements in the Northern Province that the Muslims must leave their homes, villages and towns, leaving all their valuables behind or face death. The ultimatum was that Muslims should leave this region within 48 hours from the 22nd of October 1990. In Jaffna town the time given was only two hours.[16]

The LTTE was unrelenting in their pressure—the Muslims were expelled, their houses looted of their contents including cash, jewellery and other valuables. The people who were thus driven out took refuge in Muslim villages in

the Sinhalese districts adjacent to the Northern Province.
Nearly 90 per cent of the total Muslim population of the
Northern Province, who became refugees went to the
Puttlam and Anuradhapura districts where they live in
appalling conditions. The hardships they endured have
been only marginally alleviated by grants from the
government and non-governmental organizations. The rest
moved to other parts of the country.

Over the last seven years they have remained where
they are, often facing the hostility of the Muslim villagers
among whom they live, and still yearning for the day when
they could go back. Their plight was politically beneficial
to the SLMC. For one thing it eroded the support the
UNP had among the Muslims in the Eastern Province
through this demonstration of the inability of the
government to afford protection to the Muslims. The
longer they remained as refugees the stronger became the
appeal of the SLMC to them as potential saviours.

When the parliamentary election of 1994 came around,
the SLMC, secure in its Eastern Province base, turned
against the UNP. They succeeded in demonstrating their
strength among the Muslims, not merely in the Eastern
Province, but elsewhere as well. The votes of Muslims
expelled from the Northern Province were added to the
national tally of the party.

By August 1994, Ashroff and the SLMC joined the new
SLFP led coalition government with Ashroff becoming a
member of the Cabinet and two of his colleagues
accommodated as Deputy Minister, and Deputy Chairman
of Committees (the third in the hierarchy after the Speaker
and Deputy Speaker) respectively. The Eastern Province
had ceased to be merely a bridgehead for the SLMC, and
had become a forward base that helped convert it to a
national party which had successfully challenged the
established Muslim organizations.

But other challenges lie ahead for Ashroff and his
SLMC as the Eastern Province has become once more an
arena of conflict between the security forces and the

LTTE. It will not be possible any longer for the SLMC to blame others; they are in charge and will have to take full responsibility for anything that goes wrong there. Besides, as Minister for Reconstruction and Rehabilitation, the welfare of the Muslim refugees is Ashroff's responsibility.

CHAPTER 8

The Indian Tamil Community

A WORLDWIDE DISPERSAL OF INDIAN WORKERS

The movement of Indians to the central hills of Sri Lanka beginning in the 1830s was a response to the demand for a reliable supply of labour in British-owned plantations then being opened in parts of the island. There were two main regional centres of labour recruitment in India for the plantations of the British Empire. The first was the present state of Bihar, and the other perhaps the bigger of the two, was the Madras presidency of which the present Tamilnadu was a part.[1] It was from this latter region that Indian plantation workers and others came to Sri Lanka during British rule in the island.

Indian labour was used, without resort to indentures, in the coffee plantations in Sri Lanka from the 1830s till the collapse of the Sri Lankan coffee enterprise in the 1870s. This labour was generally seasonal, but the nature of the demand changed fundamentally with the opening and expansion of Sri Lanka's tea and rubber enterprises, also in the last quarter of the 19th century; these needed many more workers than the coffee plantations and they needed resident rather than mainly seasonal migrants. The indigenous population in the plantation districts of Sri Lanka refused to put up with the rigours and discipline of plantation labour. There was some indigenous labour on the plantations no doubt, but the vast bulk of the workers on the plantations in Sri Lanka was Indian.

There was also a demand for Indian labour in fields other than plantation enterprise. Indian labour was obtained for the clearing of the bush for the construction of railways in British East Africa. Skilled Indian labour was in great demand in the railway workshops in Colombo, Sri Lanka; and unskilled labour for the hard and grimy work in the dark, cavernous and dusty structures which stored coal for use of the railways. There was work, skilled and unskilled, but generally rigorous and disciplined, also in the dockyards in Colombo and in Rangoon, Burma. Another area of activity in which the native population generally refused to engage because it was regarded as low status employment was the cleaning of the streets, and sanitation work in the towns before flush toilets became a requirement of health authorities, and before the introduction of a modern sewage system in the city of Colombo. All this became the purview of Scheduled Caste Indians who settled down in the poorer working-class suburbs and slums of Colombo and other towns. There was a similar pattern of settlement observed in British controlled Burma.

Another category that emerged was the Indian trading community in the Indian Ocean region, East Africa, the Gulf states, and in Sri Lanka. In Sri Lanka, Indian traders controlled the wholesale and retail distribution of food; and as in many other parts of the British colonies the Indian money-lender was ubiquitous and usually unpopular. British banks which generally had a monopoly of the banking business seldom if ever lent money directly to a Sri Lankan; an intermediary was required. The shroffs, many of whom were Indians, helped to serve this purpose.

In Sri Lanka, the vast majority of Indians were plantation workers and from the working class, settled in Colombo and its suburbs as well as in other urban areas. The bulk of them belonged to the so-called depressed castes, described also as Scheduled Castes. Class status, caste origin and their location, a considerable distance away from main centres of the indigenous Tamil population, kept the two Tamil groups apart. Besides, the Indian Tamils had their own leadership distinct from that of the indigenous Tamils, and Sinhalese trade union leaders and Marxist parties alike. In the person of S. Thondaman the Indian leadership showed remarkable political longevity, from the late 1940s to the present day, without a break, until March 1997 when that leadership lost its electoral base to representatives of the UNP at the national local government elections.

The problem of the political status and voting rights of Indian communities overseas came to the fore first of all in Sri Lanka, and as long ago as 1928-31, with the introduction of universal suffrage, sixteen years before the country became independent. Except for a small left-wing minority, the vast majority of the Sri Lankan politicians refused to accept the position that *all* the Indians resident in the country were entitled to citizenship. The controversies over this issue which began in 1928 and continued for two decades throughout the transfer of power negotiations, are reviewed later. But in the 1940s, the Sri Lankan politicians insisted upon and succeeded in getting Whitehall to accept the position that the independent government of Ceylon, or Sri Lanka as it later became, had the right to determine who its citizens were. The politicians were responding to the most compelling of political calculations, the arithmetic of electoral systems, and the size of ethnic minorities—to prevent the unrestricted increase in the size of Sri Lanka's second Tamil community.

The situation is neatly summarized in a recent article by Myron Weiner:

> When Sri Lanka became independent there was no clear notion as to what constituted Sri Lankan citizenship. In the 1949 [sic][2] elections anyone who was a British subject in Sri Lanka including [the resident Indians] could vote. But the new government lost no time in introducing the Ceylon Citizenship Act of 1948 and the Indian and Pakistani Residents (Citizenship) Act of 1949. These Acts along with various agreements subsequently signed with the Indian government in 1964 and 1974, added up to a set of policies to end all further migration into Sri Lanka, to expatriate [sic][3] as many of the Indian estate workers as Indians would accept . . .
>
> The Sri Lankan government was hardly alone in wanting

the expatriation of migrants who had entered when the country was under colonial rule. Many post-colonial regimes regarded their migrants as an illegitimate presence if the migrants did not belong to the dominant indigenous ethnic community. Uganda and Burma expelled their Indian and Pakistani settlers and in Indonesia large numbers of Chinese were massacred or expelled. Sri Lanka, however, had a democratic government. It sought to remove the Indians through legitimate means, in accordance with the law and with due regard for its international obligations. However, one may fault successive Sri Lanka governments for their policies of seeking to expatriate the Indian community, one should note that the Sri Lanka government at no point engaged in the forcible expulsion or killing of estate workers. Its repatriation policies were constrained by whatever agreements were reached with India.[4]

The Sri Lankan experience was unique for another reason. India generally refused to accept repatriation of people of Indian origin from former colonial territories to India. Only in the case of Indians in Sri Lanka was this accepted. Significantly, this came in the early 1960s after Nehru's death, and the defeat India had suffered at the hands of China in 1962.

A QUESTION OF NUMBERS

For 60 years, from 1928, the political arithmetic of how many Indians should be granted citizenship rights was a matter of one of the principal debates among Sri Lanka's political parties. At the time the debate began the number of Indians in Sri Lanka was as high as 11 per cent of the population, that is to say, there were almost as many Indian Tamils as there were indigenous Tamils—perhaps more. By the time the problems were resolved between 1964 and 1988, the number of Indians granted citizenship had been reduced to 5 per cent of the total population in the island. Throughout this period this question of numbers—how many Indians would qualify as citizens of

Sri Lanka—was also a matter of acute controversy between
the Sri Lankan political leaders, and Indian officials—
prior to independence—and thereafter with their
counterparts in the political leadership in India. The
senior politicians of both countries had been involved in
negotiations on this issue even before the two countries
attained independence. The 20 years from 1929 are crucial
in this regard: they were notable for a series of lost
opportunities when this problem could have been resolved
without resort to the legislation introduced unilaterally by
Sri Lankan leaders after independence, if the Indian
negotiators, especially Jawaharlal Nehru, had shown greater
flexibility.

As in Burma, the depression of the late 1920s and
early 1930s created problems for the Indians; working
class Indians in the urban areas, especially in and around
Colombo, were resented as competitors in a tight labour
market. The plantation workers were seen—to a greater
extent than in the past—as a privileged group, and trade
union leaders like A.E. Goonesinha, who had earlier
worked with their Indian counterparts in the island and
championed the cause of the underprivileged workers,
indigenous and Indian alike, turned against the latter. But
there was, fortunately, no violence.

Above all else the depression focussed jealous attention
on a small but wealthy section of the Indian community in
the island; on the Indian moneylenders foreclosing on
mortgages on land and houses; and on Indian traders who
controlled the wholesale distribution of rice and other
food items and textiles, and had a commanding position
in their retail distribution throughout the island. The
prominence attained in their respective spheres by the
moneylenders and traders attracted hostile criticism on
the Indian community as a whole, from vocal sections of
the Sinhalese, including influential politicians, at this time
of high unemployment and persisting fears of the economic
and political threat to the Sinhalese population from the
Indian minority in the island.

The Board of Ministers with J.L. Kotelawala, Minister for Transport and Works in the lead, responded by imposing restrictions, in 1939, on the employment of Indians in the government service. These restrictions affected skilled as well as unskilled workers employed in the railways, in road construction and sanitation services among others. The government of India retaliated, by placing an embargo on the emigration to Sri Lanka of unskilled labour from India, which in turn inevitably produced an outcry from the planters who feared that the supply of Indian labour on which they were so dependent would be reduced as a result. Over and above all this the voting rights of Indians in Sri Lanka became a matter of acute controversy in early 1940.

The following extract from a minute by K.W. Blaxter, a senior Colonial Office principal provides a succinct summary of the issues involved:

> . . . On the existing register of voters a large number of Indians have been wrongly included owing to the lax interpretation of a memorandum by the Legal Secretary. The Board of Ministers are assuming that the election next January [i.e. January 1941] will duly take place and it is therefore necessary during the present year to carry out a further revision of the register. The Legal Secretary has recently issued a further memorandum impressing upon the registering authorities the procedure they must adopt for enroling Indian voters. The strict observance of this memorandum will result in the removal of a large number of voters from the rolls. The Ministers have become thoroughly alarmed by the realization of what the position is and are not disposed to introduce in the State Council the necessary financial supplementary estimate for the money required to carry out the revision of the register until certain changes had been made in the Election Order in Council relating to Indian voters. They wish the Order in Council to be amended so as to provide for the payment of a rupee fee and also to ensure that Indians who obtain the vote in Ceylon should renounce the special privileges which they had as

Indians. They propose to move a resolution in the State Council on the 14 May to the effect that the serious condition of the Electoral Register demands that immediate steps be taken to give effect to paragraph 35 of Sir Herbert Stanley's despatch of the 2nd June 1929 and to paragraph 10 of Lord Passfield's despatch of the 10th October 1929.[5]

These conflicts showed little signs of abating, wartime conditions notwithstanding. Two integral units of the empire were bickering like two sovereign states over the protection of their respective interests, almost oblivious to the larger interests of an empire whose very existence was under severe threat from its enemies. Governor Sir Andrew Caldecott was aware of the dangers of the continuation of this conflict and endeavoured to cool tempers among Sri Lankan politicians. He realized that the planters were apprehensive about the threat posed to the efficient running of their plantations from potential labour shortages as a result of the ban imposed from India on the emigration of unskilled labour. In addition, there were hints from India, of trade sanctions. The Colonial Office was anxious that these controversies should be brought to an end through a process of negotiation.

Attempts at resolving these issues had been made towards the end of 1939 but these failed almost at once. A terse communiqué issued by the Government of India on 5 January 1940 announced the failure of these talks. In the meantime, under pressure from the Board of Ministers, senior British officials in the island proceeded with plans to tighten the regulations on registering Indians resident in the island. The Government of India was perturbed by this and sought an opportunity to comment on changes proposed. In early July 1940, moves were afoot to resume talks between the two governments. The Colonial Office suggested on 15 July that the first conversations with the Indian side be of an exploratory nature, a proposal that found acceptance both in Colombo and Delhi.

Representatives of the two governments met to discuss

outstanding issues 'at informal and preparatory talks' in November 1940, in New Delhi. The four member ministerial delegation from Sri Lanka was led by D.S. Senanayake and included G.C.S. Corea, Minister for Labour, Industry and Commerce, S.W.R.D. Bandaranaike, and a British official H.J. Huxham, the Financial Secretary. In their official report the delegation from Colombo stated that

> As no agreement could be reached on the question of the status of Indian immigrants in Ceylon, the Indian delegation was unwilling to proceed to the consideration of other questions noted for discussion. The talks thus came to an end.

Caldecott struggling very hard to control the damage to Indo-Ceylon relations that could have flowed from the abrupt failure of these preparatory talks, successfully prevailed upon the Sri Lankan Ministers in the official delegation to Delhi to refrain from publishing their version of the talks, for fear that any hasty public official statement by the Ministers could make things worse than they already were. He succeeded in this to the extent that no official statement was issued, but he could not prevent D.S. Senanayake from making a reference to the talks in the course of addressing the annual sessions of the Ceylon National Congress on 22 December 1940. His explanation of why, in his opinion, the talks in Delhi had failed, was given wide coverage and great prominence in the local newspapers.

In this speech D.S. Senanayake explained that:

> We proposed that the franchise should be given to all Indians now in Ceylon who have permanently settled down here and that full rights of citizenship should be given only to the second generation of such Indians. Their proposal is that full rights of citizenship with very minor restrictions should be given to all Indians who have lived five years in Ceylon and have their families here.

Their proposals would practically amount to our having to confer full rights of citizenship on the entire 900,000 Indians now in Ceylon irrespective of the fact that their real home is India and not Ceylon . . .

We found it impossible to agree to these proposals and so the conference had to end in this unsatisfactory manner . . .

A second and more fruitful round of talks was held in Colombo in September 1941 between a delegation led by Sir G.S. Bajpai representing the Indian government and a delegation of Sri Lankan ministers and officials. Both sides were in a more conciliatory mood on this occasion, the Sri Lankans more so than the Indians. This time the Sri Lankan delegation offered the status of permanent settlers—with the right to vote—to Indians with a minimum of seven years residence in the island, with those admitted to the country thereafter being treated as temporary residents. This was part of a six point formula designed to resolve the problem. To the relief of both governments agreement was reached on this basis. However, this opportunity was missed because the Indian government, under pressure from the leadership of the Indians resident in Sri Lanka refused, or failed, to ratify the agreement which its representative had already initialled in Colombo. Indeed the fact that an agreement had been reached had been given publicity; the terms of the settlement reached were also published.[6] This bitter experience made Sri Lankan politicians and officials extremely wary in future negotiations on this issue.

The unresolved issues relating to the position of the Indians in the Sri Lanka polity, and the conflicting grievances involved in these, were ventilated afresh when the Soulbury Commission began its sittings in Colombo in 1945. In their submissions to the Commission, spokesmen for the Indian community argued that Indians resident in the island had been clearly discriminated against in regard to the franchise, and urged that this subject as well as immigration in general should be among those reserved for the British government under the terms of the declaration of July 1943.

The Soulbury Commission devoted a chapter of its report[7] to these issues. That chapter came down very much on the side of the Board of Ministers in declaring that the policies pursued by the latter on the franchise

> did not seem to His Majesty's government to involve any racial discrimination against Indians, whereas some of the Indians protests amounted in effect to a claim to a position of privilege rather than of equality.

Besides, in paragraph 242, it recommended that:

(i) Any Bill relating solely to the prohibition or restriction of immigration into Ceylon shall not be regarded as coming within the category of Bills which the Governor-General is instructed to reserve for the signification of His Majesty's pleasure . . .

(ii) Any Bill relating solely to the franchise shall not be regarded as coming within the category of Bills which the Governor-General is instructed to reserve for the signification of His Majesty's pleasure.

The Indian leadership in the island regarded these comments and recommendations as a grievous setback to their cause and began a campaign of opposition to the recommendations embodied in the Soulbury report, but to no avail.

A second opportunity was missed in 1945. When the vote was taken on the White Paper on Sri Lanka's passage to semi-independence status, on 9 November, two Indian representatives joined a solitary Sinhalese radical in opposition to Senanayake's motion for acceptance of Britain's offer. This motion was approved by 51 members of 54 present and voting. The Indian representatives had been inclined to vote in favour even though the *quid pro quo* they asked for was not forthcoming, but M.S. Aney[8] the agent for the government of India[9] seated in the gallery of the house, sent down a note asking them to vote against the motion. It was, as Governor Sir Henry Monck-Mason-Moore, Caldecott's successor, observed in a confidential letter to a senior official at the Colonial Office, 'a stupid and improper piece of interference' on the part of the representatives of the Indian government.[10]

Senanayake was elated at the majority he had won. But Aney's indiscretion did not pass unnoticed. If anything, it tended to confirm fears of undue Indian influence on the affairs of Sri Lanka through the Indian minority once both India and Sri Lanka had won their independence. Indeed, relations between Senanayake and his associates on the one hand and the leadership of the Indian community in the island on the other remained strained throughout the year 1946-7. Had Aney refrained from his tactless intervention, and permitted the two Indian representatives to vote with Senanayake the latter may have been in a more conciliatory and generous mood.

Once Sri Lanka's independence was decided upon in 1946-7, there was some unease at the Colonial Office that negotiations had not been resumed on the thorny issue of the Indian franchise. On the questions relating to the status of the Indian minority in Sri Lanka, Senanayake's hand had been strengthened considerably with the publication of the Soulbury report. The Soulbury Commissioners themselves had considered this problem in all its ramifications and, as we have seen, had come down very much on the side of the Sri Lankan ministers. They had been convinced that Sri Lanka's political leadership had made a genuine effort to reach an agreement on this issue. Besides, independence was in the offing, and Sri Lanka was now in a stronger position—as a would-be dominion talking to another dominion—to get a favourable settlement.

Governor Sir Henry Monck-Mason-Moore, informed the Colonial Office on 17 October 1947 that Senanayake had arranged for negotiations with India. Senanayake was aware that Britain herself was preparing a UK Nationality bill, and fearing that this could affect his forthcoming negotiations with Nehru, had suggested that discussions on the UK Nationality bill be postponed till his negotiations with India were over. He clarified his views further on 8 November 1947 in another telegram which he sent through Moore explaining that a definition of Ceylon citizenship was being planned, but that he would not proceed with it till after his talks with the Indians scheduled for December 1947.

The substance of the offer he made to Nehru on this occasion was the grant of citizenship for all Indians who had lived in the island for a 'prescribed number of years'. Senanayake defined the prescribed period as seven years continuous residence for married persons and ten for single persons, with 31 December 1945 as the operative date. This, in fact, was a much more generous offer than the one made in 1941, but even so it did not satisfy Nehru who held out for a qualification of eight years for all persons, married or single, with January 1948 as the qualifying date.[11] Senanayake, with memories of what had happened at the negotiations in 1941 very much in mind would not go beyond this offer. The talks collapsed. Hugh Tinker, the historian of the Indian communities settled in British colonies, had no doubt that the blame should go to Nehru for the failure of these talks. Tinker identified Nehru's rigidity and his refusal to bargain or compromise, on what he—Nehru—thought were matters of principle, as the reasons why the talks failed. Eventually, an unilateral decision on this issue was imposed by Senanayake's independent government in 1948-9.[12]

One of the first political initiatives of Senanayake's government after independence was the definition of Sri Lankan citizenship that he had referred to in his telegram to the Colonial Office of 8 November 1947. The Ceylon Citizenship Act No. 18 of 1948 restricted the status of a national of Sri Lanka to those who could claim it by descent or registration. The application of these conditions to Indians in Sri Lanka was defined in The Indian and

Pakistani Residents (Citizenship) Act No. 3 of 1949. The requirements were much the same that Senanayake had offered Nehru in 1947. A third piece of legislation, The Ceylon (Parliamentary Elections) Amendment Act No. 48 of 1949, removed the voters of Indian origin from the electoral rolls.

Under the second of these Acts, applicants were required to produce documentary evidence in support of their claims to Sri Lankan citizenship. Such evidence was hard to come by, but the difficulties involved in this were compounded by the initial refusal of the Ceylon Indian Congress (later the Ceylon Workers' Congress) to co-operate in implementation of this legislation. By the time they changed their minds, it was too late for most potential applicants seeking Sri Lankan citizenship to stake their claims. S. Thondaman, then a young Ceylon Indian Congress leader, and a MP in the new Parliament, first gained national prominence through his involvement in this exercise in miscalculation.

RESOLUTION OF THE PROBLEM[13]

The citizenship legislation of 1948-9 and subsequent amendments had provided a legal definition of citizenship which excluded most of the Indians and the suffrage was limited to citizens of Sri Lanka. The vast majority of Indians resident in Sri Lanka were classified as stateless persons. It was never intended that they would remain permanently in this state of limbo. If far fewer Indians than anticipated secured Sri Lankan citizenship this was due as much to the mismanagement of the campaign of opposition to this legislation led by the Ceylon Indian Congress as to the zeal with which Sri Lankan officials stuck doggedly to the letter of the law. The Ceylon Indian Congress leadership had responded to this legislation with symbolic gestures of opposition in the Gandhian tradition, fasts in public places, *satyagrahas* and the like, all intended to use moral pressure on the Sri Lankan government and to rouse public opinion both in the island and outside it to the cause of the Indians here.[14] They had the support at all times of left-wing and Marxist opinion. Outside the country they had the moral and political support of the Indian government, and the state government of Madras. The latter's support could on occasion be more enthusiastic than was diplomatically acceptable, while other political groups and individuals in Madras and other parts of the state would go well beyond the level of support extended by the state government in sustaining the cause of the Indians in Sri Lanka. Indeed when in 1952, the Ceylon Workers' Congress (as the old Ceylon Indian Congress then called itself) embarked on a 100-day *satyagraha*, it required considerable tact and diplomacy to prevent 'volunteers' from coming over from Madras to join the campaign.[15]

But the advantages were now clearly with the Sri Lanka government. They had compelled the Indians to come to terms with the reality that citizenship would be determined on rules and regulations designed by the Sri Lanka government with very little influence on these from India. Nevertheless, the Indians were physically present in Sri Lanka, and the Indian government for its part refused to accept any responsibility for repatriating any significant number of them to India.

The issue came up for discussion once more between the two Prime Ministers in 1953 at a Commonwealth Prime Ministers' Conference in London. There, D.S. Senanayake's son and successor as Prime Minister, Dudley Senanayake, faced Nehru whose single-minded opposition to repatriation was well known. The talks between the two Prime Ministers were more important for the formula that Dudley Senanayake introduced on that occasion than for any great success achieved in reaching an agreement on it. That formula, set out below, was to be the essence of all future negotiations on this issue.

The formula recognized three categories of Indian residents in Sri Lanka: firstly, those who qualified for Sri Lankan citizenship under the prevailing citizenship laws;

secondly, those who did not qualify for citizenship but, subject to future review, would be granted permanent residence status on work permits; and the third category would be Indian citizens who would be gradually but compulsorily repatriated to India. The figures Senanayake had in mind for each of these categories were as follows: 400,000 for the first category, 200,000 for the second, and 300,000 for the third.[16]

Once more, as in 1947, there was agreement, in principle, on the formula of three categories, but once more the talks collapsed in regard to the details in its implementation. Some part of the blame for the failure attaches to Nehru whose attitude on this has been described as 'both unyielding and unreal'.[17] When Nehru insisted on a reduction of the numbers in the third category from 300,000 to 250,000, the younger Senanayake understood it to indicate that the Indian Prime Minister was testing his staying power and tenacity of purpose in what was their first personal encounter. The reduction by a sixth seemed to be too small to be anything other than an attempt to stall on an offer that, for all its advantages to India, still required a repatriation of a large number of Indians from Sri Lanka. Indeed Nehru, with the fate of the Indian minority in Burma very much in mind, was unhappy about accepting the principle of repatriation of Indians, even those with Indian passports. A stronger personality than the inexperienced Sri Lankan Prime Minister, may have seized on Nehru's haggling to seal the agreement. But the younger Senanayake was not inclined to do so.

Significantly enough, after Dudley Senanayake had resigned office in September 1953, his successor Sir John Kotelawala, resumed negotiations with India in January 1954. On this occasion, a firm agreement was reached, endorsing the three-categories formula of 1953. At this stage the Sri Lanka government was anxious to reach an agreement, and not merely because of the physical presence of the 'stateless' Indian Tamils in Sri Lanka. There was the equally important issue of the surreptitious addition to their numbers through a process of illicit immigration from across the Palk Straits. A promise was extracted of Indian assistance in checking this traffic, a task which had hitherto been performed by Sri Lanka's minuscule security forces.

One important feature of this agreement was that Indians accepted as Sri Lankan citizens under its terms would be placed on a separate register, and a special constituency, an 'Indian and Pakistani district' which would return up to four MPs. In insisting on this the Kotelawala government was safeguarding its own political base and demonstrating its interest in protecting the Kandyan constituencies from being swamped at a future date by Indian Tamils. Once more, the agreement broke down over implementation. All parties concerned, the two governments on the one hand, and the Ceylon Workers' Congress on the other, were suspicious of each other's motives and intentions. The Ceylon Workers' Congress was hostile to the principle of a separate register and a separate communal electorate which they regarded as flagrantly discriminatory, and one has reason to believe that their opposition to this had much to do with the eventual failure to implement the agreement. S.W.R.D. Bandaranaike never had time to focus attention on this issue during his administration and by the early 1960s it had become an intractable one with neither government prepared to make concessions to the other's point of view. When an agreement eventually emerged in 1964 with Mrs Bandaranaike as Prime Minister of Sri Lanka, and Lal Bahadur Shastri as Nehru's successor, its basis was the three-categories formula introduced by Dudley Senanayake in 1953. Nehru's death and India's discomfiture in the border war with China had more to do with the success of these negotiations than the negotiating skills and techniques of the Sri Lankan delegation. Nehru's successor, Shastri, had fewer compunctions than him about accepting the need to concede this principle. Besides, he had a more modest vision of India's position in the world than

Nehru's lofty aspiration to the role of the conscience of the world, or at least of the Third World.

The agreement Shastri reached with Mrs Bandaranaike provided for the repatriation over a 15-year period of 525,000 Indian residents in Sri Lanka to India, along with their natural increase; the absorption of 300,000 as citizens by Sri Lanka; the future of the remaining 150,000 to be negotiated later on by the two countries. The practical benefits to all parties were quite considerable, not least to the Indians in Sri Lanka, 300,000 of whom were to become Sri Lankan citizens. But two parties—the Indian government and the Indians in Sri Lanka—had their reservations about the principle of compulsory repatriation of those who opted for and obtained Indian citizenship.

In a reversion to a line of policy originally devised by the Kotelawala government in 1954, Mrs Bandaranaike decided to place all persons of recent Indian origin, those who had already obtained Sri Lanka citizenship, as well as those who were entitled to it under the agreement of 1964, on a separate electoral register. This move was designed to protect the political interests of the Kandyans. It antagonized all sections of Indian opinion resident in the island. They reiterated their opposition to a separate electoral register and a separate constituency because it established two categories of voters, one of which was distinctly inferior because its basis was ethnic identity.

The result was a remarkable change in political alignments. The Ceylon Workers' Congress, the most powerful trade union *cum* political party among the plantation workers, withdrew its support from the SLFP-dominated government and, in a surprising *volte-face*, swung over to an alliance with the UNP which it had hitherto treated as its principal opponent. The reconciliation was based on the understanding that the UNP would repudiate the policy of a separate register for Indians, and examine afresh the requirement that those who obtained Indian citizenship would be immediately repatriated. With the establishment of the UNP-led coalition government of

1965 these pledges were honoured. Those Indians who secured Sri Lankan citizenship remained on the general electoral roll and those who were granted Indian citizenship were permitted to remain in the island, if necessary to the end of their working days, to be repatriated thereafter, or at a time to be determined by the Sri Lankan government. The SLFP for its part did not revive the principle of a separate electoral register for Indians, but when in office in the 1970s insisted on a linkage between immediate repatriation and the conferment of Indian citizenship.

The UNP-CWC entente has been a prominent feature of Sri Lankan politics since the mid-1960s to 1994, to the advantage of both parties. On the part of the CWC it reflected a more pragmatic and less doctrinaire approach to politics than that of the Federal Party and its successors; it also demonstrated that the linguistic nationalism of the Tamils had its own limits and could not bring all Tamils together within the Sri Lanka polity on a common political programme.

One of Mrs Bandaranaike's most constructive achievements in her second term as Prime Minister was the virtual settlement of the problems relating to persons of recent Indian origin resident in Sri Lanka. Through negotiations with the Indian Prime Minister, Mrs Gandhi, she brought to a successful conclusion a settlement initiated originally in 1964. The primary objective was to eliminate statelessness for good. For the moment the more urgent requirement was an agreement on how to deal with the balance of 150,000 left over for later consideration in terms of the 1964 pact. The decision was that there would be an equal division of these into Indian and Sri Lankan citizens. Not all the stateless were covered by this 1974 agreement; there were a number, variously computed at between 50,000 to 75,000, left over for further consideration, the last of the stateless. But much more important for Mrs Bandaranaike was that the Indian government accepted the principle that those who were recognized as Indian citizens must be repatriated to India, upon the granting of such citizenship, and that the process of repatriation itself must be expedited in order to make up for the time lost between 1965 and 1970.

From the point of view of the Indians who obtained Sri Lanka citizenship there was the distinct advantage that no attempt was made by her to revive the scheme of a separate electoral register for them. Thus nearly half a million of them would eventually be integrated into the Sri Lankan polity, and Sri Lankan citizenship would confer on them the political legitimacy which, as an ethnic group, they did not have since 1949. But these long-term political implications of the Prime Minister's diplomacy and skilfully crafted settlement of this issue seem to have had very little effect on the thinking of some members of her own Cabinet.

And relations between the leadership of the Ceylon Workers' Congress and the government were as unfriendly as those of the latter with the Federal Party. It is almost inevitable that a government in which Kandyan influence is predominant would be inclined towards attitudes of apprehension and a suspicion of, if not open hostility to, the Indian community resident in the island. And so it proved to be. It was not the Prime Minister herself a Kandyan Sinhalese, but the Minister for Agriculture and Lands, H. Kobbekaduwa, who gave expression to the traditional Kandyan hostility to the Indians through word and deed. His speeches against them were unabashedly racist in tone.[18] And he followed them up with administrative acts avowedly discriminatory in intent and effect, a policy of unconcealed hostility more vigorous and far more severe in impact than anything in the past.

He used his authority as minister in charge of land acquisitions to take over almost all the plantations owned by political activists among the Indian residents in Sri Lanka. This was done *well before* the Land Reform Act of 1972, which placed a ceiling on landholdings, was introduced. Among those affected were the Ceylon Workers' Congress leader S. Thondaman, and

V. Annamalai, who had been an appointed MP in the Parliament of 1965-70. Evidently the Minister for Agriculture and Lands, if not the United Front government, was hoping to destroy the economic base which sustained the leadership of the Ceylon Workers' Congress.

As the guiding spirit of the first phase of the nationalization of the plantations, i.e. 1972, Kobbekaduwa made the impact of nationalization on the Indian workers harsher than it may have been under a more sympathetic and understanding Minister. The United Front government had just such a minister in the person of Dr Colvin R de Silva of the LSSP. Fortunately for the Indian plantation workers some of the larger state-run plantations came under the Ministry of Plantation Industries of which Dr de Silva was the minister. The treatment of Indian plantation workers under this ministry was exemplary. Even so the larger section of the plantations were still privately owned and managed by British commercial firms. When these were nationalized in 1975 the LSSP had been expelled from the coalition. Nevertheless some of the worst features of the first phase of nationalization under Kobbekaduwa, especially the harsh treatment of Indian plantation workers, were largely avoided. There was the danger of parcelling out of some of the better, if not the best, plantations in small lots among the Sinhalese peasants who lived in the vicinity of the plantations. By 1976 and 1977 the danger was very real.[19] Among the plantations identified for this purpose were some of the best in the Nuwara Eliya district, the heart of the plantation enterprise. The danger was avoided through the defeat of the SLFP at the general election of 1977 during which the CWC worked enthusiastically for the UNP.

The immigrant plantation workers have been, since independence, the most economically depressed group in Sri Lanka, but never more so than in the early and mid-1970s. In this they were the victims of impersonal market forces, declining yields and falling prices of plantation products rather than of any policy of discrimination. All sections of the population felt the impact of the inflationary pressures of the 1970s, the unprecedented increase in food prices accompanied by a drastic curtailment of government expenditure on food subsidies. But the effect of these on the plantation workers was devastating, a precipitous decline from a bare subsistence to grinding poverty. The grimmest, and most telling, evidence of this lay in the maternal and infant mortality rates of this period. These were considerably higher among the plantation workers than the national average. Deaths by starvation were a frequent occurrence in the plantations in the 1970s, especially in late 1973 and through much of 1974. The UF government's lack of concern in the face of this appalling fall in living standards of the plantation workers was explicable only in terms of powerful anti-Indian sentiment so deeply rooted among influential cabinet ministers that it was proof against appeals to conscience and humanitarianism.

The situation was aggravated, no doubt, by increasing unemployment on the plantations. The plantations were in no position to provide employment to the natural increase of the estate population when the regular workers were themselves generally under-employed. The leadership of the Indian plantation workers complained that the latter had been by-passed in the provision of welfare facilities in health and education. These were usually provided by the plantations rather than directly through the state and none but the most financially stable and viable of the plantations were able to maintain their welfare facilities unimpaired much less expand them. The plantation economy was, up to the mid-1970s, in a generally depressed state.

Because most of the plantation workers were without votes they were at a great disadvantage in the search for employment outside the plantations since no politicians, other than the plantation workers leadership itself, were interested in their cause. Certainly they—even those who have a vote—did not have the same access to land on irrigation projects, much less to state-owned land in the vicinity of plantations, that the Sinhalese have. All that was available to them, apart from work on plantations, was occasional employment in the vicinity of the estates and in the bazaars and towns in the plantation districts as casual labourers.

1977 AND AFTER

The general election of 1977 was a decisive turning point in the recent history of Sri Lanka's Indian community. Its re-integration into the national political process, thwarted if not interrupted since the early 1950s by the restrictions placed on the voting rights of Indians in Sri Lanka, began that year, the product of the alliance between the CWC and the UNP. For the first time since the general election of 1947, the Indians had enough votes to send a representative to Parliament through the ballot— S. Thondaman who won the third seat in the multi-member constituency of Nuwara Eliya.

Politically, the UNP and the CWC made an odd couple, the former generally regarded as the authentic voice of the Sri Lankan capitalist class, the latter unique in South Asia as a trade union that functioned as a political party, and the party itself as the voice of an ethnic group the great majority of whom were workers on the plantations. Beginning in the mid-1960s as an electoral alliance this unusual combination of political forces became a governing coalition in 1978, a coalition of convenience rather than of necessity or ideology, and which remained intact till the general elections of August 1994 and the defeat of the UNP on that occasion. That political alliance benefitted both groups. The UNP was assured of a solid block of votes, a votebank in the parlance of Indian political reportage, which kept increasing in size over the 1980s till it became a very sizeable one in the 1990s, large enough to command special attention as a potential swing vote. The Indian leadership, for its part, secured support for its political and social agendas. These agendas are reviewed below.

One part of that social agenda does need special mention. We have seen how the CWC had gained a seat on each of the two state controlled management structures that ran the plantations. Part of the influence it had was used to improve living conditions on the plantations and to increase the wages there for the first time for over a decade. But some of that influence has been directed against attempts at privatization of the plantations even though there is a strong economic cause for it. Indeed if Sri Lanka's plantations show some of the dynamism of their Kenyan or Thai counterparts, all run by private companies, wages could increase to the levels in these countries, and living standards would improve on the plantations. But it was feared that the process could also lead to a reduction in the number of those employed on the plantations; or a shifting of workers from areas of excess labour to others in which there is a shortage of labour. The CWC has objected to privatization for both these reasons. The trade union is strongly opposed to the latter process, especially any movement from the Nuwara Eliya district where there is an excess of labour for fear of diluting its voting strength there, its most significant and conspicuous electoral stronghold.

Despite being a trade union primarily, the CWC as a political party is as leader-dominated as the UNP or SLFP. Like the SLFP which has been controlled by the Bandaranaike family from its establishment in 1951, the leadership of the CWC has an extremely narrow personal base. S. Thondaman, in fact, is the most durable political- and trade union-leader in Sri Lanka's history, surpassing the Bandaranaikes in this. He has been an important figure in the affairs of the then Ceylon Indian Congress since the 1940s and the major figure in the CWC since the 1950s by which time he had established himself as its leader, a position he has held over the last four decades. Throughout this period—indeed till March 1997—he has seldom if ever been out of step with the wishes and opinions of his constituents except in one matter. He maintains his Indian ties, especially with the district from which his ancestors came to Sri Lanka. These ties include a home and investments in India. Many of the younger, second rung leaders, are endeavouring to disavow any ties with India, and speak of themselves as Hill Country Tamils, very much an indigenous group.

Under Thondaman's leadership the CWC and its constituency regards itself as part of the political mainstream unlike the principal parties of the indigenous Tamils. Only once has the CWC actually linked its fortunes, politically, to those of the main Sri Lanka Tamil groups. This was in the 1970s when it became part of the short-lived Tamil United Front (TUF). The link was severed by mid-1970s, not indeed with any great fanfare but Thondaman and his group steered clear of any activity that could be construed as sympathy for, much less, support for Tamil separatism. Nevertheless, Thondaman left room for himself to play a mediatory role between the Sri Lanka government and Tamil separatist groups, using his Indian links on occasion, for this purpose.

Thondaman has proved to be a master of the step by step approach in securing the principal elements in the political agenda of his trade union cum party. He campaigned with great patience, from within the UNP government between 1978 and 1988, to complete the process begun in 1964 and 1974 of bringing an end to statelessness among the workers in his community. The process was completed in 1988, sixty years after the question of voting rights for Indians in Sri Lanka became a divisive issue in the island's politics. The legislation of 1988 that ensured this was no more than a footnote to the principal agreements reached between Sri Lanka and India in 1964 and 1974 under the leadership of Mrs Bandaranaike. One consequence of riots of 1983, and the subsequent Indian mediation and intervention, is that the repatriation to India of plantation workers deemed to be Indian citizens, and even those holding Indian passports, has ceased, despite the clause in the Indo-Sri Lanka Accord which sought to ensure that they would be sent to India. This group, whose numerical strength is a matter for speculation and debate represents one more item of unfinished business in a 60-year controversy between India and Sri Lanka.

When the CWC switched its support to the present left of centre People's Alliance coalition in 1994, the integration of the Indian community into the Sri Lankan political system was complete. The Indian vote had become a swing vote that could be switched from one major Sri Lanka party to another as the Muslim vote had done on several occasions. Thondaman had led the CWC out of its 30-year alliance with the UNP, just as he had led them into it in 1964.

The CWC has many challenges ahead, many of them stemming from Thondaman's durability as the leader, and his attempt to designate his grandson as his political heir, overlooking the claims of the second-rung leadership. Because Thondaman has succumbed to the South Asian malady of dynasty-building, his political legacy. is likely to be dissipated in the struggle for the succession that would ensue with his departure from the scene. He is now in his early 80s. The power struggle to fill the huge void he will leave could even result in the disintegration of the CWC. Almost certainly everyone who aspires to the succession of the whole or part of it is likely to make a greater effort than Thondaman to emphasize the Sri Lankan orientation of both the leadership and the community.

CHAPTER 9

Conclusion

The difference between happy families and unhappy ones, it is often said, is that the happy families are very much alike while unhappy ones are unhappy each in its own different way. So is the difference between multi-ethnic states with a record of good governance and given to the maintenance of harmonious relations among its component ethnic and religious groups, and those others with a record of violent conflict of varying intensity. The difference is best posed in terms of what might have been. How is it that Malaysia succeeded in maintaining a stable political structure and relatively harmonious relations between potentially antagonistic if not hostile ethnic groups, while Sri Lanka failed to do so? Or again what common factors do we see in the breakdown in Sri Lanka which we have analysed in this book, the virtual collapse of the state in Lebanon, and the persistence of violent confrontations in Ulster?

If the problems of Ulster demonstrate anything at all it is that partition of acutely divided polities with a long record of violent internal conflict creates as many new problems as it solves when the minority in the former larger entity becomes a majority in a smaller separate one.[1] Lebanon has always been a collection of minorities brought together by former colonial powers to form an artificial political entity.[2] Yet a system of balancing religious, ethnic and clan identities through a contrived electoral compromise gave Lebanon several decades of political stability and a level of economic prosperity that was the envy of its neighbours. The breakdown came in the 1970s through the operation of a complex set of factors one of which was a demographic change which rendered obsolete the electoral compromise imposed in the 1940s. More relevant for purposes of comparison with Sri Lanka is Malaysia. Like Sri Lanka, Malaysia is a multi-ethnic society in which the component elements increased under colonial rule with the immigration of Chinese and Indians. At independence the Malays were a bare majority, unlike the Sinhalese in Sri Lanka. The Sinhalese-Buddhists were just under two-thirds of the island's population at the transfer of power, while the Sinhalese—Buddhist and Christian— were over 70 per cent of the population at that time. As in Sri Lanka, so in Malaysia, one of the principal issues that came up for discussion and settlement prior to the transfer of power was the question of citizenship rights of immigrants, two sets of them, Chinese and Indians, in this instance, and not merely Indians as in Sri Lanka. For Malaysia (or Malaya as it was before independence) the time of troubles started before independence not after (with the single exception of the riots of 1969) as was the case in Sri Lanka. The prognosis for Malaysia, in the years following independence, was far from encouraging. Yet the prophets of gloom were proved wrong.

There are many reasons for the relatively peaceful operation of the Malaysian political system. Among the most important of these is the existence of a pragmatic political bargain between the principal ethnic groups in the country, Malays and the Chinese. This bargain is more implicit than explicit but it acts as a powerful restraining influence on both. Its basic principle is that the Malays would treat the Chinese economic interests as the engine of the national economy, and agree to absorb the young Chinese into the political system while the Chinese, for their part, would accept Malay political dominance and an increasing share for the Malays in the economy in return.[3] The origins of this bargain go back virtually to the early days of independence, and while it has been re-interpreted particularly after May 1969, it has lasted to the present day. The crucial difference between Malaysia and Sri Lanka is that there has been no similar 'agreement' on common interests between the Sinhalese and Tamils since the mid-1950s; indeed since the early 1920s.

Malaysia's electoral and parliamentary system which encourages multi-racial cooperation, particularly among the racially based component parties of the ruling coalition, is a second factor. This difference between the Malaysian and Sri Lankan political systems reflects the difference in the spatial distribution of the various ethnic groups in the two countries. The third factor, the nearly continuous economic growth and development of the country since 1957, has been emphasized more than the others. Undoubtedly, this has given the ruling coalition greater leeway in keeping all ethnic groups more or less satisfied with their lot.[4] Even so the demographic pattern of the country with its almost even balance[5] between the Malays and non-Malays at the time of independence has also contributed substantially to the maintenance of this political bargain and has acted as a powerful deterrent to any attempt to radically change the ethnic composition of the ruling coalition for fear of the possible devastating consequences of a national racial conflagration. This is one point the leaders of the coalition, especially the Malays, always emphasize in their appeal to the electorate just before elections. By and large the electorate seems to accept the argument.

While the minorities in Malaysia are much larger numerically than in Sri Lanka there is no large territory with a Chinese or non-Malay majority. The nearest to such a situation is the island of Penang (a state in the federation) where there is a Chinese majority. An independent Penang has not been regarded as a viable proposition and no serious attempt has been made at establishing a Chinese 'homeland' based on Penang. Equally important is the distance between the Chinese in Malaysia and China itself, separated by hundreds of kilometers of land or sea, and not a mere 35 kilometers at the narrowest point as it is between the Tamils of the Jaffna peninsula in Sri Lanka and Tamilnadu in southern India. In short, there is no territorial base to encourage aspirations to separatism, as there was and is in Sri Lanka.

Sri Lanka, as the earlier chapters of this volume have shown, was the model colony, the one post-independence state emerging from the British *raj* and empire in South Asia, to manage a peaceful transition from colonial rule to government by an indigenous elite. The first stage in the model colony's fall from grace came in the mid-1950s and early 1960s in the transformation of its nationalism from a multi-ethnic form to a more inclusive if more democratic version based on language. The question that needs to be answered is why the clash of competing linguistic nationalisms should have erupted in violence, when the more long drawn out conflict of religions, Buddhism and Christianity, did not do so? This is partly explained by the fact that the latter was essentially a conflict among the Sinhalese. The former was a conflict between the Sinhalese and the island's principal minority, the Tamils. Both conflicts had deep historical roots.

Ethnic conflict between the Sinhalese and Tamils is a twentieth century manifestation of an age-old rivalry, very much like that between the Vietnamese and the Chinese. One needs to keep in mind the historical dimension of the rivalries, a palimpsest with layer upon layer of troubled historical memories, where the events of several centuries ago assume the immediacy of the previous weekend, and those of a thousand years, that of the last year. The country is haunted by a history which is agonizing to recall but hazardous to forget. This is not a peculiarly Sri Lankan or even a South Asian or South-east Asian phenomenon; one turns to the contemporary situation in the Balkans— Bosnia, Serbia, Macedonia and Albania—or if one ventures further into the east of Europe, to the Caucasus region, for powerful reminders of the play of historical memories on the political aspirations and on the fears—rational and irrational—of people.

The Sinhalese outnumber the Tamils six to one within Sri Lanka, and yet far from this overwhelming majority status giving them a sense of security they regard themselves as a historically beleaguered minority facing an ancient antagonist whose main stronghold lies across the seas in Tamilnadu in South India. The Tamils of South Asia—of Tamilnadu and Sri Lanka—outnumber the Sinhalese by more than four to one. We thus confront the powerful influence of the Sinhalese sense of historical destiny, of a small and embattled people who have preserved Theravada Buddhism when it was obliterated in southern India under a Hindu revivalist tide, and whose language, despite its roots in classical Indian languages, is uniquely Sri Lankan. And along with it there is the perception of the Tamils as the traditional national enemy against whom their ancestors fought at various times in the past. There is, above all, the perception of southern India as the source from which scores of invasions of the heartland of ancient Sri Lanka were launched.

These historical memories reinforce the present sense of Sinhalese insecurity in dealing with the Tamils, and reinforce too their belief that they are a 'minority'. Yet, to accept the Sinhalese perception of themselves as a 'minority' facing a massive and implacable Tamil phalanx is to ignore several facts of Sri Lankan politics. First of all, the Sri Lankan Tamils living outside the Tamil areas of the north and east of the island have a distinct political outlook of their own, and if this has been distinct from the outlooks of the Sinhalese majority, just as often they were distinct also from those of the Tamils of the Jaffna peninsula. Secondly, we have seen how the Indian Tamils have had strong political links with the UNP, in a political alliance that has withstood the vicissitudes of Sri Lanka's changing political system for 30 years since 1964; at present they have shifted their allegiance to the ruling Peoples' Alliance.

If the Sinhalese were—and are—insecure because of the burden of history and memories of the past, the Tamils are insecure because of fears for their future. And just as the Sinhalese sense of insecurity lies behind the misguided policies intent on forcing the pace of change, when change in their favour was inevitable if somewhat slower than they wished it to be, the Tamils sought to protect their interests and to redress the balance which was now shifting markedly against them by making exaggerated claims to a special status in the Sri Lanka polity. These claims were asserted in a number of forms and at various times, all of which made the management of ethnic tensions harder than it might have been without them. Among the most controversial of these is the claim for control over what is called the 'Traditional Homelands' of the Tamils.[6]

And here it needs to be underlined that the unusual prominence the Sri Lanka Tamils have had in Sri Lankan public life in the early 20th century has left an indelible mark on their political attitudes. Thus, in 1918, a document presented by the Jaffna Association to the Colonial Office made the point that:

> . . . The Tamils of Ceylon have hitherto, in spite of their inferiority in numbers, maintained a position of equality with their Sinhalese brethren, whether in official of unofficial life.[7]

This special position they owed to a number of exceptional circumstances, but one of them undoubtedly was the skilful leadership and political dexterity of the two brothers, Ponnambalam Ramanathan and Ponnambalam Arunachalam.

Up to the early 1920s, the Tamils did not regard themselves as a minority, nor were they regarded as a minority. At that time the term 'minorities' had a much more restricted meaning in the Sri Lankan context than it has today: it included the Europeans, Burghers and Muslims but not always the Christians or the Tamils. In fact, the political thinking of that period accepted the concept of two majority communities, the Sinhalese and the Tamils. The situation changed in the 1920s: instead of *two* majority communities there was now one majority community, the Sinhalese, and several minorities which included the Tamils.

Ramanathan gloried in the role of being a minority spokesman, or rather the spokesman for the minorities, but even so old assumptions died hard, for we have that shrewd observer of the Sri Lankan scene, Governor Sir Hugh Clifford, commenting in November 1926 that:

> . . . the Sinhalese resent the reluctance of the Tamils to accord themselves merely a minority section of an united Ceylonese nation . . .[8]

Thus, we see the emergence of a duality in the Tamil political attitudes, their assertion of minority rights, always accompanied by a search for a wider and larger role. In Ramanathan's time this duality took the form of a leadership of a phalanx of minorities, with the Tamils in the lead. This duality inevitably led to confusion about the nature of the Tamils' role or position in the Sri Lankan polity, and this confusion has continued to affect the political vision of the Tamils' leadership ever since. The '50-50' campaign can only be explained as an attempt to perpetuate this duality. The sharp terms in which it was rejected by both Sir Andrew Caldecott, who as Governor of the island first confronted the political pressures that emerged from that agitation, and by the Soulbury Commissioners, sprang from their clear grasp of its implications for the management of ethnic tensions in Sri Lanka. The latter viewed the '50-50' campaign as an 'inequitable' and 'artificial means to convert a majority into a minority'.[9]

Traces of this duality linger on in contemporary Tamil politics in Sri Lanka. It takes various forms. It appears in the concept of the 'Tamil-speaking peoples of Sri Lanka' with its assumption of tutelage over the Muslims; it is immanent in the insistence on federalism; and it lies at the heart of the campaign for separatism. Thus, the present conflict between the Sinhalese and the Tamils takes on an unusual complexity. It is much more than a conflict between a majority and minority, or indeed a conflict between two minorities. The conflict is between a majority with a minority complex, and a minority with a yearning for majority status, a minority with a majority complex.

EFFORTS AT MANAGEMENT AND RESOLUTION

The principal issues in dispute in Sri Lanka's ethnic conflicts have been reviewed in earlier parts of this book. While many of these issues were once regarded as intractable, some of the more salient among them, issues that divided the people of the country sharply over the last 50 years or more, have been resolved. Partly, a surprisingly resilient spirit of compromise has succeeded in the face of dogmatism and rigidity. Despite the tensions and violence that have been a feature of life in post-independence Sri Lanka, there has been an irrepressible strand of pragmatism which eventually helped in moderating the outcome of many of the very contentious issues.

For instance, religious strife in the form of tensions and conflict between Buddhists and Christians—in particular the Buddhists and Roman Catholics—one of the most divisive factors in Sri Lanka public life for about 80 years or so beginning in the last quarter of the 19th century, has ceased to be a contentious issue in politics since the early 1970s. These religious tensions had been, at times, so sharp that they gave every impression of remaining an abiding divisive factor in Sri Lankan public life. Many of these tensions had been linked to controversies on state control over education. By the end of the 1960s the Roman Catholics had reconciled themselves to a more limited role in education and in Sri Lankan public life. Within the church there were groups who argued that it needed to move away from its traditional attitudes on education of its flock. The bitterness engendered by it had reached a peak in the 1930s and 1940s when the state began to stake out a greater share for itself in education at the expense of the missionaries. The struggle for state control over education brought the Marxists and Buddhist activists together in a campaign which reached its finale in

1960-1. But the rancour it generated and left behind caused divisions among the Sinhalese rather than between them and the Tamil minority. The wounds began to heal only in the 1970s when the Roman Catholics, after the Vatican Council of 1963-5, started showing evidence of a greater readiness towards acceptance of religious pluralism, and sought an accommodation with the forces of nationalism just as the smaller Protestant groups had done almost half a century earlier. The point that needs to be made, and as emphatically as possible, is that these religious disputes were principally among the Sinhalese, between the Christians and the Buddhists and not between the latter and the Tamils, and also that religious tensions are only of very limited significance in the current conflict between the Sinhalese and Tamils.[10]

Then again there is the settlement reached on the status of Indian Tamils in Sri Lanka. The problem of the political status and voting rights of Indian communities overseas came to the fore first of all in Sri Lanka, and as long ago as 1928-31. The accommodation reached between 1964 and 1974[11] as well as the elaboration of this made between 1977 and 1988[12] constitute a major political accomplishment considering the passions and fears that this question has aroused since the late 1920s and the violence associated with societies in other parts of the world that had to cope with large-scale immigration of Indians. Once agreement was reached on the number of Indians to whom Sri Lankan citizenship was to be granted, their inclusion within the 'political nation' was accomplished over a 20-year period. Eventually, the number of Indians admitted to Sri Lankan citizenship has proved to be larger than that agreed to in 1964 and 1974.

The accommodation reached on language policy is even more significant. One needs to reiterate the price the country paid in the breakdown of ethnic harmony, and in the distortion of national priorities, outweighed the undeniable benefits the emphasis on indigenous languages brought to the people at large. We have seen how 'Sinhala

Only' proved to be an elusive objective, an abstraction rather than a well-formulated policy. 'Sinhala Only' was never more than a convenient piece of rhetorical fiction maintained for political purposes by sections of the Sinhalese elite.

At the same time, modifications of language policy made between 1958 and 1978, through political necessity (in 1958) and a realistic adjustment to life in a plural society (1978), had all but conceded parity of status to the Tamil language. The clauses on language in the constitution of 1978 reflected a recognition of an existing reality. The explicit reversion to parity of status to the two languages which came in 1987 and 1988 as a part of a political settlement, brokered by the Indian government, was also a recognition of this. And yet the political benefits of these concessions, and the anticipated political advantages, have proved to be just as elusive as the quest for 'Sinhala Only' because Tamil politicians did not see it in their interest to make public acknowledgment of the importance of these changes, much less to concede that the 'Sinhala Only' policy was never really implemented as rigidly as its ideologues intended it to be. Instead, they have persisted in concentrating on some of the practical difficulties involved in the transaction of business in the Tamil language in the Sinhalese areas of the country.

The bitterness underlying the controversies on employment is explained in part by the conflict between Tamils' traditional anxiety to maintain the levels of employment in the state services they had grown accustomed to under British rule and the attempts of Sinhalese to insist on what they regard as their legitimate share of it. The economic resources of the Northern Province are severely limited and as early as the last quarter of the 19th century it was evident that the increasing population of the region could not be accommodated in the traditional occupations based on land. The Tamils turned to state employment and the professions, much more than to plantation agriculture and trade, in search of avenues of employment; and they emigrated in large numbers to the British territories in what is now peninsular Malaysia. Indeed, by the early years of the 20th century the Tamils had come to be singularly dependent on government service and precisely because they had no deep roots in the island's plantation economy or trade for that matter, they were moved to defend their position in the public service all the more zealously.

By the 1930s Tamils dominated the public sector as clerks, teachers, and technicians and were well-established in the professional services as doctors and engineers as well. More significantly, they now faced Sinhalese competition, and their advantageous position in government employment became a point of contention and division in politics. The Soulbury Commissioners reported in 1945 that appointment to the public services

> . . . provides a common source of dissension between majority and minority communities . . . [The] Ceylon Tamils appear, at any rate as late as 1938, to have occupied a disproportionate number of posts in Public Services . . . That they have won for themselves a much larger share is a consequence of the higher standard of literacy and education which this community has so long enjoyed, and of its energy and efficiency. For similar reasons the Burghers have achieved an even more remarkable position.[13]

The Commission viewed

> . . . the Sinhalese challenge to the predominant position of the Tamils in public appointments . . . [as] the natural effect of the spread of education and of the efforts being made to bring other portions of the island up to the intellectual level of one portion of it . . .[14]

Having identified the problem they turned to the British experience to reassure the Tamils:

> In this connection, we cannot help recalling a period in our own history when, as the result of the superior educational facilities and better teaching prevalent in

Scotland, a minority was enabled to secure a larger
share of administrative and executive posts in the United
Kingdom than could have been justified on any
proportional allocation. Since then the English have
made strenuous and not altogether unsuccessful
endeavours to redress the deficiencies of their past.[15]

Thus, at the time of the transfer of power, the Tamil
minority was warned in the clearest possible terms—even
though the style chosen for the warning was understatement
rather than exaggeration—that hard times lay ahead of
them as educational standards improved among the
Sinhalese. Unlike some achievement-oriented minorities
in other parts of the world, the Chinese in Malaysia and
other parts of South-east Asia, for instance, the Sri Lankan
Tamils grew accustomed to state employment. Their
position in commerce and industry and plantation
agriculture did not match their stake in their chosen field
of concentration, and the determining factor was a quest—
almost a passion—for security and a steady income, a
reflection of their awareness of the limited opportunities
for employment available to them in the Jaffna peninsula.
This made them exceptionally vulnerable and exceptionally
sensitive to changes in language policy, to educational
reform, and changes in the mechanisms for determining
admission to tertiary education in a country in which
expansion in university education lagged far behind the
expansion of secondary and primary education.

After independence, competition increased, especially
with the rapid expansion of educational opportunities in
the Sinhalese areas. This greatly reduced the prospects of
the Tamils in their search for positions in government
service. Over the next 25 years they would be overtaken in
almost every sector of state employment and in the
professions by the Sinhalese, overtaken but far from being
overwhelmed. For a while they retained their advantageous
position in some of the professions—medicine, law and
engineering—but lost it by the early 1980s. This represented
the intellectual capital of the past, carefully gathered, and

protected and augmented but, in their eyes, not expanding rapidly enough to overcome what they saw as the disadvantages of the new policy changes which would adversely effect the next generation of Tamils.

The drop in the numbers of Tamils in the state service was very marked after 1956. While representatives of Tamil opinion often argue that this was the inevitable result of the change in language policy adopted in that year, there were other powerful forces of change at work. Given the demographic structure of the country, the Tamils could hardly have maintained the percentage of posts they held up to the 1930s.

In an assessment of this complex situation made in 1984 S.W.R.de.A. Samarasinghe points out that:

> The Tamils have already lost the relative position in central government employment that was enjoyed in the past. Apart from the obvious economic loss this entails, there is the psychological adjustment that many Jaffna (Tamil) families must make in the wake of this change. There is the fact that government jobs are no longer as easily obtained as they were a generation or two ago. The Sinhalese, on the other hand, are bound to view the change as a natural and inevitable adjustment that bestows on them their 'due' share. Clearly there are two different perceptions of the same phenomenon. The result is the Tamils have begun to feel they are 'discriminated' against and the Sinhalese feel recent changes have simply reversed the 'discrimination' they had been subjected to in the past.[16]

Samarasinghe's assessment holds true for the last 14 years as well, i.e. for the post-1984 period. Indeed, if one excludes the state-owned plantation sector, where the vast majority of the employees are Indian Tamils, the number of Tamils in *all* grades of state employment has declined to less than 10 per cent. This is about a third or a fourth of what it was in the early 1940s.

Many factors have contributed to this sharp decline in numbers after 1984: first, there is the large-scale emigration of Tamil youth from all strata of society to Australia, to western countries such as Canada,[17] Scandinavia (largely to Norway and Sweden) and mainly Britain, in the wake of Sri Lanka's ethnic conflict and, in particular, the disturbed political situation in the Jaffna peninsula. They desire to flee the rigours of life under the LTTE and escape the harsh reality of compulsory military service in the LTTE's army. Second, there has also been a steady stream of 'economic refugees' to Denmark, Germany, France and Switzerland in western Europe and to Canada. There is next, the collapse of civil administration of the north of the island and in parts of the east. This has greatly reduced opportunities for state employment for the Tamils who live there. In addition, there is another factor, the expansion of the private sector for the first time since the mid-1950s. Since the late 1970s, the private sector (including import-export trade) has provided opportunities for employment, outside the control of government and the political processes—including the system of patronage—that often govern admission to state employment. The expansion of the private sector was on a scale that would have seemed impossible in the early 1970s. Among the principal beneficiaries of the expansion of the private sector are the minorities, Tamils and Muslims. More to the point, state employment is no longer as attractive as it once was in comparison to the private sector with its greater flexibility in wages, and promotions, greater recognition given to merit and personal initiative and above all its freedom from political interference. Nevertheless, remedial measures—perhaps a form or forms of affirmative action—are required to get the country's public services to reflect more accurately than it does today the country's ethnic profile in the composition of its cadres.

We have seen how changes in university admissions policy have contributed substantially and dramatically to the sharp deterioration of ethnic relations in Sri Lanka in the last two decades, and to radicalizing the politics of the

Tamil areas in the north and east of the island. The crux of the problem was that the Sri Lankan Tamils who constitute no more than an eighth of the island's total population, had a dominant position in the science-based faculties of the then University of Ceylon at Peradeniya and Colombo for years. In 1970, for instance, the Tamils gained just over 35 per cent of the admissions to the science-based faculties; in Engineering and Medicine it was as high as 40 per cent. In 1970, the United Front coalition introduced a fundamental change by instituting a system of standardization of marks by language media at the university entrance examination. The effect of this was to place the Tamil students at a disadvantage in that they had to obtain a higher aggregate of marks to enter the university—in the medical, science and engineering faculties—than the Sinhalese. Thereafter, a district quota system was also introduced which gave weightage to students in rural areas and from backward communities. All this represented a departure from the traditional practice of selecting students on the basis of actual marks obtained at an open competitive examination. The Tamils, justifiably, saw this change in university entrance policy as patently and deliberately discriminatory.[18]

In the late 1970s and early 1980s the newly-elected UNP government changed this policy, and moved towards a more equitable admissions system, a mixture of district quotas and merit, and affirmative action for rural areas—Sinhalese, Tamil and Muslim.[19] Nevertheless, memories of the unilateral and discriminatory change in university policy made in the early 1970s still remain fresh in the minds of Tamils, although the policy has been changed, and despite the very substantial expansion of university places in medicine and engineering that has taken place after 1979 providing greater opportunities to students from all sections of the population. The Tamils' share of places in the engineering and medical faculties has varied from 35 per cent to 25 per cent since 1978-9, to very recent times when it has fallen to around 15 per cent.

This system has now developed powerful vested interests which resist all attempts to return to a merit-based system. The most vocal supporters of the system are the Muslims and the 'Indian-Tamils' with the Tamils of the Eastern Province and from parts of the Northern Province (outside the Jaffna peninsula) being joined by Sinhalese from more rural parts of the country in this.[20] The most recent (1994-5) development is that the Tamils from the Jaffna peninsula, hitherto the most vocal critics of the system, have also joined in. They are demanding the status of a disadvantaged district for Jaffna itself. They succeeded in securing this advantage when, without much fanfare, Jaffna was recognized as a disadvantaged district. It remains to be seen whether this reversal of the position taken by the Jaffna politicians, from being the most vigorous advocates of a merit system to the somewhat low-key claimants for the benefits of district quotas, will be purely temporary, or become permanent.

Quite apart from tertiary education, there have been sharp rivalries among the minorities over access to facilities in primary and secondary education (e.g. the Muslims against the Tamils in the Eastern Province). The most recent manifestation of this lies in the Central Province in the rivalries between the Muslims and 'Indian' Tamils. In a bizarre development the Central Provincial Council in Kandy has, at present, the unusual feature of two regional Ministers of Education, one 'Indian' Tamil and one Muslim. The 'Indian' Tamil community has insisted on securing this 'portfolio', and the Muslims have responded with the demand that they needed a minister of their own to look after the educational needs of their community. The UNP which controls the Provincial Council had to concede the demands of both groups to ensure its continuing control over that body.

Next, there is the accommodation reached on one of the long-standing grievances of the Tamils, the distribution of state-owned land among landless peasants. Tamil politicians have generally claimed that the Sri Lankan state has used state-owned land as a means of changing the demographic pattern in what they—i.e. the Tamil politicians—call the 'traditional homelands of the Tamils', primarily state-owned land in the Eastern Province. Researchers[21] have shown how little validity there is in these criticisms, but advocates of the Tamil cause have persisted with them nevertheless and through sheer repetition these charges have gained widespread acceptance among Tamil politicians, Tamil scholars as well as others.

A formula for the distribution of state land was devised in 1984 after long negotiation between representatives of the Sri Lanka government, and Tamil politicians led by the TULF. This formula was endorsed by the All Parties Conference (APC). It came up for review by the Political Parties Conference (PPC) of 1986, and was examined afresh by the two Indian politicians representing the Indian government, P. Chidambaram and Natwar Singh, who visited the island in late 1986 for negotiations on a resolution of Sri Lanka's ethnic conflict. The 1984 formula was endorsed by them, as well as the delegates to the PPC.

The essence of that formula is as follows—state-owned land on major irrigation schemes would be distributed on a quota which reflected accurately the population profile of the island, with the Sinhalese getting 74 per cent and the Tamils, Muslims and Indians 12 per cent, 6-7 per cent and 5 per cent respectively. The Tamils were permitted to use their island-wide quota in any area they chose, and naturally it was assumed that they would fill their quota, concentrating on the Eastern and Northern Provinces. On minor irrigation schemes, the distribution of state land would reflect the demographic pattern of the district or province in which the scheme was based.

The wide support this formula has received from almost all parties to the dispute, including the TULF, reflects a recognition, once again implicit more than explicit, that the criticisms levelled at state policies on land distribution did not bear serious examination. For the fact is that the formula devised in 1984 and endorsed in 1986 recognized the inevitability of a larger number of Sinhalese rather than others being the beneficiaries because much the largest number of landless peasants were Sinhalese.

Finally, we turn to the most intractable problem of all—devolution. Differences of opinion over devolution[22] have proved to be altogether more difficult to resolve than on other issues. This has been despite the great deal that has been achieved between 1980 and 1987 in establishing a second tier of government, a major political achievement given the failure of the attempts made in 1957-8, and 1965-8. Politicians are caught between the Sinhalese electorate's deep-rooted suspicions about the political consequences of devolving more power to the provinces and the Tamils' insistence on transferring greater extents of power to the provinces or regions at the expense of the central government, their demands ranging from the creation of a large Tamil-dominated North-Eastern Province, to the establishment of a federal political structure with a weak centre and more powerful provinces or regions. This is quite apart from the LTTE's insistence on a separate state as a non-negotiable demand. Beginning in the late 1930s and early 1940s as an eminently non-controversial issue, a largely administrative or technical matter on which there was a large measure of support— indeed virtually unanimous support—from all sections of opinion in the national legislature, it became by the mid-1950s the one issue that has eluded all efforts at resolution, the nut that cracked governments. An examination of why it has proved to be an inseparable obstacle to practical political management will show that it touches some of the most durable fears, suspicions and prejudices that divide the country.

The fact that there is little agreement among academic experts, no less than politicians, on the capacity of devolution of power to regional units, be they districts or provinces or something larger than provinces, to reduce ethnic conflict contributes to the polarization of Sri Lankan political opinion on devolution that we have referred to earlier. Indeed, the evidence available from other parts of world would show that the success of devolution in reducing ethnic conflict is more limited than enthusiastic advocates of it—in Sri Lanka, almost entirely Tamils—are willing to concede. The great success stories often cited range from Switzerland, to India and—rather surprising given its actual record of perennial political crises—contemporary Nigeria. Only Switzerland is a real success story, and there are special historical reasons for that. In the first and third of these the dominance of national politics by the largest ethnic group, the German Swiss and the Hausa respectively, is softened by the multiplicity of territorial units, provinces or states, all of which have some role to play in the control and exploitation of national resources. Unlike in the case of Switzerland, the number of states in the Nigerian Federation has increased exponentially—from the original three (in 1959) to 31 in 1991 and there has been a persistent demand for a further increase in this number, ranging from 38 to 80. Although the problem is not as acute as in contemporary Nigeria, India too is facing demands for the creation of an ever increasing number of states. As a leading article in *The Hindu* of 28 September 1996 put it:

> The announcement . . . on independence day on the creation of Uttarkhand has opened the Pandora's box indeed as this has emboldened the activists demanding statehood for the Darjeeling hills in West Bengal, the Jharkhand region in Bihar, Vidharba in Maharashtra and elsewhere . . . .

In both Nigeria and India the principal states of the union vary in size and power, but none dominates the polity, or could seriously threaten secession without facing the political consequences which separatism invites when the acceptable and tolerable limits of its expression are exceeded as was the case with the Biafran crisis in Nigeria in the 1960s and in regard to Kashmir, Punjab and Assam in India.

Twenty years ago, the US political scientist Milton Esman, warned that '. . . the conflict regulation potential of territorial autonomy [is limited] . . . when territorial units make extravagant and even incompatible demands . . . which the polity cannot accommodate, thus escalating rather regulating conflict . . .'[23] Recent events in the Punjab, and currently in Kashmir, not to mention the problems of India's North-east provide powerful supporting evidence for Esman as does the agitation for a separate state in the north-east of the island by the Tamils of Sri Lanka. Two years ago Esman returned to this theme arguing that,

> For statecraft, the principal risk associated with federalism is that territorial autonomy may be the prelude to demands for complete separation . . . .[24]

The resistance to transferring greater power to the provinces in Sri Lanka, springs from such fears.

There is the close proximity of the Jaffna region in the north of Sri Lanka to Tamilnadu, formerly a great reservoir of Tamil separatist sentiment in India, and which has encouraged, nurtured and protected Tamil separatist groups from Sri Lanka. Even when it has been introduced, the devolution of power to provincial councils is suspect because of the fear that it could serve to spur separatist pressures rather than act as an effective check on them in the north and east of the island. Large sections of the Sinhalese view the Tamils' pressure for devolution of power as the first step in an inevitable progression to separation of the Tamil majority areas of the country from the Sri Lankan polity. Historical memories contribute greatly to the disquiet and apprehensions the Sinhalese have about South India: the popular perception of events of centuries past, especially, that of South India as the single most powerful and persistent threat confronting Sri Lanka and the Sinhalese.

In the early years of independence the Tamils of the north and east of the island had showed little inclination to identify themselves with the Tamils of Tamilnadu. Nevertheless, the Sinhalese feared this possibility and the campaign for a federal structure for the island served to aggravate these fears. Those in the forefront of the Tamils' agitation for devolution of power have always been vague, deliberately or unconsciously, in the terminology used in their arguments, and the distinction between provincial autonomy, states' rights in a federal union, and a separate state have been blurred by a fog of verbiage, and obfuscation. The close links that were established in more recent times between the TULF, and various separatist groups, with the government and opposition in Tamilnadu have naturally aggravated the situation; and more so the establishment of training camps in Tamilnadu for separatist activists who made forays into the northern and eastern coastal regions of Sri Lanka from there. The result is that decentralization which was, and should be, a purely Sri Lankan matter has taken on a transnational dimension of which India's role as mediator in the political negotiations between the Sri Lankan government and representatives of Tamil opinion in the 1980s was the most conspicuous feature.

Pressure for decentralization of administration is limited to the Tamils, and largely to the Tamils living in the north and east of the island, where they are either a majority or form a substantial minority. There is no pressure—on the contrary strong opposition to decentralization—from other ethnic groups. Quite apart from the opposition of the Sinhalese majority to most schemes of devolution of power, the Muslim minority, especially those living outside the Eastern Province, have been deeply concerned about the dangers of their political marginalization in a decentralized political and administrative structure. Devolution of power to a unit larger than a province is perceived as threatening the interests of the smaller group—the Muslims—since the larger group—the Tamils—seem likely to dominate the affairs of a large territorial unit linking two provinces. The demographic profile of the Eastern Province, where the Tamils are less than the majority, being only 40 per cent of the population thus remains a critical stumbling block in the long drawn out negotiations on the creation of a province or region amalgamating the Northern Province with parts or the whole of the Eastern Province. The main Tamil separatist group the LTTE, for its part, will accept nothing short of a separate Tamil state. The deadlock over this issue continues to the present day. A section of the Muslims, led by the Sri Lanka Muslim Congress, has reacted to this by urging the creation of a separate administrative unit in the Eastern Province in which the Muslims would constitute a majority. A more elaborate version of this demand calls for a Muslim province with its main base in the Eastern Province, but with enclaves or sub-units elsewhere such as in the Mannar district of the Northern Province.

One of the unfortunate consequences of concentrating attention on district and provincial units, and on supra-provincial units has been a neglect of one of the less controversial and more viable forms of decentralization— local government institutions at the municipal and urban council levels and village council levels. The three principal municipalities, Colombo, Kandy and Galle, were established in 1865-6, while the origins of smaller urban and town councils and village councils go back to the early 20th century. The last comprehensive examination of local government institutions and their problems took place as long ago as 1954-5. Thereafter, largely because of the agitation of Tamil parties for the creation of District and Provincial Councils, the focus of attention has been almost exclusively on the second tier of government.

Over the last 30 years or more very little has been done to strengthen the financial bases of local government institutions or their powers to initiate local development projects. On the contrary there was till the late 1970s an ever-increasing control over them by the central government, in the name, generally of efficiency and co-ordination of services and economic development, but in fact in the pursuit of political objectives designed to benefit the party in power. That tendency reached its peak in the period 1970-7 when the operations of a large number of local government bodies ranging from municipalities (including the Colombo Municipality) to village councils were suspended—their elected heads and members deprived of office—and placed under bureaucrats nominated by the government. No local government elections were held between April 1977 and the end of the United Front government's term of office in 1977. The result was that an important range of institutions which could have contributed to a genuine devolution of power through participatory democracy and local initiatives lost a great deal of their vitality. The UNP government elected in 1977 revived local government bodies and held the first set of elections for Municipalities and Urban and Town Councils in 1979. Elections to Village Councils scheduled for 1979 and 1980 had to be put off because, once again, the establishment of District Councils took precedence.

The decision of the Presidential Commission on Development Councils of 1980 to abolish village councils and to transfer the functions of these bodies to local level units of the District Development Councils, and to informal (theoretically, non-political) village organizations did not yield any of the benefits anticipated on that occasion. That decision was based on a mixture of political considerations and a misplaced idealism. The TULF who argued in favour of the abolition of village councils hoped thereby to strengthen the district councils, and in any case to bring all other local government institutions under the purview and supervision of the district councils. Others argued that the administrative costs of running these village councils had kept increasing to the point where very little money was left for development programmes and that, in any event, such programmes were of a distinctly *ad hoc* nature. In addition, there was the belief that informal but popular village bodies could cut across party alignments and bring the people of the village together for common development projects. It soon became clear that the mechanisms and informal institutions substituted for village councils did not provide either the administrative efficiency or the responsiveness to local needs anticipated when they were instituted. Village councils were re-established in 1988-9 and the first elections to them were held in 1991.

After 1977, local government elections have been held at regular intervals at a national level and generally—like parliamentary elections—on a single day. Again in stark contrast to the situation between 1970 and 1977 government controls over such councils were relaxed, and certainly no council was brought under central control. Nevertheless, there has been no systematic attempt to examine the financial viability of village and urban councils, or the power, functions and resources of municipalities. While Sri Lanka has avoided the worst features of South Asian urbanization so far, its continued ability to do so will depend very much on the effective functioning of its local government institutions, especially its municipalities.

THE LTTE AND OPPOSITION TO ACCOMMODATION

Since the late 1970s the principal opponents of any politically viable accommodation on Sri Lanka's ethnic conflict has been the LTTE. A study of the LTTE's brief and tempestuous history provides, at one level, a classic example of a small, violent and determined group dominating regional politics in the Jaffna peninsula and systematically rendering its opponents within the Tamil community peripheral and dispensable, if not actually destroying them physically. At a second, and much more important level, it provides an example of how a single group could, through its intransigence, obstruct the search for accommodation at a national level. From its early beginnings in 1975-6, up until 1983, it was one of several separatist groups operating in the Jaffna peninsula. The LTTE's origins were rather modest: its cadres began as foot soldiers in the TULF campaign of opposition to the United Front government in the 1970s. Both parties drew sustenance and nourishment from the association; the armed separatist groups gained respectability in the Tamil electorate by their association with the TULF. Once the TULF was absorbed into the national political process after 1977, the separatist groups' activities were governed by a firm determination to keep the TULF 'honest', that is to say, honest to their publicly proclaimed separatist programme and aspirations. The riots of 1977 greatly strengthened the separatists, and made it more difficult for the TULF to repudiate their association, howsoever inconvenient. Thereafter, sporadic acts of violence continued, as did the intimidation of people who might, normally, object to transgressions of the law in a society that was well-known for its social conservatism and its law-abiding people.

Between 1977 and 1986 the LTTE established a dominance in the political life of Jaffna and the Tamils of the peninsula that it retained and consolidated through their resistance to the Sri Lankan army (1986-7) and the IPKF (1987-90). All the while it has been engaged internally in a dual conflict, a systematic campaign against its rivals and allies in the separatist movement, and the marginalization of the TULF. This second process was accelerated in the early 1980s and especially after the anti-Tamil riots of 1983, and the short-sighted decision of the TULF leadership to seek refuge in Madras. The first process was nothing short of internecine warfare in which it ruthlessly eliminated all rival groups, culminating in the massacre of the TELO group and the killing of its leader Sri Sabaratnam, between 1 and 3 May 1986 in Jaffna. Thus one of the three figures in the separatist triumvirate of the 1970s and 1980s, that included Prabhakaran and Uma Maheswaran, had been eliminated. From this point onwards the LTTE was the principal Tamil political group in the island, the one that set the pace, imposed their own political agenda and established the political priorities of the Tamil minority.

The size of the LTTE's forces during this period in the early 1980s and thereafter has been variously estimated; the range was from 1,500 to 3,000. Considering that the Sri Lankan armed services never mustered more than 20,000 up to the end of 1984, the Tamil separatist forces were large enough to pose a serious threat to the Sri Lankan security forces. In time, the LTTE's forces grew larger and more battle-hardened through campaigns against the Sri Lankan army and the IPKF. Currently in 1997, the trained cadre is estimated at round 4,000 with 5,000 to 6,000 others serving as 'reserve' force. Unlike the rag-tag forces maintained by other separatist activist groups, the LTTE has generally created a well-trained, highly disciplined army and its cadres have a degree of commitment to their cause that its rivals cannot match.[25] The culture of the cyanide capsule dangling from a gold (or gold plated) chain is evidence of the ultimate commitment to a cause, a readiness to commit suicide on its behalf rather than surrender or be captured, a level of commitment which a more conventionally trained regular army cannot match, and cannot be expected to match.

Quite apart from their ruthless elimination of hundreds of their Tamil rivals, they have been pitiless—like most guerrilla bands operating in other parts of the world—in killing any person, irrespective of age or sex, on the slightest suspicion of being an informer or collaborator, or if he or she stood up to them by refusing to obey orders, or to respect their *diktats*. They have enforced their will on the civilian population with a purposeful inflexibility that no regular army can match even under martial law because the penalty for failure or refusal to accept this arbitrary authority is death, a penalty that has generally been vigorously imposed. They have relentlessly pursued and eliminated cadres of rival separatist organizations and defectors from their own ranks: in the process they have killed more Tamils than either the Sri Lankan army or the IPKF. Hundreds of their opponents languish in their jails. These include members of the civilian population of Jaffna.

Their treatment of minorities who live or lived in their midst in the Jaffna peninsula has been extraordinarily brutal. The Sinhalese population of the Jaffna peninsula has either been killed or compelled to flee. The Sinhalese were a much smaller minority than the Muslims there. The LTTE attacked the Muslims of the Northern and Eastern Provinces at regular intervals between 1984 and 1990 and killed hundreds of them, culminating in a horrifying exercise in ethnic cleansing in which the whole Muslim population of the Northern Province, (estimated at 75,000 persons) was expelled *en masse* on 22 October 1990.

Although the LTTE was driven out of the Jaffna peninsula in the period 1987 to 1990 by the IPKF, they nevertheless maintained a shadowy existence there, while their leadership and many of their cadres moved to jungle hideouts in the Northern Province (outside the Jaffna peninsula) and the Eastern Province. They returned to the Jaffna peninsula in 1990 once the IPKF left, thanks largely to the shortsightedness of President Premadasa who permitted them to do so, overruling the objections of the service chiefs. They managed to maintain control over the Jaffna peninsula till 1995-96. The LTTE enjoyed a stroke of luck twice. In July 1987, the intervention of the Indians saved them from the Sri Lanka army; in 1990 the roles were reversed when the Sri Lankan government saved them from the Indians.

Separatist groups which indulge in acts of calculated violence are often accused of being terrorist organizations. Few separatist groups operating in South and South-east Asia have deserved this epithet more than LTTE. Such separatist groups generally have a terrorist section operating in association with it or as a peripheral unit. With the LTTE, terrorism is part of its core, and has been so from its inception. How much of this terrorism derives from the political culture of internecine warfare, and of fratricidal violence, in which the LTTE has had to operate, and how much is due to the nature of its leadership and of its leader, Velupillai Prabhakaran, are matters for debate. There is no doubt however that the latter's—the leader's— personal attributes have much to do with it. A recent *New York Times* article[26] put it fairly when it stated that:

> . . . He has shown a bloodthirstiness, in dealing with opponents, that has been compared with some of the cruellest figures in recent Asian history, including Pol Pot of Cambodia.

> Prabhakaran, who is 40, leads a movement whose deeds, in scale, pale alongside the genocide committed by Pol Pot's Khmer Rouge of the 1970s . . . But what they lack in scope, they make up in brutality . . .

> . . . [He] has established a rule of terror in the city of Jaffna. According to scores of accounts from defectors and others who have escaped the Tiger tyranny, many of his own lieutenants have been murdered; Tamils who have criticized him, even mildly or in jest have been picked up, tortured, and executed; others have been held for years in dungeons, half-starved, hauled out periodically for a battering by their guards.

The finances required for equipping and maintaining the LTTE's armed forces and civilian cadres are formidable even taking into account the resources available either voluntarily or otherwise from the Tamils in the north and east of the island, not to mention Colombo. The Sri Lankan state also provides some of the funds—involuntarily or inadvertently—since it supplies the salaries of public servants and teachers in the parts of the island which the LTTE controls. Apart from the taxes the LTTE collects from these officials, based on their earnings, there are also large numbers of absentees, and the dead, whose salaries continue to be paid and, of course, the salaries and wages of 'ghost' employees whose names have been entered by pliant senior officials, or by officials who are political sympathizers. The LTTE also gets part of the revenue from sales of consumer items sent from Colombo for the civil population and provided free of charge. They either control the sales and pocket the proceeds or extract a 'fee'. The hospitals are run at the expense of the state, and so is the University of Jaffna and the bulk of the schools.

Before the LTTE's armed forces became as large and well-equipped as they were by 1984, the question of finances to maintain and equip them was not as exacting a problem as it became thereafter. The expatriate Tamil communities in the West are a source of financial assistance, especially its United States and Canadian components, the former with its relatively affluent professionals and the latter because of the sheer numbers involved; the expatriate communities in Britain and Europe are in no position to match the North American group in the extent of financial support rendered.[27] The large refugee groups now in many western countries, Canada, in particular, are a ready source of income. Some of this money is extracted under duress, through the LTTE's enforcers, but a lot of the contributions are quite voluntary. But even these sources are inadequate to sustain the LTTE's organization and to maintain and equip its forces. Thus, reliance has to be placed on other sources of money, of which the narcotics trade is the principal one. This is not so much through the control and direction of local sources of supply—indeed, there are no local supplies—but as couriers, part of a link in a wider narcotics trade which comes down from Afghanistan and Pakistan, to India and thence to Sri Lanka. And as often happens the smugglers are the main suppliers to the couriers. Above all, they have built an intricate narcotics smuggling operation to Europe, and a distribution network in European cities which includes links to the Mafia. A British newspaper first drew attention to this narcotics trade from Sri Lanka in 1985;[28] since then there have been regular reports on this enterprise, including a recent one in *India Today* which identified the ramifications of the trade in Tamilnadu, through the LTTE connection. Ports and airports in that state, serve as 'a transit point for drug traffickers between the northern part of the Indian sub-continent and Sri Lanka', with Tamilnadu.

. . . being increasingly used as a base to smuggle narcotics to Sri Lanka from where it finds its way to other countries.[29]

The US State Department's report on Patterns of Global Terrorism, 1994, provides confirmation of much of this:

Information obtained since the mid-1980s indicates that some Tamil communities in Europe are also involved in narcotics smuggling. Tamils historically have served as drug couriers moving narcotics into Europe.[30]

If this flourishing narcotics trade helps sustain, or actually sustains, the LTTE as a political and military organization, the survival of the LTTE against the IPKF and the Sri Lanka armed forces is explained by another factor—the LTTE has the inestimable advantage of easy access to the sea, something that few other separatist organizations in South and South-east Asia possess. The indented coast of the Jaffna peninsula with its isolated coves provides both access and security, access to men and arms from abroad, India and South-east Asia, in particular, and security because the state's large naval craft are much less effective in such waters than the small boats and catamarans used by the smugglers. The Moros of Philippines have a similar advantage of access to the sea, and like the Tamils they have access to parts of neighbouring states with friendly co-religionists.

Parallel to its narcotics distribution network in Europe the LTTE has built a support base among the diaspora communities in Europe and North Australia (primarily Canada with Toronto as the principal base). It has

a significant overseas support structure for fund-raising, weapons procurement and propaganda activities. . . . [Its] overt organizations support Tamil separatism by lobbying foreign governments and the United Nations. The LTTE also uses its international contacts to procure weapons, communications, and bomb-making equipment . . . [exploiting the] Tamil communities in North

America, Europe and Asia to obtain funds and supplies
for its fighters in Sri Lanka.[31]

Apart from Toronto in Canada, the LTTE has two
important propaganda centres, London and Paris, with an
office in each of these cities, and with London very much
the principal international 'headquarters' of the LTTE. In
addition to its own network of cadres overseas, the LTTE
has the support of several front organizations: of these the
most active are the World Tamil Association (WTA), World
Tamil Movement (WTM), and the Federation of
Associations of Canadian Tamils (FACT). There is also the
Ellalan Force which operates in Sri Lanka and overseas.[32]

The fact, however, is that, as the *New York Times*
pointed out on 29 May 1995, 'the Tigers . . . despite their
record, have paid hardly any price, until recently, on their
standing outside Sri Lanka . . .' The assassination of
former Indian Prime Minister Rajiv Gandhi in May 1991,
along with 18 others at an election rally near Madras,
shocked regional and international opinion. Earlier, in
March 1991, they had assassinated the then Foreign
Minister and Deputy Minister of Defence Ranjan Wijeratne.
The death toll had been larger than it was in Madras on
the fateful evening when Rajiv Gandhi was killed. This was
followed by the assassination of Admiral Clancy Fernando,
the head of the Sri Lanka Navy, killed by a suicide bomber
on a motor bicycle. Then came the assassination of
President Premadasa on 1 May 1993, in Colombo, in a
carbon copy performance of the Rajiv Gandhi assassination
except that the suicide killer on this occasion was a man.
A few days earlier Lalith Athulathmudali had been shot
and killed when he was addressing an election rally.
Because Athulathmudali had directed the campaign against
the LTTE and other separatist groups from 1984 to 1989,
the LTTE are the principal suspects in this killing.
Athulathmudali was a potential presidential candidate at
the time of his assassination. He was the sole victim on
that occasion. The most recent in this series came on 24
October 1994. The target was Gamini Dissanayake, Leader

of the Opposition and the UNP's presidential candidate who was killed along with 55 others, including two former Cabinet Ministers, the general secretary of the UNP, and a former presidential candidate of the Sri Lanka Mahajana Pakshaya (SLMP), a splinter group of the SLFP. This time the *modus operandi* was almost exactly as in the Rajiv Gandhi killing—a female suicide bomber.

To this list must be added Prabhakaran's rivals in the separatist movement, Sri Sabaratnam (killed in 1986) and K. Pathmanabha of the EPRLF. Four TULF MPs, were killed, two in 1985, and two in 1990, including A. Amirthalingam, the Leader of the TULF. It was widely suspected that Uma Maheswaran (killed in 1990), an erstwhile colleague and later rival of Prabhakaran was also a victim of the latter's campaign of elimination of opponents in the Tamil political parties, but it is now believed that Maheswaran was killed in a factional dispute within his own organization.

Despite this long list of political rivals eliminated by Prabhakaran and the LTTE, international opinion turned against the LTTE only after Prabhakaran was indicted in India on the charge of complicity—i.e. planning—in the assassination of Rajiv Gandhi. Early in 1995 the Indian government made a formal request from Sri Lanka for the extradition of Prabhakaran and two of his associates (one a female) wanted in India as prime suspects in the Rajiv Gandhi killing. Further evidence of the international opposition to the LTTE came when on 8 October 1997, the US State Department included it in its black list of 30 of the world's terrorist organizations and proscribed it in terms of the US Anti-Terrorism Act of 1996. Surprisingly the LTTE has not been banned in Sri Lanka.

The situation with regard to Sri Lanka's Tamil regions, some parts of them still under the grip of the LTTE despite the loss of the Jaffna peninsula, is a parable of our times. At one level, it reveals the pathology of separatism, its capture by the most violent advocates of the cause under the leadership of a man charged with murder in a neighbouring state, and with a long string of political assassinations to his credit. At another level, the island as a whole provides a case-study of a democratic state successfully maintaining a multi-party, non-racial political structure in a social system riven by ethnic conflict but confronting the reality of a small part of the country being controlled by a political group which has imposed a one-party dictatorship on, what was up to very recently, a comparatively large Tamil political entity from which all ethnic minorities have been eliminated (the Jaffna peninsula and the Northern Province) or where Sinhalese and Muslims are under great pressure as in the multi-ethnic Eastern Province.

Sri Lanka's current government, the People's Alliance coalition having inherited these problems, placed great emphasis on the restoration of peace in the country, and its leader projected herself as the peace candidate in the parliamentary and presidential campaigns of August and November 1994. In the presidential election she secured an overwhelming majority, 62 per cent of the poll. The principal feature was the massive vote received from the Tamil minority, including the Indian Tamils, wherever it was possible for the Tamils to vote (i.e. outside the Jaffna peninsula). With this unmistakable mandate, the government turned almost immediately to resume negotiations with the LTTE—begun in the wake of the victory at the parliamentary elections and interrupted only briefly after the assassination of Gamini Dissanayake—intent on exploiting its electoral triumph to devise a political settlement. This was the second set of direct negotiations with the LTTE by a Sri Lankan government. The first had been in 1989 and 1990 under R. Premadasa. The negotiations with Premadasa had lasted for over a year before they broke down. The second set of talks collapsed within a few weeks, by 19 April 1995, because of the intransigence of the LTTE and its attacks on the Sri Lankan security forces notwithstanding the formal ceasefire. Later, this violence was directed against the Sinhalese living in the Eastern Province.

Eventually, the government decided on a more vigorous course of action, a military campaign in the Jaffna peninsula, the LTTE's stronghold. The campaign began in July 1995 and despite some early setbacks its first stage culminated later in the year in the capture of Jaffna town and parts of the Jaffna peninsula, with a surprisingly small number of civilian casualties. The next stage began in May 1996 when the army drove the LTTE out of the whole of the Jaffna peninsula. This was the second time in the space of 10 years that the Sri Lanka army was engaged in a military campaign in the Jaffna peninsula, but already there is a significant difference. In May 1987 when the first attack was made, it was stopped in its tracks, after some early success, by the threat of Indian intervention. On this present occasion, India maintained a studied silence, evidence that it has no intention of intervening. Indeed, having asked for Prabhakaran's extradition it could hardly object to the military action directed against the LTTE. There were signs of some agitation in Tamilnadu, but nowhere near the scale in the 1980s. The situation has not changed with the election of a new coalition government in Delhi after the defeat of the Congress. In addition, the US State Department has blamed the LTTE for the present situation of conflict, and implicitly endorsed the military action that the government has been compelled to take.

As they had done in 1987-90 when the Indian army brought the Jaffna peninsula under their control, the LTTE moved their operations headquarters to the areas just south of the peninsula, Kilinochchi and Mullaitivu and retained control of it till the IPKF left. In September 1996, the Sri Lanka army captured Kilinochchi town after a long battle with the LTTE. After the fall of Kilinochchi, the Mullaitivu area serves as the last LTTE stronghold and its *soi disant* administrative capital. The low-intensity conflict in the country's north and north-east is likely to continue for some time. It may be remembered that the LTTE survived in the forests of the Kilinochchi and Mullaitivu districts for over two years against the efforts of the IPKF to dislodge them.

The government's military campaign is based on the assumption that the LTTE can be defeated militarily, or at least weakened to the point where it is likely to settle for something much less than the separate state for which it has fought for so long. Certainly, the fall of Jaffna town and the loss of control over the Jaffna peninsula is a significant reverse for the LTTE, a reversal which could yet be a decisive defeat if they are unable to prevent the Sri Lankan armed forces from consolidating their hold on that densely populated region. Comparisons with similar campaigns against armed separatist groups in other parts of South and South-east Asia, and India in particular, would appear to justify the hopes placed in such an outcome: Punjab, Assam and India's North-east, and to some extent, Kashmir itself. In South-east Asia, the Myanmar army has conducted a 50-year war of attrition against the forces of that country's dissident minorities. Even the most powerful of these latter have had to come to terms with the state or are now willing to settle for something much less than the proclaimed objectives for which they had fought in Myanmar's prolonged civil war. And so it is also with the Malay minorities of Thailand's southern states. Admittedly this conflict in southern Thailand has lacked the intensity and the systematic violence of the others referred to here, although the origins of the struggle in its current manifestation go back to the early years of this century. Then there is the oldest internal conflict in South-east Asia, the struggle of the Moros against the Phillipine state which goes back to the 16th century. Recent events in the Philippines where a powerful section of the Moros have come to terms with the government, on an autonomous status far short of what they were willing to accept 25 years ago, provide further evidence that separatist campaigns in South and South-east Asia seldom succeeded unless as in the case of Bangladesh a regional power makes a decisive intervention.

In most instances of prolonged ethnic strife, pragmatism and compromise combine to thwart even the most obdurate champions of a struggle to the bitter end and to compel a settlement even when there seemed no hope of one. Time, it would appear, is not merely a great healer, but an ally of governments in their struggle against separatists.

Appendices

Table 1. SRI LANKA POPULATION, 1960-1997

Year	Population ('000)	Rate of growth (%)	Year	Population ('000)	Rate of growth (%)
1960	9896		1979	14471	2.0
1961	10168	2.7	1980	14747	1.9
1962	10443	2.7	1981	15011	1.8
1963	10646	1.9	1982	15195	1.2
1964	10903	2.4	1983	15416	1.4
1965	11164	2.4	1984	15599	1.2
1966	11439	2.5	1985	15837	1.5
1967	11703	2.3	1986	16117	1.8
1968	11992	2.5	1987	16361	1.5
1969	12252	2.2	1988	16586	1.4
1970	12516	2.1	1989	16806	1.3
1971	12690	1.4	1990	16993	1.1
1972	12861	1.3	1991	17247	1.5
1973	13091	1.8	1992	17405	0.9
1974	13284	1.5	1993	17619	1.2
1975	13496	1.6	1994	17865	1.4
1976	13717	1.6	1995*	18112	1.4
1977	13942	1.6	1996**	18337	1.2
1978	14190	1.8	1997**	18547	1.1

*1995-provisional; **1996, 1997-Estimated mid year projections

[Source: Department of Census and Statistics, Statistical Abstracts (Annuals)]

Table 2. SRI LANKA: POPULATION AND ETHNICITY, 1921-1981

Census Year	Total Population '000	per cent of total population					
		Sinhalese	Sri Lankan Tamils	Indian Tamils	Moors & Malays	Burghers	Others
1921	4,498.6	67.1	11.5	13.4	6.6	0.6	0.8
1931	5,306.9	65.5	11.3	15.4	6.4	0.6	0.8
1946	6,657.3	69.4	11.0	11.7	6.5	0.6	0.8
1953	8,907.9	69.4	10.9	12.0	6.6	0.6	0.5
1963	10,582.0	71.0	11.0	10.6	6.8	0.4	0.2
1971	12,689.8	72.0	11.2	9.3	7.0	0.4	0.1
1981	14,850.0	74.0	12.7	5.5	7.3	0.3	0.2

(Source: Dept. of Census and Statistics)

Table 3. SRI LANKA: POPULATION AND RELIGION, 1921-1981

Census Year	Total Population '000	per cent of total population				
		Buddhists	Hindus	Muslims	Christians	Others
1921	4,498.6	61.6	21.8	6.7	9.9	..
1931	5,306.9	61.5	22.0	6.7	9.8	..
1946	6,657.3	64.5	19.8	6.6	9.1	..
1953	8,097.9	64.3	19.9	6.7	8.9	0.2
1963	10,582.0	66.2	18.5	6.8	8.4	0.1
1971	12,689.8	67.3	17.6	7.1	7.9	0.1
1981	14,850.0	69.3	15.5	7.6	7.5	0.1

Note: .. Denotes less than 0.1%

(Source: Dept. of Census and Statistics)

Table 4. VITAL STATISTICS: SRI LANKA COMPARED WITH SELECTED COUNTRIES IN ASIA

	Year	Sri Lanka	Bangladesh	India	Pakistan	Indonesia	Malaysia	Philippines	Singapore	Thailand	Rep. of Korea
Mid year Population in Millions	1993	17.6	113.2	898.0	122.8	189.3	19.1	65.0	2.9	58.6	44.1
Population Growth Annual Avg. Growth %	1980-1993	1.4	2.2	2.4	3.7	2.1	2.9	2.7	2.0	1.9	1.2
Density of Population per Sq. Km (a)	1992	279	774	264	150	98	56	211.0	4666	113	441
Urban Population (As a % of Total Population)	1993	22	20	26	32	31	43	43	100	34	74(b)
Crude Birth Rate (per '000)	1993	20	35	29	40	24	28	30	16	19	16
Crude Death Rate (per '000)	1993	6	11	10	9	8	5	6	6	6	6
Fertility Rate (Births per Woman)	1993	2.4	4.3	3.7	6.1	2.8	3.5	3.9	1.7	2.1	1.7
Infant Mortality Rate (per '000 Live Births)	1993	17	106	80	88	56	13	42	6	36	11
Expectation of Life at Birth (Years)	1993	72	56	61	62	63	71	67	75	69	71

(a) Population/Total Land Area   (b) For the year 1990
(Sources: Human Development Report 1994, UNDP; World Development Report 1995.
Key Indicators of Developing Asian and Pacific Countries—1994, ADB
Central Bank of Sri Lanka)

Notes

Chapter 1

1. Sir Charles Jeffries, *Ceylon, The Path to Independence*, Pall Mall, London, 1962, *Preface.*
2. Nicholas Mansergh, *Survey of British Commonwealth Affairs, Problems of Wartime Cooperation and Post-war Change, 1939-1952*, Oxford University Press, Oxford, 1958, p 246.
3. Dennis Austin, *Democracy and Violence in India and Sri Lanka*, Royal Institute of International Affairs, London, 1994, *Preface.*
4. W.W. Isajiw, 'Definition of Ethnicity', *Ethnicity* 1 (July 1974), pp 111-24.
5. See particularly, Anthony D. Smith, *Theories of Nationalism*, Duckworth, London, 1971; John Breuilly, *Nationalism and the State*, Manchester, 1982 and older works such as, Elie Kedourie, *Nationalism*, Hutchinson, London, 1960; Hans Kohn, *The Idea of Nationalism*, MacMillan, New York, 1967 and Carlton Hayes, *The Historical Evolution of Nationalism*, New York, 1931.
6. Paul Brass, *Language, Religion and Politics in North India*, Cambridge, 1974, pp 9-10.
7. V. Pareto, *The Mind and Society: A Treatise on General Sociology*, Harcourt Brace, New York, 1923, reprinted 1963, p 1837.
8. Edmund Leach, *Political Systems of Highland Burma*, Cambridge University Press, Cambridge, 1954, p 15.
9. Frederik Barth, 'Introduction' in Frederik Barth (ed.), *Ethnic Groups and Boundaries*, Little Brown, Boston, 1969, pp 9-38.
10. The reference is to Leach's, *Political Systems of Highland Burma* and Barth's 'Introduction' to the book he edited on *Ethnic Groups and Boundaries*.
11. Edward Shils, 'Primordial, Personal, Social and Civil Ties', *British Journal of Sociology*, 7(1957), pp 113-45.
12. C. Geertz, 'The Integrative Revolution: Primordial Sentiments and Civil Policies in the New States' in C. Geertz (ed.), *Old Societies and New States*, New York, 1963, pp 105-57.

13. Charles Keyes, 'Towards a New Formulation of the Concept of Ethnic Group', *Ethnicity*, 3(1976) pp 202-13 and 'The Dialectic of Ethnic Change' in C. Keyes (ed.), *Ethnic Change*, University of Washington Press, Seattle, 1981, pp 3-30.

14 Paul Brass, *Language, Religion and Politics in North India*, Cambridge, 1974, p 8.

15. Joseph Rothchild, *Ethnopolitics: A Conceptual Framework*, Columbia University Press, New York, 1981, p 3.

16. Frederik Barth, 'Introduction', in Frederik Barth (ed.), *Ethnic Groups and Boundaries*, p 34.

17. A.J. Stockwell, 'The White Man's Burden and Brown Humanity: Colonialism and Ethnicity in British Malaya', *The South East Asian Journal of Social Science*, 10(1), 1982, p 44.

18. This existed in the north and some parts of the east of the island from the 13th century till the early part of the 17th century.

19. See K.M. de Silva, *The Traditional Homelands of the Tamils, Separatist Ideology in Sri Lanka: A Historical Appraisal*, International Centre for Ethnic Studies, Kandy, 1994.

20. Senanayake is in danger of becoming one of the forgotten men in Sri Lankan politics. Apart from a rather unsatisfactory biography by H.A.J. Hulugalle published in 1973, *The Life and Times of Don Stephen Senanayake*, Colombo, Lake House Publishers, there is no serious study of the man and his career.

21. For a brief review of Senanayake's work see K.M. de Silva, 'Senanayake's Political Settlement and its Critics, 1947-1952', in K.M. de Silva, *Managing Ethnic Tension in Multi-Ethnic Societies, Sri Lanka, 1880-1985*, Lanham, Md, 1986, pp 140-58.

22. At the time he arrived in the island in 1942 he was still in his late 30s, but he had three major works to his credit, including the standard work on *Cabinet Government*.

23. On linguistic nationalism and the Buddhist resurgence, see Donald E. Smith, 'The Sinhalese Buddhist Revolution', Chapter 21, in Donald E. Smith (ed.), *South Asian Politics and Religion*, Princeton, NJ, 1969, pp 453-509. See also George Bond, *The Buddhist Revival in Sri Lanka*, University of South Carolina Press, 1988.

24. There are a number of good studies on the creation of Bangladesh. Among the best is T Maniruzzaman, *The Bangladesh Revolution and its Aftermath*, Dhaka, 1980.

25. The present People's Alliance consists of the SLFP, LSSP, CP and a section of the Sri Lanka Mahajana Pakshaya (SLMP); others including the Sri Lanka Muslim Congress and the Ceylon Workers Congress joined after the PA had secured a majority at the parliamentary elections of August 1994.

26. On the background to the introduction of a system of PR in the island and its implications for the resolution of ethnic conflict see C.R. de Silva, 'The Constitution of the Second Republic of Sri Lanka (1978) and its Significance', *The Journal of Commonwealth and Comparative Politics*, XVII(2) pp 192-209 and K.M. de Silva 'A Tale of Three Constitutions: 1946-8, 1972 and 1978,' *Ceylon Journal of Historical and Social Studies* (CJHSS) n.s. VII(2), pp 1-17.

27. For an assessment of the benefits gained by the Indian plantation workers after 1978, see G.H. Peiris, 'Changing Prospects of the Plantation Workers of Sri Lanka', in S.W.R. de A. Samarasinghe and Reed Coughlan (eds), *Economic Dimensions of Ethnic Conflict: International Perspectives*, Frances Pinter, London, 1991, pp 156-93.

28. S. Thondaman has published two volumes of a projected three-volume autobiography. Vol. II is entitled *Tea and Politics. An Autobiography, My Life and Times*, Navrang, Delhi and Vijitha Yapa, Colombo, 1994, deals with the period 1939 to 1978.

29. David Little, *Sri Lanka: The Invention of Enmity*, United States Institute of Peace, Washington D.C., 1994. For a critical review of this book see G.H. Peiris, *Ethnic Studies Report*, XII(2), July 1994, pp 258-264; David Little's rejoinder and Peiris's response are published in *Ethnic Studies Report*, XIII(2), July 1995, pp 237-246 and 247-263. See also my comments on Little's book in 'Buddhism, Politics and Violent Ethnic Conflict in Modern Sri Lanka—A Review Article', in *Ethnic Studies Report*, XII(2), pp 222-257; see particularly pp 225-228.

Chapter 2

1. See, Jane Russell, 'Language, Education and Nationalism The Language Debate of 1944', *CJHSS*, new series VIII(2),

1982, pp 38-64. The text of the resolution is as it appeared in the official record, see *Hansard* [State Council] Vol. 1, 1944, column 745.

2. On the general election of 1956 see Chapter IX in Wriggins, *Ceylon: Dilemmas of a New Nation*, Princeton, 1960.

3. On this see G.P. Malalasekera's articles in the *Ceylon Daily News*, 10-12 October 1955.

4. S. Nadesan published a 4-part series of articles on 'Ceylon's Language Problems' in the *Ceylon Daily News* of 12, 13, 14 and 15 October 1955. These were subsequently reprinted as a pamphlet entitled *Ceylon's Language Problems*, Colombo, 1955.

5. S. Nadesan, *Ceylon's Language Problems*, Colombo, 1955, p 22.

6. H. Wriggins, *op.cit.*, p 260.

7. See, K.M. de Silva, *Managing Ethnic Tensions in Multi-Ethnic Societies in Sri Lanka 1880-1985*, Chapter XIV for discussion of this theme. See also G.P. Malalasekera's article in the *Ceylon Daily News*, 12 October 1955.

8. See K.M. de Silva, 'Ethnicity, Language and Politics: The Making of Sri Lanka's Official Language Act No. 33 of 1956', *ESR* XI(1) 1993, pp 1-29.

9. *ibid.*

10. On the UNP's march to Kandy in October 1956, see, K.M. de Silva and Howard Wriggins, *J.R. Jayewardene of Sri Lanka, A Political Biography*, Vol. II, 1994, pp 35-43.

11. *ibid.*, pp 96-100.

12. See his article in the *Ceylon Daily News*, 10 October 1955.

13. On opposition to assimilation see G.G. Ponnambalam's speech in the State Council, *Hansard* [State Council] 1939 column 960; see also S. Nadesan, *Ceylon's Language Problems*, Colombo, 1955, *passim.*

14. While students entered the universities on the basis of the language medium in which they sat the qualifying examination for admission to the universities, they had a free choice in regard to the medium of instruction in which they preferred to read for university examinations once they gained admission.

15. On the significance of this change see the assessment by N. Satyendra, 'Language in the New Constitution', the *Ceylon Daily News*, 4 October 1978. Satyendra is Nadesan's

son, and like his father a lawyer.

16. *SPV* 1980, *Report of the Presidential Commission on Development Councils*, pp 86-7, for a memorandum by two Muslim members of the Commission pointing out the importance of the changes made to the benefit of Tamil speakers in the island.

17. See, S.G. Samarasinghe, 'Language Policy in Public Administration, 1956-1994: An Implementor's Perspective', pp 79-111 in K.N.O. Dharmadasa (ed.), *National Language Policy in Sri Lanka, 1956 to 1996: Three Studies in Its Implementation*, Kandy, International Centre for Ethnic Studies Occasional Papers, No. 6, 1996.

18. *ibid.*

19. See, for example, S. Nadesan, *Ceylon's Language Problems*.

20. Cynthia H. Enloe, *Ethnic Conflict and Political Development*, Boston, 1973, p 97.

21. Article 21(1) of the Constitution.

22. These rights are consolidated and incorporated through Articles 21(2) and 21(3) of the 1978 constitution.

23. Carol L. Schmid, *Conflict and Consensus in Switzerland*, Berkeley and Los Angeles, 1982, p 20.

24. *ibid.*

Chapter 3

1. S. Arasaratnam, 'Oratorians and Predikants. The Catholic Church in Ceylon under Dutch Rule', Review article in *CJHSS*, I, 1958, pp 216-22. C R Boxer, 'Christians and Spices: Portuguese Missionary Methods in Ceylon, 1518-1658', *History Today*, VIII, 1958, pp 346-54; 'A Note on Portuguese Missionary Methods in the East: 16th-18th Centuries', *Ceylon Historical Journal*, X, 1960, pp 77-90.

2. On British missionary organizations in Sri Lanka see, K.M. de Silva, *Social Policy and Missionary Organizations in Ceylon, 1840-55*, London, 1965. 'The Government and Religion: Problems and Policies, c.1832 to c.1910', in K.M. de Silva (ed.), The University of Ceylon, *History of Ceylon*, Vol. III, Colombo, 1973, pp 187-212. 'Christian Missions in Sri Lanka and their Response to Nationalism, 1919-1948', in P.L. Prematilleke, K. Indrapala, and J.E. van Lohuizende Leeuw (eds), *Senarat Paranavitana Commemoration Volume. Studies in South Asian Culture*, Vol. V, pp 221-33, Institute of

South Asian Archeology, University of Amsterdam, Leiden, 1978.

3. See K.M. de Silva, *Social Policy and Missionary Organizations in Ceylon, 1840-55*, London, 1965, pp 29-63, for the early 19th century, and 'The Government and Religion, Problems and Policies, c.1832 to c.1910', *op.cit.*, for the rest of the country.

4. K.M. de Silva, *A History of Sri Lanka*, London, 1981, pp 347-349.

5. For a study of these problems see, K.M. de Silva, *Social Policy and Missionary Organizations in Ceylon 1840-55*, London, 1965, pp 64-137; K. Malalgoda, *Buddhism in Sinhalese Society, 1750-1900*, University of California Press, Berkeley, California, 1976 and 'The Buddhist-Christian Confrontation in Ceylon, 1800-1880', *Social Compass*, XX(2), 1976, pp 171-200.

6. K. Malalgoda, *Buddhism in Sinhala Society, 1750-1900*, California, 1976 and 'The Buddhist-Christian Confrontation in Ceylon, 1800-1880', *Social Compass*, XX(2), 1976, pp 171-200.

7. For a succinct review of the 19th century Buddhist revival see George D. Bond, *The Buddhist Revival in Sri Lanka*, University of South Carolina Press, 1988, pp 4-74.

8. Cited in M.T. Price, *Christian Missions and Oriental Civilizations*, (privately printed) Shanghai, 1924, p 15.

9. *ibid.*, p 164.

10. For a study of the 're-indigenisation' movement see, K.M. de Silva, 'Christian Missions in Sri Lanka and their Response to Nationalism, 1910-1948', in Prematilleke, *et.al.*, (eds), *op.cit.*

11. There is a considerable body of literature on Dharmapala but no biography as yet. See particularly A. Guruge (ed.), *Return to Righteousness*, The Government Press, Colombo, 1965. Two articles by S. Amunugama are very insightful. Of these one has been published. 'Anagarika Dharmapala (1864-1933) and the Transformation of a Sinhala Buddhist Organization in a Colonial Setting', *Social Science Information*, 24(4) 1985, pp 697-730. The other article, 'A Sinhala Buddhist Babu: Anagarika Dharmapala (1864-1933) and the Bengal Connection', n.d. but probably 1991, remains unpublished.

12. The reference is to the Buddhist Temporalities Ordinance of 1931.

13. For discussion of this see K.M. de Silva, 'The High Politics of the Transfer of Power in Sri Lanka: 1942-1946', *The Sesquicentennial Commemorative Volume of the Royal Asiatic Society of Sri Lanka 1845-1995*, Colombo, 1995, pp 487-520.

14. *ibid.*, pp 491-7.

15. See K.M. de Silva, 'Buddhist Revivalism, Nationalism and Politics in Modern Sri Lanka', in James W Bjorkman (ed.), *Fundamentalism, Revivalists and Violence in South Asia*, Manohar, Delhi, 1988, p 127.

16. On Burmese Buddhism of this period see, E. Sarkisyanz, *Buddhist Backgrounds of the Burmese Revolution*, E.J. Brill, The Hague, 1965. See also D.E. Smith, *Religion and Politics in Burma*, Princeton University Press, Princeton NJ, 1965.

17. D.E. Smith, *op.cit.*, p 158.

18. The political campaign of 1956 is analysed comprehensively in W. Howard Wriggins, *Ceylon: The Dilemmas of a New Nation*, Princeton, 1960.

19. See K.M. de Silva, 'Ethnicity, Language and Politics: The Making of Sri Lanka's Official Language Act No. 33 of 1956', *ESR*, XI(1), 1993, pp 1-29.

20. See K.M. de Silva, *Managing Ethnic Tensions in Multi-Ethnic Societies: Sri Lanka 1880-1985*, Lanham, Md, 1986, pp 196-200.

21. The technical details, from a lawyer's angle, are handled admirably in L.G. Weeramantry's *Assassination of a Prime Minister*, (privately printed) Geneva, 1960. Weeramantry was one of the defence lawyers on this occasion. See also *The Report on the Assassination of Prime Minister S.W.R.D Bandaranaike, Sessional Paper III of 1965*, Colombo, 1965.

22. See K. Malalgoda, *Buddhism in Sinhalese Society, 1750-1900*, Berkeley, California, 1976.

23. K.M. de Silva, 'Buddhist Revivalism, Nationalism and Politics in Modern Sri Lanka', *op.cit.*, pp 152-3.

24. *ibid.*, see also, K.N.O. Dharmadasa, 'Buddhist Resurgence and Christian Privilege in Sri Lanka, c.1940-1965', in K.M. de Silva *et.al.* (eds), *Ethnic Conflict in Buddhist Societies: Sri Lanka, Thailand and Burma*, London, 1988, pp 110-25.

25. K.M. de Silva, 'Buddhist Revivalism, Nationalism and Politics in Modern Sri Lanka', *op.cit.*, pp 152-3.

26. *ibid.*
27. 'Munificent Financial Assistance to Buddhism' is principally for the preservation and maintenance of archaeological sites, which are largely Buddhist. Again, there are no 'restrictions on the efforts of other religious organizations to propagate their faith.' There are, however restrictions since the late 1950s, on the building of new Christian churches, but all it requires is formal permission if a *new* church is to be built. There are no such restrictions on the building of Hindu temples and for mosques serving the Islamic community.
28. See, S. Amunugama, 'Buddhaputra and Bhumiputra? Dilemmas of Modern Sinhala Buddhist Monks in Relation to Ethnic and Political Conflict', *Religion* (21) 1991, pp 115-39. M. Juergensmeyer, 'What the *Bhikkhu* Said: Reflections on the Rise of Militant Religious Nationalism', *Religion* (20) 1990, pp 130, 165.
29. Thus on 23 October 1988, four senior *bhikkhus* including the two *Mahanayakes* of Malvatta and Asgiriya, joined together in calling upon President Jayewardene to establish a caretaker government as a prelude to a general election.
30. This included official recognition of the trade union activities of one such monk who heads a nurses union.
31. The *bhikkhu* concerned abandoned the venture.
32. In the diocese of Kandy, Indian Tamils constitute an overwhelming majority of the flock, 57,000 out of a total of 72,000. I owe this point to the Bishop of Kandy, the very Revered Vianney Fernando.
33. R.L. Stirrat's *Power and Religiosity in a Post-Colonial Setting, Sinhala Catholics in Contemporary Sri Lanka*, Cambridge University Press, Cambridge, 1992. While this monograph discusses the efforts by Roman Catholics to accomodate themselves to a situation of Buddhist dominance of the Sri Lanka polity he makes no reference, however to similar moves by the Protestants which began well before independence. See also A.J.V. Chandrakantha, *Catholic Revival in Post-Colonial Sri Lanka*, Social and Economic Development Centre, Colombo, 1994. Apart from its rather optimistic title, one that flies in the face of all the evidence, Chandrakantha's book is disappointing because of its poor grasp of the historical and contemporary background. He

is a Roman Catholic priest based in Jaffna.

34. There is a brief analysis of the current problems of the Roman Catholic Church in Sri Lanka, see R.L. Stirrat, 'The Riots [of 1983] and the Roman Catholic Church in Historical Perspective', in James Manor (ed.), *Sri Lanka in Change and Crisis*, Croom Helm, London, 1984, pp 196-213.

35. See, for example, his paper, 'Let My People Go' presented at the International Conference on the Conflict in Sri Lanka: Peace with Justice, Canberra, Australia, 1996. The paper published in the proceedings of the conference, is an unabashed defence of the LTTE's position and policies.

36. Protests against proselytization have figured prominently in the corresponding columns of Sri Lankan newspapers in recent years. See the article entitled 'Conversions and Humanitarian Service', in the *Sunday Times*, 17 July 1994. Earlier, on 16 June 1994, the same newspaper had carried a joint statement from 23 Christian organizations justifying their stand on conversions.

Chapter 4

1. See Marguerite Ross Barnett, *The Politics of Cultural Nationalism in South India*, Princeton University Press, Princeton, New Jersey, 1976; Eugene F. Irschick, *Tamil Revivalism in the 1930s*, Cre-A, Madras, 1986.

2. These issues are reviewed in Tariq Rahman, 'Language Policy in Pakistan', in *Ethnic Studies Report*, XIV(1), 1996, pp 72-98. For the opposition to Urdu in East Pakistan, see pp 74-79 in the same article. See also his *Language and Politics in Pakistan*, Oxford University Press, Karachi, 1996, pp 79-102.

3. See, K.M. de Silva, 'Ethnicity, Language and Politics: The Making of Sri Lanka's Official Language Act No, 33 of 1956', in *Ethnic Studies Report*, XI(1), 1993, pp 1-29.

4. See, K.M. de Silva and Howard Wriggins, *J.R. Jayewardene of Sri Lanka, A Political Biography*, Vol. II, Leo Cooper, London, 1994, pp 7-23.

5. On the riots of 1915 see, A.P. Kannangara, 'The Riots of 1915 in Sri Lanka: A Study in the Roots of Ethnic Violence', *Past and Present*, 102 ,1983, pp 130-165. Charles Blackton, 'The Action Phase of the 1915 Riots', *Journal of Asian*

Studies, 29(2), 1970, pp 235-254.

6. Tarzie Vittachy, *Emergency '58: The Story of the Ceylon Race Riots,* Andre Deutsch, London, 1958.

7. For a more recent assessment of these riots see, Stanley J. Tambiah, *Leveling Crowds: Ethnonationalist Conflicts and Collective Violence in South Asia,* University of California Press, Berkeley, 1996, pp 82-94.

8. The background to the two failed *coups d'état* is reviewed in K.M. de Silva and Howard Wriggins, *J.R. Jayewardene of Sri Lanka, A Political Biography,* Vol. II, pp 100-125, 142-164.

9. Howard Wriggins, *Ceylon: The Dilemmas of a New Nation,* Princeton University Press, Princeton, New Jersey, 1960, pp 150-151.

10. *ibid.,* p 151.

11. On the constitution of 1972 see particularly, J.A.L. Cooray, *Constitutional And Administrative Law of Sri Lanka,* Hansa Publishers, Colombo, 1973. An expanded second edition of this book was published in Colombo in 1995. See also the very perceptive article by L. Wolff-Philips, 'Post-Independence Constitutional Changes in the Commonwealth', *Political Studies,* XVIII (1), 1970, pp 18-43, especially p 35 where he predicted that 'some kind of constitutional innovation (most likely a new autochthonous constitution) will be necessary in [Sri Lanka] in the early 1970s.'

12. On the background to these developments see, A. Jeyaratnam Wilson, *S.J.V. Chelvanayakam and the Crisis of Sri Lankan Tamil Nationalism, 1947-1977,* C Hurst, London, 1994, particularly pp 113-132.

13. Sir Charles Jeffries, *Ceylon, The Path to Independence,* Preface.

14. Lord Soulbury's foreword to B.H. Farmer, *Ceylon: A Divided Nation,* Oxford University Press, Oxford, 1963.

15. In 66, *New Law Reports,* 73, 1964.

16. On this issue see C.R. de Silva, 'Weightage in University Admissions: Standardization and Ethnic Quotas in Sri Lanka, 1970-75', *Modern Ceylon Studies,* V(2) pp 152-78. 'The Politics of University Admissions: A Review of Some Aspects of University Admissions Policy, 1971-1978', *The Sri Lanka Journal of Social Sciences,* 1(2), pp 85-123.

17. C.R. de Silva, 'The Politics of University Admissions . . .' *op.cit.,* p 85.

18.   *ibid.*, p 87.

19.   *ibid.*, pp 89-90.

20.   *ibid.*, p 90.

21.   Thomas Sowell, *Preferential Politics. An International Perspective*, New York, W.M. Morrow, 1990, pp 76-87; Donald L. Horowitz, *Ethnic Groups in Conflict*, University of California Press, Berkeley, 1985, pp 663-6. See also Myron Weiner, 'Affirmative Action: The International Experience', pp 1-15, in *Development and Democracy*, (IV) May 1993, Johannesburg, South Africa; and S.W.R. de A. Samarasinghe, 'Sri Lanka: Affirmative Action and Equity in a Multi-Ethnic Society', pp 41-52, in *Development and Democracy*, VI, September 1993.

22.   There is no comprehensive study as yet of the JVP insurrection of 1971. The most informative study is A.C. Alles, *The JVP, 1969-1989*, Lake House, Colombo, 1990. See also, R.N. Kearney and Janice Jiggins, 'The Ceylonese Insurrection of 1971', *The Journal of Commonwealth and Comparative Politics*, XIII(1) 1975, pp 40-64.

23.   For discussion of this see S.W.R de A. Samarasinghe, 'Ethnic Representation in Central Government Employment and Sinhala-Tamil Relations in Sri Lanka, 1948-1981', in R.B. Goldmann and A.J. Wilson (eds), *From Independence to Statehood*, London, 1984, pp 173-84.

24.   Donald L. Horowitz, *Coup Theories and Officers' Motives: Sri Lanka in Comparative Perspective*, Princeton University Press, Princeton, New Jersey, 1980 provides a detailed study of the abortive *coup d'état* of 1962.

25.   K.M. de Silva and Howard Wriggins, *J.R. Jayewardene of Sri Lanka, A Political Biography*, Vol. II, *op.cit.*, pp 142-164.

26.   On the politics of Tamilnadu during this period see, Lloyd Rudolph, 'Urban Life and Populist Radicalism: the Dravidian Movement in Madras', *The Journal of Asian Studies*, XX, 1961, pp 283-97; and Robert L. Hardgrave Jnr., 'The DMK and the Politics of Tamil Nationalism', *Pacific Affairs*, XXXVII, (1964-65), pp 396-411, and 'Riots in Tamilnadu: Problems and Prospects of India's Language Crisis', *Asian Survey*, V, 1965, pp 399-407.

27.   There were frequent visits of Federal Party leaders to Tamilnadu in 1960s and 1970s, where they were welcomed by the Chief Minister of the state and his ministerial

colleagues. A.J. Wilson's political biography of his father-in-law, S.J.V. Chelvanayakam has a photograph of the latter being greeted by M.G. Ramachandran in Madras (now Chennai) in 1970. See the 86-87 in A.J. Wilson, *S.J.V. Chelvanayakam and the Crisis of Sri Lanka Tamil Nationalism, 1947 1977*, C. Hurst, London, 1994.

28. Norman Cutler, 'The Fish-Eyed Goddess Meets the Movie Star: An Eyewitness Account of the Fifth Tamil Conference', *Pacific Affairs*, LVI(2), 1983, pp 270-87. The quotation is from p 277.

29. This is discussed in K.M. de Silva, *Managing Ethnic Tensions in Multi-Ethnic Societies: Sri Lanka, 1880-1985*, University Press of America, Lanham Md, 1986, pp 273-274.

30. This same combination of factors was seen in operation when the International Tamil Conference was held 21 years later in Tanjavur, Tamilnadu, in January 1995. History repeated itself, on this occasion, with farce following tragedy. The research element was marginalized in a bizarre atmosphere of grossly partisan politics (of Tamilnadu) and a virtual beatification of Jayalalitha, Tamilnadu's corpulent Chief Minister of that time. The Sri Lankan Tamil cause entered the picture again, and in a political form, with the expulsion from India of two Sri Lankan Tamil scholars for alleged LTTE sympathies, along with a German academic based in Sweden well-known for his LTTE sympathies. For an account of the deportation of these scholars see *Frontline* (27/1/95).

31. For an impartial assessment of the incidents relating to the deaths caused on this occasion see, *Sessional Paper*, (hereafter *SP*) VII of 1980, *Report of the Presidential Commission on the Inquiry into Incidents that took place between 13 August and 15 September 1977*, (The Commissioner was M.C. Sansoni, former Chief Justice of Sri Lanka, a Burgher), pp 66-70. The Commissioner supported the findings of the magisterial inquiry held in 1974, at which it was established that the deaths had been caused by electrocution when some electric wires were accidentally dislodged. It was 'unreservedly held that not a single rifle bullet was fired [by the police on that occasion].'

32. See, *India Today*, 30 June, 1986, the article entitled, 'Profile of a Tiger'. Durayappah was unarmed at the time of his

killing—he was returning from a *kovil* (a Hindu temple). He was unsuspecting as well.

33. There is a large and growing literature on separatist or secessionist movements. See particularly, J. Nagel, 'The Conditions of Ethnic Separatism', *Ethnicity*, 7(2) 1980; D.L. Horowitz, 'Patterns of Ethnic Separatism', *Comparative Studies in Society and History*, 23(2) 1981; J. Wood, 'Secession: A Comparative Analytic Framework', *Canadian Journal of Political Science*, 14, 1981; R. Premdas, S.W.R. de A. Samarasinghe and A Anderson (eds), *Secessionist Movements in Comparative Perspective*, London, 1990; R. Premdas, 'Secessionist Movements in Comparative Perspective', in R. Premdas, *et.al. Secessionist Movements . . . , op.cit.*, pp 12-29.

34. See particularly Surin Pitsuwan, *Islam and Malay Nationalism: A Case Study of the Malay-Muslims of Southern Thailand*, Bangkok, 1985, and W.K. Che Man, *Muslim Separatism: The Moros of Southern Philippines and the Malays of Southern Thailand*, Manila, 1990.

35. This aspect of the Moro struggle is reviewed in Cesar A. Majul, *The Muslims in the Philippines*, Quezon City, 1973.

36. See K.M. de Silva, *The 'Traditional Homelands' of the Tamils. Separatist Ideology in Sri Lanka: A Historical Appraisal*, 2nd edition, International Centre for Ethnic Studies, Kandy, 1994, for a comprehensive study of this problem, and for the background to the Cleghorn Minute.

37. *The Journal of the Royal Asiatic Society, (Ceylon Branch)* hereafter *JRAS(CB)*, n.s., Vol. 3, 1954, p 131.

38. These issues are discussed in K.M. de Silva, *Managing Ethnic Tensions in Multi-Ethnic Societies: Sri Lanka, 1880-1985*, Lanham, Md, 1986; W. Howard Wriggins, *Ceylon: The Dilemmas of the New Democracy*, Princeton, N.J. 1960.

39. Permanent Tamil settlements in parts of the north of Sri Lanka became fairly extensive only in 11th century AD. See K. Indrapala, 'Early Tamil Settlements in Ceylon', *JRAS(CB)* XIII, 1969, pp 43-63.

40. See C.R. de Silva and S. Pathmanathan, 'The Kingdom of Jaffna up to 1620', and 'The Expulsion of the Portuguese from Sri Lanka', in K.M. de Silva (ed) The University of Peradeniya, *History of Sri Lanka*, Vol. II, University of Peradeniya, Peradeniya, 1995, pp 105-21 and 163-81 respectively.

Chapter 5

1. The riots of 1977 are discussed in some detail in K.M. de Silva and W. Howard Wriggins, *J.R. Jayewardene of Sri Lanka: A Political Biography*, Vol. II, London, 1994, pp 338-58.

2. On the constitution of 1978 the standard work is A. Jeyaratnam Wilson, *The Gaullist System in Asia: The Constitution of Sri Lanka, 1978*, Macmillan, London, 1980.

3. The discussion of this theme here is based on my chapter 'University Admissions and Ethnic Tensions in Sri Lanka, 1977-83', in R.B. Goldmann and A.J. Wilson (eds), *From Independence to Statehood: Managing Ethnic Conflict in Five African and Asian States*, Frances Pinter, London, 1984, pp 97-110.

4. C.R. de Silva, 'The Politics of University Admissions', *op.cit.*, pp 100-1.

5. These were: Anuradhapura, Badulla, Batticaloa, Hambantota, Moneragala, Mullaitivu, Nuwara Eliya, Polonnaruwa, Mannar, Vavuniya, Ampara and Trincomalee. Of these, Batticaloa, Mullaitivu, Mannar and Vavuniya are Tamil majority areas, while Trincomalee had a sizeable Tamil population. The Muslims are a significant group in Ampara, Batticaloa, Trincomalee and Mannar.

6. *Report of the Committee Appointed to Review University Admissions Policy*, University Grants Commission [UGC], Colombo 1984. The five districts retained were Ampara, Mannar, Mullaitivu, Hambantota and Badulla.

7. Virginia Leary, *Ethnic Conflict and Violence in Sri Lanka*, International Commission of Jurists, Geneva, 1981, p 80.

8. *Emergency: Sri Lanka*, International Alert, London, 1986, p 13.

9. S.J. Tambiah, *Sri Lanka, Ethnic Fratricide and the Dismantling of Democracy*, University of Chicago Press, Chicago, 1986, pp 29-30. Tambiah is Professor of Anthropology at Harvard University.

10. See the *Ceylon Daily News*, 30 June 1979; *The Catholic Messenger*, 1 July 1979.

11. See, N. Tiruchelvam, 'The Politics of Decentralization and Devolution: Competing Conceptions of District Development Councils in Sri Lanka', in R.B. Goldmann

and A.J. Wilson (eds), *From Independence to Statehood, op.cit.*, pp 196-209.

12. This is discussed in my essay, 'Bandaranaike and the National Debate on Devolution 1926-1957', pp 3-20 in K.M. de Silva (ed.), *Devolution in Sri Lanka*, International Centre for Ethnic Studies, Kandy, Occasional Paper No. 4, 1996. This monograph contains the introductory survey referred to above and eleven documents, pp 21-97.

13. *SP V* of 1980, *Report of the Presidential Commission on Development Councils*, pp 37-46.

14. For a study of the riots of 1958 see Tarzie Vittachy, *Emergency '58—The Story of the Ceylon Race Riots*, London, 1960.

15. This is a reference to the British Commonwealth of Nations. Generally, this organization is now known as the Commonwealth or Commonwealth of Nations.

16. The close links that developed between the TULF leadership, and militant youth groups emerge very clearly through the evidence given before, and gathered by the Sansoni Commission, *SP VII* of 1980, and in its report itself.

17. Among the groups that began to take an interest in the problems of Sri Lanka's Tamil minority from the early and mid-1970s were, the London-based Minority Rights Group, Amnesty International and the Geneva-based International Commission of Jurists.

18. For this viewpoint see Virginia Leary, *Ethnic Conflict and Violence in Sri Lanka, op.cit.*, pp 43-55.

19. The background to these events is discussed in K.M. de Silva, *Managing Ethnic Tensions in Multi-Ethnic Societies: Sri Lanka 1880-1985, op.cit.*, pp 331-2.

20. On the riots of 1983, see, T.D.S.A. Dissanayake, *The Agony of Sri Lanka*, Colombo, 1983; and Sinha Ratnatunga, *The Politics of Terrorism: The Sri Lanka Experience*, Canberra, 1988, pp 11-68. There are some discerning eyewitness accounts in the essays in James Manor (ed.), *Sri Lanka in Change and Crisis*, London, 1984.

21. Contrary to C. Manogaran in *Ethnic Conflict and Reconciliation in Sri Lanka*, University of Hawaii Press, Honolulu, 1987, p 134, not a single factory in the Free Trade Zone near Negombo was destroyed during the riots of 1983. Nor was

it true to say as he does that 'many successful labour-intensive industries were financed and operated in the Free Trade Zone by Tamils before they were destroyed by mob violence in 1983.' There were no such Sri Lankan Tamil-owned factories in the Free Trade Zone.

22. On the Malaysian riots of May 1969, see, Karl von Vorys, *Democracy without Consensus: Communalism and Political Stability in Malaysia*, Princeton University Press, Princeton, 1975, pp 308-38.

23. The *New York Times*, 4 November 1984, p 10, a report under the title 'Mob's Wrath Brings Death to Sikh Area', by Barbara Crossette.

24. S.J. Tambiah, *Sri Lanka-Ethnic Fratricide . . . op.cit.*, p 32.

Chapter 6

1. James Laue, 'The Conflict Resolution Field: An Overview with some Critical Questions', in *Dialogue on Conflict Resolution: Bridging Theory and Practice*, Washington DC, United States Institute of Peace, 1993, p 24. •

2. *ibid.*, p 25.

3. H.A. Indorf, *Strategies for Small State Survival*, Institute of Strategic Studies, Kuala Lumpur, 1985.

4. For Senanayake's views on this see, Colonial Office Records London, CAB 129/18 CP (47)144, Cabinet-Ceylon Constitution, 2 May 1947.

5. This concept in relation to India's borders is reviewed in Steven A. Hoffman, *India and the China Crisis*, Berkeley, 1990.

6. These issues are discussed in K.M. de Silva and Howard Wriggins, *J.R. Jayewardene of Sri Lanka: A Political Biography*, Vol. II, *op.cit.*, pp 419-22 and K.M. de Silva, *Regional Powers and Small State Security, India and Sri Lanka 1977-1990*, Washington DC, Woodrow Wilson Center Press and Johns Hopkins University Press, 1995, pp 116-8.

7. See K.M. de Silva, 'Decentralization and Regionalism in the Management of Sri Lanka's Ethnic Conflict', *International Journal of Group Tensions*, 14(4), 1989, pp 317-38.

8. These issues are treated in detail in K.M. de Silva, *Regional Powers and Small State Security: India and Sri Lanka, 1977-1990, op.cit.*, pp 105-107.

9. *ibid.*

10. Hansard [Rajya Sabha] 16 August 1988, columns, 358-359.

11. See K.M. de Silva, *Regional Powers and Small State Security: India and Sri Lanka 1977-1990, op.cit.*, pp 105-12.

12. *ibid.*, pp 123-46, for a discussion of G. Parathasarathy's negotiations in Sri Lanka.

13. On Mrs Gandhi's attitudes, see J.N. Dixit, *Assignment Colombo*, Delhi, 1997, p 20.

14. For a brief review of the problems relating to the voting rights of immigrant Indians in Sri Lanka see K.M. de Silva, *Managing Ethnic Tensions in Multi-Ethnic Societies, op.cit.*, pp 105-10.

15. The discussion here is based on P.A.T. Gunasinghe, *The Tamils of Sri Lanka*, (privately printed) Colombo, 1985, pp 9-24, and Tikiri Abeyasinghe (ed.), *A Study of the Portuguese Regimentos of Sri Lanka at the Goa Archives*, Department of National Archives, Colombo, n.d. published probably in 1984, pp 89.

16. S.C. Canagaratnam, *Monograph of the Batticaloa District of the Eastern Province, Ceylon*, The Government Press, Colombo, 1921, p 102.

17. *ibid.*, p 2.

18. This monograph was published as a special issue of the *JRAS(CB)*, n.s. vi, 1963.

19. G.H. Peiris, 'An Appraisal of the Concept of a Traditional Tamil Homeland in Sri Lanka'. A mimeographed paper presented at a conference on 'The Economic Dimensions of Ethnic Conflict in Sri Lanka', 8 August 1985, Kandy, Sri Lanka.

20. *ibid.*

21. See *India Today*, 31 March 1984, pp 84-99, see particularly the essay of investigative reporting entitled, 'Sri Lanka Rebels: An Ominous Presence in Tamilnadu', also *The Sunday Times*, London, 1 April 1984, and Reuter reports on these bases published in Sri Lanka in the *Sun* of 23 May 1984, and the *Island* of 25 May 1984. See also the London-based journal *South: The Third World Magazine*, March 1985, pp 14-5. See *Time International*, 3 April 1989, pp 10-1, for a later account.

22. K. Mohandas, *MGR: The Man and the Myth*, Panther Publications, Bangalore, 1992, p 118.

23. Two visits by General Vernon Walters, a special emissary sent to Sri Lanka by the Reagan administration discussed the issue of these bases with the Indian government in 1984. Walters made two visits to Sri Lanka, the first in October 1983 and the second late in 1984. On both occasions he informed the Indian government that US administration had photographs of the training camps for Tamil separatists in Tamilnadu, as well as the addresses of the main separatist groups operating from Tamilnadu. See K.M. de Silva and Howard Wriggins, *J.R. Jayewardene of Sri Lanka, A Political Biography*, Vol. II, pp 581-2.

24. One of the Indian delegates to the UN General Assembly was S. Ramachandran, a Minister of the Tamilnadu State government. On 21 October 1983 he addressed the special Political Committee and raised the question of Sri Lankan refugees in Tamilnadu. See the official publication issued by the Indian Mission to the United Nations, *Indian News*, 21 October 1983. Ramachandran's speech was on Agenda Item 74: International Co-operation to Avert New Flows of Refugees. On 27 September 1984, Mr Ram Niwas Mirdha, an Indian delegate, made much the same points in a statement on behalf of his country at a general debate at the 39th session of the UN General Assembly.

25. Official records of the UN Geneva office show that in 1983, 1984 and 1985 Indian delegates raised the issue of human rights violations in Sri Lanka at meetings of the Commission on Human Rights, and the Subcommission on Prevention of Discrimination and Protection of Minorities. Of particular interest in this regard is the speech of M.C. Bandhare, a member of the Subcommission on Prevention of Discrimination and Protection of Minorities in Geneva, 21 August 1984.

26. Bhandari's efforts at mediation in Sri Lanka are reviewed in detail, in K.M. de Silva, *Regional Powers and Small State Security, op.cit.*, pp 147-76.

27. Personal knowledge. I was in the US in 1985-1986 and have seen the literature put out by the Indian Embassy in Washington, and the Indian High Commissions in London and Ottawa in support of the Sri Lanka Tamils. They were in the form of newsheets or articles in official 'newspapers'.

28. K.M. de Silva, *Regional Powers and Small State Security op.cit.*, pp 175-6.

29. For discussion of Bhandari's role in the mediation process see, K.M. de Silva, *Regional Powers and Small State Security: India and Sri Lanka, 1977-1990, op.cit.,* pp 221-244.

30. On the military situation in Sri Lanka at this time, see Colonel Edgar O'Ballance, 'Sri Lanka and its Tamil Problem', in *Armed Forces*, Vol. 5 (12), December 1986. *Armed Forces* is published by Ian Allan Ltd., in conjunction with the Royal United Services, Institute for Defence Studies.

31. . See the statement made by Dr G.S. Dhillon, Leader of the Indian delegation to the 42nd Session of the Commission on Human Rights, under Agenda item 12, on 5 March 1986. This brief statement was in response to a very comprehensive one made by Dr H.W. Jayewardene leading the Sri Lankan delegation on 4 March 1986, setting out in detail the negotiations conducted between the two governments, and also details of attacks by Tamil separatist groups on civilians, and clashes between the Sri Lankan security forces and Tamil separatist groups.

32. For an account of this clash between the LTTE and the TELO group, see *The Hindu*, 13 May 1986.

33. A.P. Venkateswaran, interview with the author, 24 April 1990.

34. On the problems of the Eastern Province and its links with the concept of the traditional homelands of the Tamils see G.H. Peiris, 'An Appraisal of the Concept of a "Traditional Homeland" of the Tamils in Sri Lanka', *ESR*, IX(1) 1991, pp 11-39.

35. See K.M. de Silva, *Regional Powers and Small State Security: India and Sri Lanka, 1977-1990,* pp 202-3 for further discussion of this.

36. The background to these events, and the events themselves are discussed in K.M. de Silva, 'The Making of the Indo-Sri Lanka Accord: The Final Phase—June-July 27 1987', in K.M. de Silva and S.W.R. de A Samarsinghe (eds), *Peace Accords and Ethnic Conflict*, London, 1993, pp 112-55.

37. Of M.G. Ramachandra's grant of $ 3.3 million, the greater part, $ 2.5 went to the LTTE, and $ 833,300 to the EROS group, close allies of the LTTE. See, M.R. Narayan Swamy, *Tigers of Lanka, From Boys to Guerrillas*, Delhi, 1994, p 233. A reputed Sri Lankan journalist, Sinha Ratnatunga in his

Politics of Terrorism: Sri Lanka Experience, Belconnen, ACT, Australia, 1988, p 366, explains that the money was handed over to the LTTE through the Syndicate Bank of Madras, 'in a blaze of publicity', see also *Hindu*, 28 May 1987.

38. For an analysis of this accord and a review of the events that preceded and followed its signing see K.M. de Silva, *Regional Powers and Small State Security: India and Sri Lanka, 1977-1990, op.cit.*, pp 221-44.

39. *ibid.*, p 240.

40. See M.S.S. Pandian's article, 'The Election that was Not', in *The Economic and Political Weekly*, 3 December 1988, where he argues out that the election was rigged by the IPKF.

41. Thanks to the LTTE boycott, no election was possible in the four districts of the Northern Province. The IPKF succeeded in securing the election of the EPRLF slate uncontested there.

42. In the Eastern Province there was an election of sorts in which the IPKF served, more or less, as election agents of the EPRLF.

43. See C.A. Chandraprema, *Sri Lanka: The Years of Terror, the JVP Insurrection, 1987-1989*, Lake House Bookshop, Colombo, 1991.

44. *ibid.*

45. Dixit played a key role in the drafting of the Indo-Sri Lanka Accord and later on as a co-ordinator of the political aspects of the IPKF's operations in Sri Lanka. See his own account of this in his memoir of his tour of duty in Sri Lanka, *Assignment Colombo*, 1997.

46. It was often alleged by Indian critics of President Premadasa's policy of *rapprochement* that the Sri Lanka government had supplied arms to the LTTE at this stage, and that these were to be used against the IPKF. In September 1991, Premadasa himself had to acknowledge that arms had been supplied to the LTTE. On 17 December 1991 the *Hindustan Times* carried a news item to the effect that one of the young officers of the Sri Lanka army who had been ordered to transport these arms to the LTTE had testified to the effect that he was aware that they were to be used against the IPKF.

47. For discussion of this see, K.M. de Silva, *Regional Powers*

and *Small State Security: India and Sri Lanka, 1977-1990,*
op.cit., pp 277-80.

48. This point was first made by Professor Ainslee Embree of
the Southern Asia Institute, Columbia University, New
York.

49. Ravi Rikhye, *The Militarisation of Mother India,* Chanakya
Publications, New Delhi, 1990, pp 77-90. His estimate of
the size of the IPKF is the largest we have.

50. There is a growing literature on the IPKF's operations in
Sri Lanka: these include, S. Bhaduri and Afsir Karim, *The
Sri Lankan Crisis:* Lancer Paper I, Delhi, 1990; R. Kadian,
India's Sri Lanka Fiasco, Vision Books, Delhi, 1990; as well
as extensive references to them in Ravi Rikhye, *The
Militarisation of Mother India, op.cit.*

Two general officers who served with the IPKF in Sri
Lanka have published accounts of their stay in the island's
north and east: Lt. Gen. S.C. Sardeshpande, *Assignment
Jaffna,* Lancer Publishers, New Delhi, 1991 and Lt. Gen.
Depinder Singh, *IPKF in Sri Lanka,* Trishul Publications,
Delhi, 1991.

Chapter 7

1. Very little research has been done on this interesting
theme. Some of the issues are outlined in the pamphlets
issued on behalf of the main participants in the controversy:
see, for instance, S.L. Mohamed, *Who are the Ceylon Moors?*
The Moors' Direct Action Committee, Colombo, 1950.

2. Vijaya Samaraweera, 'Orabi Pasha in Ceylon, 1883-1901',
Islamic Culture, 49, October 1976, pp 219-27.

3. P Ramanathan, 'The Ethnology of the "Moors" of Ceylon',
JRAS(CB), 10(36), 1888, pp 234-62.

4. I.L.M. Abdul Azeez, *A Criticism of Mr Ramanathan's Ethnology
of the 'Moors' of Ceylon,* Colombo, Moors' Union, 1907; repr.
Colombo, Moors Islamic Cultural Home, 1957.

5. Kaleel was a founder member of the UNP from 1946, and
remained faithful to the party through all its vicissitudes.
He was the president of the party from 1990 to the time
of his death.

6. The unicameral legislature of this period had seven
executive committees whose chairmen, elected by the

members, became the minister of the subject under the purview of the executive committee. The committees had a powerful influence on policy-making, and even on the implementation of policy.

7. *Hansard*, Vol. 1, State Council, 1944, p 812.

8. For discussion of this, see K.M. de Silva, *Managing Ethnic Tensions in Multi-Ethnic Societies: Sri Lanka 1880-1985*, Lanham, MD; University Press of America, 1986, pp 229-231 for details.

9. *SP V* of 1980, *Report of the Presidential Commission on Development Councils*, pp 83-102.

10. One of the points made was that although the Muslims had voted in larger numbers for the UNP than the SLFP, Muslim members of UNP Cabinets generally held rather unimportant portfolios such as labour, whereas Muslim Cabinet Ministers of the SLFP were entrusted with more important areas of responsibility such as health and education.

11. K.M. de Silva, 'Hinduism and Islam in Post-Independence Sri Lanka', *CJHSS* 4(1-2), pp 98-103.

12. M.A.M. Hussain, 'Muslims in Sri Lanka Polity', *The Muslim World League Journal*, September 1982, pp 46-50; October 1982, pp 53-7; November 1982, pp 45-7; December 1982, pp 44-8.

13. M.S. Kariapper, Kalmunai, and M.M. Mustapha, Pottuvil.

14. For discussion of this see K.M. de Silva and Howard Wriggins, *J.R. Jayewardene of Sri Lanka: A Political Biography*, Vol. II, pp 690-1, 699, 705.

15. *ibid.*, pp 581-2.

16. See Dr S.H. Hasbullah's unpublished seminar paper, 'The Ethnic Crisis and Internal Displacement: The Muslim Minority of the Northern Province of Sri Lanka', presented at the ICES, Kandy/Michigan State University Seminar, May 1995. An earlier (1991) paper by him presented at an ICES conference on Ethnic Peace Accords, entitled, 'Muslims and Ethnic Conflict: Dynamics of Muslim Politics with Special Reference to the Indo-Lanka Accord', also deals with this episode, pp 29-33.

Chapter 8

1. On this see, C.Z. Guilmoto, 'The Tamil Migration Cycle, 1830-1950, in India', *EPW*, 16-23 January 1993, pp 111-20.

2. These elections were held in 1947 not 1949.

3. The technical term used is repatriate.

4. Myron Weiner, 'Rejected Peoples and Unwanted Migrants in South Asia', *EPW*, 21 August 1993, pp 1738-46: the extracts are from p 1739.

5. C[olonial] O[ffice] records series, 54/987, K.W. Blaxter's minute of 13 May 1940. The references in the last two sentences of Blaxter's minute were to the modifications of the Donoughmore Commission's recommendations on the voting rights of Indians resident in the island. The Donoughmore Commission had recommended that 5 years residence in the island was adequate for this purpose. The Sri Lankan political leadership refused to accept this. There was the very real possibility that the national legislature would reject the Donoughmore reforms just on this one issue. At this stage, the Governor Sir Herbert Stanley, and the Secretary of State, Lord Passfield (Sydney Webb) agreed to a more restrictive set of rules.

6. See, Hugh Tinker, *The Banyan Tree: Overseas Emigrants from India, Pakistan and Bangladesh*, Oxford University Press, Oxford, 1977, p 40; see also the same author's *Separate and Unequal: India and Indians in the British Commonwealth, 1920-1950*, C. Hurst, London, 1976, pp 198-9.

7. Chapter XI of that report, pp 60-4; See also Chapter X in it, pp 56-60.

8. Dr Madhao Shihari Aney; member for Overseas Indians, Viceroy's Executive Council, 1941-3; he had been appointed agent for Ceylon (Sri Lanka) of the government of India in July 1943.

9. In the 1920s the government of India had insisted on the appointment of an agent (generally an Indian Official) to British colonies admitting Indians for labour either on plantations or other areas of economic activity. Among the first countries to which such agents were sent were Sri Lanka and Malaysia.

10. CO 54/986 file 55541/5. Governor Sir Henry Monck-Mason-Moore to G.E.J. Gent, private and confidential letter of 20 November 1945.

11. Hugh Tinker, *The Banyan Tree, op.cit.*, pp 38-40; and *Separate and Unequal, op.cit.*, pp 198-9.

12. Hugh Tinker, *The Banyan Tree, op.cit.*, p 42.

13. This section of the present chapter is based on K.M. de Silva, *Managing Ethnic Tensions in Multi-Ethnic Societies: Sri Lanka 1880-1985, op.cit.,* pp 222-5, 276-80.

14. In a self-destructive mood the Ceylon Indian Congress (later the Ceylon Workers' Congress) began by actively discouraging its membership from applying for Sri Lanka citizenship under the new legislation. The result was a flood of applications at the last moment or just after the prescribed time limit. Thus scrutiny of these applications was delayed and it became easier to reject many on purely technical grounds.

15. S.U. Kodikara, *Indo-Ceylon Relations since Independence,* Ceylon Institute of World Affairs, Colombo, 1965, pp 220-37.

16. *ibid.,* pp 123-5.

17. Hugh Tinker, *The Banyan Tree, op.cit.,* p 42.

18. A good example is a speech reported in *The Ceylon Daily News,* 1 August 1973.

19. See M.H. Gunaratne, *The Plantation Raj,* Cave and Company, Colombo, 1980, for a participant's account of the tensions between the plantation workers and the government at this time; see also K.M. de Silva, *Managing Ethnic Tensions in Multi-Ethnic Societies . . . op.cit.,* pp 276-81.

Chapter 9

1. On Northern Ireland see, Frank Wright, *Northern Ireland: A Comparative Study,* Gill and Macmillan, Dublin, 1992. The effects of partition are reviewed in Robert Schaeffer, *Warpaths: The Politics of Partition,* Hill and Wang, New York, 1990.

2. See Helena Cobban, *The Making of Modern Lebanon,* Hutchinson, London, 1985; Itamar Rabinovich, *The War for the Lebanon, 1970-1985,* Cornell University Press, Ithaca, revised edition, 1985.

3. Diane Mauzy, 'Malaysia: Malay Political Hegemony and Coercive Consociation' in John McGarry and Brendan O'Leary (eds), *The Politics of Ethnic Conflict Regulation,* Routledge, London, 1993, pp 112-3.

4. On this economic policy see, Goh Ban Lee, 'Restructuring Society in Malaysia: Its Impacts on Employment and Investment', and S. Husin Ali, 'Development, Social Stratification and Ethnic Relations: The Malaysian Case'.

pp 74-95 and 96-118, respectively in S.W.R. de A. Samarasinghe and Reed Coughlan (eds), *Economic Dimensions of Ethnic Conflict: International Perspectives*, Pinter Publishers, London 1991.

5. At the moment Malaysia's population of 17 million is composed of 58 per cent Malays, 32 per cent Chinese, 8 per cent Indians, Kadazans, Ibans and other indigenous groups.

6. See K.M. de Silva, *The 'Traditional Homelands' of the Tamils. Separatist Ideology in Sri Lanka: A Historical Appraisal*, Kandy, revised second reprint, 1995.

7. Memorial of the Jaffna Association to W.H. Long, Secretary of State for the Colonies, 2 January 1918. It was enclosed in a despatch from Governor Sir John Anderson to Long, 81 of 8 April 1918, in CO 54/854.

8. CO 527/697 Sir Hugh Clifford's secret despatch to L.S. Amery of 20 November 1926.

9. *The Soulbury Report*, p 70.

10. See, Stanley J. Tambiah, *Buddhism Betrayed? Religion, Politics and Violence in Sri Lanka*, University of Chicago Press, Chicago, 1992 and David Little, *Sri Lanka: The Invention of Enmity*, United States Institute of Peace, Washington, D.C, 1994. For a refutation of the views of Tambiah and Little, see K.M. de Silva, 'Buddhism, Politics and Violent Ethnic Conflict in Sri Lanka', *Ethnic Studies Report*, XI(2), July 1994, pp 223-58.

11. K.M. de Silva, *Managing Ethnic Tensions in Multi-Ethnic Societies, op.cit.*, pp 221-5.

12. K.M. de Silva, 'Politics and the Political System', in K.M. de Silva (ed.), *Sri Lanka: The Problems of Governance*, Delhi, 1993, pp 30-1, for the political effects of the increase in the number of voters among the Indian Tamils in Sri Lanka.

13. *Soulbury Report*, p 49.

14. *ibid.*, p 50.

15. *ibid.*

16. S.W.R. de A. Samarasinghe, 'Ethnic Representation in Central Government Employment and Sinhala-Tamil Relations in Sri Lanka: 1948-1981', in Robert B. Goldmann. and A.J. Wilson (eds), *From Independence to Statehood: Managing Ethnic Conflict in five African and Asian States*, London, 1984, pp 179-80.

17. In the 20 year period, 1973-1992 there were over 40,000 immigrants to Canada from Sri Lanka, of whom the vast majority came in after 1984. The great bulk of them were Tamils from the Jaffna peninsula. See, *Refuge*, XIII(3), June 1993, Special issue on Sri Lanka, p 36. *Refuge* is Canada's periodical on refugees, published by the Centre for Refugee Studies, York University, Ontario. The current estimate is around 125,000 Tamils almost all of them from Jaffna and the north of Sri Lanka, living in and around Toronto.

18. On the controversies on university admissions policy see, C.R. de Silva, 'Weightage in University Admissions, Standardization and District Quotas in Sri Lanka', *Modern Ceylon Studies*, 5(2), 1974, pp 152-78; 'The Politics of University Admissions: A Review of Some Aspects of Admissions Policy in Sri Lanka', *Sri Lanka Journal of Social Sciences*, 1(2) 1978, pp 85-123.

19. K.M. de Silva, 'University Admissions and Ethnic Tension in Sri Lanka: 1977-1982', in R.B. Goldmann and A.J. Wilson (eds), *From Independence to Statehood . . . op.cit.*, pp 97-110.

20. See K.M. de Silva, 'The Sri Lankan Universities from 1977 to 1990: Recovery, Stability and the Descent to Crisis', *Minerva*, XXVIII(2), Summer, 1990, pp 156-216.

21. G.H. Peiris, 'Irrigation, Land Distribution and Ethnic Conflict in Sri Lanka: An Evaluation of Criticisms, with Special Reference to the Mahaveli Programme', in *ESR* XII(1), 1994, pp 43-88; and 'An Appraisal of the Concept of a Traditional Tamil Homeland in Sri Lanka', *ESR*, XI(1), pp 13-39.

22. On the problems of devolution in Sri Lanka see, G.R.T. Leitan, *Local Government and Decentralized Administration in Sri Lanka*, Lake House Bookshop, Colombo, 1979. B.S. Wijeweera, *A Colonial Administrative System in Transition: The Experience of Sri Lanka*, Lake House Bookshop, Colombo, 1988. See also K.M. de Silva, 'Regionalism and Decentralization of Power', in K.M. de Silva (ed.), *Sri Lanka: Problems of Governance, op.cit.*, pp 99-126.

23. Milton T. Esman, 'The Management of Ethnic Conflict', *Public Policy*, XXI(1972), pp 49-78. The quotation is from p 64.

24. Milton T. Esman, *Ethnic Politics*, Cornell University Press, Ithaca, 1994, p 43.

25. For a study of the LTTE in its struggle against its rivals in the Tamil separatist movement, see M.R. Narayan Swamy, *Tigers of Sri Lanka: From Boys to Guerrillas*, Konarak, Delhi, 1994, and Dayan Jayatilleka, *Sri Lanka. The Travails of a Democracy: Unfinished War, Protracted Crisis*, Vikas, New Delhi, 1995.

26. See the issue of 29 May 1995, an article by John F. Burns. Prabhakaran's career in political assassination began 20 years ago when as a young man of 18 or 19, he shot and killed the then SLFP Mayor of Jaffna, a fellow Tamil. In an interview he gave *India Today*, for its issue of 30 June 1986 he proclaimed this his 'first military encounter'. In this bizarre elevation of a cold-blooded killing of a single individual to a 'military encounter', Prabhakaran was proclaiming to the world that he had personally killed a political opponent.

27. See, Anthony Davis, 'Tamil Tiger International', *Jane's Intelligence Review*, October 1996, pp 464-473. Christopher McDowell, *A Tamil Asylum Diaspora: Sri Lankan Migration, Settlement and Politics in Switzerland*, Berghan Books, Providence RI, and Oxford, 1996.

28. See *The Guardian*, weekly, 11 August 1985, p 11, an article by Laurent Crellsamer, 'Tamil Emigrants could be Europe's Major Source of Heroin'. The article made the point that 'frightening quantities of heroin are being smuggled into Europe from a completely new source—Colombo, the capital of Sri Lanka . . . the quantity of heroin transiting via the Sri Lanka route is on the way to overtaking all other complications in the field.' See also *The Asian Wall Street Journal*, 9 September 1985, an article entitled 'Drugs, Guns and Terrorism'.

29. *India Today*, 30 September 1994, p 125.

30. *Patterns of Global Terrorism*, Washington D.C., 1995, The US Department of State, pp 48-9.

31. *ibid.*, p 48.

32. *ibid.*, all these front organizations are identified in this report. One that is not included is the UK based International Federation of Tamils (IFT).

Bibliography

GENERAL WORKS ON ETHNICITY AND POLITICS

Alter, Peter. *Nationalism*, London, Edward Arnold, 1989.

Anderson, Benedict. *Imagined Communities: Reflections on the Origin and Spread of Nationalism*, London, Verso Revised edition, 1991.

Austin, Dennis. *Democracy and Violence in India and Sri Lanka*, London, Royal Institute of International Affairs, 1994.

Azar, Edward E. *The Management of Protracted Social Conflict: Theory and Cases*, Aldershot, Hampshire, Dartmouth, 1990.

——and John W. Burton. *International Conflict Resolution, Theory and Practice*, Boulder, Colorado, Wheatsheaf, 1986.

Banton, Michael. *Racial and Ethnic Competition*, Cambridge, Cambridge University Press, 1983.

Barnett, Marguerite R. *The Politics of Cultural Nationalism in South India*, Princeton, Princeton University Press, 1976.

Barth, F. (ed.) *Ethnic Groups and Boundaries: The Social Organization of Culture Difference*, London, Allen and Unwin, 1969.

Bjorkman, James W. (ed.) *Fundamentalism, Revivalists and Violence in South Asia*, New Delhi, Manohar, 1988.

Brass, Paul. (ed.) *Ethnic Groups and the State*, Tatawa, N.J., Barnes and Noble, 1985.

——*Ethnicity and Nationalism: Theory and Practice*, New Delhi, Sage Publications, 1991.

Breuilly, John. *Nationalism and the State*, Manchester, Manchester University Press, 1982.

Brown, Sherlyn J., and Kimber M Schraub, *Resolving Third World Conflict: Challenges for a New Era*, Washington D.C., United States Institute of Peace, 1992.

Connor, Walker. *The National Question in Marxist Leninist Theory and Strategy*, Princeton, Princeton University Press, 1984.

——*Ethnonationalism: The Quest for Understanding*, Princeton, Princeton University Press, 1994.

de Silva, K.M. *et.al.*, (eds) *Ethnic Conflict in Buddhist Societies: Sri Lanka, Thailand and Burma*, London, Pinter Publishers, 1988.

——and R.J. May (eds) *Internationalization of Ethnic Conflict*, London, Pinter Publishers, 1991.

——and S.W.R. de A. Samarasinghe (eds) *Ethnic Peace Accords and Ethnic Conflicts*, London, Pinter Publishers, 1993.

Deutsch, Karl W. *Nationalism and its Alternatives*, New York, 1969.

——(ed.) *Nationalism and Social Communication*, Cambridge, Mass., 1966.

Edwards, J. *Language, Society and Identity*, Oxford, Blackwell, 1985.

Emerson, R. *From Empire to Nation: The Rise to Self-Assertion of Asian and African Peoples*, Cambridge, Mass., 1960.

Enloe, Cynthia H. *Ethnic Conflict and Political Development*, Boston, Little Brown & Co., 1973.

——*Ethnic Soldiers: State Security in a Divided Society*, Harmondsworth, Penguin, 1980.

Esman, Milton J. *Ethnic Politics*, Ithaca, Cornell University Press, 1994.

Gellner, Ernest. *Nations and Nationalism*, Oxford, Blackwell, 1983.

——*Encounters with Nationalism*, Oxford, Blackwell, 1994.

Ghosh, Partha S. *Cooperation and Conflict in South Asia*, New Delhi, Manohar Publications, 1989.

Glazer, Nathan, and Daniel P Moynihan (eds) *Ethnicity: Theory and Experience*, Cambridge, Mass., Harvard University Press, 1975.

Gurr, Ted Robert. *Why Men Rebel*, Princeton, Princeton University Press, 1971.

Heraclides, Alexis. *The Self-Determination of Minorities in International Politics*, London, Frank Cass, 1991.

Hobsbawm, E J. *Nations and Nationalism since 1780*, Cambridge, Cambridge University Press, revised edition 1993.

Horowitz, Donald L. *Ethnic Groups in Conflict*, Berkeley, University of California Press, 1985.

Isaacs, Harold R. *Idols of the Tribe: Group Identity and Political Change*, New York, 1976.

Kedourie, Elie. *Nationalism*, London, 1960.
——(ed.) *Nationalism in Asia and Africa*, London, 1970.

Kellas, James G. *The Politics of Nationalism and Ethnicity*, London, Macmillan, 1991.

Lijphart, Arend. *Democracy in Plural Societies*, New Haven, CT: Yale University Press, 1977.

Little, Richard. *Intervention: External Involvement in Civil Wars*, London, 1975.

McDowell, C.A. *Tamil Asylum Diaspora: Sri Lankan Migration, Settlement and Politics in Switzerland*, Berghan Books, Providence RI and Oxford, 1996.

Montville, Joseph V. (ed.) *Conflict and Peacemaking in Multiethnic Societies*, Lexington, Mass., Lexington Books, 1991.

Moynihan, Daniel P. *Pandemonium: Ethnicity in International Politics*, New York, 1993.

Mayall, James. *Nationalism and International Society*, Cambridge, Cambridge University Press, 1990.

Nash, Manning. *The Cauldron of Ethnicity in the Modern World*, Chicago, University of Chicago Press, 1989.

Nordlinger, Eric A. *Conflict Regulation in Divided Societies*, Harvard, Mass., Harvard University, 1972.

Patterson, Orlando. *Ethnic Chauvinism: The Reactionary Impulse*, New York, Stein and Day, 1977.

Periwal, Sukumar (ed.) *Notions of Nationalism*, Budapest, Central European Press, 1995.

Phadnis, Urmila. *Ethnicity and Nation Building in South Asia*, New Delhi, Sage, 1990.

Porter, J N., and T. Taplin, *Conflict and Conflict Resolution*, New York, 1978.

Premdas, Ralph., S.W.R. de A. Samarasinghe & Alan B. Anderson (eds) *Secessionist Movements in Comparative Perspective*, London, Pinter Publishers, 1990.

Rothschild, Joseph. *Ethnopolitics: A Conceptual Framework*, New York, Columbia University Press, 1981.

Ryan, Stephen. *Ethnic Conflict and International Relations*, Aldershot, Dartmouth, 1990.

Samarasinghe, S.W.R. de A., and Reed Coughlan (eds) *Economic Dimensions of Ethnic Conflict*, London, Pinter Publishers, 1991.

Schaeffer, Robert. *Warpaths: The Politics of Partition*, New York, Hill and Wang, 1990.

Seton-Watson, H. *Nations and States: An Enquiry into the Origins of Nations and the Politics of Nationalism*, London, 1977.

Smith, A.D. *Theories of Nationalism*, 2nd ed., New York, Holmes and Meier, 1983.

——*The Ethnic Revival in the Modern World*, New York, Cambridge University Press, 1981.

——*The Ethnic Origin of Nations*, Oxford, Basil Blackwell, 1987.

——*National Identity*, Harmondsworth, Penguin, 1991.

——*Nations and Nationalism in a Global Era*, Oxford, Polity Press and Blackwells Publishers, 1995.

Smith, D.E. (ed.) *South Asian Politics and Religion*, Princeton, Princeton University Press, 1966

Stavenhagen, Rodolfo. *The Ethnic Question: Conflicts, Development and Human Rights*, Tokyo, United Nations University, 1990.

Stone, John. *Racial Conflict in Contemporary Society*, London, 1985.

Suhrke, Astri., and Lela Garner Noble (eds) *Ethnic Conflict in International Relations*, New York, Praeger, 1977.

Sureda, A. Rigo. *The Evolution of the Right to Self Determination*, Leiden, 1973.

Tambiah, S.J. *Leveling Crowds: Ethnonationalist Conflicts and Collective Violence in South Asia*, Berkeley and Los Angeles, University of California Press, 1996.

Tinker, H. *The Banyan Tree: Overseas Emigrants from India, Pakistan and Bangladesh*, Oxford, Oxford University Press, 1977.

Tonnesson, Stein and Hans Antlov. *Asian Forms of the Nation*, London, Curzon Press for the Nordic Institute of Asian Studies, 1996.

van den Berghe, P.L. *The Ethnic Phenomenon*, New York, Elsevier, 1991.

Weiner, Myron. *Sons of the Soil: Migration and Ethnic Conflict in India*, Princeton, Princeton University Press, 1978.

Wriggins, W. Howard. (ed.) *Dynamics of Regional Politics: Four Systems on the Indian Ocean Rim*, New York, University of Columbia Press, 1992.

Young, Crawford. *The Politics of Cultural Pluralism*, Madison, 1976.

Young, Oran R. *The Intermediaries: Third Parties in International Crises*, Princeton, Princeton University Press, 1967.

GENERAL WORKS—ARTICLES

Ayoob, Mohammed. 'The Primacy of the Political: South Asian Regional Cooperation in Comparative Perspective', *Asian Survey*, 25(4) April 1985, pp 443-57.
——'India in South Asia: The Quest for Regional Predominance', *World Policy Journal*, 7(1) 1989, pp 107-33.

Birch, A.H. 'Minority Nationalist Movements and Theories of Political Integration', *World Politics*, Vol. 33, 1978, pp 325-44.

Connor, Walker. 'Nation Building or Nation Destroying?' *World Politics*, XXIV(3) 1972, pp 319-55.

——'The Politics of Ethnonationalism', *Journal of International Affairs*, Vol. 27, 1973, pp 1-21.

——'Ethnonationalism in the First World', in Milton J. Esman (ed.), *Ethnic Conflict in the Western World*, Ithaca, Cornell University Press, 1977, pp 19-45.

——'A Nation is a Nation, is a State, is an Ethnic Group, is a . . .', *Ethnic and Racial Studies*, 1(4) 1978, pp 377-400.

——'The Impact of Homelands upon Diasporas', in Gabriel Sheffer (ed.), *Modern Diasporas in International Politics*, London, 1986, pp 16-68.

Esman, Milton J. 'The Management of Ethnic Conflict', *Public Policy*, XXI(1) 1973, pp 49-78.

——'Perspectives on Ethnic Conflict in Industrialized Societies', in M.J. Esman (ed.), *Ethnic Conflict in the Western World*, Ithaca, Cornell University Press, 1977, pp 371-90.

——'Ethnic Pluralism and International Relations', *Canadian Review of Studies in Nationalism*, XVII(1-2) 1990, pp 83-93.

Fishman, Joshua A. 'Nationality-Nationalism', in Joshua A Fishman, *et.al.*, (eds), *Language Problems of Developing Nations*, pp 39-51.

Geertz, C. 'The Integrative Revolution', in C Geertz (ed.), *Old Societies and New States: The Quest for Modernity in Africa and Asia*, New York, 1963, pp 105-57.

Gladstone, Jack A. 'Theories of Revolution: The Third Generation', *World Politics*, XXXII(3), 1980, pp 425-53.

Gurr, Ted Robert. 'Theories of Political Violence and Revolution in the Third World', in Francis M·Deng and I William Zartman (eds), *Conflict Resolution in Africa*, Washington D.C., Brookings Institution, 1991, pp 153-89.

Halsey, A.H. 'Ethnicity: A Primordial Social Bond', *Ethnic* and *Racial Studies*, 1(1) 1978, pp 124-8.

Hare, A.P. 'Third Party Role in Ethnic Conflict', *Social Dynamics*, 1(1), 1975, pp 81-107.

Hechter, Michael. 'The Political Economy of Ethnic Change', *The American Journal of Sociology*, 79(5) 1973, pp 1151-78.

Horowitz, Donald L. 'Ethnic Identity', in Glazer and Moynihan (eds), *Ethnicity: Theory and Experience*, 1975, pp 111-40.

Juergensmeyer, Mark. 'What the *Bhikkhu* Said: Reflections on the Rise of Militant Religious Nationalism', *Religion*, 20, 1990, pp 53-75.

Keyes, Charles F. 'Towards a New Formulation of the Concept of Ethnic Group', *Ethnicity*, 3, 1976, pp 203-13.

Lijphart, Arend. 'Consociational Democracy', *World Politics*, XXI, 1969, pp 207-25.

Lustick, Ian. 'Stability in Deeply Divided Societies: Consociationalism versus Control', *World Politics*, XXXI(3) 1979, pp 325-44.

McKay, James., and Frank Lewins, 'Ethnicity and the Ethnic Group: A Conceptual Analysis and Reformulation', *Ethnic and Racial Studies*, 1(4) 1978, pp 412-27.

Mitchell, C.R. 'Civil Strife and the Involvement of External Parties', *International Studies Quarterly*, XIV(2) 1970, pp 166-94.

——'External Peace-Making Initiatives and Intra-National Conflict' in M Midlarsky (ed.), *The Internationalization of Communal Strife*, London, 1992, pp 274-97.

Petersen, William. 'Ethnicity in the World Today', *International Journal of Comparative Sociology*, XX(1&2) 1979, pp 3-13.

Roberts, Michael. 'Nationalism, the Past and The Present: The Case of Sri Lanka', (Review Essay) *Ethnic and*

Racial Studies, Vol. 16, No. 1, January 1993, pp 133-66.

Ross, Marc Howard. 'A Cross-Cultural Theory of Political Conflict and Violence', *Political Psychology*, 7(3) 1986, pp 427-69.

——'The Role of Evolution in Ethnocentric Conflict and its Management', *Journal of Social Issues*, 47, 1991, pp 167-85.

——'Ethnic Conflict and Dispute Management' in Austin Sarat and Susan Silbey (eds), *Studies in Law, Politics and Society*, Vol. 12, Greenwich Ct, 1992, pp 107-146.

Rothchild, Donald. 'Ethnicity and Conflict Resolution', *World Politics*, XX(1) 1969, pp 597-616.

——'An Interactive Model for State-Ethnic Relations' in Francis M Deng and I William Zartman (eds), *Conflict Resolution in Africa*, Washington D.C.: The Brookings Institution, 1991, pp 190-215.

Smith, A D. 'The Diffusion of Nationalism', *I   Journal of Sociology*, Vol. 29, 1978, pp 234-48.

Stavenhagen, Rodolfo. 'Ethnic Conflicts and Their Impact on International Society', *International Social Science Journal*, 127 (February 1991), pp 117-32.

Touval, Saadia. 'Biased Intermediaries', *Jerusalem Journal of International Relations*, 1(1) 1975, pp 51-69.

——'Gaining Entry to Mediation in Communal Strife', in M. Midlarsky (ed.), *The Internationalization of Communal Strife*, London, 1992, pp 255-73.

van Dyke, Vernon. 'Self-Determination and Minority Rights', *International Studies Quarterly*, 111(3) 1969, pp 226-33.

Wibers, Hakan. 'Self-Determination as an International Issue', in I.M. Levis (ed.), *Nationalism and Self-Determination in the Horn of Africa*, London, 1983, pp 43-65.

Wittman, Donald. 'How a War Ends—A Rational Model Approach', *Journal of Conflict Resolution*, 23(4) 1979, pp 743-63.

Wood, John R. 'Secession: A Comparative Framework', *Canadian Journal of Political Science*, 1(1) 1981, pp 107-34.

White, N.R. 'Ethnicity, Culture and Cultural Pluralism', *Ethnic and Racial Studies*, Vol.(2) 1978, pp 139 53.

Yapp, Malcolm. 'Language, Religion and Political Identity: A General Framework', in D. Taylor & M. Yapp (eds), *Political Identity in South Asia*, London, Curzon Press, 1979, pp 1-34.

Young, Crawford. 'The Temple of Ethnicity', *World Politics*, XXXV(4) 1983, pp 652-62.

BOOKS AND MONOGRAPHS ON HISTORY AND POLITICS OF SRI LANKA—

Alles, A.C. *Insurgency 1971*, Colombo, Colombo Apothecaries, 1976.
——*The JVP 1969-1989*, Colombo, Lake House, 1989.

Bhaduri, Shankar, and Afsir Karim, *The Sri Lankan Crisis*, Lancer Paper 1, New Delhi, Lancer International, 1990.

Bond, George. *The Buddhist Revival in Sri Lanka: The Religious Tradition, Reinterpretation and Response*, Columbia, S.C.: University of South Carolina, 1988.

Bullion, Alan J. *India, Sri Lanka and the Tamil Crisis 1976-1994: An International Perspective*, London, Pinter, 1995.

Chandraprema, C.A. *Sri Lanka: The Years of Terror—The JVP Insurrection 1987-1989*, Colombo, Lake House, 1991.

de Silva K.M. (ed.) University of Ceylon, *History of Ceylon*, Vol III, University of Ceylon, Peradeniya, 1973 and University of Peradeniya, *History of Sri Lanka*, Vol II, Peradeniya, 1995.
——(ed.) *Sri Lanka, A Survey*, London, C. Hurst, 1977.
——*A History of Sri Lanka*, London, C. Hurst, 1981
——(ed.) *Universal Franchise, 1931-1981: The Sri Lankan Experience*, Colombo, Department of Information, 1981.

———*Managing Ethnic Tensions in Multi Ethnic Societies: Sri Lanka, 1880-1985*, Lanham, Md.: University Press of America, 1986.

———(ed.) *Sri Lanka: The Problems of Governance*, New Delhi, Konarak, 1993.

———*Regional Powers and Small State Security. India and Sri Lanka, 1977-1990*, Washington D.C., Woodrow Wilson Center Press, 1995.

———*The Traditional Homelands of the Tamils. Separatist Ideology in Sri Lanka. A Historical Appraisal*, Kandy, International Centre for Ethnic Studies, 2nd revised ed, 1994.

———with Howard Wriggins, *J.R. Jayewardene of Sri Lanka. A Political Biography*, Vol I, 1906-1956, London, Quartet Press, 1988 and Vol II, 1956 to his retirement, London, Leo Cooper, 1994.

Dharmadasa, K.N.O. *Language, Religion and Ethnic Assertiveness: The Growth of Sinhalese Nationalism in Sri Lanka*, Ann Arbor, Michigan University Press, 1992.

———(ed.) *National Language Policy in Sri Lanka, 1956-1996: Three Studies in Its Implementation*, ICES, Kandy, 1996.

Dissanayaka, T.D.S.A. *The Agony of Sri Lanka: An In-depth Account of the Racial Riots of July 1983*, Colombo, Swastika (Pvt) Ltd., 1983.

———*The Dilemma of Sri Lanka*, Colombo, Swastika (Pvt) Ltd., 1993.

Dixit, J.N. *Assignment Colombo*, Delhi, Konarak Publishers, 1997.

Fernando, Tissa., and Robert N Kearney (eds), *Modern Sri Lanka: A Society in Transition*, Syracuse, Maxwell School of Citizenship and Public Affairs, 1979.

Gunaratna, Rohan. *Sri Lanka: A Lost Revolution? The Inside Story of the JVP*, Colombo, Institute of Fundamental Studies, 1990.

———*Indian Intervention in Sri Lanka: The Role of India's Intelligence Agencies*, Colombo, South Asian Network on Conflict Research, 1993.

Jayatilleka, Dayan. *Sri Lanka. The Travails of a Democracy:*

Unfinished War, Protracted Crisis, New Delhi, Vikas, 1995.

Jayawardena, Visakha Kumari. *Ethnic and Class Conflicts in Sri Lanka*, Dehiwala, Centre for Social Analysis, 1986.

Jayaweera, Neville. *Sri Lanka: Towards a Multi-Ethnic Democracy?*, (Report of a fact-finding mission), Oslo, International Peace Research Institute, 1990.

Jayewardene, J.R. *Men and Memories: Autobiographical Recollections and Reflections*, New Delhi, Vikas, 1992.

Jennings, Sir Ivor. *The Constitution of Ceylon*, (3rd ed.), London, Oxford University Press, 1953.

Jiggins, Janice. *Caste and Family in the Politics of the Sinhalese 1947-1976*, Cambridge, Cambridge University Press, 1979.

Jupp, James. *Sri Lanka, Third World Democracy*, London, Frank Cass, 1978.

Kadian, Rajesh. *India's Sri Lanka Fiasco: Peace Keepers at War*, New Delhi, Vision Books, 1990.

Kapferer, Bruce. *Legends of People, Myths of State: Violence, Intolerance and Political Culture in Sri Lanka and Australia*, Washington D.C.: Smithsonian Institution Press, 1967.

Kearney, Robert N. *Communalism and Language in the Politics of Ceylon*, Durham, N.C., Duke University Press, 1967.

——*The Politics of Ceylon* (Sri Lanka), Ithaca, N.Y., Cornell University Press, 1973.

Kemper, Steven. *The Presence of the Past: Chronicles, Politics and Culture in Sinhala Life*, Ithaca, N.Y., Cornell University Press, 1991.

Kodikara, Shelton U. *External Compulsions of South Asian Politics*, New Delhi, Sage, 1993.

——*Foreign Policy of Sri Lanka*, 2nd ed., New Delhi, Chanakya Publications, 1992.

——(ed.) *Indo-Sri Lanka Agreement of July 1987*, Colombo, University of Colombo, 1989.

——*Indo-Ceylon Relations since Independence*, Colombo, Ceylon Institute of World Affairs, 1965.

Little, David. *Sri Lanka: The Invention of Enmity*, Washington, D.C., United States Institute of Peace, 1994.

Manogaran, Chelvadurai. *Ethnic Conflict and Reconciliation in Sri Lanka*, Honolulu, University of Hawaii Press, 1987.

Manor, James. (ed.) *Sri Lanka in Change and Crisis*, London, Croom Helm, 1984.

——*The Expedient Utopian: Bandaranaike and Ceylon*, Cambridge, Cambridge University Press, 1989.

Mohandas, K.. *M.G.R.: The Man and the Myth*, Bangalore, Panther, 1992.

Muni, S.D. *Pangs of Proximity: India and Sri Lanka's Ethnic Crisis*, Oslo, PRIO, 1993.

Narayan Swamy, M.R. *Tigers of Lanka : From Boys to Guerrillas*, Delhi, Konarak, 1994 revised and 1997.

O'Ballance, Edgar. *The Cyanide War: Tamil Insurrection in Sri Lanka 1973-88*, London, Brassey's, 1989.

Pfaffenberger, Brian. *Caste in Tamil Culture: The Religious Foundations of Sudra Domination in Tamil Sri Lanka*, Syracuse, Syracuse University, 1982.

Phadnis, Urmila. *Religion and Politics in Sri Lanka*, New Delhi, Manohar, 1976.

Ponnambalam, Satchi. *Sri Lanka, the National Question and the Tamil Liberation Struggle*, London, Zed, 1983.

Ratnatunga, Sinha. *The Politics of Terrorism: The Sri Lanka Experience*, Canberra, International Fellowship for Social and Economic Development, 1988.

Roberts, Michael. *Caste Conflict and Elite Formation. The Rise of a Karava Elite in Sri Lanka, 1500-1931*, Cambridge, Cambridge University Press, 1982.

——*Exploring Confrontation. Sri Lanka: Politics, Culture and History*, Victoria, Harwood Academic Publishers, 1994.

Ross, Russell R., and Andrea Matles Savada (eds), *Sri Lanka: A Country Study*, Washington D.C., 1991.

Russell, Jane. *Communal Politics under the Donoughmore*

Constitution, 1931-1947, Colombo, Tisara Press, 1983.

Ryan, Bryce. *Caste in Modern Ceylon*, New Brunswick, Rutgers University Press, 1953.

Sardeshpande, S.C. *Assignment Jaffna*, New Delhi, Lancer, 1992.

Seevaratnam, N. (ed.) *The National Question and the Indo-Sri Lanka Accord*, New Delhi, Konarak, 1989.

Singer, Marshall R. *The Emerging Elite: A Study of Political Leadership in Ceylon*, Cambridge, Mass., MIT Press, 1964.

Singh, Depinder. *The IPKF in Sri Lanka*, New Delhi, Trishul, 1992.

Spencer, Jonathan. (ed.) *Sri Lanka: History and the Roots of Conflict*, London, Routledge, 1990.

Suriyanarayana, P.S. *The Peace Trap: An Indo-Sri Lankan Political Crisis*, New Delhi, Affiliated East-West Press, 1988.

Tambiah, Stanley J. *Sri Lanka: Ethnic Fratricide and the Dismantling of Democracy*, Chicago, University of Chicago Press, 1986.

——*Buddhism Betrayed? Religion, Politics and Violence in Sri Lanka*, Chicago, University of Chicago Press, 1992.

Thondaman, S. *My Life and Times, An Autobiography*, Vol. 1, Colombo, The Ceylon Workers' Congress, 1987; *Tea and Politics*, Vol II, New Delhi, Navrang, 1994.

Tiranagama, R., and others, *The Broken Palmyra: The Tamil Crisis in Sri Lanka, An Inside Account*, California, The Sri Lanka Studies Institute, 1990.

Vanniasingham, Somasundaram. *Sri Lanka: The Conflict Within*, New Delhi, Lancer, 1988.

Vijayavardhana, D.C. *The Revolt in the Temple*, Colombo, Sinha Publications, 1953.

Vittachy, Tarzie, *Emergency '58: The Story of the Ceylon Race Riots*, Andre Deutsch, London, 1958.

Weerakoon, Bradman. *Premadasa of Sri Lanka: A Political Biography*, New Delhi, Vikas, 1992.

Wickremaratne, L.A. *Buddhism and Ethnicity in Sri Lanka: A Historical Analysis*, New Delhi, Vikas, 1995.

Wilson, A. Jeyaratnam. *Electoral Politics in an Emergent State: The Ceylon General Elections of May 1970*, Cambridge, Cambridge University Press, 1975.

——*Politics in Sri Lanka, 1947-1979*, London, Macmillan, 1979.

——*The Gaullist System in Asia, The Constitution of Sri Lanka, 1978*, London, Macmillan, 1980.

——*The Break-up of Sri Lanka: The Sinhalese-Tamil Conflict*, Honolulu, University of Hawaii Press, 1988.

Warnapala, W.A. Wiswa. *Ethnic Strife and Politics in Sri Lanka: An Investigation into Demands and Responses*, New Delhi, Navrang, 1994.

Woodward, Calvin. *The Growth of a Party System in Ceylon*, Providence, Rhode Island, Brown University Press, 1969.

Wriggins, W. Howard. *Ceylon: Dilemmas of a New Nation*, Princeton, N.J.: Princeton University Press, 1960.

ARTICLES AND PAMPHLETS ON SRI LANKA

Amunugama, Sarath. 'Buddhaputra and Bhumiputra? Dilemmas of Modern Sinhala Buddhist Monks in Relation to Ethnic and Political Conflict', *Religion* XXI(1991), pp 115-39.

de Silva, C.R. 'The Constitution of the Second Republic of Sri Lanka (1978) and its Significance', *The Journal of Commonwealth and Comparative Politics*, XVII(2), pp 192-209.

de Silva, H.L. 'The Indo-Sri Lanka Agreement (1987) in the Perspective of Inter-State Relations', *Ethnic Studies Report*, Vol. X, No.2, July 1992, pp 10-17.

de Silva, K.M. 'Buddhist Revivalism, Nationalism and Politics in Modern Sri Lanka', in James W Bjorkman (ed.), *Fundamentalism, Revivalists and Violence in South Asia*, New Delhi, Manohar, 1988, pp 107-58.

——'Multi-Culturalism in Sri Lanka—Historical Legacy and Contemporary Political Reality', *Ethnic Studies Report*, 15(1), January 1997, pp 1-44.

Fernando, Tissa. 'Elite Politics in the New States. The Case of Post-Independence Sri Lanka', *Pacific Affairs*, XLVI(3), pp 361-83.

Halliday, F. 'The Ceylonese Insurrection', in *New Left Review*, in October 1971, reprinted in R. Blackburn (ed.), *Explosion in a Sub-Continent*, Harmondsworth, 1975, pp 151-220.

Kearney, R.N. 'Ethnic Conflict and the Tamil Separatist Movement in Sri Lanka', *Asian Survey*, XXV(9), pp 898-917.

——'Sinhalese Nationalism and Social Conflict in Ceylon', *Pacific Affairs*, XXXVII, pp 125-136.

——and J Jiggins, 'The Ceylon Insurrection of 1971', *The Journal of Commonwealth and Comparative Politics*, XIII(1), pp 40-64.

Obeyesekere, Gananath. 'The Sinhalese-Buddhist Identity', in G de Vos and L Romanucci-Ross (eds), *Ethnic Identity, Cultural Continuities and Change*, Palo Alto, 1976.

Peiris, G.H. 'An Appraisal of the Concept of a Traditional Tamil Homeland in Sri Lanka', *Ethnic Studies Report*, IX(1), pp 13-39.

——'Irrigation, Land Distribution and Ethnic Conflict in Sri Lanka: An Evaluation of Criticisms, with Special Reference to the Mahaveli Programme', *Ethnic Studies Report*, XII(1), pp 43-88.

Pfaffenberger, Brian. 'The Cultural Dimension of Tamil Separatism in Sri Lanka', *Asian Survey*, XXI(12), pp 1145-57.

Roberts, Michael. 'Elites, Nationalism, and The Nationalist Movement in Ceylon', xxix to ccxxii, introduction to

Michael Roberts (ed.), *Documents of the Ceylon National Congress*, Vol. 1, Colombo, 1978.

——'Ethnic Conflict in Sri Lanka and Sinhalese Perspectives: Barriers to Accommodation', *Modern Asian Studies*, VII(3), pp 353-76.

Samarasinghe, S.W.R. de A.. 'Ethnic Representation in Central Government Employment and Sinhala-Tamil Relations in Sri Lanka, 1948-81', in R.B. Goldmann and A. Jeyaratnam Wilson (eds), *From Independence to Statehood*, London, Frances Pinter, 1984, pp 86-108.

Schwarz, W. *The Tamils of Sri Lanka*, Minority Rights Group Report No. 25, (revised ed.), London, 1979.

Smith, Donald E. 'The Political Monks and Monastic Reform', in Donald E. Smith (ed.), *South Asian Politics and Religion*, Princeton, Princeton University Press, 1965, pp 489-501.

——'The Sinhalese-Buddhist Revolution', *ibid.*, pp 453-88.

Stiratt, R.L. 'The Riots and the Roman Catholic Church in Historical Perspective', in James Manor (ed.), *Sri Lanka in Change and Crisis*, London, Croom Helm, 1984, pp 196-213.

Wilson, A.J. 'The Tamil Federal Party in Ceylon Politics', *The Journal of Commonwealth Political Studies*, IV(2), pp 117-39.

Wriggins, W. Howard. 'Impediments to Unity in New Nations: The Case of Ceylon', *The American Political Science Review*, LV(2), pp 313-21.

BIBLIOGRAPHIES ON SRI LANKA

Daya and C.R. de Silva, *Sri Lanka (Ceylon) since Independence (1948-1976)*, Hamburg, Institute of Asian Affairs, 1978.

——*Sri Lanka since Independence: A Reference Guide to the Literature*, New Delhi, Navrang, 1992.

Goonetileke, H.A.I. *A Bibliography of Ceylon: A Systematic Guide to the Literature on the Land, People, History and Culture Published in the Western Languages from the Sixteenth Century to the Present Day*, 5 Volumes, Zug, Switzerland, Inter Documentation Co., 1970-1983.

Samaraweera, V.K. *Sri Lanka*, World Bibliographical series, Vol 20, Santa Barbara, Clio Press, 1987.

Index

Afghanistan (Soviet Union's involvement in) 198

Ali, M.E.H. Mohamed 265

All Ceylon Buddhist Congress 84, 86-7, 89-91, 103

All Ceylon Moors Association 254, 259

All Ceylon Muslim League 254, 259

All Party Conference (APC) 106, 189, 203-4, 217, 313

All Sri Lanka Muslim League 259

Amirthalingam, A. 124, 157, 163, 328

Ampara district (Eastern Province) 209, 228-9, 253, 265, 269

Aney, M.S. 281-2

Anglicans (Anglican Church) 76, 116

Anti-Tamil riots of-1983 7, 106, 188-92, 193, 200, 321

Anti-Terrorism Act of 1996, 328

Anuradhapura 81, 270

APC, see, All Party Conference

Arunachalam, Sir Ponnambalam 302

Athulathmudali, Lalith 234, 238, 327

Ashroff, M.H.M. 265-6, 268-71

Bajpai, G.S. 280

Balasingham, Anton 229

Bandaranaike, S.W.R.D. 24-6, 28-30, 46-55, 84, 86, 88-93, 98, 100, 110, 123-4, 142, 176, 206, 279, 287, 294

assassination 93, 98

devolution of power 52-5

language policy 24-5, 45-62, 100, 123

Provincial Councils and 52-55, 176

Sinhalese-Buddhist populism 24-6, 47-52, 84, 86, 88-93

Bandaranaike, Sirimavo 33, 55-56, 60, 94, 97, 102, 124, 241, 262, 266, 287-9, 294-5

Bangladesh 25, 150, 199-200, 331

Bhandari, Romesh 217-21, 224-225

Bhikkhus 50, 54, 72, 81, 84, 86, 88-91, 93-5, 98-102, 106-11, 122-3

activists 50, 54

educational reforms and 89-90, 95, 99

in politics 84, 88-91

opposition to devolution of power to District Development Councils 101, 108

opposition to Indo-Sri Lanka Accord 107-9

Roman Catholics 99

Bodhi tree, 79

British Prevention of Terrorism Act 185

British raj 16-7, 25, 46, 149, 195-7, 300

India's assumption role 196

Sri Lanka not part of 195-7

Buddha, see, Buddhism

Buddha Jayanthi 24, 87

Buddha Sasana Act 1312 BE (1950), 85

Buddha Sasana Commission 91-2, 94-5, 98, 108
Buddha Sasana Council 87
Buddharakkita, M. 93
Buddhism 8, 23-4, 26, 29-30, 40-2, 70, 72-5, 77, 79-87, 89-92, 94; 98, 103-5, 300
  and Christianity 300
  and Sinhalese 23-7, 29-30, 79, 105
  and State 40-2, 80-6, 89-92, 94, 103-5 109-10
  restriction as practice of 70
  resurgence 77, 79
  revival of 72-5, 79-80, 87, 98
  temporalities 75
Burghers 302, 307
Burma 149-50 273, 276, 286

Caldecott, Andrew 278-9, 282, 303
Canagaratnam, S.C. 209
Caste,
  among Tamil 273
Ceylon Citizenship Act of 1948 274, 283
Ceylon Indian Congress 284 294
Ceylon National Congress 255, 279
Ceylon (Parliamentary Election) Amendment Act No 48 of 1949 284
Ceylon Workers Congress (CWC) 37-8, 125-7, 177-79, 284-5, 287-91, 293-6
  alliance with UNP 37-8, 177-9, 288-91, 293-4
  relations with UF Government 125-7, 177, 295

Chelvanayakam, S.J.V. 111, 123, 162-3
Chidambaram, P. 224, 229, 313
Christianity,
  colonialism and 69-76
  conflicts with Buddhists 79, 82, 300
  conversion to 71
  education and 96-7
  language policy and 26
  minority 111-8
  response to nationalism 76-88, 111-88
  Roman Catholics and 48
  'westernness' of 75
Citizenship issue, 275, 283-96
Clapham House 72
Cleghorn, Hugh 152, 155, 205
Cleghorn Minute 152-3, 157
Clifford, Hugh 303
Communist Party (CP) 36-9, 56, 61, 239
Constitution of India 144
Constitution of 1972, 62-3, 164-6
Constitution of 1978, 165-6
Corea, G.C.S. 279
Cyprus 199

Dahanayake, W. 92, 262
Decentralization of administration, *see,* Devolution of power
De-induction, see, IPKF
Delhi Accord 219-21, 223-5
Desai, Morarji 197
Devolution of power 52-5, 123, 175-6, 314-5, 317
Dharmapala, Anagarika 78-81
Dissanayake, Gamini 327, 329
District Councils 101, 126

District Development Councils 174-7, 186-9, 198, 202, 204, 319

District Development Councils Act (1980) 198

district vs. provinces 202

Dixit, Jyotindra Nath 240, 242

Dominion status 23

Donoughmore Commission 176

Donoughmore Constitution 1931, 80

Donoughmore System 257

Dravida Kazhagam (DK) 143-44

Dravida Munnetra Kazhagam (DMK) 143-4, 199

Durayappah, Alfred 148

East Pakistan *see*, Bangladesh, Urdu as official language 119-21

Eastern Province (Sri Lanka) 163, 207-14, 227-30, 236-7, 239, 253, 257, 264-71, 313-14, 318

Muslim politics of 264-71

Education,
Christianity and 96-7
Committee of 1942 257
Muslims and 60-1, 257-8, 261-3
reforms 45-7, 59-60, 86-7, 96-97
state control of 79

Eelam, *see*, Tamil separatist movements

Eelam National Democratic Liberation Front (ENDLF) 240

Eelam People's Revolutionary Liberation Front (EPRLF) 219, 239-40, 243, 245, 268, 328

Elections, in Sri Lanka 27-8, 31, 33-9, 55, 121, 126, 177

Electoral system 32-9, 264

Emigration of Tamils 272-96, 305

Ethnic communities, distribution of 10

Ethnic conflict in Sri Lanka, India as mediator in 193-240
management and resolution 304-20
politics 119-58
reconciliation policies 161-92

Ethnicity,
concept 12-13
politicization of 15

Evangelicalism 77-8

Federal Party (FP) 28, 35, 38-39, 48-9, 52-7, 111, 119, 121, 123-4, 126-7, 130, 139, 152-55, 157, 162, 176, 202, 206, 209, 211, 256, 266, 289-90

Federation of Association of Canadian Tamils (FACT) 327

'Fifty-fifty' campaign 303

Fundamental rights issue 164-65

Gal Oya irrigation project 154, 209-10

Gandhi, Indira 191, 193, 196-207, 217-8, 223, 246, 289
and Sri Lanka 197-207
assassination 191 246

Gandhi, Rajiv 205-6, 217-8, 220-1, 223-5, 228-9, 233-6, 242, 245-6, 327-8
assassination 245-6, 327-8

Gnanasiha, bhikkhu
Henpitagedera 100
Good Friday bus massacre 230
Goonesinha, A.E. 276
Gordon, Arthur 73-4, 91, 103
Grant of Citizenship to
Stateless Persons Act No. 39
of 1988, 204
Great Buddhist Council 87
Gregory, William 73, 91, 103
Gujral, Inder Kumar 242

Hindus 79, 88, 96, 104, 106,
108, 111-12
Horowitz, Donald 136
Human Rights Commission
216
Huxham, H.J. 279

Ilankai Thamil Arasi Kachchi
(ITAK) 153-5
India, relations with Sri Lanka
193-245
India Today 214, 325
Indian and Pakistani Residents
(Citizenship) Act No. 3 of
1949 284
Indian immigrants, in Sri
Lanka 272-96, 305
Indian National Congress 32
Indian Peace-Keeping Force
(IPKF) 231-45, 266, 268, 321-
23, 326, 330-1
intermediary phase 231-40
last phase 240-5
Indian Tamils 177-8, 273, 286,
305, 312
Indian workers, worldwide
dispersal 272-75
Indo-Sri Lanka Accord 63, 107,
178, 232-5, 238-39, 241-2,
244, 260, 266, 296
Islamic fundamentalism 208

Islamic revival 41, 251-71
Islamic Socialist Front 135, 260
Israel 267-8

Jaffna Association 302
Jaffna peninsula (Sri Lanka)
12, 19, 89, 130-1, 138, 140-
41, 144, 148, 150, 154, 156,
163-4, 171, 180-1, 183, 185-
88, 229-30, 237, 244, 251,
253, 268-9, 299, 301, 308,
310, 312, 316, 320, 323, 326,
328-30
Janatha Vimukthi Peramuna
(JVP) 34, 54, 108 136-9, 180,
232, 235, 237-46
Janatharan 146
Jatika Vimukti Peramuna 54
Jayah, T.B. 257-8
Jayatilaka, D.B. 80-82, 92
Jayewardene, J.R. 30, 32, 46-
47, 53, 63-4, 106-8, 110, 173,
177, 197, 202-3, 218, 225-6,
228-9, 232-4, 236, 238-42,
247, 258, 266-7
Jeffries, Charles 5-6, 127
Jennings, Ivor 23, 83, 127

Kaleel, M.C.M. 257
Kannangara, C.W.W. 262
Karunanidhi, M. 199
Kilinochchi (Sri Lanka) 330
Kobbekaduwa, H. 290-1
Kotelawala, (J.L.) John 24, 32,
277, 286-88
Kotle Kingdom 156
Kumaratunga, Chandrika 32,
110

Labour Parties 35
Land Reform Act of 1972 290
Language 40-42, 45-68, 94, 166,
301, 308

and religion 40-2
devolution of power and 52
dilution of Sinhala Only
 policy 55-61
policy 40-2, 94, 166, 301,
 308
problem, 45-68
rights, 62-8
Sinhala Only policy 47-52,
 55-61
Lanka Sama Samaja Party
 (LSSP) 27, 36-7, 56-8, 61,
 98, 124-5, 128-9, 136, 239,
 291
Laue, James 194
Leary, Virginia 172-72
Lebbe, M.C. Siddi 255
Liberal Democratic Party
 (Japan) 32
Liberation Tigers of Tamil
 Eelam (LTTE) 115, 148,
 158, 180-4, 200, 219, 221-5,
 227-8, 230-2, 235-7, 240-7,
 251, 266-9, 271, 310, 314,
 318, 320-32
 opposition to
 accommodation 320-2
Linguistic nationalism 84, 88
Link language 64-5
Longowal, Sant Harchand
 Singh 223

Mahajana Eksath Peramuna
 (MEP) 36, 48, 50, 54, 56,
 88-9
Mahanayakes of Asgiriya and
 Malvatta 100-1
Maheswaran, Uma 219, 321,
 328
Mahmud, Badi-ud-din 60, 130-
 31, 135, 260, 262, 265
Malalasekera, G.P. 58
Malaysian riots of 1969, 191

Mansergh, Nicholas 5-6
Maran, Murasoli 199
Marrs, Robert 47
Marx 21
Marxist parties 21, 26-31, 36-
 37, 48, 51, 56-7, 61, 98-9,
 138, 155, 304
May, Erskine 21
Migration, to Eastern
 provincial 212
Ministers' Draft Constitution
 (1944) 23
Minority 23, 176, 301, 317
Mohandas, K. 215
Monck-Mason, Moore, Sir
 Henry 282
Moor 253-5, 257
Muslims,
 and Sinhalese 122, 130-1,
 252, 254-5, 259, 261-2,
 264
 clashes with Tamils 121, 138,
 251, 262, 268-71, 323
 education 60-1, 130-1, 177,
 257-8, 261-3
 opposition to District
 Development Council
 177, 317
 politics of Eastern Province
 209, 264-71
 post-independence
 perspectives 259-64
 pre-independence political
 attitude 255-9
 rivalry with Tamils 9, 121,
 262-4, 312, 323
Muslim Charitable Trusts 261
Muslim Intestate Succession
 and Wakfs Ordinances of
 1931, 256, 261
Muslim League 119

Muslim Provincial Council 269
Mustapha, M.M. 265

Nadesan, S. 48-9
Nalliah, V. 258
Narcotics 325-7
National Language issue 58, 64, 166
Nationalism,
  and language 24-5
  Christian response to 76-88, 111-88
  linguistic 25, 45-68
Nationalist movement 257
Nava Sama Samaja Party 239
Nehru, Jawaharlal,
  and Indians in Sri Lanka 143, 196, 275-6, 283-4, 286-88
North Eastern Province (Sri Lanka) 52-3, 55, 152, 154-55, 157, 205-6, 208, 212, 227-8, 232-3, 235, 239
North Eastern Provincial Council 268
Northern Province (Sri Lanka) 9, 163, 181-2, 185, 237, 253, 266, 269, 306
Nu, U. 87-8
Nuwara Eliya district 211, 291, 293-4

Official Languages Act No. 33 of 1956, 51, 54
Official Languages Commission 64-5
Official Languages Commission Act No. 18 of 1991 64
Operation Liberation 230

Pakistani Residents (Citizenship) Act of 1949 274

Parathasarathy, G. 201-3, 217-18
Pathmanabha, K. 328
Pearce, Lord 129
Peiris, G.H. 210, 213
Peoples' Alliance (PA) 35, 296, 301, 329
Peoples' Liberation Organization of Tamil Eelam (PLOTE) 219
Perera, N.M. 27
Plantation Workers 178-9, 272, 276, 291-6
Police and security forces 123-24, 140-2, 180-2, 186, 188, 195
Political Parties Conference (PPC) 107, 226-7, 313
Political Reform movement 80
Ponnambalam, G.G. 163
  and 'fifty-fifty' campaign 303
Population, growth of 333-5
Portuguese, in Sri Lanka 69
Poya week-end holiday scheme 99-100, 104
Prabhakaran, Velupillai 148, 219, 229, 236, 321, 324, 328, 330
Premadasa Ranasinghe 31-2, 64, 108-10, 234, 241-2, 268, 323, 327, 329
Presidential Commission 175, 263, 319
Prevention of Terrorism (Temporary Provisions) Bill 185
Provincial Councils 239
Provincial Councils Act (1987) 226

Rahiman, W.M.A. 257
Rahula, Walpola 81
Ramachandran, M.G. 199, 231

Ramanathan, Sir Ponnambalam 208, 255-6, 302-3
Razik, A.R.A. 257-8, 263, 265
Re-indigenisation movement 76-7
Regional Councils Bill 52-4
Religion,
  language and 40-2
  state 102-18
Religious groups, ethnic composition 111-12
Repatriation of Indian Tamils 286
Research and Analysis Wing (RAW) 219
Rikhye, Ravi 244
Riots in Sri Lanka,
  of 1900-17 257
  of 1915 130, 255-6
  of 1950 161
  of 1956 42, 119, 121-3, 141
  of 1958 42, 52, 54, 122-3, 141, 179, 189-90
  of 1970 121
  of 1977 7, 161-2, 164, 166, 177, 179, 183, 198, 321
  of 1980 121
  of 1981 187
  of 1983 7, 188-92
Roman Catholicism 40, 69-71, 75, 77-80, 86, 96, 99, 101-6, 111-8, 173-4, 190, 304-5

Sabaratnam, Sri, 219, 321, 328
Samarasinghe, S.W.R. de A. 309
Sangha 81, 91, 94-5, 98, 100-1, 104-5, 108, 116, 203-4
Sansoni, M.C. 183
Satyagraha 52, 54, 285
Savundranayagam, Thomas 115

Security forces 23, 123-4, 140-43, 181, 188, 195
  conflicting perception 195
  intervention politics 123-4
Senanayake, D.S. 22-4, 32, 35, 68, 81-4, 86, 89-92, 108, 111, 151, 195-6, 279, 281-5
Senanayake, Dudley 24, 32, 39, 263, 285-7
Separatism 16-17, 140-3, 147, 149-58, 179-92, 295, 299, 303, 316, 321, 323, 326-8
Singh, Natwar 224, 229, 313
Sinhala Only Act of 1956 55-56, 59, 62
Sinhala Only policy 47-53, 67-68, 121, 166, 305-6
  dilution of 55-63, 67-8
Sinhalese-Buddhist populism 23-7, 29-30, 35-6, 41-2, 49, 58, 84, 86-8
Sinhalese-Muslim riots of 1915, 122, 254
Siyam, *nikaya* 95, 100
Soulbury 127-8
Soulbury Commission 280-2, 303, 307
Soulbury Constitution 6, 92, 97, 127-9, 137
South Asian Association for Regional Cooperation (SAARC) 228
Sri Lanka,
  Buddhist activism in 88-102
  Christian minority 111-8
  coalition governments 31-40
  devolution of power 52-5
  ethnic politics 119-58
  IPKF in 240-5
  India and,
  as mediator 193-5, 197-207, 214-31, 246-7

ethnic conflict in Sri Lanka 231-40
Indian Tamils 272-96
Islamic factor 251-71
language and religion as divisive factors 40-2
language problem 45-68
language rights 62-7
linguistic nationalism 45-68
modern 69-118
multiparty system 31-40
policies of reconciliation 161-92
political culture 20-31
political violence 119-49
polity of 1956-1972 88-102
polity of 1972-1997 102-11
population 333-5
post-colonial state 20-31
religion and politics in 69-118
resistance to invaders 18-20
security perceptions 195-7
Sinhala Only policy 47-52, 55-62
Tamil separatism 149-58
Tamilnadu connection 143-49
traditional homelands theory 207-14
vital statistics 335
Sri Lanka Freedom Party (SLFP) 26, 28, 33-4, 36-40, 51, 56-8, 61, 84, 86, 88, 93-4, 97-100, 102, 104, 124-5, 128-29, 136, 145, 148, 155, 162, 173, 177, 203, 226, 235, 237-39, 241, 260, 263, 266, 268, 270, 288-89, 291, 294
Sri Lanka Mahajana Pakshaya (SLMP) 239, 328

Sri Lanka Muslim Congress (SLMC) 11, 39-40, 240 264-71, 318
Sri Lankan army 141-3, 180, 223, 267, 321-3, 330
Sri Lanka's Buddhist Society 40
Stanley, Herbert 278
States Re-organization Commission 143
Swabashá movement 46-7, 133

Tamil Congress (TC) 35-6, 38-9, 48, 121, 127, 154, 260
Tamil Eelam Liberation Organization (TELO) 219, 225, 321
Tamil language 120-1, 126, 133-5, 144, 162, 166, 300
Tamil Language (Special Provisions) Act No. 28 of 1958 54-5, 57, 59, 61, 100
Tamil Language (Special Provisions) Regulations of 1966 55-7, 61
Tamil Muslim conflicts 251
Tamil National Army (TNA) 243
Tamil separatism 16-17, 138-43, 147, 149-58, 179-92, 295, 299, 303, 316, 321, 323, 326-28
maturation of 155-8
rise of 149-55
Tamil United Front (TUF) 127, 139, 147-8, 152, 163, 295
Tamil United Liberation Front (TULF) 39, 111, 124, 138, 152-3, 155-7, 162-4, 174, 176, 181-3, 187-90, 192, 198,

200-6, 208, 211, 216-21, 223-27, 232, 240, 256, 313, 317, 319, 321, 328

Tamilnadu 140, 143-9, 181, 183, 193-5, 197-9, 214-7, 221-2, 245, 301, 325
and Sri Lanka 143-9, 193-95, 197, 301
INC in 143-4
immigration to Sri Lanka 140
training camps and bases in 198-9, 214-7, 221-2, 245

Tamils,
attitude to security forces 141
university education among 132-5, 311

Terrorism 190, 323-6

Thaninayagam, Fr Xavier 145

Theravada Buddhism 19, 87-88, 301

Thimpu (Bhutan) talks 219

Thondaman, S. 38, 178, 273, 284, 290, 294-6

Tiruchelvam, M. 56, 163

Traditional homelands of Tamils, theory of 19, 151-3, 156, 205, 211, 213, 269, 302, 313

Trincomalee 207, 209, 237, 269

Unemployment 292

United Front (UF) 37, 124-6, 128, 130-1, 133, 136-7, 139, 142, 145, 166, 168, 171, 183-84, 291-2, 311, 319, 321

United National Party (UNP) 6, 26-30, 32-3, 35-40, 47-8, 51, 53-8, 61, 64, 86, 89, 98-100, 102-4, 108, 121, 128, 130, 143, 161, 173, 176-8, 180-1, 183, 186, 190-91, 196-97, 203, 239, 241-2, 260, 263, 266-8, 270, 274, 288-89, 291, 293-6, 301, 311-2, 319, 328

University education,
admission policy 131-6, 166-72, 174
ethnic conflict and 133, 136, 170-2

University Grants Commission 168

Vadamarachchi campaign (Sri Lanka) 230

Vaddukodai resolution of 1976 155, 157

Vatican Council of 1962-3 102, 305

Vaz, Fr Joseph 116

Venkateswaran, A.P. 225, 227

Vipulasara, Mapalagama 102

Wickremasinghe, Lakshman 116

Wickremasinghe, R. 32

Wijeratne, Ranjan 327

Wijetunga, D.B. 32, 110

World Tamil Association (WTA) 327

World Tamil Movement (WTM) 327

Wriggins, Howard 123-4